SCHAUM'S OUTLINE OF

THEORY AND PROBLEMS

OF

MACROECONOMICS

Third Edition

•

EUGENE DIULIO, Ph.D.
Associate Professor of Economics
Fordham University

•

SCHAUM'S OUTLINE SERIES

McGRAW-HILL

New York   St. Louis   San Francisco   Auckland   Bogotá   Caracas   Lisbon
London   Madrid   Mexico City   Milan   Montreal   New Delhi
San Juan   Singapore   Sydney   Tokyo   Toronto

EUGENE A. DIULIO, currently Associate Professor of Economics at Fordham University, received his Ph.D from Columbia University. He is the coauthor of *Schaum's Outline of Principles of Economics,* 2nd ed. His research has been in the area of financial institutions and financial markets. He is an educational consultant to numerous banks.

Schaum's Outline of Theory and Problems of
MACROECONOMICS

4 5 6 7 8 9 10 11 12 13 14 15 16 17 18 19 20 PRS PRS 9 0 2

ISBN 0-07-017053-3

Sponsoring Editor: Barbara Gilson
Production Supervisor: Pamela Pelton
Editing Supervisor: Maureen B. Walker
Project Supervision: Keyword Publishing Services

Library of Congress Cataloging-in-Publication Data

Diulio, Eugene A.
    Schaum's outline of theory and problems of macroeconomics / Eugene
Diulio—3rd ed.
        p.   cm.—(Schaum's outline series)
    Rev. ed. of: Schaum's outline of theory and problems of
macroeconomic theory / Eugene Diulio. 2nd ed. ©1990.
    Includes index.
    ISBN 0-07-017053-3
    1. Macroeconomics—Problems, exercises, etc.   I. Diulio, Eugene
A.   Schaum's outline of theory and problems of macroeconomic theory.
II. Title.   III. Series.
HB172.5.D58   1997
339.3'076—dc21   97-37207
                                                           CIP

McGraw-Hill
A Division of The McGraw-Hill Companies

Preface

Macroeconomics is the study of employment, output, and prices in a decentralized, market economy. This book presents in a clear and systematic way the theoretical core of macroeconomics found in most intermediate macroeconomics textbooks. The book is eclectic and embraces Keynesian, monetarist, and rational expectations approaches. The book can be used by undergraduates or graduate business students as a supplement to current standard texts or by instructors as an independent text supplemented by empirical and/or policy readings. The book may also be useful to graduate economics students as a review of the analytical core of macroeconomic theory.

Each chapter begins with a concise presentation of concepts and theory with fully illustrated examples. Solved problems are presented with detailed, step-by-step solutions, which illustrate and amplify concepts and theories. Solved problems appear in a numerical, graphical, and algebraic format and focus upon points about which students often feel uncertain. The learning-by-doing methodology involves the student in macroeconomic analysis and provides repetition of the analytical core which is imperative to the learning process.

Macroeconomics is approached from a short-run and a long-run perspective. The short-run Keynesian perspective advances from a simple spending model, to one that includes monetary equilibrium, to an analysis of aggregate supply and aggregate demand. The long run is presented through Solow's model of economic growth. Chapters on the supply of and demand for money, consumption, and investment appear at the end of the book but can be integrated at any point.

The content and methodology of this book have been tested in my macroeconomic theory classes at Fordham University. I would like to thank my colleagues Joseph Cammarosano, Henry Schwalbenberg, and Parantap Basu who commented on portions of the book. The patient assistance of the Schaum staff at McGraw-Hill is greatly appreciated as is the continuous encouragement and support of my wife, Rosemary.

EUGENE A. DIULIO

Contents

vi

CONTENTS

Chapter 1

Introduction to Macroeconomic Analysis

Chapter Summary

1. Macroeconomics focuses upon economic growth, business cycles, unemployment, inflation and the output effects of globalization.

2. To help understand the complexity of macroeconomic events, economists use economic models which reduce the complexity of the real world. Models allow economists to link a phenomenon which they wish to explain (the dependent variable) to one or two variables (the independent variables) believed to be largely responsible for the behavior of the phenomenon under study.

3. Variables in a model are endogenous or exogenous. A variable is endogenous when its value is determined by the model. A variable is exogenous when its value is determined by forces outside the model. A dependent variable is endogenous.

4. Macroeconomics uses the power of supply and demand to analyze output and the price level. Macroeconomics considers the possible existence of equilibrium and disequilibrium. The traditional Keynesian model utilizes a disequilibrium model to explain business cycles.

Chapter Outline

1.1 THE FOCUS OF MACROECONOMIC ANALYSIS

Macroeconomics is concerned with current output, long-run economic growth, economic fluctuations, unemployment, inflation and the effect of increasing globalization upon domestic output. Microeconomics, by contrast, analyzes household and firm behavior to understand the determinants of price and output in individual markets. Macroeconomics seeks not only to understand macroeconomic phenomena, but to find policies which promote maximum output, employment and price stability over time. Economists hold differing views on the need for and effectiveness of economic policy. Positions can be categorized as interventionist (Keynesian or nonmonetarist) and noninterventionist (classical or monetarist). Although each school of thought supports different policies, common theoretical models are used to analyze macroeconomic activity.

Gross Domestic Product

Gross domestic product is the most frequently quoted macroeconomic measure. Gross domestic product (GDP) measures the domestic economy's output of final goods and services. GDP is measured in current prices, classified as nominal GDP, or in prices of a given year, classified as real GDP. When presented in current prices, GDP measures total output using prices that existed each year. By measuring output with prices that existed during a reference year, the economist is able to isolate changes in output from changes in the price level.

EXAMPLE 1.1.   Real GDP for the years 1966 through 1996 is presented in Fig. 1-1. GDP is measured in 1992 prices to exclude the effect of price changes. In 1992 dollars, real output increased from \$3060.2 billion in 1966 to \$6993.3 billion in 1996. During this period, output more than doubled. Note, however, that the secular increase in output includes periods where output growth slows and in some cases contracts. Two important topics in macroeconomics are economic growth (the growth of real output over time) and recessions (the decline in real GDP that occurs periodically).

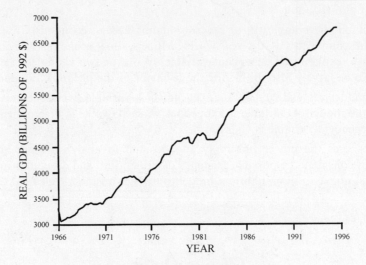

Fig. 1-1   Real gross domestic product.

Economic Growth

Economic growth refers to the increase in real GDP over time. An economy's ability to produce increases over time when there is capital accumulation and technological change, which enhance labor productivity, and growth of population, which, with a lag, increases the economy's labor supply. Economic growth is a major topic in macroeconomics because it directly affects economic well-being. Economic growth not only increases the standard of living for many individuals in the labor force, but also allows society to care better for those who are unable to work.

EXAMPLE 1.2.   Fig. 1-2 presents real GDP per capita from 1959 to 1995. (Real GDP per capita is real GDP divided by the economy's population.) Growth is frequently presented as real GDP per capita, since it draws our attention to the material well-being of individuals. Note in Fig. 1-2 that real GDP per capita increased more than two-fold between 1959 and 1995: from \$12,441 in 1959 to \$25,763 in 1995. While each individual in the U.S.A. did not experience a doubling of his or her material well-being, the likelihood is that there was an overall improvement in the living standard for a large majority of the U.S. population.

Business Cycles

As noted in Fig. 1-1, real GDP does not increase continuously over time. For example, Fig. 1-1 shows that output decreased during 1974–1975, 1980, 1981–1982, and 1990–1991. Periods of economic decline (recessions) followed by periods of sustained increases (expansions) are classified as business cycles. Between 1966 and 1996, the U.S. economy was in a recession from January 1974 to March 1975, from January 1980 to July 1980, from July 1981 to January 1982, and from July 1990 to March 1991.

Fig. 1-2   Real GDP per capita.

Business cycles are a concern because of the economic hardship associated with recessions. (Note that recessions are also evident in Fig. 1-2; real GDP per capita falls during each recession.) One of the central topics in macroeconomics is the implementation of a monetary and/or fiscal policy to moderate an economic decline or contain an inflation.

Unemployment

An individual is unemployed when he or she is looking for a job and cannot find one. The rate of unemployment, the ratio of the number of people unemployed to the number in the labor force, coincides with the business cycle. The unemployment rate rises during a recession and falls during an expansion. Obviously, an economic policy which moderates an economic downturn also reduces unemployment.

Inflation

Inflation exists when there is a sustained increase in the price level. The consumer price index (CPI), the producer price index (PPI), and the GDP deflator are frequently used measures of the price level. The consumer price index measures price changes for goods and services purchased by urban consumers. The producer price index measures price changes for goods at the wholesale level, specifically finished goods, intermediate goods, and crude materials. The GDP deflator measures changes in price for goods and services included in GDP. An inflation rate can be calculated from each of these indices by relating the change in the price index between two years to the price index in the first of the two years being compared.

EXAMPLE 1.3.   The inflation rate from 1966–1995, measured by the rate of change in the GDP deflator, is plotted in Fig. 1-3. Note that the inflation rate in the U.S.A. soared between 1974 and 1984. Unexpected inflation results in economic uncertainty because of its selective and uneven impact upon individuals and businesses. Frequently, an acceleration in the economy's rate of inflation can depress spending and thereby cause output to contract. Understanding the causes of inflation and finding ways to contain it is another focus of macroeconomics.

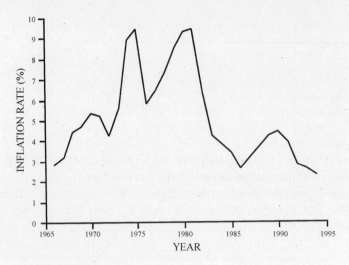

Fig. 1-3 Inflation rate measured by the rate of change in GDP deflator.

Exports

In an open economy there is extensive importing and exporting of goods and services among countries. As an economy becomes more open, its level of economic activity is increasingly tied to spending levels in other countries. It is imperative, therefore, to take a global approach to macro-economics when an economy is open.

EXAMPLE 1.4.   Fig. 1-4 presents U.S. exports as a percentage of total GDP. Note that U.S. exports are 4% of U.S. output in 1965; during that time, the U.S.A. was largely a closed economy, since exports were not a significant force affecting domestic output. By 1995, however, note that exports account for approximately 12% of U.S. output. In this setting, output in the U.S. economy is not only linked to spending by consumers, businesses, and government in the U.S.A., but to spending by its major trading partners.

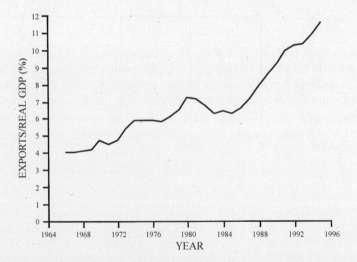

Fig. 1-4 Exports as a percentage of real GDP.

1.2 ECONOMIC MODELS

Economists use models to cut away unnecessary detail and reduce the complexity of reality. In a simple two-variable model, the variable to be explained is linked to one believed to be largely responsible for its behavior. For example, economists generally link consumption to current disposable income. Such behavior is specified by stating that consumption (C) is a function of current disposable income (Yd), or $C = f(Yd)$, meaning that consumption depends systematically upon current disposable income. A functional statement, such as $C = f(Yd)$, is both a concise and convenient way of presenting hypothesized behavior. Furthermore, it defines the economic relationship under study, i.e., it indicates which variable is dependent and which is independent. In the expression, $C = f(Yd)$, consumption is the dependent variable and current disposable income is the independent variable.

In most instances, the dependent variable (the variable to be explained) is influenced by more than one independent variable. For example, consumption may not only depend upon current disposable income, but also upon the rate of interest and expected disposable income. It is customary to present consumption as a function of only one independent variable, with the values of the other independent variables held constant. This is noted by the term *ceteris paribus*, which indicates that the values of the other independent variables are unchanged, e.g., $C = f(Yd)$, *ceteris paribus*.

Observations on consumption and current disposable income can be presented in a table or plotted in a graph. Through statistical analysis, a linear equation for the relationship of consumption and current disposable income can be estimated (see Example 1.5). In the absence of statistical analysis, one can specify the expected form of the relationship. For instance, one could hypothesize that $C = \bar{C} + cYd$, where $\bar{C}$ and c are expected to have values greater than zero. Accordingly, consumption is a positive, linear function of current disposable income. The behavioral coefficient c measures the influence of current disposable income upon consumption. (c is in effect the slope of the consumption function.) The parameter $\bar{C}$ represents the influence of other independent variables whose values are unchanged.

EXAMPLE 1.5. Suppose the actual level of consumption and current disposable income is as follows: year 1, $Yd = \$400$ and $C = \$360$; year 2, $Yd = \$500$ and $C = \$440$; year 3, $Yd = \$600$ and $C = \$520$; year 4, $Yd = \$700$ and $C = \$600$; year 5, $Yd = \$800$ and $C = \$680$; year 6, $Yd = \$900$ and $C = \$760$. These observations could be presented in a table (see Table 1-1) and in a graph (see Fig. 1-5). Using statistical analysis, we derive a linear equation $C = \$40 + 0.80\,Yd$ from these observations.

Table 1-1

Yd (\$)	C (\$)
400	360
500	440
600	520
700	600
800	680
900	760

Variables in a model are either endogenous or exogenous. A variable is endogenous when its value is determined within the model and exogenous when its value is determined by forces external to the model. A change in the value of an exogenous variable is classified as an autonomous change. Models allow one to see how a change in an exogenous variable affects the value of the endogenous variable.

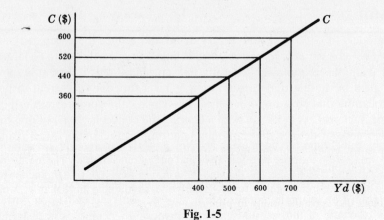

Fig. 1-5

EXAMPLE 1.6.   Suppose the consumption equation is $C = 0.80\,Yd + 0.05\Delta Yd^e$ where C is the amount consumed, Yd is current disposable income, and ΔYd^e is the change in expected disposable income. In a model of domestic product, output and current disposable income (Yd) are endogenous since their values are determined within the model. Models normally do not determine the level of or change in expected disposable income; ΔYd^e is thereby exogenous. Since consumption depends upon current disposable income, consumption is in part endogenously determined. Consumer spending, however, is also influenced by ΔYd^e and therefore by exogenous forces. Hence, a positive change in expected disposable income would increase consumer spending, output, and, in turn, current disposable income.

1.3 EQUILIBRIUM AND DISEQUILIBRIUM

The power of supply and demand analysis is used in macroeconomics to analyze output and the price level. Here demand represents aggregate demand; supply, aggregate supply; and price, the economy's price level. Aggregate demand is the sum of spending by individuals, businesses, and government, and net exports at each price level. Aggregate supply is the amount that businesses can produce and thereby supply at each price level (see Fig. 1-6). In market-clearing, equilibrium models, output, and the price level are determined by the intersection of aggregate demand and aggregate supply. When dis-

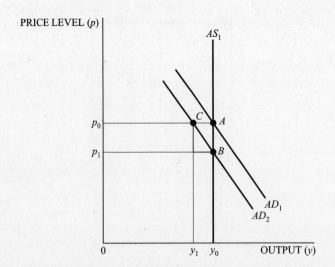

Fig. 1-6

equilibrium exists, the market does not clear; output and the price level then exist at a level other than the one determined by the intersection of aggregate demand and aggregate supply. The Keynesian model is built upon disequilibrium analysis, where prices and wages do not immediately adjust to a change in aggregate supply and/or aggregate demand. When markets are in disequilibrium for an extended period of time, some form of government intervention is necessary.

EXAMPLE 1.7.   Suppose the initial aggregate demand curve is AD_1 in Fig. 1-6 and aggregate supply is AS_1. There is equilibrium and therefore a clearing of markets at point A when, for AD_1 and AS_1, the price level is p_0 and output is y_0. A market-clearing equilibrium condition exists at point B, when a decrease in government spending shifts aggregate demand inward to AD_2, the price level falls to p_1 and output remains at y_0. The market does not clear and there is disequilibrium at point C when aggregate demand shifts inward from AD_1 to AD_2 and the price level remains at p_0. At price level p_0, aggregate spending is y_1 for AD_2; businesses produce no more than y_1, which is the amount they can sell, even though they have the ability to produce y_0.

Solved Problems

THE FOCUS OF MACROECONOMIC ANALYSIS

1.1   Explain and differentiate nominal GDP and real GDP.

Gross domestic product measures the total market value of all final goods and services produced in the domestic economy during a one-year period; quantitatively, it is the product of the quantity of goods and services produced and their respective prices. When current year prices are used in measuring output, nominal (current dollar) GDP includes the effect of price changes during the current year. To eliminate the effect of price changes, prices in a selected year (a reference year) can be used to measure output in preceding and proceeding years; this provides a measure of real (constant dollar) GDP.

1.2   (a) What is a price index? (b) What does the GDP deflator measure?

(a)   A price index measures the relationship between prices for a given year and prices for a selected (base) year. It is found by dividing the current year's prices by the base-year prices and multiplying by 100.

(b)   The GDP deflator is a price index found by dividing nominal GDP by real GDP and then multiplying by 100. The GDP deflator is a measure of changes in prices for aggregate output relative to prices that existed in the base year used to calculate real GDP.

1.3   (a) What is the relationship between labor employment and real GDP? (b) What is the relationship between the rate of growth in real GDP and the rate of unemployment?

(a)   Production occurs when economic resources—human, capital and natural—are employed. Hence, the greater the employment of labor the higher the level of real GDP.

(b)   Because greater output is associated with higher levels of employment, there should be fewer unemployed workers at higher output levels. It thereby follows that increases in the rate of economic growth would be associated with decreases in the rate of unemployment. Arthur Okun (Okun's law) found that an annual 2.5% increase in the rate of real growth above trend growth results in a 1% decrease in the rate of unemployment.

1.4   Explain the terms (a) *business cycle*, (b) *stabilization policy*, and (c) *monetary and fiscal policy*.

(a)   Business cycles are recurrent, but not periodic, fluctuations in economic activity that occur around the secular trend of GDP over a period of several years. The expansionary phase of the business cycle normally peaks at a point above trend growth, whereas the trough for the contractionary phase is normally below trend growth.

(b) A stabilization policy is an action taken by government to impact aggregate demand to moderate the expansion and contraction phases of the business cycle. During an expansion, the objective is to moderate the growth of spending; the objective during a recession (economic contraction) is to reduce the rate of decrease in spending.

(c) Monetary policy aims to stabilize economic activity by controlling the money supply or interest rates while fiscal policy utilizes a change in tax rates and/or the level of government spending for the same objective.

1.5   Suppose real output in countries A and B is \$392 in year 1 and \$504 in year 5. (a) Find output per worker for each country when the population in countries A and B is 49 workers in year 1 and when there are 80 workers in country A in year 5 and 49 workers in country B in year 5. (b) What is the probable cause for the increase in output in countries A and B? (c) Why is output per worker or output per capita a better measure of economic growth?

(a) Output per worker is \$8.00 (\$392/49 = \$8.00) in both country A and country B in year 1. Output per worker is \$6.30 in country A in year 5 and \$10.29 in country B in year 5.

(b) Country A's increase in output appears to be primarily due to an increase in its labor supply. Country B has no increase in its labor supply; therefore, increased output is either the result of technological change and/or an increase in the country's capital stock.

(c) Both countries had the same increase in total output. But we find that workers in country A had a decrease in output per worker, while those in B had an increase. Thus, workers in A had a decrease in economic well-being while those in B had an increase. When one is only interested in the increase in total output, growth in real GDP is a relevant measure. However, when the focus of economic growth is economic well-being, output per worker or output per capita is the better measure of economic growth.

1.6   Output for country C between year 1 and year 5 is presented in Fig. 1-7. From this figure, identify periods of economic recession and economic expansion.

Output falls during a recession and output increases during an expansion. Output is decreasing from year 1 quarter 3 (1:3) through year 2 quarter 2 (2:2), and decreasing from 4:2 through 5:1. It is increasing

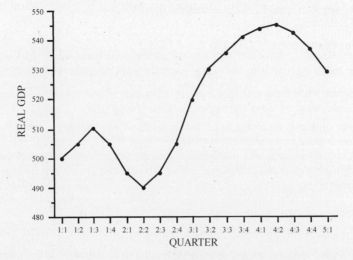

Fig. 1-7

during the other quarters. Thus, the economy is in a recession from 1:3 through 2:2 and from 4:2 through 5:1. An economic expansion exists from 1:1 through 1:3 and from 2:2 through 4:2.

ECONOMIC MODELS

1.7 Explain the following functions and identify the dependent and independent variables for (a) $I = f(i)$ and (b) $I = f(\Delta Y)$.

(a) Investment I is a function of (depends upon) the rate of interest i. Investment is the dependent variable; the rate of interest is the independent variable.

(b) Investment I is dependent upon the change in income Y. Investment is the dependent variable; the change in income is the independent variable.

1.8 (a) Explain the following statement: Consumption depends upon current disposable income, *ceteris paribus*. (b) What is the relevance of the *ceteris paribus* assumption?

(a) Consumption is systematically related to (is a function of) current disposable income. *Ceteris paribus* indicates that there is no change in the value of other variables which influence consumption, allowing one to make a precise statement about the dependency of consumption upon current disposable income.

(b) *Ceteris paribus* allows one to make precise statements about the relationship between an independent and a dependent variable. For example, when consumption is assumed to be a function of disposable income, *ceteris paribus*, one is able to specify in the model how a change in current disposable income affects consumption.

1.9 (a) Explain the components of the equation $C = \bar{C} + cYd$. (b) Explain the components of the equation $C = \$20 + 0.90Yd$.

(a) $\bar{C}$ represents other variables which affect consumption but whose value is unchanged. Behavioral coefficient c measures the change in consumption that results from a change in disposable income $(c = \Delta C/\Delta Yd)$. Since c is positive, consumption and disposable income move in the same direction.

(b) Consumption is \$20 regardless of the level of disposable income. $0.90Yd$ indicates that consumption changes by 90¢ each time there is a \$1 change in disposable income.

1.10 Use the equation $C = \$20 + 0.90Yd$ to construct a schedule for consumption when disposable income is \$200, \$250, \$300, \$350, and \$400.

The schedule for consumption is shown in Table 1-2.

Table 1-2

Yd (\$)	200	250	300	350	400
C (\$)	200	245	290	335	380

1.11 (a) Construct an equation from the consumption and current disposable income relationship in Fig. 1-8. (b) Which components of this equation represent exogenous consumption and endogenous consumption?

(a) Consumption is \$30 when current disposable income is zero. There is an \$80 increase in consumption for each \$100 increase in current disposable income; thus, $c = 0.80$, since $\Delta C/\Delta Yd$ is \$80/\$100. The equation for the consumption line is $C = \$30 + 0.80Yd$.

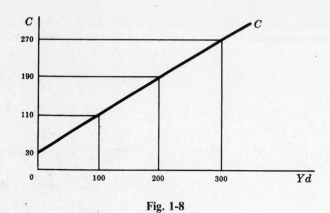

Fig. 1-8

(b)   The $30 in the consumption equation represents exogenous consumption, consumption which is determined by variables other than current disposable income but whose influence is external to the model. $0.80Yd$ represents endogenous consumption, since models of output determine current disposable income.

1.12   There is a consumption equation for each of the five individuals in Table 1-3. Identify the individuals who have had a change in autonomous consumption (a change in exogenously determined consumption) between period 1 and 2.

Table 1-3

Household	Period 1	Period 2
A	$C_A = \$10 + 0.90Yd$	$C_A = \$20 + 0.90Yd$
B	$C_B = 5 + 0.95Yd$	$C_B = 5 + 0.95Yd$
C	$C_C = 30 + 0.80Yd$	$C_C = 30 + 0.80Yd$
D	$C_D = 15 + 0.85Yd$	$C_D = 10 + 0.85Yd$
E	$C_E = 10 + 0.80Yd$	$C_E = 10 + 0.80Yd$

Individual A had a $10 increase in autonomous consumption; individual D had a $5 decrease in autonomous consumption.

1.13   Identify the exogenous and endogenous variables in the investment demand equation $I = \bar{I} + aY - bi$.

The value of an exogenous variable is determined by forces outside the model, while the value of an endogenous variable is determined within the model. $\bar{I}$ is obviously an exogenous variable. In the model of income determination, Y is an endogenous variable. The variable i is an endogenous variable if the rate of interest is determined in the model of income determination and exogenous if not.

EQUILIBRIUM AND DISEQUILIBRIUM

1.14   (a) What is the difference between equilibrium and disequilibrium? (b) When disequilibrium exists, is the amount produced determined by aggregate supply or aggregate demand?

(a) Equilibrium exists when the price level clears the market with aggregate supply equal to aggregate demand. There is disequilibrium when the price level exists at a level where the quantity that can be produced does not equal the quantity that is being demanded. In economics we normally focus upon the clearing of markets, and therefore equilibrium. The Keynesian model is built upon the belief that prices and wages do not adjust rapidly to changes in supply and/or demand, and that disequilibrium can persist for a period of time.

(b) When prices are above the market-clearing level and quantity demanded is less than quantity supplied, businesses elect to produce an amount equal to the quantity demanded. Therefore, they produce an amount determined by a specific price level and aggregate demand. When prices are below the market-clearing level, the business sector produces an amount determined by the specific price level and aggregate supply.

1.15 Suppose the price level is p_1 and output is y_1 in Fig. 1-9 for aggregate supply and aggregate demand curves AS_1 and AD_1. What happens to output and the price level when aggregate demand shifts leftward from AD_1 to AD_2 to AD_3 to AD_4 and prices are flexible, adjusting rapidly to shifts in supply and/or demand?

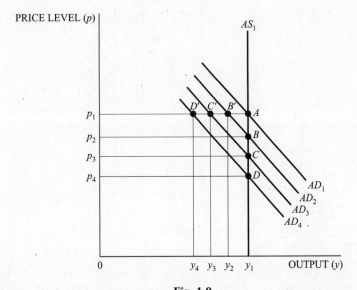

Fig. 1-9

With flexible prices, the price level is always determined by the intersection of aggregate supply and aggregate demand. Thus, for each of the aggregate demand curves AD_1, AD_2, AD_3, and AD_4, there is a new equilibrium, identified by points A, B, C, and D. The decreases in aggregate demand put downward pressure on prices but leave output unchanged. The price level falls from p_1 to p_2 to p_3 to p_4 in successive time periods and output remains at y_1.

1.16 Suppose the price level is p_1 and output is y_1 in Fig. 1-9 for aggregate supply and aggregate demand curves AS_1 and AD_1. What should happen to output and the price level when aggregate demand shifts leftward from AD_1 to AD_2 to AD_3 to AD_4 and inflexible prices keep the price level at p_1?

When the price level remains at p_1 in Fig. 1-9, although there are decreases in aggregate demand, the business sector produces a quantity determined by the price level and aggregate demand. This corresponds to points A, B', C', and D' for aggregate demand curves AD_1, AD_2, AD_3, and AD_4 with output at y_1, y_2, y_3, and y_4, respectively. Thus, when there are decreases in aggregate demand and the price level is unchanged, there are decreases in output.

1.17 Suppose the economy's ability to produce increases over time. This is indicated in Fig. 1-10 by the shift of aggregate supply from AS_1 to AS_2 to AS_3 to AS_4, where AS_1 represents supply in year 1; AS_2 supply in year 2; AS_3 supply in year 3; and AS_4 supply in year 4. Find output and the price level in year 1 through 4 when prices are flexible and adjust rapidly to changes in supply and/or demand and aggregate demand increases from AD_1 in year 1, to AD_2 in year 2, to AD_3 in year 3, and to AD_4 in year 4.

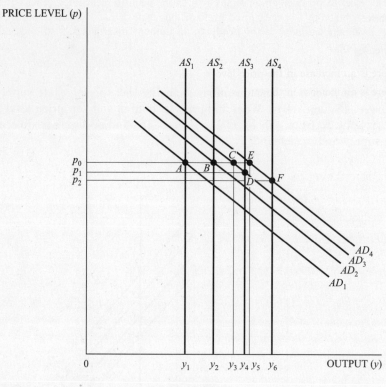

Fig. 1-10

When prices adjust rapidly to changes in supply and/or demand, output and the price level are determined by the intersection of aggregate supply and aggregate demand. In Fig. 1-10, this exists at points A, B, D, and F for curves AD_1 and AS_1, AD_2 and AS_2, AD_3 and AS_3, and AD_4 and AS_4, respectively. Output and the price level are therefore p_0 and y_1 for point A, p_0 and y_2 for point B, p_1 and y_4 for point D, and p_2 and y_6 for point F. The economy remains at full employment output (intersection of aggregate supply and aggregate demand) over time because of changes in the price level.

1.18 Suppose the economy's ability to produce increases over time. This is indicated in Fig. 1-10 by the shift of aggregate supply from AS_1 to AS_2 to AS_3 to AS_4, where AS_1 represents supply in year 1; AS_2 supply in year 2; AS_3 supply in year 3; and AS_4 supply in year 4. Suppose prices are not flexible and remain at p_0. Find output for year 1 through 4 when prices do not adjust to changes in supply and/or demand and aggregate demand increases from AD_1 in year 1 to AD_2 in year 2 to AD_3 in year 3 and to AD_4 in year 4.

Because the price level is unchanged at p_0, disequilibrium is likely. Points A, B, C, and E identify points on the aggregate demand curve which determine output. Output is now y_1 in year 1, y_2 in year 2, y_3 in year 3, and y_5 in year 4. Outputs y_3 and y_5 represent positions of disequilibrium, since they represent output levels which are below the production capability during years 3 and 4.

Multiple Choice Questions

1.   Macroeconomics is concerned with

  (*a*)   The level of output of goods and services.

  (*b*).   The general level of prices.

  (*c*)   The growth of real output.

  (*d*)   All the above.

2.   Real GDP increases

  (*a*)   When there is an increase in the price level.

  (*b*)   When there is an increase in the output of goods and services.

  (*c*)   When there is an increase in the population.

  (*d*)   At a constant rate over time.

3.   The equation $C = \$20 + 0.90\,Yd$ predicts that consumption is

  (*a*)   \$90 when disposable income is \$100.

  (*b*)   \$100 when disposable income is \$90.

  (*c*)   \$110 when disposable income is \$100.

  (*d*)   \$180 when disposable income is \$200.

4.   In the equation $C = \bar{C} + cYd$, the behavioral coefficient is (*a*) $\bar{C}$, (*b*) Yd, (*c*) c, or (*d*) all the above.

5.   In the equation $C = \bar{C} + cYD$, $\bar{C}$ is

  (*a*)   A parameter helping to determine the level of consumption.

  (*b*)   A parameter whose value depends upon the level of disposable income.

  (*c*)   A behavioral coefficient.

  (*d*)   A dependent variable.

6.   *Ceteris paribus* means that

  (*a*)   Other factors are held constant.

  (*b*)   No other variable affects the dependent variable.

  (*c*)   No other model can explain the dependent variable.

  (*d*)   The model is logical.

7.   Which of the following statements is correct?

  (*a*)   A variable is endogenous when its value is determined by forces outside the model.

  (*b*)   A change in an exogenous variable is classified as an autonomous change.

  (*c*)   A variable is exogenous when its value is determined by forces within the model.

  (*d*)   A variable is autonomous when its value is determined by forces within the model.

8.   In stating that $C = f(Yd, W)$

  (*a*)   It is hypothesized that Yd is a more important determinant of C than W.

  (*b*)   It is hypothesized that W is a more important determinant of C than Yd

  (*c*) W and Yd are dependent variables explaining C.

  (*d*) Yd and W are independent variables explaining C.

9.   In a market-clearing model

   (a)   The price level always exists at the intersection of aggregate supply and aggregate demand.

   (b)   Output is determined by the intersection of aggregate supply and aggregate demand.

   (c)   Shifts of aggregate demand or aggregate supply immediately change price and/or output.

   (d)   All of the above.

10.   In a disequilibrium model where the price level remains above the price level at which aggregate supply and aggregate demand intersect,

   (a)   Output is determined by the aggregate supply curve.

   (b)   Output is determined by the aggregate demand curve.

   (c)   There is an output shortage.

   (d)   There is an output surplus.

True or False Questions

11.   _____ Keynesian economists take a noninterventionist approach to macroeconomic problems.

12.   _____ Nominal GDP measures current output with current prices.

13.   _____ An increase in real GDP indicates that there is an increase in the material well-being of all individuals in an economy.

14.   _____ The U.S.A. is not an open economy because gross exports are less than 10% of its GDP.

15.   _____ In the expression $C = f(Yd)$, disposable income is the dependent variable.

16.   _____ The term *ceteris paribus* indicates that the value of other variables which influence the dependent variable are unchanged.

17.   _____ Real GDP declines during a recession.

18.   _____ When the consumption equation is $C = \$40 + 0.90\,Yd$, consumption is $940 when disposable income is $1000.

19.   _____ The Keynesian model assumes that prices and wages do not adjust immediately to a change in aggregate supply and/or aggregate demand.

20.   _____ There is disequilibrium when the market does not clear.

Answers to Multiple Choice and True or False Questions

1. (*d*); **2**. (*b*); **3**. (*c*); **4**. (*c*); **5**. (*a*); **6**. (*a*); **7**. (*b*); **8**. (*d*); **9**. (*d*); **10**. (*b*); **11**. F; **12**. T; **13**. F; **14**. F; **15**. F; **16**. T; **17**. T; **18**. T; **19**. T; **20**. T.

Chapter 2

Measures of Output, Prices, and Employment

Chapter Summary

1. Gross domestic product is the value of final sales; it is also equal to the value added at each stage of production. The value-added approach to measuring GDP is a cost approach, where the value of final output is the sum of payments to the factors of production (wages + rent + interest + profit) plus indirect taxes and depreciation.

2. Other output measures include national income, which is the payments made to the factors of production; personal income, which is the amount of national income that is received by individuals plus transfer payments; and disposable personal income, which is the amount that individuals have after income taxes.

3. A price index measures the relative change in prices over time. The consumer price index (CPI) is a fixed-weight index which measures the price change in a fixed basket of goods. The producers price index (PPI) measures the change in wholesale prices, the prices at wholesale for finished goods, intermediate goods, and crude materials. The GDP deflator measures the price change of all goods and services included in domestic ouptut.

4. Inflation exists when there is a sustained increase in the price level. Disinflation occurs when the rate of inflation decreases; deflation exists when the rate of change in the price level is negative.

5. A person who does not have a job and is actively looking for work is frictionally, structurally, or cyclically unemployed. Frictional unemployment exists because a search period is necessary to find a first job or a new job when one is laid off or resigns from a current one. One is structurally unemployed when a permanent decrease in demand and/or a technological change results in layoff because a business needs fewer individuals to produce a particular good or service. Cyclical unemployment exists when the economy contracts and people are laid off because of insufficient spending.

6. A country's balance of payments is a summary statement of its transactions with the rest of the world. A country has credit (+) entries in its balance of payments when it receives foreign currency and debit (−) entries when it remits foreign currency. Subsets of the balance of payments statement measure the balance of trade, current account balance, and capital account balance.

Chapter Outline

2.1 MEASURING GROSS DOMESTIC PRODUCT

There are two approaches to measuring domestic output: an expenditure approach, which measures the value of final sales; and a cost approach, which measures the value added at each stage of production. The following two-sector, three-sector, and four-sector models illustrate how GDP is measured by the expenditure and cost approaches.

A Two-Sector Model

A two-sector model consists of a business sector, which hires resources and produces goods and services, and a household sector, which supplies resource services to the business sector and purchases the goods and services produced by them. Presented as a circular flow (Fig. 2-1), the upper portion of the inner flow shows the household sector providing resource services to the business sector; the lower portion of the inner loop shows the flow of output to individuals (the household sector). The upper portion of the outer loop traces the financial payments made by the business sector to individuals for the use of resource services. Individuals receive wages, interest, and rent for the use of resource services, and profits for entrepreneurial talents. In the lower portion of the outer flow, individuals spend their money income purchasing goods and services produced by the business sector.

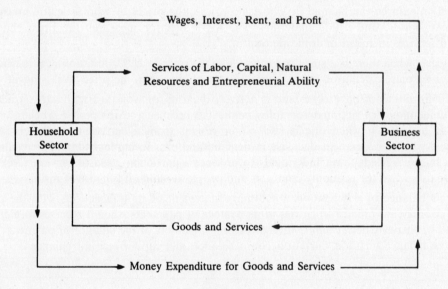

Fig. 2-1

EXAMPLE 2.1.   Suppose individuals receive the following payments from the business sector: wages $3900; interest $400; rent $150; and profit $550. One thousand items are produced and sold to the household sector at an average price per unit of $5. The market value of final output is $5,000 [$5(1,000 items)], which is the sum of total spending on final output; the cost of producing this output is also $5,000 [$3900 + $400 + $150 + $550].

Fig. 2-2 presents the circular flow of financial payments associated with the production and sale of final output; it differs from the financial payments in the outer flow in Fig. 2-1 in that individuals save a portion of their money income. The amount that individuals save equals the amount of new plant and/or equipment purchased by the business sector. Household saving is a leakage from the circular flow; saving leakages are reinjected into the circular flow by investment spending, i.e., by the business sector's purchase of plant and equipment.

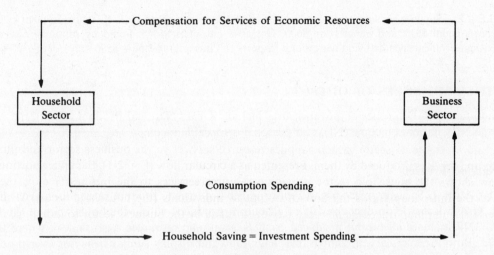

Fig. 2-2

A Three- and Four-Sector Model

Fig. 2-3 presents a closed economy circular flow among the household, business, and government sectors. In the upper loop, individuals are paid for factor services and government receives indirect taxes, which it imposes upon the output of goods and services. Individuals use their income payments to consume, save, and pay income taxes to the government. Government spends its tax receipts; individuals lend their savings to the business sector, which invests in new plant and equipment. In the lower loop, the spending flow includes consumption (C), investment (I), and government expenditures (G).

A four-sector model adds international transactions to the three-sector model. Goods and services available for U.S. purchase include those that are domestically produced (Y) and those that are imported (Mg); thus, goods and services available for domestic purchase equal $Y + Mg$. Expenditures for U.S. and foreign-made goods include consumption, investment, government, and exports (Xg). Thus, $Y + Mg = C + I + G + Xg$. Subtracting Mg from both sides of the equation, we have $Y = C + I + G + Xg - Mg$, where Y represents domestic output.

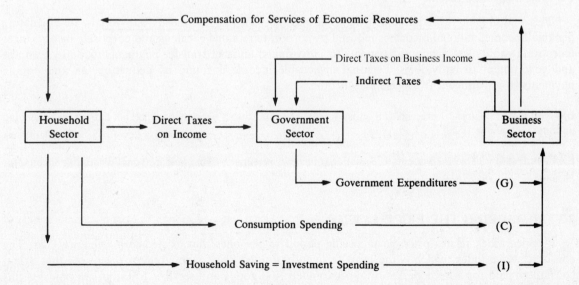

Fig. 2-3

EXAMPLE 2.2. Suppose consumption spending is $4600; investment spending is $500; government spending is $935; exports equal $630; and imports are $600. Domestic output is $6065, found by summing consumption, investment, government spending, and net exports (exports less imports) ($4600 + $500 + $935 + [$630 − $600]).

2.2 OTHER MEASURES OF OUTPUT

In addition to GDP, other output measures include: Gross National Product (GNP), net national product (NNP), national income (NI), and personal disposable income (Yd).

Gross National Product

In 1992, the U.S. government began reporting gross domestic product rather than gross national product. Gross domestic product consists of all output produced within the boundaries of the U.S.A., whereas GNP includes all output produced by U.S. economic resources regardless of where they are domiciled. Both measures are of comparable magnitude and display similar behavior over time.

Net National Product

Net national product equals GNP less replacement investment (capital consumption allowances). Each year, some of the economy's capital stock wears out. Thus, investment each year, i.e., gross investment (Ig), includes additions to the capital stock (In) and replacement of worn-out capital stock (D). Thus, $GNP = C + Ig$ (gross investment) $+ G + Xn$ (gross exports less gross imports), while $NNP = C + In$ (net investment) $+ G + Xn$.

National Income

The costs associated with producing net national product include payments to the factors of production (national income) and taxes imposed by government at production or final sale. Examples of indirect taxes at production or sale include taxes on tobacco and liquor products when these goods are packaged, sales taxes, and business and property taxes. National income is found by adding wages + interest + rent + profit or by subtracting indirect business taxes from net national product.

Personal Disposable Income

Personal income is the amount of national income which is received by individuals. In calculating personal income, national income is reduced by corporate retained earnings and corporate income taxes (corporate profits less dividend payments to individuals) and net transfer payments made by business and government to individuals. Personal disposable income is found by deducting tax and nontax payments to government from personal income.

EXAMPLE 2.3. Table 2-1 presents U.S. gross domestic product, gross national product, net national product, and national income for 1995.

EXAMPLE 2.4. Table 2-2 presents U.S. national income, personal income, and personal disposable income for 1995.

2.3 MEASURING THE PRICE LEVEL

A price index relates prices in a specific period to the ones that existed in a reference year. The consumer price index, which is the most frequently quoted price index, relates the prices that urban consumers paid for a fixed basket of approximately 400 goods and services to the prices paid for this same basket during a reference year. As such, the CPI is a fixed-weight index, where it is assumed that

Table 2-1   Gross Domestic Product, 1995 (Billions of Dollars)

(1)	(2)	(3)	(4)
Compensation of employees	4222.7	Personal consumption expenditures	4924.9
Rents	122.2	Gross private domestic investment	1065.3
Interest	403.6	Government expenditures	1358.3
Profit		Net exports	−94.7
Proprietors' income	478.3	Gross domestic product	7253.8
Corporate	586.6		
National income	5813.5		
Indirect business taxes	679.0		
Net national product (NNP)	6492.5		
Capital consumption allowances	754.2		
Gross national product (GNP)	7246.7		
Plus: Payments of factor income to rest of the world	215.3		
Less: Receipts of factor income from the rest of the world	−208.3		
Gross domestic product	7253.8		

Source: *Economic Report of the President*, 1997

Table 2-2   Personal Disposable Income, 1995 (Billions of Dollars)

National income		5813.5
Less:		
Corporate profits	586.6	
Contributions to social security plus net interest	1066.3	
Plus:		
Government and business transfers to individuals	1022.6	
Net interest paid to individuals	717.1	
Dividends paid by corporations to individuals	214.8	
Personal income		6115.1
Less:		
Personal tax and nontax payments to government	794.3	
Personal disposable income		5320.8

Source: *Economic Report of the President*, 1997

individuals do not change spending patterns in response to price changes. The CPI is a good measure of price changes over time in that it compares the relative change in the cost of a fixed basket of goods. It may not, however, be a good measure of the cost of living, in that consumers usually substitute lower-priced goods for higher-priced ones as prices increase. The GDP deflator is the ratio of nominal GDP to real GDP. Nominal GDP is the market value of all final goods and services measured in current-year prices; real GDP is the market value of all final goods and services measured with the prices of a reference year. The GDP deflator is the most comprehensive measure of the price level, since it includes all output; it is also a better measure of the price level, since it includes changes in spending which occur because of increased prices. The producers price index (PPI) is an index of prices in the large-volume wholesale markets. Components of the PPI selectively measure the prices of finished goods, intermediate goods, and crude materials. Because wholesale prices eventually impact retail prices, a change in the PPI for consumer goods is usually a good predictor of a change in the CPI. Because each index does not measure the same basket of goods, each index will not change at the same rate over time. Note, however, in Fig. 2-4, the similarity of their movement.

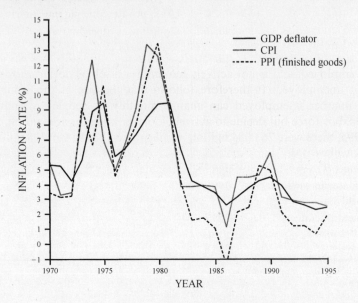

Fig. 2-4   Measures of inflation.

Inflation measures the annual rate of increase in a price index. The measures of inflation plotted in Fig. 2-4 were calculated by finding the rate of change in each index in successive years. For example, an increase in a price index from 100 in year 1 to 104 in year 2 indicates that there is a 4% annual rate of increase in the price level. The term disinflation is used when there is a decrease in the annual rate of increase in a price index. Deflation exists when there is a decrease in the annual rate of change in a price index.

EXAMPLE 2.4.   Table 2-3 presents the CPI and the annual rate of increase in the CPI from 1985 through 1995. A price index is always 100 for the base or reference year; 1982–1984 are the reference years for the consumer price index. The annual rate of inflation is calculated by finding the rate of change in the price index each year. For

Table 2-3   The CPI as a Measure of Inflation, 1985–1995 (1982–1984 = 100)

Year	CPI	Inflation Rate (%)
1985	107.6	3.6
1986	109.6	1.9
1987	113.6	3.6
1988	118.3	4.1
1989	124.0	4.8
1990	130.7	5.4
1991	136.2	4.2
1992	140.3	3.0
1993	144.5	3.0
1994	148.2	2.6
1995	152.4	2.8

example, the inflation rate for 1995, as measured by the CPI, is 2.8%, which is the rate of change in the CPI between 1994 and 1995. [4.2 (152.4 − 148.2 = 4.2) is the change in the CPI between 1994 and 1995; 4.2 divided by the consumer price index in 1994 (4.2/148.2) is 2.8%.]

2.4   MEASURING UNEMPLOYMENT AND THE UNEMPLOYMENT RATE

The labor force in the U.S.A. consists of individuals, 16 years of age or older, who are employed or are actively looking for a job and therefore unemployed. According to this definition, a person who is of working age, is not employed, and is not actively looking for a job, is not a member of the labor force and is therefore not unemployed. It therefore follows that the size of the labor force, the number employed, and the number unemployed can change monthly as people voluntarily leave the labor force, are not in the labor force but decide to actively look for a job, or are laid off or quit their current job. In December 1995, there were 263.034 million people in the U.S.A.; 199.508 million were of working age and available to work; of this number 132.034 million were in the labor force, 124.904 million were employed and 7.380 million were unemployed. The unemployment rate in December 1995 (the ratio of those unemployed to those in the labor force) was 5.6% (7.380/132.284 = 5.6%).

Economists categorize unemployment as frictional, structural, and cyclical. An individual is frictionally unemployed when he or she (1) quits a current job before securing a new one, (2) is not immediately hired when first entering the labor force, or (3) is let go by a dissatisfied employer. Frictional unemployment exists because there is a search period associated with finding a first job or another job after the current one is terminated. An individual is structurally unemployed when he or she loses a job because of a permanent decrease in demand for the good or service produced by the employing firm and/or technological advance necessitates that fewer individuals need to be employed. Those who are structurally unemployed normally have a longer search period because they usually do not possess skills which are in demand. Individuals are cyclically unemployed when there is a decrease in output (a recession) and fewer workers are needed because of lower spending levels. An economy always has frictional and structural unemployment, since people are always entering the labor force, looking for a new job or losing an existing job because of technological change. Thus, an economy has a natural rate of unemployment, a rate that is determined by a normal level of frictional and structural unemployment. Full employment therefore exists when the actual rate of unemployment equals the natural rate of unemployment. It is possible for the actual rate of unemployment to be above or below the natural rate. When the unemployment rate is greater than the natural rate, output is below its potential; when the unemployment rate is less than the natural rate, the economy is operating beyond its potential and inflationary pressures usually develop.

EXAMPLE 2.5.   Fig. 2-5 presents the U.S. unemployment rate from 1970 through 1995. Increases in the unemployment rate in 1970, 1975, 1982, and 1991 were the result of economic recessions. Note that the unemployment rate returns to a 5–6% level during expansions. In the 1980s, many economists believed that the natural rate of unemployment was 6%; current experience suggests that the natural rate is below 5.5%.

2.5   THE BALANCE OF PAYMENTS

A balance of payments statement is a record of all economic transactions between the residents of a country and those of foreign countries for a one-year period. A debit (−) entry represents a home country's payment to another country; and a credit (+) entry represents a payment received by the home country. Thus, a country earns foreign currency when there is a credit (+) entry, e.g., when a country exports goods or services or has a capital inflow.

International transactions are placed into categories to measure a country's balance of trade, balance on goods and services, balance on current account, balance on capital account, and official reserve transactions. A country's trade balance is the net balance on its commodity exports and imports. The current account balance is the net balance for all trade transactions, international service transactions (tourism, transportation, and royalty fees) and international unilateral transfers (gifts and foreign aid).

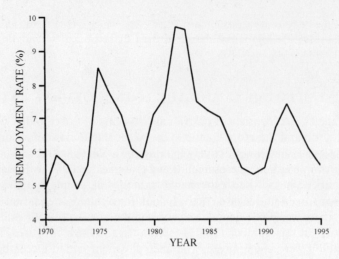

Fig. 2-5 U.S. unemployment rate, 1970–1995.

Financial transactions (consisting of direct investment and purchases of interest-bearing financial instruments, non-interest-bearing demand deposits, and gold) comprise the capital account balance. Official reserve transactions consist of movements of international reserves among governments and official agencies to accommodate imbalances arising from the current and capital accounts.

EXAMPLE 2.6. Table 2-4 presents a hypothetical balance of payments statement for the U.S.A. The negative balance on merchandise trade of −124.3 indicates that the U.S.A. had a trade deficit. The balance on current account is also in deficit. The +$117.4 capital account balance indicates that the U.S.A. had a capital inflow. In this example, the official reserve transaction balance is zero. When this occurs, the balance on capital account is the financial counterpart of the current account—in this case −$117.4 is offset by +$117.4.

Table 2-4   ($ billions)

Exports of goods	+214.0	
Imports of goods	−338.3	
Balance on merchandise trade		−124.3
Income from current services	+55.2	
Income on foreign assets	+90.5	
Payments for current services	−58.2	
Interest paid on foreign-owned assets	−65.8	
Balance on goods and services		−102.6
Unilateral transfers	−14.8	
Balance on current account		−117.4
Capital outflows	−29.5	
Capital inflows	+146.9	
Balance on capital account		+117.4

Solved Problems

MEASURING GROSS DOMESTIC PRODUCT

2.1 Suppose, in a two-sector model, that individuals receive the following payments from the business sector: wages $520, interest $30, rent $10, and profits $80. Consumption spending is $550 and investment is $90. (*a*) Find the market value of output and household saving. (*b*) What is the relationship of saving and investment?

   (*a*) The market value of final output is $640, found by adding wages of $520 + interest of $30 + rent of $10 + profits of $80 or by adding consumption and investment ($550 + $90). Saving is $90, found by subtracting the $550 that individuals consume from their $640 income.

   (*b*) Both saving and investment equal $90. This relationship always holds true in a two-sector model, since leakages must always equal injections.

2.2 (*a*) What is a leakage from the circular flow? (*b*) Why is investment spending viewed as an injection into the circular flow?

   (*a*) A leakage occurs when income received is not spent by its recipient; for example, when households are the sole recipient of income from production, their decision to save is a leakage from the flow of income and spending.

   (*b*) Investment represents an injection of spending into the circular flow. Those who desire to invest obtain funds from those who save.

2.3 (*a*) What are the components of gross investment? (*b*) Why are additions to inventory a component of net investment? (*c*) Can inventory additions be negative?

   (*a*) Gross investment consists of commercial and residential construction, the purchase of machinery, equipment and tools, and the change in business inventory.

   (*b*) Businesses hold materials as well as semifinished and finished goods, i.e., inventory, to facilitate the production and sale of goods. Inventory is held for the same reason that a firm purchases machinery, equipment, and tools, namely to acquire assets which are necessary for the production and sale of goods. Additions to a firm's inventory represent net investment, since these goods, like plant and investment, contribute to future sales.

   (*c*) Yes. When expected sales do not materialize, firms hold less materials and finished and semifinished goods inventory. The reduction of inventories, *ceteris paribus*, results in a negative change in inventory investment.

2.4 Posit a closed economy with household, business, and government sectors. Individuals receive income of $760 and pay taxes of $100 to the government; consumer spending is $560; gross investment is $110; depreciation is $40; government spending is $130. (*a*) Find GDP and household saving. (*b*) What are the leakages and injections for this closed economy model? What is the relationship of these leakages and injections?

   (*a*) GDP is $800, the sum of consumption ($560), gross investment ($110), and government spending ($130). Household saving is $100, the sum of income received by individuals ($760) less taxes ($100) and consumption ($560).

   (*b*) Household saving, government taxes, and depreciation are leakages from the circular flow, whereas gross investment and government spending are injections. Leakages of $240 (saving of $100 plus taxes of $100 and depreciation of $40) equal the $240 in injections from gross investment ($110) and government spending ($130). Note that household saving does not have to equal investment when there is depreciation and a government sector.

2.5   What are direct and indirect taxes?

Direct taxes are taxes levied upon earned income. Examples of direct taxes include federal, state and/or local taxes imposed upon household and/or business income. Indirect taxes are taxes levied on goods and services at production or at final sale and are thereby passed on to the final buyer through higher prices. Examples of indirect taxes include excise taxes, sales taxes, business property taxes, import duties, and license fees.

2.6   (*a*) Find GDP from the payment and expenditure flows for the closed economy in Fig. 2-6. Assume that individuals own all economic resources. (*b*) Find the sum of leakages and injections.

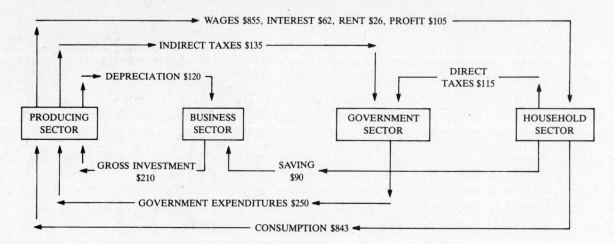

Fig. 2-6

(*a*)   Since individuals own all economic resources, individuals have an income of $1048 (wages $855 + interest $62 + rent $26 + profit $105); government collects indirect taxes of $135; depreciation is $120. The sum of payment flows, and therefore GDP, is $1303. Spending flows consist of consumption $843, gross investment $210, and government expenditures $250. The expenditure approach also gives us a value of $1303 for GDP.

(*b*)   Leakages consist of saving, indirect taxes, income taxes, and depreciation. Injections consist of government spending and gross investment. Leakages of $460 ($90 + $135 + $115 + $120) equal injections of $460 ($250 + $210).

2.7   (*a*) From the following data for the U.S.A., establish the amount of domestic output available for U.S. purchase and the total amount of goods and services available for U.S. purchase: GDP is $1000; gross exports equal $100 while gross imports are $150. (*b*) Does U.S. GDP always equal U.S. purchases of goods and services when there are international transactions? (*c*) What happens to U.S. GDP when U.S. imports increase *ceteris paribus*?

(*a*)   The amount of domestic output available for U.S. purchase is $900—the $1000 U.S. GDP less the $100 of U.S. output which is exported. The total amount of goods and services available for U.S. purchase is $1050—the $900 from domestic production plus the $150 of imported goods and services.

(*b*)   Purchases of goods and services can be equal to, less than, or greater than domestic output depending upon gross exports and gross imports. When gross imports (Mg) exceed gross exports (Xg) and there is a negative net export (Xn) balance, U.S. purchases of goods and services exceed U.S. output [the situation depicted by the data for part (a)]. However, when there is a positive net export balance (gross exports exceed gross imports), U.S. output is greater than U.S. purchases of goods and services.

(c)   GDP in the U.S.A. falls since there are increased purchases of foreign-made goods and decreased purchases of U.S.-made goods.

OTHER MEASURES OF OUTPUT

2.8   (a) GDP is the market value of final output. What is the difference between a final good and an intermediate good? (b) Why would inclusion of intermediate goods in measuring GDP involve double counting?

(a)   A final good does not require further processing and is purchased for final use (e.g., clothing purchased by a consumer or a machine by a manufacturer). An intermediate good (1) requires further processing during the year before it is ready for final use, (2) is being purchased for modification before final use, or (3) will be resold during the year for a profit.

(b)   Intermediate goods are components of final goods. If the value of both intermediate and final goods is included in the measurement of final output, there would be a double counting of value and therefore an overstatement of GDP.

2.9   What is the difference between personal income and national income?

Personal income is the income received by households during a given year. National income is the sum of payments made to economic resources. In a free enterprise economy, economic resources are owned by households, but government and the corporate form of business organization divert some of the income flow from households when corporations earn profits and government mandates that households make contributions to social security. Some of these diverted funds, however, are returned to households as government and business transfers and interest on the public debt. Thus, personal income can be less than, equal to, or greater than national income, depending upon the net diversion of funds from households by government and corporations.

2.10   From the following data, find (a) national income, (b) personal income, (c) personal disposable income and (d) personal saving.

Compensation of employees	$1866.3
Business interest payments	264.9
Rental income of persons	34.1
Corporate profits	164.8
Proprietors' income	120.3
Corporate dividends	66.4
Social security contributions	253.0
Personal taxes	402.1
Interest paid by consumers	64.4
Interest paid by government	105.1
Government and business transfers	374.5
Personal consumption expenditures	1991.9

(a) National income = compensation of employees + business interest payments + rental income of persons + corporate profits + proprietors' income. National income = $1866.3 + $264.9 + $34.1 + $164.8 + $120.3 = $2450.4.

(b) Personal income:

National income			$2450.4
Minus:	Corporate profits	$164.8	
	Social security contributions	253.0	(417.8)
Plus:	Government and business transfers	374.5	
	Interest paid by government	105.1	
	Corporate dividends	66.4	546.0
Personal income			$2578.6

(c) Personal disposable income = Personal income − personal taxes = $2578.6 − $402.1 = $2176.5.

(d) Personal saving = Personal disposable income − (personal consumption expenditures + interest paid by consumers).
Personal saving = $2176.5 − ($1991.9 + $64.4) = $120.2.

MEASURING THE PRICE LEVEL

2.11   Table 2-5 presents the price of and units of aggregate output for 199x and 199y. (a) Present in Table 2-6, nominal GDP for 199x and 199y. (b) Also calculate in Table 2-6 real output for 199y

Table 2-5   Aggregate Output in a Five-Good Economy

Good	199x Units Produced	199x Price	199y Units Produced	199y Price
A	25	$1.50	30	$1.60
B	50	7.50	60	8.00
C	40	6.00	50	7.00
D	30	5.00	35	5.50
E	60	2.00	70	2.50

Table 2-6   Nominal and Real GDP for 199x and 199y

Good	Value of 199x Output 199x prices	Value of 199y Output 199y prices	Value of 199y Output 199x prices
A	$ 37.50	$ 48.00	$ 45.00
B	375.00	480.00	450.00
C	240.00	350.00	300.00
D	150.00	192.50	175.00
E	120.00	175.00	140.00
GDP	$922.50	$1245.50	$1110.00

by measuring 199*y* output in 199*x* prices. What is the purpose of such a calculation? (*c*) What is the GDP deflator in 199*y*?

(*a*) Nominal GDP for 199*x* and 199*y* is found by multiplying the units produced each year by the respective price of each unit for that year and then summing the calculated values. Thus, as presented in Table 2-6, the value of good A in 199*x* is \$37.50; nominal GDP (value of output for goods A through E for 199*x*) is \$922.50 in 199*x*; it is \$1245.50 in 199*y*.

(*b*) Measuring 199*y* output in 199*x* prices gives a measure of real output for 199*y*. The right column measures the value of 199*y* output for goods A through E in 199*x* prices; real GDP for 199*y* is \$1110. A comparison of the first and last column (both measured at 199*x* prices) reveals the change in output, whereas a comparison of the first and second columns reveals a combined change in both output and prices.

(*c*) The GDP deflator for 199*y* is 112.2, found by dividing 199*y* nominal GDP (199*y* output measured in 199*y* prices) by 199*y* real GDP (199*y* output measured in 199*x* prices) and multiplying by 100: (\$1245.50/\$1110)100 = 112.2.

2.12 What is a GDP deflator?

The GDP deflator is an index of price changes for goods and services included in GDP. Thus, the deflator reflects changes in the price of goods and services purchased by consumers, businesses, and government. The GDP deflator is found by dividing current-dollar GDP by constant-dollar GDP, with the spending components (C, I, G) of constant-dollar GDP derived separately.

2.13 (*a*) What is the CPI? (*b*) Does an increase in the CPI always indicate an increase in the consumer's cost of living?

(*a*) The CPI is a measure of the prices paid by the typical urban working-class family for a fixed basket of goods and services. Statisticians have sampled "typical" consumers to establish a relevant basket of goods which is purchased and the appropriate relative importance (weight) of each good. The basket consists of goods and services divided into the following categories: food and beverages, housing, apparel, transportation, medical care, entertainment, and other.

(*b*) Although the CPI is the most reliable measure of the cost of living, it may overstate the prices individuals pay for goods and services that they actually purchase over time. Because it is a fixed-weight index, it does not allow for substitution effects, where consumers may "shop" for goods whose prices are rising and/or select a substitute good whose price has experienced a smaller relative increase. The quality of goods also changes, so that a price increase may reflect improved quality rather than inflation. For these reasons, the CPI may not truly reflect consumers' cost of living.

2.14 Suppose households purchase the categories of goods and services listed in Column 1 of Table 2-7; the relative importance of each category is given by the weight assigned in column 2. The price index for each category during year 1 and year 2 is found in columns 3 and 4, respectively. (*a*) From the data, calculate the CPI for year 1 and year 2. (*b*) What is the rate of inflation between year 1 and year 2 as measured by the change in the CPI?

(*a*) In Table 2-8 the price index for each spending category is multiplied by its respective weight and then summed. The CPI for year 1 is 280.80 and 301.87 for year 2.

(*b*) The rate of inflation is calculated by taking the change in the CPI between year 1 and year 2 and dividing by year 1 CPI. The rate of inflation indicated by the CPI is 7.50%. [(301.87 − 280.80)/280.80 = 0.075, or 7.50%.]

Table 2-7

Category	Weight	Price Index for Each Category	
		Year 1	Year 2
Food and beverages	0.175	270	270
Housing	0.460	300	330
Apparel	0.046	180	180
Transportation	0.193	280	308
Medical care	0.049	300	330
Entertainment	0.036	230	241
Other	0.041	250	250
	1.000		

Table 2-8

Category	Year 1	Year 2
Food and beverages	0.175(270) = 47.25	0.175(270) = 47.25
Housing	0.460(300) = 138.00	0.460(330) = 151.80
Apparel	0.046(180) = 8.28	0.046(180) = 8.28
Transportation	0.193(280) = 54.04	0.193(308) = 59.44
Medical care	0.049(300) = 14.70	0.049(330) = 16.17
Entertainment	0.036(230) = 8.28	0.036(241) = 8.68
Other	0.041(250) = 10.25	0.041(250) = 10.25
CPI	280.80	301.87

2.15 What does the producers price index measure?

The PPI is an index of the prices charged by businesses for crude, intermediate, and finished goods. Because these prices represent various stages of production, some goods enter the PPI as many as three times: as a crude good (e.g., wheat sold by the farmer), as an intermediate good (flour sold by the mill), and as a finished good (bread sold by the baker to a food retailer). A PPI is published for crude goods, intermediate goods, and finished goods to avoid the double counting that exists in the PPI for goods at all stages of production. Prices in the PPI are weighted as they are in the CPI. Movements in the PPI can be used to forecast the CPI; however, because the PPI does not include services, such forecasts are subject to error when the principal cause of inflation derives from increases in the prices of services.

MEASURING UNEMPLOYMENT AND THE UNEMPLOYMENT RATE

2.16 What are the causes of unemployment?

Unemployed workers can be placed into three categories: frictional, structural, and cyclical unemployment. Frictional unemployment is short-term, usually up to six months; it consists of temporary layoffs (perhaps due to a temporary decrease in the demand for labor), labor which has voluntarily left a job, and reentrants and new entrants into the labor force, who have a longer job search. Structural unemployment is longer term; it exists because of skill and/or location mismatching in the labor markets. For example, a job applicant may not have the required skill for a particular job; or a job may exist in another region but labor is unaware of its availability or is unwilling to relocate. Cyclical unemployment exists because of the business cycle. A deficiency of labor demand relative to supply periodically develops when decreases occur in economic activity.

2.17   What is a natural rate of unemployment?

The natural rate of unemployment is the rate that exists when there is no cyclical unemployment. Because frictional and structural unemployment are always present in a dynamic market economy, the natural rate of unemployment equals the percentage of the labor force that is frictionally and structurally unemployed at a point in time. The labor markets are considered to be at full employment when equilibrium exists at the natural rate of unemployment.

THE BALANCE OF PAYMENTS

2.18   What does a balance-of-payments statement measure?

A balance-of-payments statement is a record of all transactions between the residents of a country and the residents of foreign countries for a specific period of time. These international transactions are categorized to record a country's trade balance (net balance for a country's commodity exports and imports), current account balance (net balance on international trade, services and unilateral transfers), capital account balance (net balance on capital inflows and outflows), and official reserve transactions (changes in the international reserves held by governments and official agencies). When there are no statistical discrepancies and no change in official reserve transactions, the capital account balance is the financial counterpart of a country's balance on current account. Thus, in the absence of a change in official reserve assets, a country's net balance on current account and capital account is zero, i.e., its balance of payments is zero.

2.19   Use the following data to measure a country's balance on merchandise trade, balance on current account, balance on capital account and balance of payments. There is no change in reserve assets held by governments and official agencies.

1. The U.S.A. exports goods valued at $19,650.

2. The U.S.A. imports merchandise valued at $21,758.

3. U.S. citizens receive interest income of $3621 from foreign investments.

4. Interest income of $1394 is paid on foreign-owned assets in the U.S.A.

5. U.S. citizens' travel expenditures equal $1919.

6. Foreign travel in the U.S.A. is $1750.

7. U.S. unilateral transfers are $2388.

8. U.S. capital outflow is $4174.

9. U.S. capital inflow is $6612.

The balance on merchandise trade is the difference between goods imported and goods exported:

Exports of goods	+$19,650
Imports of goods	−$21,758
Balance on merchandise trade	−$2,108

The balance on current account is the balance on merchandise trade, interest paid and received, travel and unilateral transfers

Balance on merchandise trade		−$2,108
Exports of services		+$5,371
Interest income	+$3,621	
Travel	+$1,750	
Imports of services		−$3,313
Interest income	−$1,394	
Travel	−$1,919	
U.S. government unilateral transfers		−$2,388
Balance on current account		−$2,438

The balance on capital account is the difference between capital inflows and capital outflows

U.S. capital outflows	−$4,174
U.S. capital inflows	+$6,612
Balance on capital account	+$2,438

The balance of payments equals the net balance on current account and capital account: Balance of payments = 0.

2.20 (a) What are official reserve transaction balances? (b) Explain why the capital account is the financial counterpart of a country's balance on current account when there is no change in official reserve transaction balances.

(a) Official reserve transaction balances consist of international reserves held by governments or official government agencies. International reserves include a government's holdings of gold, balances in the International Monetary Fund, and foreign currencies.

(b) International transactions are recorded on a system of double-entry accounting where each debit entry necessitates a credit entry. Thus, the sum of all debit items in the balance of payments must equal the sum of all credit items. When there is no change in official reserve assets held by governments, the balance on current account plus the balance on capital account must equal zero. Hence, a deficit (−) current account balance must be countered by a surplus (+) capital account balance, i.e., the capital account is the financial counterpart of a country's balance on current account when there is no change in the holding of official reserve transaction balances.

Multiple Choice Questions

1. In a private sector model,

(a) Household saving is a leakage from the circular flow.

(b) Investment is a spending injection.

(c) Saving leakages equal investment injections.

(d) All of the above.

2. In an open economy model, GDP is the sum of

(a) Consumption, gross investment, government spending, and net exports.

(b) Consumption, net investment, government spending, and net exports.

    (*c*) Consumption, gross investment, government spending, and gross exports.

    (*d*) Wages, rent, interest, profit, and depreciation.

3.   In a closed economy, three-sector model,

    (*a*) Household saving equals net investment.

    (*b*) Household saving equals gross investment.

    (*c*) Household saving plus depreciation equals gross investment plus government spending.

    (*d*) Household saving plus taxes plus depreciation equals gross investment plus government spending.

4.   If personal income is \$570, personal income taxes are \$90, consumption is \$430, personal interest payments total \$10, and personal saving is \$40, disposable income equals

    (*a*) \$500

    (*b*) \$480

    (*c*) \$470

    (*d*) \$400

5.   When nominal GDP is \$1100 and real GDP is \$1000, the GDP deflator is

    (*a*) 9.09

    (*b*) 90.91

    (*c*) 1.11

    (*d*) 110

6.   Suppose nominal GDP is \$500 in year 1. If the GDP deflator doubles by year 6 while real output has increased 40%, nominal output in year 6 is

    (*a*) \$2000

    (*b*) \$1400

    (*c*) \$1000

    (*d*) \$750

7.   In the U.S.A., the labor force includes

    (*a*) Those who are employed and unemployed.

    (*b*) Those who are employed.

    (*c*) Those who are of working-age.

    (*d*) The entire population.

8.   Frictional unemployment exists

    (*a*) When there is a decrease in real GDP.

    (*b*) Because it takes time to find a job when one is first entering the labor force.

    (*c*) As a result of technological change.

    (*d*) When an individual retires.

9.   The natural rate of unemployment equals the sum of those who are

    (*a*) Frictionally and structurally unemployed.

    (*b*) Frictionally and cyclically unemployed.

(*c*)   Structurally and cyclically unemployed.

(*d*)   Frictionally, structurally, and cyclically unemployed.

10.   When there is no change in central bank holding of international reserves, a country's

(*a*)   Trade balance always equals 0.

(*b*)   Current account balance always equals 0.

(*c*)   Capital account balance always equals 0.

(*d*)   Balance of payments always equals 0.

True or False Questions

11.   _____ Gross domestic product is the sum of wages, rent, interest, and profit plus indirect taxes and depreciation.

12.   _____ National income is the amount of income received by individuals.

13.   _____ The GDP deflator is a variable-weight price index which is published monthly.

14.   _____ Disinflation exists when the inflation rate is negative.

15.   _____ GDP is $1000 when consumption is $800; investment is $150; government expenditures total $70; gross exports equal $100; and gross imports are $120.

16.   _____ A country which has cyclical unemployment has an unemployment rate greater than its natural rate.

17.   _____ A college graduate is structurally unemployed when he or she looks for a job upon graduation from college.

18.   _____ When a U.S. resident imports a foreign-produced good, the transaction is recorded as a debit in the U.S. trade balance.

19.   _____ A country which experiences a net outflow of capital has a deficit balance in its capital account.

20.   _____ An official reserve transaction consists of the purchase or sale of international reserves by a government unit.

Answers to Multiple Choice and True or False Questions

1. (*d*); **2.** (*a*); **3.** (*d*); **4.** (*b*); **5.** (*d*); **6.** (*b*); **7.** (*a*); **8.** (*b*); **9.** (*a*); **10.** (*d*); **11.** T; **12.** F; **13.** F; **14.** F; **15.** T; **16.** T; **17.** F; **18.** T; **19.** T; **20.** T.

Chapter 3

Output in the Short and Long Run

Chapter Summary

1. Potential output depends upon the quantity and productivity of natural, capital, and human resources. In the short run, potential output is influenced by supply shocks and/or changes in the labor markets.

2. The marginal productivity of labor is the incremental output due to a one unit increase in labor, with the amount of capital and productivity unchanged. Each additional labor input results in diminishing marginal productivity. The marginal productivity of capital is the incremental output due to a one unit increase in capital, with the amount of labor and productivity unchanged. There is diminishing marginal productivity for each additional unit of capital.

3. The marginal revenue product of labor (MRPL) is the incremental revenue generated by each additional labor unit. The number of labor units demanded (the demand for labor) depends upon the marginal revenue generated by each labor unit and the wage paid to the last worker hired. The supply of labor is positively related to the wage paid to each labor unit. Equilibrium in the labor markets exists when the quantity of labor supplied equals the quantity of labor demanded.

4. The labor markets and supply shocks determine output in the short run. In the absence of supply shocks, potential output increases or decreases with increases or decreases in the quantity of labor units hired. An adverse supply shock reduces productivity and thereby output for a given amount of capital and labor.

5. Output in industrialized countries increases along a cyclical path: a sustained decline in output (recession) followed by a much longer period of economic expansion. Recessions can be explained by adverse supply shocks and by an environment in which prices respond slowly to a decrease in aggregate demand.

Chapter Outline

3.1 THE ECONOMY'S PRODUCTION FUNCTION

An economy's ability to produce depends upon the quantity and productivity of its natural, capital, and human resources. An economy's production function can be presented as $y = f(R, K, L; A)$, where y represents potential output, R natural resources, K capital resources, L human resources, and A the productivity of resources. For most industrialized nations, the contribution of natural resources to total output is relatively small and unchanged over time; thus, it is customary to use the Cobb–Douglas production function $y = A(K^{\alpha} L^{1-\alpha})$, where α represents the share of income received by capital and $1 - \alpha$ the share received by labor. Potential output increases over time as a result of additions to the amount of capital or human resources and/or increases in productivity. It decreases when A, K, and/or L

decline. Over long periods of time, potential output increases as a result of advances in productivity and/ or larger amounts of human and capital resources. In the short run an adverse supply shock, which reduces productivity, can lower potential output. Potential output will also change in the short run when there is a change in the amount of labor units. (See Example 3.2.)

EXAMPLE 3.1.   Suppose an economy's production function is $y = A(K^{0.5}L^{0.5})$ or $y = A(\sqrt{K}\sqrt{L})$. When $A = 12$, $K = 36$, and $L = 4$, potential output for the economy is \$144 units.

$$y = A(\sqrt{K}\sqrt{L})$$
$$y = 12(\sqrt{36}\sqrt{4})$$
$$y = 12(6[2])$$
$$y = 144$$

EXAMPLE 3.2.   Suppose an economy's production function is $y = A(K^{0.5}L^{0.5})$. When $A = 12$, $K = 36$, and labor inputs increase from 4 to 5, potential output increases from 144.0 to 161.0 units. The levels of output associated with a productivity of 12, capital inputs of 36, and 1 through 10 units of labor are presented in Table 3-1. The data from Table 3-1 are plotted in Fig. 3-1, with the production function labeled P'. Note that this production function relates labor inputs to total output, keeping productivity and the amount of capital unchanged.

Table 3-1   Production Function (when $A = 12$ and $K = 36$)

Labor inputs	Units of Output
1	72.0
2	101.8
3	124.7
4	144.0
5	161.0
6	176.4
7	190.4
8	203.6
9	216.0
10	227.7

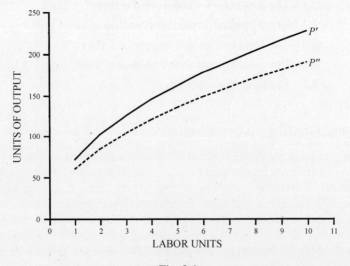

Fig. 3-1

EXAMPLE 3.3. Suppose there is an adverse supply shock; productivity is reduced and the value of A in Example 3.2 decreases from 12.0 to 10.0; capital is unchanged at 36 units. Potential output is now 120 units when there are 4 labor units. Potential output for 1 through 10 labor units is plotted in Fig. 3-1, with the production function labeled P''. Note that this decrease in productivity shifts the production function in Fig. 3-1 downward from P' to P''. If A had increased, P' in Fig. 3-1 would shift upward.

3.2 THE MARGINAL PRODUCTIVITY OF LABOR AND CAPITAL

The marginal productivity of labor is the incremental output associated with a one unit increase in labor, with productivity and capital unchanged. From Table 3-1, we find that output increases from 144.0 to 161.0 when labor units increase from 4 to 5. Thus, the marginal productivity of labor is 17 units, which is the incremental output associated with a one unit increase in labor. The marginal productivity of additional labor for the sixth labor unit is 15.4; the marginal productivity of additional labor units is derived from the production function in Table 3-1 and plotted in Fig. 3-2. Note that the marginal productivity of labor decreases as additional labor units are added to a fixed amount of capital. There is a diminishing marginal product of labor since, with technology unchanged, incremental units of labor are less productive when combined with a fixed amount of capital.

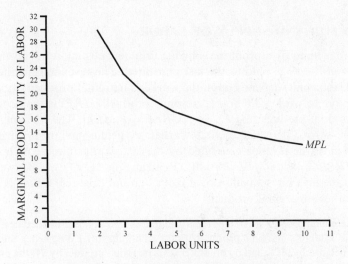

Fig. 3-2 Marginal productivity of labor.

EXAMPLE 3.4. The marginal productivity of labor measures the incremental output associated with one unit increases in labor. From Table 3-1, we find that output increases 29.8 units (101.8 units less 72.0 units) when labor increases from 1 to 2 units. Thus, the marginal productivity of the second labor unit is 29.8 units. The marginal productivity of the third labor unit is 22.9, the fourth unit 19.3; the fifth unit 17.0; the sixth unit 15.4; the seventh unit 14.0; the eighth unit 13.2; the ninth unit 12.4; and the tenth unit 11.7. The marginal productivity of labor is plotted in Fig. 3-2, with the curve labeled *MPL*.

The marginal productivity of capital is the incremental output associated with one unit increases in capital, keeping technology and the amount of labor unchanged. Example 3.5 calculates the incremental output associated with each additional unit of capital. Note that with technology unchanged the marginal productivity of capital also diminishes as additional capital inputs are added to a fixed amount of labor.

EXAMPLE 3.5. Suppose an economy's production function is $y = A(K^{0.5}L^{0.5})$. When $A = 12$, $K = 9$, and $L = 4$, potential output is 144. The output associated with 7 through 14 capital units, with A and L unchanged, is presented in Table 3-2. The marginal productivity of capital for each additional unit of capital is also presented in Table 3-2. Note that, like the marginal productivity of labor, the marginal productivity of capital decreases for each additional unit of capital when there is a fixed amount of labor and technology is unchanged.

Table 3-2 Total Output and the Marginal Productivity of Capital
(when $A = 12$ and $L = 4$)

Capital inputs	Total Output	MPK
7	63.5	
8	67.9	4.4
9	72.0	4.1
10	75.9	3.9
11	79.6	3.7
12	83.1	3.5
13	86.5	3.4
14	89.8	3.3

3.3 THE DEMAND FOR AND SUPPLY OF LABOR

The quantity of labor hired by a profit-maximizing firm depends upon the revenue generated by an additional labor unit and the wage paid to the last unit hired. The revenue generated by an additional worker (an additional labor unit) depends upon the worker's marginal productivity and the price of the good produced. Therefore, a worker's marginal revenue product (MRP) is the product of the price of output (P) and its marginal product (MPL), i.e., $MRPL = P[MPL]$. The incremental cost of the last labor unit hired is the wage (W) paid to that worker. A profit-maximizing firm will thereby hire additional labor units until the revenue generated by the last worker hired equals the wage paid that worker, i.e., where $MRPL = W$ or $MPL(P) = W$. Rearranging $MPL(P) = W$, we get $MPL = W/P$. From this we find that the firm hires an additional labor unit until the real wave (W/P) paid to the last worker equals that worker's marginal product.

EXAMPLE 3.6. The marginal productivity of labor, derived in Example 3.4, is presented in Column 2 of Table 3-3. (We shall assume that this is labor's marginal productivity for an 8-hour day.) When each unit of output is sold for $4, labor's marginal revenue product is found by multiplying its marginal product by $4, the price at which each unit can be sold. $MRPL$ is presented in Column 3 of Table 3-3. When each labor unit is paid $7 an hour, each worker receives $56 for an 8-hour day. Six workers are thereby hired, since the marginal revenue product of the sixth labor unit equals the $56 wage payment to the last worker hired.

Table 3-3

Labor inputs	MPL	$MRPL$
2	29.8	$119.20
3	22.9	91.60
4	19.3	77.20
5	15.4	61.60
6	14.0	56.00
7	13.2	52.80
8	12.4	49.60
9	11.7	46.80

The demand for labor in the short run depends upon labor's marginal revenue product. D_1 in Fig. 3-3(a) represents labor's marginal revenue product and therefore the demand for labor. Since labor normally attaches a positive value to leisure, additional labor units are supplied when there is a higher wage. S_1 in Fig. 3-3(a) represents the amount of labor units supplied at each wage. Equilibrium exists in the labor markets at wage W_1, where the L_1 quantity of labor units supplied equals the L_1 quantity of labor units demanded.

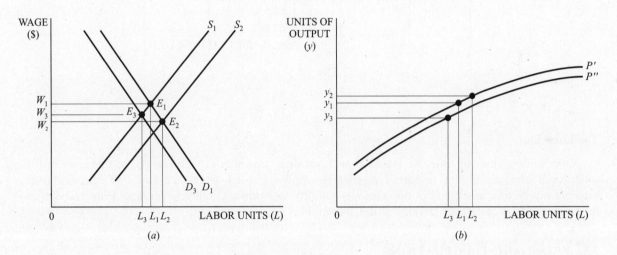

Fig. 3-3

3.4 POTENTIAL OUTPUT IN THE SHORT AND LONG RUN

The Short Run

When technology and capital resources are unchanged, potential output in the short run depends upon the equilibrium condition in the labor markets. For example, in Fig. 3-3(a) there is equilibrium in the labor markets for labor demand curve D_1 and labor supply curve S_1 when L_1 labor units are employed. We find in Fig. 3-3(b) that employment of L_1 labor units results in an output of y_1 for production function P'. When the labor supply is S_2, L_2 labor units are employed at a wage of W_2. For production function P' in Fig. 3-3(b), output is y_2 when L_2 labor units are employed. Thus, potential output in Fig. 3-3(b) could be y_1 or y_2 in the short run, depending upon the supply of labor.

An adverse supply shock decreases labor's productivity and reduces potential output in the short run. For example, an adverse supply shock would shift the demand for labor curve in Fig. 3-3(a) inward from D_1 to D_3 and shift production function P' in Fig. 3-3(b) downward from P' to P''. Equilibrium in the labor markets for curves D_3 and S_1 exists when L_3 labor units are employed; potential output is then y_3 for production function P''. In the short run, then, an adverse supply shock or a change in the supply of labor can generate a y_3 or y_2 rather than a y_1 level of output. These different output levels are presented in Fig. 3-4 and labeled AS_1, AS_2, and AS_3, with each output level representing the economy's ability to produce and thereby supply goods and services in the short run.

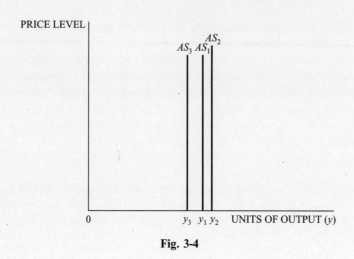

Fig. 3-4

The Long Run

Over long periods of time, we would expect not only advances in technology but increases in the quantity of labor and capital resources. Aggregate supply curve AS_1 would thereby shift rightward over long periods of time as a result of the economy's ability to produce goods and services. Potential output in the long run is more fully developed in Chapter 11.

3.5 ECONOMIC FLUCTUATIONS

Output increases over long periods of time for most industrialized nations. During shorter time intervals, however, there are periods in which output falls. The repeated sequence of a sustained decline in output followed by a longer interval of rising output is classified as a business cycle. Short-run fluctuations in output for the U.S. economy are presented in Fig. 3-5. Between 1974 and 1995, there are four recessions—four periods in which a sustained decline occurred in real GDP: November 1973 to April 1975; January 1980 to July 1980; July 1981 to November 1982; and July 1990 to March 1991. Output during the other time periods is for the most part rising.

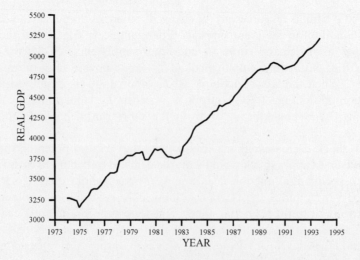

Fig. 3-5

Business cycles can be explained from a classical and a Keynesian perspective. A classical approach attributes recurrent recessions to changes in labor markets and/or to adverse supply shocks. For example, the y_1 to y_2 decrease in real output in Fig. 3-3(b) might be the result of an adverse supply shock and/or a decrease in the supply of labor. A Keynesian approach would attribute a recession to a slow wage and/or price response to a change in aggregate demand. For example, output declines whenever there is a decrease in aggregate spending and an insufficient decline in prices in response to the lower spending level. In the chapters that follow, we explain recessions from a Keynesian and then a classical perspective.

EXAMPLE 3.7. Keynesians contend that recessions occur because prices respond slowly to a decrease in aggregate demand. Aggregate demand (AD_1) in Fig. 3-6 represents the amount of goods and services that individuals, government, and business plan to purchase at different price levels. Aggregate supply (AS_1) represents potential output and therefore the economy's ability to produce. We initially assume that output is y_1 and the price level is p_1 for curves AD_1 and AS_1. Suppose a decrease in spending shifts the aggregate demand curve AD_1 downward to AD_2. Output remains at y_1 when the price level falls from p_1 to p_2. Output falls to y_2, however, when the price level remains at p_1. Thus, an economy enters a recession in the short run when aggregate demand declines, but the response of the price level is insufficient to keep spending levels at their full employment level.

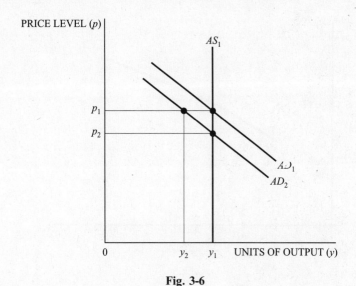

Fig. 3-6

Solved Problems

THE ECONOMY'S PRODUCTION FUNCTION

3.1 (a) What is meant by the term productivity? (b) What are the sources of increased productivity?

   (a) Productivity refers to the effective utilization of an economy's resources; specifically, it is the output associated with a fixed quantity of economic resources. Resources are more productive when an unchanged amount of resources produces a larger quantity of output.

(b) Productivity increases are the result of knowledge and are frequently referred to as technological advances. Increased knowledge may be associated with the introduction of new capital, which is more efficient. Increased knowledge could also be the result of better labor skills, the direct result of education, and from new ideas which result in new products or more efficient ways of using existing resources.

3.2 Suppose an economy's production function is specified by $y = A(\sqrt{K}\sqrt{L})$, where A represents the productivity of resources, K the quantity of capital resources, and L the quantity of labor resources. (a) Find potential output when $A = 10$, $K = 49$, and $L = 9$. (b) Find potential output when $A = 10$, $K = 49$, and labor resources are 3, 6, and 12. (c) Plot the levels of output associated with 3, 6, 9, and 12 labor units; label the production function P'. What happens to this production function when productivity increases (the value of A is larger) and/or there is more capital?

(a) $y = 10(\sqrt{49}\sqrt{9})$; $y = 210.00$; potential output $= 210.00$ units.

(b) Output is 121.24 units when labor inputs are 3; 171.46 when $L = 6$; and 242.49 when $L = 12$.

(c) The production function plotted in Fig. 3-7 shifts upward when improved technology increases the productivity of a fixed amount of labor and/or each labor unit works with more capital, since more capital increases the output of each worker.

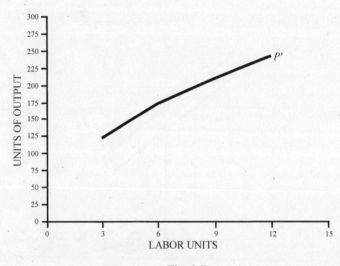

Fig. 3-7

3.3 Suppose an economy's production function is specified by $y = A(\sqrt{K}\sqrt{L})$, where A represents the productivity of resources, K the quantity of capital resources, and L the quantity of labor resources. (a) Find potential output when $A = 10$, $K = 25$, and $L = 9$. (b) Find potential output when $K = 15$, 20, and 30, and there is no change in the value of A or L. (c) Are changes in potential output in the short run more likely to be associated with changes in the quantity of labor or capital? Why?

(a) Output $= 150.00$ units.

(b) Output is 116.19 units when $K = 15$; 134.16 when $K = 20$; and 164.32 when $K = 30$.

(c) In the short run, changes in potential output are most likely the result of changes in labor rather than capital. Since capital is human-made, its quantity is unlikely to change in the short run. The supply of labor is likely to vary in the short run since (1) individuals, who previously were not looking for work, may decide to seek employment and thereby enter the labor force; (2) individuals who have jobs may look for a second one; and/or (3) currently employed individuals may be willing to work overtime.

3.4   What is meant by the term "supply shock?"

A supply shock means that there is a change in the productivity of economic resources, i.e., there is a change in the value of A in the production function $y = A(\sqrt{K}\,\sqrt{L})$. An adverse supply shock means that there has been a decrease in productivity and thereby an increase in the cost of producing goods and services. An adverse supply shock could be the result of unfavorable weather, a natural disaster, new environmental protection laws, a higher minimum wage, an escalation of wages due to a union settlement, and/or the organization of an international cartel which raises the price of a basic raw material. A favorable supply shock increases productivity and is the result of an increase in the value of A.

THE MARGINAL PRODUCTIVITY OF LABOR AND CAPITAL

3.5   (*a*) What is meant by the term marginal productivity of labor? (*b*) Suppose $y = A(\sqrt{K}\,\sqrt{L})$; $A = 10$; $K = 9$; and labor varies from 1 to 6 units. (1) Find the output associated with 1 through 6 labor units. (2) Find the marginal productivity of labor for the second through sixth labor unit. (*c*) Plot the marginal productivity of labor derived in part (*b*) and label the curve MPL'.

(*a*)   The marginal productivity of labor is the extra output which results from employing an additional labor unit, with technology and the amount of capital unchanged. The marginal productivity of labor declines with each additional labor unit, reflecting the diminishing marginal productivity of labor.

(*b*)   (1) Output is 30 units when 1 labor unit is employed $\{y = 10(\sqrt{9}\sqrt{1})\}$. Output is 42.4 units when 2 labor units are employed; 52.0 units when $L = 3$; 60.0 units when $L = 4$; 67.1 units when $L = 5$; and 73.5 units when $L = 6$. (2) The second labor unit increases output 12.4 units; therefore, the marginal productivity of the second labor unit is 12.4. The marginal productivity for the third labor unit is 9.6; 8.10 for the fourth; 7.1 for the fifth; and 6.4 for the sixth labor unit.

(*c*)   See Fig. 3-8.

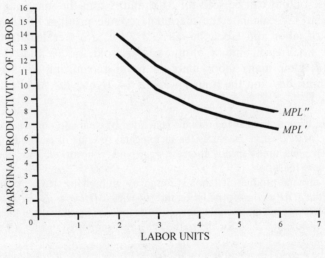

Fig. 3-8

3.6   (*a*) Suppose there is an increase in productivity and the value for A in Problem 3.5 increases from 10 to 12. The quantity of capital remains at 9 and the amount of labor varies from 1 to 6 units. (1) Find the output associated with 1 through 6 labor units. (2) Find the marginal productivity of labor for the second through sixth labor units. (*b*) Plot the marginal productivity of labor derived in part (*a*) and label the curve MPL''. What happens to the marginal productivity of labor when there is an increase in productivity, *ceteris paribus*? (*c*) What happens to the marginal productivity curve MPL' in Fig. 3-8 when there is an adverse supply shock? What has happened to the value of A?

(*a*)   (1) Output is 36.0 units when 1 labor unit is employed $\{y = 12(\sqrt{9}\,\sqrt{1})\}$. Output is 50.9 units when 2 labor units are employed; 62.4 units when $L = 3$; 72.0 units when $L = 4$; 80.5 units when $L = 5$; and 88.2 units when $L = 6$. (2) The marginal productivity of the second labor unit is 13.9. The marginal productivity of labor for the third unit is 11.5; the fourth is 9.6; the fifth 8.5; and the sixth 7.7.

(*b*)   The marginal productivity of labor increases when there is an increase in productivity; this results in a rightward shift of MPL' in Fig. 3-8 to MPL''.

(*c*)   The MPL' curve shifts inward. The value of A decreases when there is a decrease in productivity.

3.7   (*a*)   What is meant by the term "marginal productivity of capital?" (*b*) What happens to the marginal productivity of capital when there is an increase in the quantity of labor and/or an increase in productivity?

(*a*)   The marginal productivity of capital measures the incremental output associated with additional units of capital, with technology and the quantity of labor unchanged.

(*b*)   An increase in the quantity of labor and/or an improvement in technology increases the marginal productivity of capital. Graphically, the negatively sloped MPK curve shifts outward and to the right.

THE DEMAND FOR AND SUPPLY OF LABOR

3.8   (*a*) Why does the marginal revenue product of labor ($MRPL$) curve represent the demand for labor? (*b*) Suppose output can be sold for $4 a unit. From the marginal productivity of labor derived in Problem 3.5, calculate the marginal revenue product of labor; plot the marginal revenue product of labor and label the curve $MRPL'$. (*c*) Recalculate the marginal revenue product of labor when each unit of output can be sold for $5. Plot the data and label the curve $MRPL''$. (*d*) How many labor units do profit-maximizing firms hire when each labor unit works an 8-hour day and the hourly wage is $4? [Note: the $MRPL$ for each labor unit is for an 8-hour day.]

(*a*)   Labor units are hired as long as the revenue generated by each additional labor unit is greater than its cost. Since the $MRPL$ curve measures the incremental revenue of each additional unit of labor, the number of labor units hired depends upon the wage paid each worker. Thus, the $MRPL$ curve becomes the demand curve for labor.

(*b*)   The marginal revenue product of labor is found by multiplying MPL by the price of each unit of output. Thus, the MRP of the second labor unit is $49.60 [$MPL(P) = MRPL$; 12.4 units at $4 a unit = $49.60]. The MRP of each additional labor unit is as follows: $38.40 for the third; $32.40 for the fourth; $28.40 for the fifth; and $25.60 for the sixth. The data are plotted in Fig. 3-9 and the curve is labeled $MRPL'$.

(*c*)   The MRP of the second labor unit is now $62.00 [$MPL(P) = MRPL$; 12.4 units at $5 a unit = $62.00]. The MRP of each additional labor unit is as follows: $48.00 for the third; $40.50 for the fourth; $35.50 for the fifth; and $32.00 for the sixth. The data are plotted in Fig. 3-9 and the curve is labeled $MRPL''$.

(*d*)   Four labor units are hired when each unit of output is sold for $4.00. At a wage of $4 an hour, each labor unit is paid $32.00 for an eight-hour day. Businesses hire no more than four labor units, since the marginal revenue product of the fourth labor unit is $32.40. [Note that businesses do not hire the fifth labor unit at a cost of $32.00, since the marginal revenue product of the fifth labor unit is $28.40.] When the price of the good is $5.00, six labor units are hired. Each labor unit still costs $32.00 for an eight-hour day, since the hourly wage is unchanged at $4. Businesses hire six labor units, since the $32 wage paid the sixth labor unit equals the $32 marginal revenue product of the sixth labor unit.

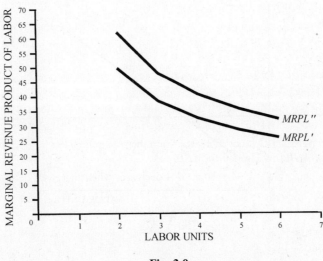

Fig. 3-9

3.9   (a) Suppose there are six labor units in an economy; each labor unit works an eight-hour day. Use the marginal revenue product of labor calculated in parts (b) and (c) of Problem 3.8 to establish the hourly wage that each labor unit will receive. (b) Explain why labor is paid a higher wage when the price of the good is $5 than when the price of the good is $4.

(a) Since each of the six labor units is willing to work, six labor units must be employed. Therefore the hourly wage is set at a rate where the labor cost for an eight-hour day is equal to the marginal revenue product of the sixth labor unit. The marginal revenue product of the sixth labor unit is $25.60 in part (b) when the price of the good is $4. Each of the six workers is thereby paid $25.60 for an eight-hour day or $3.20 an hour. When the price of the good is $5 [part (c)], the marginal revenue product of the sixth worker is $32.00. Each worker now receives $32.00 for an eight-hour day or $4 an hour.

(b) Labor receives a higher wage in part (c) because its marginal revenue product is higher, i.e., there is a greater demand for labor. An increased demand for labor occurs when output can be sold at a higher price and/or there is an increase in labor's marginal productivity.

3.10   (a) How would an adverse supply shock affect the marginal revenue product of labor? (b) Suppose labor receives a fixed wage. What happens to the number of labor units employed when there is an adverse supply shock?

(a) An adverse supply shock reduces the productivity of economic resources: in this case, it decreases the marginal productivity of labor. When the price of output is unchanged, a decrease in labor productivity translates into a decrease in labor's marginal revenue product.

(b) Businesses hire labor units based upon the revenue they generate. Since labor's wage is unchanged and its marginal revenue product has decreased, profit-maximizing firms hire fewer units of labor.

3.11   (a) Explain why the number of labor units supplied is positively related to the wage paid. (b) A labor supply curve is presented in Fig. 3-10. Explain what should happen to this labor supply curve when (1) there is an increase in the working-age population, *ceteris paribus*; (2) there is a sudden decline in the wealth of individuals, *ceteris paribus*; (3) government imposes a mandatory retirement age of 65, *ceteris paribus*.

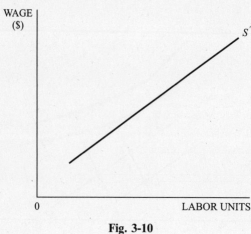

Fig. 3-10

(*a*) Work competes with leisure. The opportunity cost of leisure is the wage that one earns when one gives up leisure for work. Many individuals are willing to give up leisure for work when there is adequate compensation for doing so. Since each individual has a different work/leisure preference, the number of labor units supplied varies with the wage rate. Thus, it is reasonable to expect more labor units to be supplied at a higher wage.

(*b*) 1. An increase in the working-age population means that more labor units are available to work at each wage. The labor supply curve S' in Fig. 3-10 shifts outward to the right.

2. When there is a loss of wealth, more individuals are willing to work at each wage to rebuild their wealth. Thus, the labor supply curve S' in Fig. 3-10 shifts outward to the right.

3. The imposition by government of a mandatory retirement age reduces the number of workers available to work at each wage. As a result supply curve S' in Fig. 3-10 shifts inward to the left.

POTENTIAL OUTPUT IN THE SHORT AND LONG RUN

3.12 Explain why potential output in the short run depends upon the equilibrium condition in the labor markets.

Potential output depends upon the productivity and quantity of labor and capital. An economy's stock of capital is unchanged in the short run since capital resources are long-lived and take time to produce. Productivity is normally unchanged in the short run. Labor units, on the other hand, are variable. Workers can enter or leave the labor force; employed workers can be asked to work overtime; employed workers can look for a second job. With a given production function, then, output in the short run depends upon the employment of labor and therefore the equilibrium condition in the labor markets.

3.13 (*a*) Find the equilibrium condition in the labor markets in Fig. 3-11(*a*) when the demand for labor is D' and the supply of labor is S'. Use production function P' in Fig. 3-11(*b*) to establish potential output. (*b*) Suppose the working-age population increases and the supply of labor curve in Fig. 3-11(*a*) shifts outward to S''. The demand for labor remains at D'. Find the new equilibrium condition in the labor markets and the new level of potential output.

(*a*) Equilibrium in the labor markets for curves D' and S' in Fig. 3-11(*a*) exists when L_1 labor units are employed at a W_1 wage. Output in Fig. 3-11(*b*) for production function P' is y_1 when L_1 labor units are employed.

(*b*) Equilibrium for curves S'' and D' in Fig. 3-11(*a*) exists when L_2 labor units are employed at a W_2 wage. Potential output is then y_2 in Fig. 3-11(*b*) for production function P'.

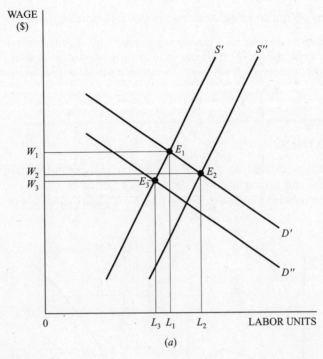

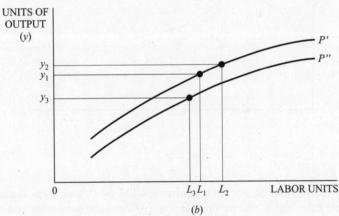

Fig. 3-11

3.14   (*a*) Suppose there is an adverse supply shock; the demand curve for labor in Fig. 3-11(*a*) shifts inward to D'' and the production function in Fig. 3-11(*b*) shifts downward to P''. Explain why an adverse supply shock shifts the demand for labor and the production function curves. (*b*) Find labor market equilibrium in Fig. 3-11(*a*) for curves D'' and S'. Find potential output along production function P''.

(*a*)   The decrease in productivity reduces the output associated with each labor unit; thus, the production function shifts downward from P' to P''. The marginal productivity of labor decreases, which lowers the marginal revenue product of labor; the demand curve for labor shifts inward from D' to D''.

(*b*)   Equilibrium in the labor markets exists in Fig. 3-11(*a*) for D'' and S' when L_3 labor units are employed at a wage rate of W_3. In Fig. 3-11(*b*), L_3 labor units are associated with a y_3 output along production function P''.

3.15   Why does potential output increase over long periods of time?

Potential output depends upon the quantity and productivity of economic resources. Over time, most nations expand their stock of capital; experience an increase in population and the size of their labor force; and enjoy the benefits of technological advances. Therefore, potential output for most nations increases over long periods of time.

ECONOMIC FLUCTUATIONS

3.16   Suppose a recession is defined as a period in which real output is falling for two or more consecutive quarters and an expansion is defined as a period in which real output is increasing over two or more consecutive quarters. From Fig. 3-12, identify periods of recession and expansion.

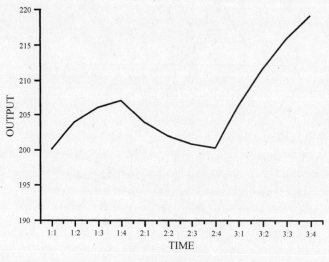

Fig. 3-12

The economy is expanding from year one, quarter one (period 1:1) through year one, quarter 4 (period 1:4). Output is falling from year 1, quarter four (period 1:4) through year 2, quarter 4 (period 2:4). There is an expansion from year 2, quarter 4 through year three, quarter 4.

3.17   Explain the recession in Fig. 3-12 as the outcome of an adverse supply shock.

An adverse supply shock exists when a decrease in productivity shifts a short-run production function downward and reduces the economy's level of output. For example, in Fig. 3-11(b), an adverse supply shock shifts production function P' downward to P'' and output is lowered from y_1 to y_3. Thus, an adverse supply shock could have reduced output in Fig. 3-12 for the period 1:4 through 2:4.

3.18   How might a Keynesian explain the recession identified in Fig. 3-12?

A Keynesian might attribute the recession to disequilibrium; aggregate demand might have declined but the price level failed to fall to a level which would equate spending and full employment output. For example, the aggregate demand curve AD' in Fig. 3-13 could have shifted leftward to AD''. If the price level remains at p_1, output falls from y_1 to y_2. Because of an inflexible price level, the economy lowers output and the business sector produces below its full employment potential.

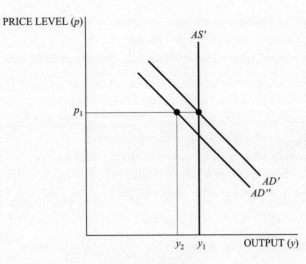

Fig. 3-13

Multiple Choice Questions

1. When graphed, a production function displays a

    (*a*) Positive relationship between output and the level of technology, *ceteris paribus*.

    (*b*) Positive relationship between output and labor inputs, *ceteris paribus*.

    (*c*) Negative relationship between output and the level of technology, *ceteris paribus*.

    (*d*) Negative relationship between output and labor inputs, *ceteris paribus*.

2. When the value of $K = 4$ and $L = 4$ with a production function of $y = A(K^{0.5}L^{0.5})$, output is

    (*a*) 80 when $A = 5$.

    (*b*) 80 when $A = 10$.

    (*c*) 40 when $A = 5$.

    (*d*) 40 when $A = 10$.

3. The marginal productivity of labor is

    (*a*) The incremental output due to an increase in capital, *ceteris paribus*.

    (*b*) The incremental output due to an increase in labor, *ceteris paribus*.

    (*c*) The incremental output due to a change in technology, *ceteris paribus*.

    (*d*) The incremental output due to a change in technology and a change in the amount of capital.

4. The marginal productivity of labor

    (*a*) Increases when the price of the good sold increases, *ceteris paribus*.

    (*b*) Decreases when there is an adverse supply shock, *ceteris paribus*.

    (*c*) Increases when more workers are hired, *ceteris paribus*.

    (*d*) Decreases when there is an increase in the quantity of capital, *ceteris paribus*.

5. The marginal revenue product of labor

    (*a*) Increases when there is an adverse supply shock, *ceteris paribus*.

    (*b*) Increases when there is an increase in the price of output, *ceteris paribus*.

    (*c*) Increases when more workers are hired, *ceteris paribus*.

    (*d*) Increases when fewer capital units are used with a fixed quantity of labor, *ceteris paribus*.

6.   The demand for labor

    (*a*) Increases when there is a technological advance, *ceteris paribus*.

    (*b*) Increases when there is an increase in the supply of labor, *ceteris paribus*.

    (*c*) Decreases when fewer labor units are hired, *ceteris paribus*.

    (*d*) Decreases when there is an increase in the supply of labor, *ceteris paribus*.

7.   Which of the following does not increase output?

    (*a*) An increase in the supply of labor, *ceteris paribus*.

    (*b*) There is a technological advance, *ceteris paribus*.

    (*c*) Government imposes new environmental laws, *ceteris paribus*.

    (*d*) There are improved methods for managing economic resources, *ceteris paribus*.

8.   Which of the following statements is incorrect?

    (*a*) Potential output increases in the short run when there is an increase in the marginal productivity of labor, *ceteris paribus*.

    (*b*) Potential output increases in the short run when there is an increase in the supply of labor, *ceteris paribus*.

    (*c*) Potential output increases when there is a favorable supply shock, *ceteris paribus*.

    (*d*) Potential output increases when government passes a law that mandates retirement at the age of 65, *ceteris paribus*.

9.   Suppose output over four successive quarters is: 1:1 $350.00; 1:2 $357.00; 1:3 $353.40; 1:4 $346.40; 2:1 $342.90; 2:2 $349.80; 2:3 $360.20; 2:4 $365.60. The economy is in a recession during which of the following quarters?

    (*a*) 1:1 through 1:4

    (*b*) 1:3 through 2:3

    (*c*) 1:1 through 2:2

    (*d*) 1:3 through 2:1

10.   Which of the following statements is true?

    (*a*) An adverse supply shock can cause a recession.

    (*b*) A substantial increase in the minimum wage can cause a recession.

    (*c*) A decline in aggregate spending can cause a recession.

    (*d*) All of the above.

    (*e*) None of the above.

True or False Questions

11. _____ Output is \$30 when $A = 10$, $K = 3$, and $L = 3$ for a production function of $y = A(K^{0.5}L^{0.5})$.

12. _____ Over long periods of time, potential output shows a cyclical pattern where increases and decreases in output are of the same length and magnitude.

13. _____ Increases in productivity are the result of increased knowledge.

14. _____ Changes in potential output, in the short run, are normally the result of increased capital resources.

15. _____ A beneficial supply shock increases the productivity of economic resources.

16. _____ Incremental labor units have a diminishing marginal productivity, *ceteris paribus*.

17. _____ An increase in capital, *ceteris paribus*, increases the marginal productivity of labor.

18. _____ An adverse supply shock reduces the marginal productivity of labor.

19. _____ Output in the short run is a function of the equilibrium condition in the labor market.

20. _____ A classical approach to recessions attributes the decline in real GDP to a rapid adjustment of prices to a change in the level of aggregate demand.

Answers to Multiple Choice and True or False Questions

1. (*b*); **2**. (*d*); **3**. (*b*); **4**. (*b*); **5**. (*b*); **6**. (*a*); **7**. (*c*); **8**. (*d*); **9**. (*d*); **10**. (*d*); **11**. T; **12**. F; **13**. T; **14**. F; **15**. T; **16**. T; **17**. T; **18**. T; **19**. T; **20**. F.

Chapter 4

Models of Spending Equilibrium

Chapter Summary

1. The short-run model of output developed in this chapter assumes that the price level remains above the intersection of aggregate supply and aggregate demand. (See Example 3.7 and Fig. 3.6.) In such a situation, businesses produce what they can sell at current prices. Although not representative of full-employment output, we designate the production level at which spending equals output as an equilibrium level of output.

2. A two-sector spending model consists of consumer and investment spending. Consumer spending (C) is positively related to current disposable income (Yd) and is also influenced by other unspecified variables. Since variables determining investment spending (I) are unspecified, investment is a fixed sum. In this model, output $(Y) = C + I$, where $C = \bar{C} + cYd$ and $I = \bar{I}$. In the two-sector model, equilibrium output equals $(\bar{C} + \bar{I})/(1 - c)$.

3. The marginal propensity to consume (MPC) relates a change in consumption (ΔC) to a change in current disposable income (ΔYd). In the equation $C = \bar{C} + cYd$, c is the MPC ($\Delta C/\Delta Yd$), which is also the slope of the consumption line. In a two-sector model, a change in exogenous spending results in a multiple change in output. This is specified as $\Delta Y = \Delta \bar{A}/(1 - c)$ where $\Delta \bar{A}$ represents a change in exogenous consumption ($\Delta \bar{C}$) or exogenous investment ($\Delta \bar{I}$).

4. In an expanded four-sector model, aggregate spending includes consumption, investment, government expenditures (G), and net exports (exports minus imports). Government spending is exogenous; net exports are exogenous and negatively related to output. Government tax revenues are positively related to output and are influenced by other unspecified variables. In the four-sector model, spending equilibrium exists where $Y = (\bar{C} + \bar{I} + \bar{G} - c\bar{T}x + \bar{X})/(1 - c + ct + m)$; $\bar{T}x$ represents lump-sum taxes, $\bar{X}$ represents exogenous net exports, t is the personal income tax rate, and m is the marginal propensity to import.

5. When an income tax and a marginal propensity to import are added to the model, the multiplier changes from $1/(1 - c)$ in the two-sector model to $1/(1 - c + ct + m)$ in the expanded model. A change in an exogenous variable now changes output by $\Delta Y = \Delta \bar{A}/(1 - c + ct + m)$, where $\Delta \bar{A}$ represents a change in exogenous consumption ($\Delta \bar{C}$), exogenous investment ($\Delta \bar{I}$), exogenous government expenditures ($\Delta \bar{G}$), exogenous taxes ($\Delta \bar{T}x$), and/or exogenous net exports ($\Delta \bar{X}$).

Chapter Outline

4.1 AGGREGATE SPENDING IN A TWO-SECTOR MODEL

A two-sector spending model consists of individuals and businesses. We shall assume in this chapter that, at the existing price level, aggregate demand is less than aggregate supply. At the existing price level, there is surplus output when production is determined by the aggregate supply curve. Thus, business sector production is determined by aggregate demand; businesses produce what can be sold at current prices. The following behavior is assumed for individuals and businesses: (1) investment (I) is unrelated to output and therefore is exogenous; and (2) consumer spending (C) is a positive linear function of current disposable income (Yd). Because consumer saving (S) equals current disposable income less consumption ($S = Yd - C$), saving is also a positive, linear function of current disposable income. Consumer disposable income (Yd) equals the value of output (Y) since there is no government sector.

EXAMPLE 4.1. Fig. 4-1 presents consumption and investment spending. In Fig. 4-1(a), consumption is $450 when disposable income is $500 and $530 when disposable income is $600. Saving equals $Yd - C$. Thus, saving, read from either Fig. 4-1(a) or (b), is $50 when disposable income is $500 and $70 when disposable income is $600. In Fig. 4-1($c$), investment is $50 regardless of the level of output.

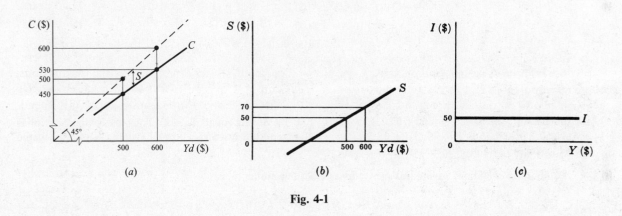

Fig. 4-1

EXAMPLE 4.2. In Fig. 4-2(a), $50 in investment spending is added to the consumption line. There is spending equilibrium when output is $500, since C of $450 plus I of $50 equals the $500 produced. In Fig. 4-2(b), there is equilibrium output when investment injections equal saving leakages.

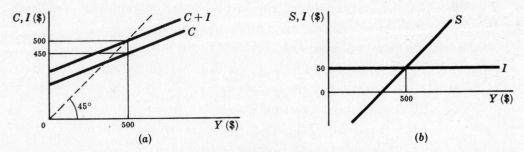

Fig. 4-2

4.2 AN ALGEBRAIC SOLUTION TO EQUILIBRIUM OUTPUT

The consumption line in Fig. 4-1(a) can be presented as $C = \$50 + 0.80\,Yd$. With investment spending at \$50, we find spending equilibrium by equating output and spending, i.e., $Y = C + I$. (See Example 4.3.) Equilibrium output is also found by equating saving leakages and investment injections (Example 4.4). Spending equilibrium can also be presented with alphabetical symbols: investment spending is $\bar{I}$, where $\bar{I}$ represents exogenous investment; consumption is $\bar{C} + cYd$, where $\bar{C}$ represents exogenous consumption and cYd represents the amount of consumption at each level of current disposable income. Spending equilibrium is then $Y = (\bar{C} + \bar{I})/(1 - c)$.

EXAMPLE 4.3. Suppose household consumption is $C = \$50 + 0.80\,Yd$, and investment is \$50. In the absence of a government sector and taxes, the value of output equals household disposable income, so that $Yd = Y$. Given the specified spending plans, *equilibrium output* is \$500.

Equilibrium condition: Output equals spending:

$$Y = C + I$$
$$Y = (\$50 + 0.80\,Y) + \$50$$
$$Y - 0.80\,Y = \$100$$
$$Y(1 - 0.80) = \$100$$
$$Y(0.20) = \$100$$
$$Y = \$100/0.20$$
$$Y = \$500$$

EXAMPLE 4.4. Suppose $C = \$50 + 0.80\,Yd$; $I = \$50$; $Y = Yd$. Saving equals $Yd - C$. Thus, the saving function is $S = -\$50 + 0.20\,Y$. [$S = Yd - C$; $Yd = Y$; $S = Y - (\$50 + 0.80\,Y)$; $S = -\$50 + 0.20\,Y$.] Equilibrium occurs where saving leakages equal investment injections.

Equilibrium condition: Saving leakages = investment injections

$$S = I$$
$$-\$50 + 0.20\,Y = \$50$$
$$0.20\,Y = \$100$$
$$Y = \frac{\$100}{0.20}$$
$$Y = \$500$$

EXAMPLE 4.5. Suppose $C = \bar{C} + cYd$; $Yd = Y$; $I = \bar{I}$; $S = -\bar{C} + (1 - c)Yd$; [$S = Yd - C$; $S = Yd - (\bar{C} + cYd)$; $S = Y - \bar{C} - cYD$; $S = -\bar{C} + (1 - c)Yd$]. Equilibrium output is $Y = (\bar{C} + \bar{I})/(1 - c)$, found by equating $Y = C + I$ and $S = I$.

Equilibrium condition: Output equals spending:

$$Y = C + I$$
$$Y = \bar{C} + cY + \bar{I}$$
$$Y - cY = \bar{C} + \bar{I}$$
$$Y(1 - c) = \bar{C} + \bar{I}$$
$$Y = \frac{\bar{C} + \bar{I}}{1 - c}$$

Equilibrium condition: Saving leakages = investment injections:

$$S = I$$
$$-\bar{C} + (1 - c)Y = \bar{I}$$
$$Y = \frac{\bar{C} + \bar{I}}{1 - c}$$

4.3 THE MARGINAL PROPENSITY TO CONSUME

The marginal propensity to consumer (MPC) relates the change in consumption to the change in disposable income, i.e., $MPC = \Delta C / \Delta Yd$. As presented in Fig. 4-3, the change in consumption is less than the change in disposable income; the MPC is assumed to have a value greater than 0 but less than 1. In the consumption equation, $C = \bar{C} + cYd$, the MPC is behavioral coefficient c, which is the slope of the consumption line. Since individuals either consume or save, the marginal propensity to save equals $1 - MPC$ or $1 - c$.

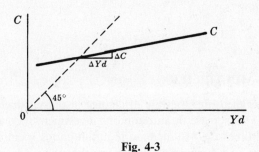

Fig. 4-3

EXAMPLE 4.6. Suppose the value of c is 0.80 for consumption equation $C = \bar{C} + cYd$. The MPC is 0.80, indicating that there is an $8 change in consumption for every $10 change in disposable income.

4.4 THE MULTIPLIER EFFECT OF A CHANGE IN EXOGENOUS SPENDING

A change in exogenous spending results in a parallel shift of the $(C + I)$ spending line in Fig. 4-2(a) and a new equilibrium level of output. In a two-sector model, a change in exogenous spending means that there is a change in either $\bar{C}$ or $\bar{I}$. (A change in exogenous spending is also reported as a change in autonomous spending.) A change in autonomous spending alters output and induces further changes in consumption because of the dependency of consumption upon disposable income. Thus, an increase in autonomous investment ($\Delta\bar{I}$), *ceteris paribus*, causes output to change by more than the autonomous change ($\Delta Y > \Delta\bar{I}$) because a change in personal disposable income induces a change in consumption.

EXAMPLE 4.7. Equilibrium output is $500 for the $C + I'$ line in Fig. 4-4; consumption is $450, and investment is $50. A $10 increase in investment shifts the spending line from $C + I'$ to $C + I''$ with equilibrium output increasing from $500 to $550. At the higher output level, investment is $60 and consumption is $490. The $10 increase in autonomous investment induces $40 in additional consumption for a $50 change in output.

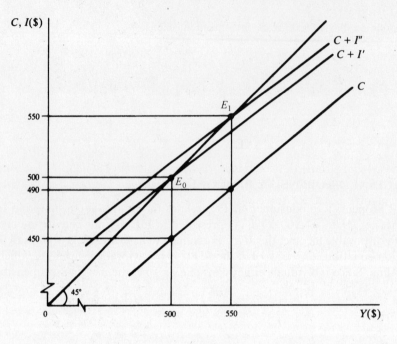

Fig. 4-4

4.5 THE EXPENDITURE MULTIPLIER

The expenditure multiplier measures the rate of change in output due to a change in autonomous spending. In Example 4.7, a \$10 increase in autonomous investment increases equilibrium output \$50, i.e., the change in output is 5 times the \$10 increase in autonomous spending. Thus, $\Delta Y/\Delta \bar{I}$ equals 5, and the expenditure multiplier k_e is 5. Example 4.8 shows that the value of the expenditure multiplier depends upon c, the marginal propensity to consume. A larger MPC increases the value of k_e while lower values reduce k_e.

EXAMPLE 4.8.   Suppose $C = \bar{C} + cY$ and $I = \bar{I}$. Equilibrium output is $Y = (\bar{C} + \bar{I})/(1 - c)$ which is derived in Example 4.5. An increase in autonomous investment, with no change in $\bar{C}$ or c, increases equilibrium output by $\Delta Y = \Delta \bar{I}/(1 - c)$. The multiplied effect on equilibrium output from the change in autonomous investment $(\Delta Y/\Delta \bar{I})$ is $1/(1 - c)$. The expenditure multiplier k_e is $1/(1 - c)$; the value of k_e depends upon c, the marginal propensity to consume:

$$Y = \frac{\bar{C} + I}{1 - c}$$

Letting $\Delta \bar{I} > 0$, *ceteris paribus* (i.e., $\Delta \bar{C} = 0$ and there is no change in c)

$$\Delta Y = \frac{\Delta \bar{I}}{1 - c}$$

Thus,

$$\frac{\Delta Y}{\Delta \bar{I}} = \frac{1}{1 - c}$$

Letting $k_e = \Delta Y/\Delta \bar{I}$,

$$k_e = \frac{1}{1 - c}$$

EXAMPLE 4.9.   The multiplier provides a short-cut method for determining the equilibrium level of output.

Equilibrium occurs where

$$Y = \frac{\bar{C} + \bar{I}}{1 - c}$$

or where

$$Y = (\bar{C} + \bar{I})\left[\frac{1}{1 - c}\right]$$

Letting $k_e = 1/(1 - c)$, and $\bar{A} = (\bar{C} + \bar{I})$,

$$Y = k_e \bar{A}$$

4.6 GOVERNMENT SPENDING, TAXES, TRANSFERS, AND OUTPUT

Government spending consists of goods purchased by federal, state, and local governments and payments to government employees, including military personnel. Transfers consist of government payments which involve no direct service by the recipient, such as unemployment insurance, interest on the public debt, and welfare payments. Taxes are imposed upon property, goods (sales and excise taxes) and income, which the government uses to make transfers and to pay for expenditures.

Output rises when there is an increase in government spending (G) and/or a decrease in the government sector's net tax revenues, *ceteris paribus*. (Net tax revenues Tn equal gross tax receipts (Tx) less government transfers (Tr).) Fiscal policy consists of a change in taxes, transfers and/or government spending to change output. In the following three-sector model, equilibrium output exists where $Y = C + I + G$ in the spending approach and $Tn + S = I + G$ in the leakages/injections approach to output. [Tn represents net tax revenues, i.e., $Tn = Tx - Tr$.]

EXAMPLE 4.10. Output is Y_0 in the two-sector ($C + I$) model in Fig. 4-5(*a*); the addition of government spending shifts the spending ($C + \bar{I}$) line upward to ($C + \bar{I} + \bar{G}$); equilibrium output increases from Y_0 to Y_1. In the leakage/injection approach in Fig. 4-5(*b*), $\bar{G}$ shifts the injection line $\bar{I}$ upward to ($\bar{I} + \bar{G}$). Note that, in the absence of taxes to finance government spending, government spending of $\bar{G}$ is financed by private sector saving of $S_0 S_1$.

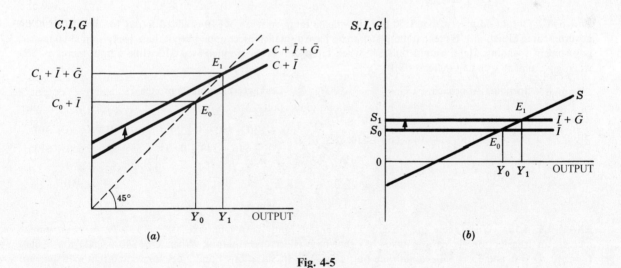

(*a*)   (*b*)

Fig. 4-5

EXAMPLE 4.11. Suppose government finances the expenditure of $\bar{G}$ in Example 4.10 through a lump-sum tax $\bar{T}x$. In Fig. 4-6(*a*), $\bar{T}x$ taxes shift spending line ($C + \bar{I} + \bar{G}$) downward to ($C + \bar{I} + \bar{G} - c\bar{T}x$) since taxes reduce consumption. Note that the reduction in output from Y_1 to Y_2 leaves output above the initial Y_0 level in the two-sector model. In Fig. 4-6(*b*), $\bar{T}x$ appears as a leakage from the circular flow, which shifts the leakage schedule upward from S to ($S + c\bar{T}x$), reducing output from Y_1 to Y_2.

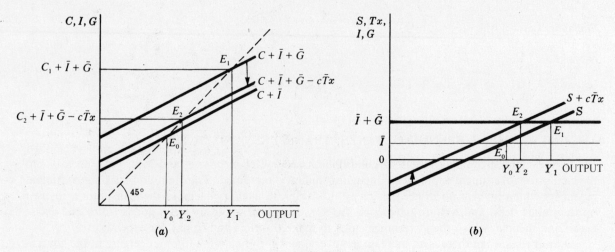

Fig. 4-6

EXAMPLE 4.12.   Equilibrium output is \$500 when $C = \$40 + 0.80 Yd$, $I = \$60$, and there are no taxes or government spending.

Situation 1: Output increases from \$500 to \$550 when \$10 in government spending is introduced. This increase in government spending has the same multiplier effect upon output as would a similar increase in investment.

Spending Approach	Leakage/Injection Approach
$Y = C + I + G$	$S = I + G$
$Y = \$40 + 0.80Y + \$60 + 10$	$0.20Y - \$40 = \$60 + \$10$
$Y = 0.80Y + \$110$	$0.20Y = \$110$
$Y = \$550$	$Y = \$550$

Situation 2: Output decreases from \$550 to \$510 when a lump-sum tax of \$10 is added to pay for the \$10 spent by government in Situation 1. Note that lump-sum taxes have a smaller effect upon output than does a similar change in government spending. Here, output falls \$40 when lump-sum taxes are increased \$10 while output increases \$50 when government spending increases \$10.

Spending Approach	Leakage/Injection Approach
	$S + Tx = I + G$
$Y = C + I + G$	$Y - \$10 - \$40 - 0.80(Y - \$10) + \$10 = \$60 + \$10$
$Y = \$40 + 0.80(Y - 10) + \$60 + \$10$	$Y - \$10 - \$40 - 0.80Y + \$8 + \$10 = \$60 + \$10$
$Y - 0.80Y = \$110 - \$8$	$0.20Y - \$32 = \$70$
$Y = \$510$	$Y = \$510$

EXAMPLE 4.13.   When there are government transfers and lump-sum taxes, $Yd = Y - Tx + Tr$. A similar increase in transfers or decrease in taxes has the same effect upon output. When $C = \$40 + 0.80 Yd$, $I = \$60$, $G = \$10$, $Tr = 0$, and $Tx = \$10$, equilibrium output is \$510. In Situations 1 and 2 below, we find that a \$5 increase in transfers or a \$5 decrease in taxes raise output from \$510 to \$530.

Situation 1: A \$5 increase in transfers

$$Y = C + I + G$$
$$Y = \$40 + 0.80(Y - \$10 + \$5) + \$60 + \$10$$
$$Y = \$530$$

Situation 2: A \$5 decrease in lump-sum taxes

$$Y = C + I + G$$
$$Y = \$40 + 0.80(Y - \$5) + \$60 + \$10$$
$$Y = \$530$$

4.7 GOVERNMENT SECTOR MULTIPLIERS

When there is a government sector, there is a lump-sum tax multiplier and a balanced budget multiplier in addition to an expenditure multiplier.

EXAMPLE 4.14.   Equilibrium output is $Y = (\bar{C} + \bar{I} + \bar{G} - c\bar{T}n)/(1 - c)$, when

$$C = \bar{C} + cYd, \; Yd = Y - Tn, \; Tn = \bar{T}x - \bar{T}r, \; I = \bar{I}, \; G = \bar{G}. \text{ For equilibrium}$$

$$Y = C + I + G$$
$$Y = \bar{C} + c(Y - \bar{T}n) + \bar{I} + \bar{G}$$
$$Y - cY = \bar{C} - c\bar{T}n + \bar{I} + \bar{G}$$
$$Y = \frac{\bar{C} + \bar{I} + \bar{G} - c\bar{T}n}{1 - c}$$

The change in equilibrium output from a change in autonomous consumption, investment, government spending and lump-sum taxes is thereby

$$\Delta Y = (\Delta \bar{C} + \Delta \bar{I} + \Delta \bar{G} - c\Delta \bar{T}n)/(1 - c)$$

The Expenditure Multiplier

The change in equilibrium output for a change in autonomous government spending of $\Delta \bar{G}$, is

$$\Delta Y = \frac{\Delta \bar{G}}{1 - c}$$

The expenditure multiplier k_e is then

$$k_e = \frac{\Delta Y}{\Delta \bar{G}} = \frac{1}{1 - c}$$

The Lump-sum Tax Multiplier

The change in equilibrium output for a change in autonomous net tax revenues of $\Delta \bar{T}n$ is

$$\Delta Y = \frac{-c\Delta \bar{T}n}{1 - c}$$

The lump-sum tax multiplier k_t is then

$$k_t = \frac{\Delta Y}{\Delta \bar{T}n} = \frac{-c}{1 - c}$$

The Balanced Budget Multiplier

The change in equilibrium output for an equal change in $\bar{G}$ and $\bar{T}n$ (i.e., $\Delta \bar{G} = \Delta \bar{T}n$) is

$$\Delta Y = \frac{\Delta \bar{G} - c\Delta \bar{T}n}{1 - c}$$

Since $\Delta \bar{G} = \Delta \bar{T} n$,

$$\Delta Y = \frac{\Delta \bar{G} - c\Delta \bar{G}}{1 - c}$$

$$\Delta Y = \frac{\Delta \bar{G}(1 - c)}{1 - c}$$

$$\Delta Y = \Delta \bar{G}$$

The multiplier for an equal change in $\bar{G}$ and $\bar{T} n$ is

$$k_b = \frac{\Delta Y}{\Delta \bar{G}} = 1$$

4.8 MULTIPLIERS FOR A MODEL WITH INCOME TAXES

While a majority of transfers are independent of income, most tax revenues for the federal government are dependent upon the level of income. Net tax revenues of government are now presented as $\bar{T}x + tY - \bar{T}r$, where $\bar{T}x$ are administered, lump-sum taxes (such as property taxes), t is a tax rate applied to personal income, and $\bar{T}r$ are exogenous transfers. For ease of analysis, it is customary to assume that t is a fixed rate income tax which is imposed upon individuals. (Note: the U.S.A. has a progressive income tax structure which means that the value of t increases with output; government also collects income taxes from corporations as well as individuals.) The inclusion of an income tax in the model reduces the value of each multiplier.

EXAMPLE 4.15.   Suppose $C = \bar{C} + cYd$, $Yd = Y - \bar{T}x - tY + \bar{T}r$, $I = \bar{I}$, $G = \bar{G}$. Equilibrium output is then

$$Y = C + I + G$$
$$Y = \bar{C} + c(Y - \bar{T}x - tY + \bar{T}r) + \bar{I} + \bar{G}$$
$$Y = \frac{\bar{C} + \bar{I} + \bar{G} - c\bar{T}x + c\bar{T}r}{1 - c + ct}$$

The change in equilibrium output from a change in autonomous consumption, investment, government spending, transfers, and lump-sum taxes is thereby

$$\Delta Y = (\Delta \bar{C} + \Delta \bar{I} + \Delta \bar{G} - c\Delta \bar{T}x + c\Delta \bar{T}r)/(1 - c + ct)$$

The Government Expenditure Multiplier

When there is a change in government spending, *ceteris paribus*, the change in output and the expenditure multiplier are:

$$\Delta Y = \frac{\Delta \bar{G}}{1 - c + ct}$$

$$k_e = \frac{\Delta Y}{\Delta \bar{G}} = \frac{1}{1 - c + ct}$$

Lump-sum Tax Multiplier

When there is a change in lump-sum taxes, *ceteris paribus*, the change in output and the lump-sum tax multiplier are:

$$\Delta Y = \frac{-c\Delta \bar{T}n}{1 - c + ct}$$

$$k_t = \frac{\Delta Y}{\Delta \bar{T}n} = \frac{-c}{1 - c + ct}$$

Balanced Budget Multiplier

When there is an equal change in government spending and lump-sum taxes, *ceteris paribus*, the change in output and the balanced budget multiplier are:

$$\Delta Y = (\Delta \bar{G} - c\Delta \bar{T}x)/(1 - c + ct)$$
$$\Delta Y = \Delta \bar{G}(1 - c)/(1 - c + ct)$$

and
$$k_b = (1 - c)/(1 - c + ct)$$

4.9 FISCAL POLICY AND *CETERIS PARIBUS*

So far, the effect of various fiscal measures has been analyzed under the assumption of *ceteris paribus*. As we shall see in Chapter 6, a fiscal action may affect private sector spending so that the fiscal measure is partially or totally offset by some other spending change. It is important, therefore, to keep in mind the methodological observations of Section 1.2. Simple models allow us to analyze with precision the result of a single parameter change. Whether we can approximate reality with such a model depends upon the importance of and possible change in other variables.

4.10 NET EXPORTS AND EQUILIBRIUM OUTPUT

A country exports domestic goods and services and imports foreign-made goods and services. Its net export balance is the sum of gross exports minus gross imports. Gross exports are exogenous, determined by the level of output in foreign countries and the foreign exchange rate. Imports are related to both the foreign exchange rate and domestic output. A country's net export balance can be presented as $X = \bar{X} - mY$, where $\bar{X}$ represents autonomous net exports (exogenous exports less exogenous imports) and m is the domestic economy's marginal propensity to import. Exogenous exports are an injection into the circular flow, while exogenous imports are a leakage. The marginal propensity to import, like the income tax, reduces the value of the multipliers.

EXAMPLE 4.16. The marginal propensity to import m represents a leakage from the domestic spending flow which reduces the value of the multipliers. Suppose $C = \bar{C} + cYd$, $I = \bar{I}$, $G = \bar{G}$, $X = \bar{X} - mY$, $Yd = Y - (\bar{T}x + tY - \bar{T}r)$. Equilibrium output is then

$$Y = \frac{\bar{C} + \bar{I} + \bar{G} + \bar{X} - c\bar{T}x + c\bar{T}r}{1 - c + ct + m}$$

For an autonomous change in $\bar{C}$, $\bar{I}$, $\bar{G}$, and $\bar{X}$, the expenditure multiplier is

$$k_e = \frac{1}{1 - c + ct + m}$$

For an autonomous change in $\bar{T}r$ and $\bar{T}x$, the lump-sum tax multiplier is

$$k_t = \frac{-c}{1 - c + ct + m}$$

EXAMPLE 4.17. The expenditure multiplier from Example 4.16 is $k_e = 1/(1 - c + ct + m)$. When $c = 0.75$, $t = 0.20$ and $m = 0$, the value for the expenditure multiplier is 2.5. The value for the expenditure multiplier is 2 when $c = 0.75$, $t = 0.20$ and $m = 0.10$. Thus, an increase in an economy's marginal propensity to import reduces the multiplier effect of a change in an autonomous variable.

Solved Problems

AGGREGATE SPENDING IN A TWO-SECTOR MODEL

4.1 From Fig. 4-7, determine consumption and saving at disposable income levels OYd_1, OYd_2, and OYd_3.

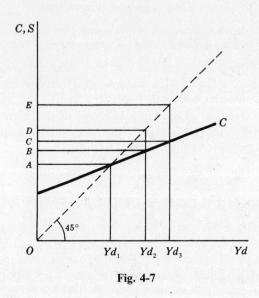

Fig. 4-7

For OYd_1, consumption is OA and saving is zero. Consumption is OB and saving is BD for disposable income OYd_2; consumption is OC, and saving is CE when disposable income is OYd_3.

4.2 (a) From Fig. 4-8, define the relationship between spending $(C + I)$ and output at points A, B, and C. Do these points represent equilibrium or disequilibrium? (b) Why does equilibrium occur when consumption plus investment intersect the 45° line?

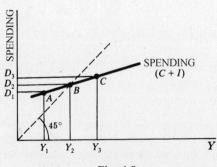

Fig. 4-8

(a)   Point A is a position of disequilibrium because spending of OD_1 is greater than output OY_1. Point B is an equilibrium position because spending OD_2 equals OY_2. Point C represents disequilibrium because spending of OD_3 is less than output OY_3.

(b)   The 45° line is equidistant from the output and spending axes. Anywhere on the 45° line output equals spending. Since the spending function is upward-sloping, it intersects the 45° line at only one point, this point being the position where spending equals output.

4.3   (a) What is meant by a saving leakage? (b) Will output expand or contract when (1) saving is greater than investment? (2) spending is greater than output?

(a)   When individuals do not consume their entire income, they are not purchasing the entire output they helped create. That is, there is a saving leakage. Investment must fill the void created by saving if output is to be maintained.

(b)   (1) Output contracts since saving leakages are not replaced by an equal amount of investment injections. (2) Output expands since planned spending exceeds output.

4.4   (a) From Fig. 4-9, find saving leakages and investment injections for output levels OY_1, OY_2, and OY_3. (b) Find equilibrium output by equating (1) spending and output and (2) saving leakages and investment injections.

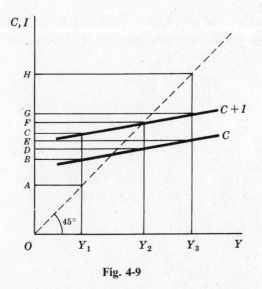

Fig. 4-9

(a)   For output OY_1, investment injections are BC and saving leakages are a negative AB. Investment injections are DF as are saving leakages at output OY_2; investment injections of EG are less than saving leakages EH at output OY_3.

(b)   Equilibrium output exists at OY_2 where (1) planned spending OF equals output OY_2 and (2) saving leakages DF equal investment injections DF.

4.5   Suppose consumption is $\$40 + 0.75Y$, and investment is $\$60$. (a) Find equilibrium output, and consumption and saving at equilibrium. (b) Show that at equilibrium spending equals output and saving leakages equal investment injections.

(a) The equilibrium condition is given by $Y = C + I$. Thus,

$$Y = \$40 + 0.75Y + \$60$$
$$Y - 0.75Y = \$100$$
$$Y = \$400 \text{ which is equilibrium output}$$

When $Y = \$400$, $C = \$40 + 0.75(\$400) = \$340$.

The saving equation is $S = Y - C$. Thus,

$$S = Y - (\$40 + 0.75Y)$$
$$S = -\$40 + 0.25Y$$

When $Y = \$400$, $S = -\$40 + 0.25(\$400) = \$60$.

(b) Spending equals output.

$$C + I = Y$$
$$\$340 + \$60 = \$400$$

Saving leakages equal investment injections.

$$S = I$$
$$\$60 = \$60$$

4.6 Suppose consumption is $\$50 + 0.80Yd$; $I = \$80$; and $Yd = Y$ since there is no government sector. (a) Derive an equation for the saving function. (b) Find equilibrium output by equating saving leakages and investment injections.

(a) Saving equals $Yd - C$; and since $C = \$50 + 0.80Yd$,

$$S = Yd - (\$50 + 0.80Yd)$$
$$S = -\$50 + 0.20Yd$$

(b) The equilibrium condition is determined by equating saving leakages and investment injections; thus

$$-\$50 + 0.20Y = \$80$$
$$0.20Y = \$130$$
$$Y = \frac{\$130}{0.20} = \$650$$

4.7 Suppose consumption is $\bar{C} + cYd$; $I = \bar{I}$; $Yd = Y$. (a) Find an expression for equilibrium output. (b) Find equilibrium output when $\bar{C} = \$50$, $c = 0.80$, and $\bar{I} = \$90$.

(a) The equilibrium condition is given by $Y = C + I$; thus,

$$Y = \bar{C} + cY + \bar{I}$$
$$Y - cY = \bar{C} + \bar{I}$$
$$Y(1 - c) = \bar{C} + \bar{I}$$
$$Y = \frac{\bar{C} + \bar{I}}{1 - c}$$

(b) Substituting, we have $Y = (\$50 + \$90)/(1 - 0.80)$; $Y = \$140/0.20 = \$700$, which is equilibrium output.

THE MARGINAL PROPENSITY TO CONSUME

4.8 (*a*) What does the marginal propensity to consume measure? (*b*) What is the relationship between the marginal propensity to consume and the marginal propensity to save?

(*a*) The marginal propensity to consume measures the change in consumption that results from a change in disposable income. It is generally assumed that individuals consume part of, but not the entire, change in their disposable income. That is, $\Delta C < \Delta Yd$.

(*b*) Individuals save that portion of disposable income that is not spent. Thus, $MPC + MPS = 1$.

4.9 (*a*) What is the *MPC* when (1) $C = \$40 + 0.75Yd$; (2) $C = \$60 + 0.80Yd$; and (3) $C = \$20 + 0.90Yd$? (*b*) What is the relationship of the *MPC* to the slope of the consumption function?

(*a*) The *MPC* is the behavioral coefficient c in the consumption equation $C = \bar{C} + cY$. Thus, the *MPC* is (1) 0.75; (2) 0.80; and (3) 0.90.

(*b*) The marginal propensity to consume measures the change in consumption due to a change in disposable income ($\Delta C/\Delta Yd$), which by definition is the slope of the consumption line.

THE MULTIPLIER EFFECT OF A CHANGE IN EXOGENOUS SPENDING

4.10 Suppose $I = \$70$; $C = \$60 + 0.80Yd$; $Yd = Y$. (*a*) Find equilibrium output. (*b*) Find equilibrium output when there is a \$10 increase in autonomous investment (investment increases from \$70 to \$80). (*c*) Establish the multiplier effect of the \$10 increase in autonomous spending.

(*a*)
$$Y = C + I$$
$$Y = \$60 + 0.80Y + \$70$$
$$Y - 0.80Y = \$130$$
$$Y = \frac{\$130}{0.20} = \$650$$

(*b*)
$$Y = C + I$$
$$Y = \$60 + 0.80Y + \$80$$
$$Y = \frac{\$140}{0.20} = \$700$$

(*c*) Equilibrium output increases \$50 (from \$650 to \$700) as a result of the \$10 increase in investment. There is a multiplier effect of 5 (that is, $\Delta Y/\Delta \bar{I} = \$50/\$10 = 5$) as a result of the increase in autonomous investment.

4.11 Explain in terms of the saving–investment equality for a two-sector model why the increase in equilibrium output is greater than the increase in autonomous investment.

In a two-sector model, equilibrium output exists where saving leakages equal investment injections. When investment increases, there is a shortage of saving leakages at the initial output level. Output must increase until saving leakages equal investment injections. Because only a portion of any increase in income is saved, output must increase by a multiple of the increase in investment to equate saving and investment.

4.12 Suppose the equilibrium condition is given by $Y = (\bar{C} + \bar{I})/(1 - c)$. (*a*) Letting $\bar{A}$ represent autonomous spending ($\bar{A} = \bar{C} + \bar{I}$), find an expression that relates output changes to changes in autonomous spending. (*b*) What is the change in equilibrium output when $\Delta \bar{C} = -\$10$, $\Delta \bar{I} = +\$30$, and $c = 0.80$.

(*a*) Equilibrium output is $\bar{A}/(1 - c)$, where $\bar{A} = \bar{C} + \bar{I}$. It therefore follows that $\Delta Y = \Delta \bar{A}/(1 - c)$.

(*b*) $\Delta \bar{A} = (-\$10 + \$30) = +\$20$. $\Delta Y = \$20/(1 - 0.80)$; $\Delta Y = \$100$.

THE EXPENDITURE MULTIPLIER

4.13 (*a*) Derive the multiplier when the *MPC* is 0.90, 0.80, 0.75, and 0.50. (*b*) What is the relationship between the marginal propensity to consume and the value of the multiplier? (*c*) Use the multiplier values found in (*a*) to establish what effect a \$20 decrease in autonomous spending has upon equilibrium output.

    (*a*)   The multiplier k_e equals $1/(1-c)$; thus, k_e is 10 when the *MPC* is 0.90; 5 when *MPC* is 0.80; 4 when *MPC* is 0.75; and 2 when *MPC* is 0.50.

    (*b*)   There is a multiplier effect because consumption spending is related to disposable income. Any change in income induces a change in consumption, with the magnitude of the change dependent on the value of the marginal propensity to consume. Thus, the value of the multiplier is directly related to the value of the marginal propensity to consume.

    (*c*)   The decline in output equals $\Delta \bar{I}(k_e)$. The decrease in equilibrium output is \$200, \$100, \$80, and \$40 for the four values of *MPC*, respectively.

4.14 If investment falls \$20 and the marginal propensity to consume is 0.60, find (*a*) the change in equilibrium output, (*b*) the change in autonomous spending and (*c*) the induced change in consumption spending.

    (*a*)   The change in equilibrium output equals $k_e \Delta \bar{I}$. Since $k_e = 2.5$, $\Delta Y = -\$50$.

    (*b*)   The \$20 decline in investment is the change in autonomous spending.

    (*c*)   The induced change in spending is the difference between the change in output and the change in autonomous spending. That is, $\Delta Y - \Delta \bar{I} = \Delta C$. Induced spending falls \$30.

GOVERNMENT SPENDING, TAXES, TRANSFERS, AND OUTPUT

4.15 Given $C = \$20 + 0.80Yd$, $I = \$50$, $G = \$20$, $Yd = Y - Tn$, $Tn = \bar{T}x - \bar{T}r$, $\bar{T}r = 0$ and $\bar{T}x = \$10$. (*a*) Find equilibrium output. (*b*) Find consumption and saving at equilibrium output. (*c*) Show the equality of leakages and injections from the spending flow at equilibrium. (*d*) How is the \$20 government expenditure financed?

    (*a*)
$$Y = \$20 + 0.80(Y - \$10) + \$50 + \$20$$
$$Y = \$410$$

    (*b*)   When $Y = \$410$, $C = \$20 + 0.80(\$410 - \$10)$; $C = \$340$. $S = Y - C - Tn$. $S = \$410 - \$340 - \$10 = \$60$.

    (*c*)   Leakages consist of $(Tn + S)$ while injections equal $(I + G)$. Thus, $Tn + S = I + G$; \$10 + \$60 = \$50 + \$20.

    (*d*)   The \$20 government expenditure is financed by \$10 from tax revenues and \$10 borrowed from household saving.

4.16 Recalculate equilibrium output for Problem 4.15 when (*a*) lump-sum taxes increase \$10 or (*b*) government spending is reduced \$10 to balance the federal budget. (*c*) Does a change in lump-sum taxes or in government spending have a similar effect upon equilibrium output?

    (*a*)   When lump-sum taxes increase \$10,

$$Y = \$20 + 0.80(Y - \$20) + \$50 + \$20$$
$$Y = \$370$$

(b) When government spending is reduced $10,

$$Y = \$20 + 0.80(Y - \$10) + \$50 + \$10$$
$$Y = \$360$$

(c) In bringing the federal budget into balance, the $10 decrease in government spending has a larger impact upon equilibrium output than the $10 increase in lump-sum taxes.

4.17 Why does a $10 increase in autonomous taxes have the same effect on equilibrium output as does a $10 decrease in autonomous transfers?

A $10 increase in autonomous taxes, *ceteris paribus*, increases net tax revenues $10 ($Tn = \bar{T}x - \bar{T}r$) as does a $10 decrease in autonomous transfers. Since each of the measures has the same effect upon net tax revenues, each measure must have the same effect upon equilibrium output.

4.18 Suppose a local government unit increases expenditures $50, funding these expenditures by a bond issue. Households in this locality, knowing that they eventually must repay the amount borrowed by the local government unit, increase saving $50. (a) Has the *MPC* or autonomous consumption changed? (b) What impact does the addition of $50 in local government spending have on equilibrium output? Assume a 0.90 marginal propensity to consume.

(a) A change in saving indicates a shift of the saving function; there has been a change in autonomous consumption (the constant of the consumption equation has changed).

(b) The $50 decrease in autonomous consumption is equal to the $50 increase in G so that there is no change in output.

4.19 Equilibrium output is $430 when $C = \$20 + 0.80(Y - Tn)$, $I = \$60$, $Tn = Tx - Tr$, $Tx = \$40$, $Tr = \$10$, and $G = \$30$. (a) Find equilibrium output when G increases from $30 to $40, *ceteris paribus*. (b) Find equilibrium output when Tx increases from $40 to $50, *ceteris paribus*. (c) Find equilibrium output when G increases from $30 to $40 and Tx increases from $40 to $50, *ceteris paribus*. (d) Compare the change in equilibrium output calculated in (a), (b), and (c).

(a) $$Y = \$20 + 0.80(Y - \$40 + \$10) + \$60 + \$40$$
                        $$Y = \$480$$

(b) $$Y = \$20 + 0.80(Y - \$50 + \$10) + \$60 + \$30$$
                        $$Y = \$390$$

(c) $$Y = \$20 + 0.80(Y - \$50 + \$10) + \$60 + \$40$$
                        $$Y = \$440$$

(d) Equilibrium output is initially $430. The $10 increase in government spending (a) raises equilibrium output $50 to $480; the $10 increase in taxes in (b) lowers equilibrium output $40 to $390; whereas the $10 increase in both G and Tx in (c) raises equilibrium output $10 to $440.

4.20 Why does an equal increase in $\bar{G}$ and $\bar{T}x$ raise output by the increase in government spending and lump-sum taxes?

In the consumption equation $C = \bar{C} + c(Y - \bar{T}x)$, disposable income is affected by any change in lump-sum taxes; any change in disposable income alters consumption by $c(\Delta Yd)$. Hence, a $10 increase in lump-sum taxes reduces disposable income $10; consumption declines by $c(\$10)$. A change in government spending has a full, direct effect on spending. Therefore, an equal increase in $\bar{G}$ and $\bar{T}x$ means that the increase in government spending has a greater effect upon output than does the increase in lump-sum taxes.

GOVERNMENT SECTOR MULTIPLIERS

4.21 Given $C = \bar{C} + cYd$, $Yd = Y - Tn$, $Tn = \bar{T}x - \bar{T}r$, $I = \bar{I}$, and $G = \bar{G}$. (a) Find equilibrium output. (b) Find an expression for ΔY that results from changes in the autonomous variables. (c) Find ΔY when $\Delta G > 0$, *ceteris paribus*. (d) Find an expression for the multiple effect of ΔG upon ΔY ($\Delta Y / \Delta G$) and label the equation k_e. (e) Find ΔY when $\Delta \bar{C} > 0$ or $\Delta \bar{I} > 0$. What is the multiplying effect of changes in autonomous spending variables $\bar{C}$, $\bar{I}$, and $\bar{G}$ upon equilibrium output?

(a)
$$Y = \bar{C} + c(Y - \bar{T}n) + \bar{I} + \bar{G}$$
$$Y - cY = \bar{C} - c\bar{T}n + \bar{I} + \bar{G}$$
$$Y = \frac{\bar{C} + \bar{I} + \bar{G} - c\bar{T}n}{1 - c}$$

(b) The autonomous variables are $\bar{C}$, $\bar{I}$, $\bar{T}n$, and $\bar{G}$. Thus,

$$\Delta Y = \frac{\Delta \bar{C} + \Delta \bar{I} + \Delta \bar{G} - c\Delta \bar{T}n}{1 - c}$$

(c) Assuming $\bar{C}$, $\bar{I}$, and $\bar{T}n$ are constant and $\Delta \bar{G} > 0$, we have

$$\Delta Y = \frac{\Delta \bar{G}}{1 - c}$$

(d) Given $\Delta Y = \Delta \bar{G}/(1 - c)$, dividing both sides of the equation by $\Delta \bar{G}$ we obtain $\Delta Y/\Delta \bar{G} = 1/(1 - c)$— an expression for the change in output due to a change in government spending. Hence,

$$\frac{\Delta Y}{\Delta \bar{G}} = \frac{1}{1 - c} \qquad k_e = \frac{1}{1 - c}$$

(e) When $\Delta \bar{C} > 0$, $\Delta Y = \Delta \bar{C}/(1 - c)$. $\Delta Y = \Delta \bar{I}/(1 - c)$ when $\Delta \bar{I} > 0$. Hence, changes in autonomous spending variables $\bar{C}$, $\bar{I}$, and $\bar{G}$ have the same k_e multiplier effect on equilibrium output.

4.22 (a) Use the equation $\Delta Y = (\Delta \bar{C} + \Delta \bar{I} + \Delta \bar{G} - c\Delta \bar{T}n)/(1 - c)$ derived in Problem 4.21(b), and find an expression for ΔY when $\Delta \bar{T}n > 0$, *ceteris paribus*. (b) Find an expression for the multiplier effect of a change in net lump-sum taxes upon equilibrium output and label the equation k_t. (c) Why is the lump-sum tax multiplier negative? (d) Do increases in $\bar{T}r$ and $\bar{T}x$ have a negative or positive effect upon $\bar{T}n$? Therefore what effect should increases in $\bar{T}r$ and $\bar{T}x$ have upon equilibrium output?

(a)
$$\Delta Y = \frac{-c\Delta \bar{T}n}{1 - c}$$

(b) Dividing both sides of the equation in part (a) by $\Delta \bar{T}n$, we have

$$\frac{\Delta Y}{\Delta \bar{T}n} = \frac{-c}{1 - c} \qquad k_t = \frac{-c}{1 - c}$$

(c) An increase in net lump-sum taxes reduces household sector disposable income, which lowers consumption and therefore output. Thus, an increase in net lump-sum taxes, *ceteris paribus*, has a negative effect upon equilibrium output.

(d) Since $\bar{T}n = \bar{T}x - \bar{T}r$, increases in $\bar{T}r$ reduce $\bar{T}n$ while increases in $\bar{T}x$ raise $\bar{T}n$. Thus, an increase in autonomous transfers has a positive effect on equilibrium output, and an increase in autonomous taxes has a negative effect.

4.23 Using the equation $\Delta Y = (\Delta \bar{C} + \Delta \bar{I} + \Delta \bar{G} - c\Delta \bar{T}n)/(1 - c)$ derived in Problem 4.21(a), find ΔY when $\Delta \bar{G}$ equals $\Delta \bar{T}n$. (b) Find the multiplier for equal changes in $\bar{G}$ and $\bar{T}n$.

(a)
$$\Delta Y = \frac{\Delta \bar{G} - c\Delta \bar{T}n}{1 - c}$$

Since $\Delta \bar{G} = \Delta \bar{T}n$, substituting we have

$$Y = \frac{\Delta \bar{G} - c\Delta \bar{G}}{1 - c} \quad \text{or} \quad \Delta Y = \frac{\Delta \bar{G}(1 - c)}{1 - c}$$

and with $(1 - c)/(1 - c) = 1$, $\Delta Y = \Delta \bar{G}$.

(b) Since $\Delta Y/\Delta \bar{G} = 1$, equal changes in $\bar{G}$ and $\bar{T}n$ impact equilibrium output by $\Delta \bar{G}$, and the balanced budget multiplier k_b is 1.

4.24 Suppose full employment occurs at a $600 level of output, equilibrium output is currently $500, and the *MPC* is 0.80. What is the necessary change in (a) government spending, (b) net lump-sum tax, and (c) net lump-sum taxes and government spending when the government is committed to a balanced budget to bring output to its full-employment level?

(a) The necessary change in Y is $+ \$100$. With $k_e = 5$, government spending must increase $20: $\Delta Y = k_e \Delta \bar{G}$; $\$100 = 5\Delta \bar{G}$; $\Delta \bar{G} = \$20$.

(b) $k_t = -4$. The necessary decrease in net lump-sum taxes is $25: $\Delta Y = k_t(\Delta \bar{T}n)$; $\$100 = -4(\Delta \bar{T}n)$; $\Delta \bar{T}n = -\$25$.

(c) $k_b = 1$. The necessary increase in net lump-sum taxes and government spending is $100.

MULTIPLIERS FOR A MODEL WITH INCOME TAXES

4.25 Suppose $C = \$35 + 0.80Yd$, $I = \$70$, $G = \$65$, $Tx = 0.10Y$. (a) Find equilibrium output. (b) What are tax revenues at equilibrium output? Does the government have a balanced budget? (c) Find equilibrium output when investment increases from $70 to $90. (d) What has happened to the relationship of government spending and tax revenues? Why?

(a)
$$Y = \$35 + 0.80(Y - 0.10Y) + \$70 + \$65$$
$$Y = \$607.14$$

(b) Tax revenues are $0.10(\$607.14) = \$60.71$. Government expenditures of $65 exceed the $60.71 in tax revenues; there is a $4.29 deficit.

(c)
$$Y = \$35 + 0.80(Y - 0.10Y) + \$90 + \$65$$
$$Y = \$678.57$$

(d) Tax revenues have increased to $67.86. There is now a budget surplus of $2.86, because more taxes are collected at a higher level of output.

4.26 When $C = \bar{C} + cYd$, $Yd = Y - Tn$, $Tn = \bar{T}x - \bar{T}r$, $I = \bar{I}$, and $G = \bar{G}$, equilibrium output is given by the equation $Y = (\bar{C} + \bar{I} + \bar{G} - c\bar{T}n)/(1 - c)$. The expenditure multiplier k_e equals $1/(1 - c)$, and the lump-sum tax multiplier k_t is $-c/(1 - c)$. (a) Find the equation for equilibrium output when $Tn = \bar{T}x + tY - \bar{T}r$ rather than $Tn = \bar{T}x + \bar{T}r$. (b) Derive k_e and k_t for changes in autonomous spending and autonomous net tax revenues for the equilibrium condition found in part (a).

(a)
$$Y = \bar{C} + c(Y - \bar{T}x - tY + \bar{T}r) + \bar{I} + \bar{G}$$
$$Y - cY + ctY = \bar{C} - c\bar{T}x + c\bar{T}r + \bar{I} + \bar{G}$$
$$Y = \frac{\bar{C} + \bar{I} + \bar{G} - c\bar{T}x + c\bar{T}r}{1 - c + ct}$$

(b) For a change in $\bar{C}$ ($\bar{I}$ or $\bar{G}$), the change in output is

$$\Delta Y = \frac{\Delta \bar{C}}{1 - c + ct}$$

and the expenditure multiplier is

$$\frac{\Delta Y}{\Delta \bar{C}} = \frac{1}{1 - c + ct}$$
$$k_e = \frac{1}{1 - c + ct}$$

For changes in autonomous taxes or autonomous transfers, the change in output is

$$Y = \frac{-c\Delta \bar{T}n}{1 - c + ct}$$

and the lump-sum tax multiplier is

$$k_t = \frac{-c}{1 - c + ct}$$

4.27 (a) Suppose the marginal propensity to consume is 0.75 and tax revenues are unrelated to income. Find the change in equilibrium output for the following autonomous changes: government spending increases $10, taxes increase $15 and transfers decrease $10. (b) Suppose the marginal propensity to consume is 0.75 and there is a 20% proportional income tax. Find the change in equilibrium output for the following autonomous changes: government spending increases $10, taxes increase $15 and transfers decrease $10.

(a) The expenditure multiplier is 4 or $k_e = 1/(1 - 0.75)$, whereas the lump-sum tax multiplier is -3 or $k_t = -0.75/(1 - 0.75)$. The change in output is found by solving the equation $\Delta Y = k_e \Delta \bar{G}$ for a change in autonomous government spending and $\Delta Y = k_t \Delta \bar{T}n$ for a change in autonomous tax revenues. Equilibrium output increases $40 for the $10 increase in autonomous government spending; equilibrium output decreases $45 for the $15 increase in autonomous taxes and increases $30 for the $10 increase in autonomous transfers.

(b) The expenditure multiplier is $k_e = 1/[1 - 0.75 + (0.20)0.75] = 2.5$, whereas the lump-sum tax multiplier is $k_t = -0.75/[1 - 0.75 + (0.20)0.75] = -1.875$. Equilibrium output increases $25 for a $10 increase in government spending, decreases $28.125 for the $15 increase in autonomous taxes and increases $18.75 for the $10 increase in transfers.

4.28 (a) Why does an income tax reduce the value of the multipliers? (b) Why is an income tax considered a "built-in" stabilizer?

(a) The multiplier derives its value from induced expenditures (i.e., induced consumption). When taxes are related to income, there is less induced consumption for each income change, since the change in disposable income no longer equals the change in output.

(b) An income tax is an automatic or built-in stabilizer, since tax revenues change with the level of output. Thus, as the economy expands, more taxes are collected, dampening the expansion; as the economy contracts, tax receipts automatically fall, slowing the contraction.

NET EXPORTS AND EQUILIBRIUM OUTPUT

4.29 Suppose $C = \$30 + 0.80Yd$, $Tn = \$50$, $I = \$60$, $G = \$50$, and $X = \$50 - 0.05Y$. (a) Find equilibrium output. (b) Find the net export balance at equilibrium output. (c) What happens to equilibrium output and the net export balance when investment increases from $60 to $70? (d)

What happens to equilibrium output and the net export balance when the net export function changes from $50 - 0.05Y$ to $40 - 0.05Y$? (e) Which has the greater effect upon an economy's net export balance: a change in autonomous domestic spending or a change in autonomous net exports?

(a) $$Y = \$30 + 0.80(Y - \$50) + \$60 + \$50 + \$50 - 0.05Y$$
$$Y = \$600$$

(b) At equilibrium, the net export balance is $X = \$50 - 0.05(\$600) = \$20$.

(c) Equilibrium output increases from $600 [part (a)] to $640 with the net export balance decreasing from $20 to $18.

(d) Equilibrium output decreases from its initial $600 level [part (a)] to $560; the net export balance decreases from $20 to $12.

(e) A $10 change in autonomous investment or in autonomous net exports has a $40 effect on equilibrium output; however, the change in autonomous net exports has the larger effect on the net export balance.

4.30 Given $C = \bar{C} + cYd$, $Tn = \bar{T}x + tY - \bar{T}r$, $I = \bar{I}$, $G = \bar{G}$, $X = \bar{X} - mY$. (a) Find an equation for equilibrium output. (b) Find the expenditure multiplier and the lump-sum tax multiplier. (c) What effect does an import function and an income tax have on the expenditure and the lump-sum tax multiplier?

(a) $$Y = \bar{C} + c(Y - \bar{T}x - tY + \bar{T}r) + \bar{I} + \bar{G} + \bar{X} - mY$$
$$Y = \frac{\bar{C} + \bar{I} + \bar{G} + \bar{X} - c\bar{T}x + c\bar{T}r}{1 - c + ct + m}$$

(b) Solving for $\Delta\bar{C}$ (or $\Delta\bar{I}$, or $\Delta\bar{G}$, or $\Delta\bar{X}$), *ceteris paribus*, we have

$$\Delta Y = \frac{\Delta\bar{C}}{1 - c + ct + m}$$

and the expenditure multiplier is

$$k_e = \frac{1}{1 - c + ct + m}$$

Solving for $\Delta\bar{T}x$ we have

$$\Delta\bar{Y} = \frac{-c\Delta\bar{T}x}{1 - c + ct + m}$$

and the lump-sum tax multiplier is

$$k_t = \frac{-c}{1 - c + ct + m}$$

(c) The import function and an income tax are induced leakages which reduce the value of the multipliers.

Multiple Choice Questions

1. When saving is greater than investment in a two-sector model,

    (a) Output should increase.

    (b) Output should decrease.

    (c) Output should not change.

2. When output exceeds spending,

    (a)   There is unsold output, and the level of output will fall.

    (b)   There is unsold output, and the level of output will rise.

    (c)   There is unsold output, and the level of spending will rise.

    (d)   There is no unsold output since the level of spending will rise.

3. In a two-sector model, when consumption is $\$40 + 0.90\,Yd$ and investment is $\$50$, equilibrium output is

    (a) $\$90$.

    (b) $\$400$.

    (c) $\$500$.

    (d) $\$900$.

4. In a two-sector model, when saving is $-\$40 + 0.20\,Yd$ and investment is $\$60$, equilibrium output is

    (a) $\$100$.

    (b) $\$400$.

    (c) $\$500$.

    (d) $\$1000$.

5. By definition, the marginal propensity to consume

    (a)   Equals $\Delta C/\Delta Yd$.

    (b)   Is the behavioral coefficient c in the equation $C = \bar{C} + cYd$.

    (c)   Is the slope of the consumption function.

    (d)   All of the above.

6. A change in autonomous spending is represented by

    (a)   A movement along a $(C + I + G)$ spending line.

    (b)   A shift of a $(C + I + G)$ spending line.

    (c)   A change in a behavioral coefficient.

7. Which of the following will not result in an increase in output?

    (a)   An increase in autonomous spending.

    (b)   A decrease in autonomous taxes.

    (c)   An increase in autonomous transfers.

    (d)   An increase in lump-sum taxes.

8. An increase in lump-sum taxes, *ceteris paribus*, causes the

    (a) $(C + I + G)$ spending line to shift upward by $c\Delta\bar{T}x$.

    (b) $(C + I + G)$ spending line to shift downward by $c\Delta\bar{T}x$.

    (c)   Leakage line $(S + Tx)$ to shift downward by $c\Delta\bar{T}x$.

    (d)   Leakage line $(S + Tx)$ to shift downward by $\Delta\bar{T}x$.

9. When there is an increase in lump-sum taxes and government spending, *ceteris paribus*, then the

    (a) $(S + Tx)$ leakage line shifts upward and the $(I + G)$ injection line shifts upward.

    (b) $(S + Tx)$ leakage line shifts downward, and the $(I + G)$ injection line shifts downward.

(c) $(S + Tx)$ leakage line shifts downward, and the $(I + G)$ injection line shifts upward.

(d) $(S + Tx)$ leakage line shifts upward, and the $(I + G)$ injection line shifts downward.

10.   When an increase in government spending is matched by an equal decrease in government transfers, output will

(a)   Stay the same.

(b)   Increase.

(c)   Decrease.

True or False Questions

11.   _____ In a two-sector model, there is an inverse relationship between the value of the MPC and the value of the expenditure multiplier.

12.   _____ The MPC has a value greater than 0 but less than 1.

13.   _____ In a $(C + I + G)$ model, there is an inverse relationship between the value of the income tax and the value of the expenditure multiplier.

14.   _____ The income tax helps moderate economic fluctuations.

15.   _____ *Ceteris paribus*, an income tax increases the value of the expenditure and the lump-sum tax multiplier.

16.   _____ An increase in the marginal propensity to import has the same effect upon the multipliers as an increase in the MPC.

17.   _____ When there is an increase in lump-sum taxes, there is a decrease in equilibrium output equal to $k_e \Delta \bar{T}x$.

18.   _____ When there is an income tax, an equal increase in government spending and lump-sum taxes increases output by less than $\Delta \bar{G}$.

19.   _____ An equal increase in autonomous taxes and autonomous transfers has no effect upon equilibrium output.

20.   _____ An increase in leakages results in a decrease in equilibrium output.

Answers to Multiple Choice and True or False Questions

1. (b); **2.** (a); **3.** (d); **4.** (c); **5.** (d); **6.** (b); **7.** (d); **8.** (b); **9.** (a); **10.** (b); **11.** F; **12.** T; **13.** T; **14.** T; **15.** F; **16.** F; **17.** F; **18.** T; **19.** T; **20.** T.

Chapter 5

The *IS–LM* Framework

Chapter Summary

1. Since all market transactions involve the exchange of money, the short-run model of Chapter 4 is expanded to include the money supply. Equilibrium output now requires that there be simultaneous equilibrium in the goods markets $[C + I + G + (X - M)]$ and the money markets (the supply and demand for money).

2. In the expanded model, investment is influenced by the rate of interest. For each rate of interest, there is a different level of investment and therefore a different level of output. The inverse relationship between the rate of interest and equilibrium output is presented graphically as a negatively sloped *IS* line.

3. The location of *IS* in space is affected by a change in autonomous spending, i.e., a change in $\Delta \bar{G}$, $\Delta \bar{I}$, $\Delta \bar{T}x$, $\Delta \bar{C}$, and $\Delta \bar{X}$. For example, *IS* shifts to the right by $\Delta \bar{G} k_e$, where there is an increase in autonomous government spending.

4. The slope of *IS* is dependent upon the interest sensitivity of investment and the expenditure multiplier. When investment is not influenced by the rate of interest, *IS* is vertical, since a change in the rate of interest does not change investment or equilibrium output. *IS* is less steeply sloped (flatter) when investment spending is highly interest-sensitive.

5. Along an *LM* line there is equilibrium between the supply and demand for money. When the demand for money is interest-sensitive, *LM* is positively sloped.

6. A change in the exogenous money supply affects the location of *LM*. For example, an increase in the money supply, *ceteris paribus*, shifts *LM* rightward by $\Delta \bar{M}/k$.

7. The slope of *LM* is dependent upon the interest sensitivity of the demand for money and the transaction demand for money. When the demand for money is unrelated to the rate of interest, *LM* is vertical. *LM*'s slope decreases (*LM* is flatter) when the demand for money is more interest-sensitive.

8. Equilibrium output can only exist at the intersection of the *IS* and *LM* lines when there are both money and goods markets.

Chapter Outline

5.1 INVESTMENT AND THE RATE OF INTEREST

When investment is dependent upon the rate of interest, there is a different level of investment for each rate of interest. For the investment line I in Fig. 5-1, we find that investment is $40 when the rate of interest is 10%, $52 when the rate of interest is 8%, $64 when it is 6%, and $76 when it is 4%. This negative relationship between investment and the rate of interest is present in the equation $I = \bar{I} - bi$, where $\bar{I}$ represents autonomous investment and b is a behavioral coefficient which measures the sensitivity of investment to the rate of interest.

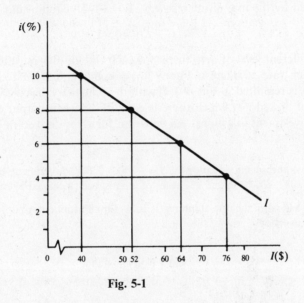

Fig. 5-1

EXAMPLE 5.1. Suppose the investment equation is $I = \$100 - 5i$. Investment is $50 when the rate of interest is 10% [$I = \$100 - 5(10)$], $60 when the rate of interest is 8%, and $70 when it is 6%. This relationship of investment and the rate of interest is plotted in Fig. 5-2, with the resulting schedule labeled I. When an increase in autonomous investment changes the investment equation to $I = \$120 - 5i$, investment is then $70, $80, and $90 for 10%, 8%, and 6% rates of interest. The relationship of investment and the rate of interest for equation $I = \$120 - 5i$ is also plotted in Fig. 5-2 and labeled I'. An increase in autonomous investment shifts the investment line rightward.

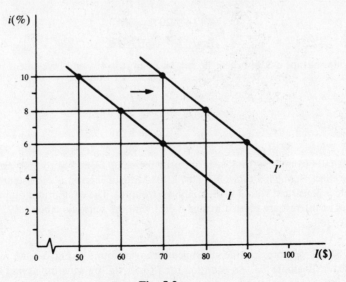

Fig. 5-2

5.2 AN *IS* SCHEDULE FOR A TWO-SECTOR MODEL

In the two-sector model of Section 4.2, equilibrium output exists where saving leakages equal investment injections or, equivalently, where output equals spending. Thus, when $C = \bar{C} + cY$ and $I = \bar{I}$, equilibrium output is

$$Y = (\bar{C} + \bar{I})/(1 - c)$$

In the preceding model, investment is exogenous (i.e., determined by forces outside the model). When investment is influenced by the rate of interest, e.g., $I = \bar{I} - bi$, equilibrium output exists where

$$Y = (\bar{C} + \bar{I} - bi)/(1 - c)$$

When there is a different level of investment for each rate of interest, there must also be a different level of output for each rate of interest. Fig. 5-3(*a*) presents equilibrium output for various rates of interest; the same data is replotted in Fig. 5-3(*b*) with the schedule labeled *IS*. The *IS* line in Fig. 5-3(*b*) shows combinations of Y and i at which there is equality between output and spending and between saving leakages and investment injections. An equation for *IS* is derived in Example 5.3.

EXAMPLE 5.2. Suppose the saving equation is $S = -\$40 + 0.20Y$; investment behavior appears in Fig. 5-1. Equilibrium outputs for 10%, 8%, 6%, and 4% rates of interest are calculated below.

Situation I: Investment is \$40 when the rate of interest is 10%. Equilibrium output is \$400, found by equating saving leakages and investment injections.

$$S = I$$
$$-\$40 + 0.20Y = \$40$$
$$Y = \$400$$

Situation II: Equilibrium output is \$460 when the rate of interest is 8% and investment is \$52.

$$S = I$$
$$-\$40 + 0.20Y = \$52$$
$$Y = \$460$$

Situation III: Equilibrium output is \$520 when the rate of interest is 6% and investment is \$64.

$$S = I$$
$$-\$40 + 0.20Y = \$64$$
$$Y = \$520$$

Situation IV: Equilibrium output is \$580 when the rate of interest is 4% and investment is \$76.

$$S = I$$
$$-\$40 + 0.20Y = \$76$$
$$Y = \$580$$

As the rate of interest falls from 10% to 8%, investment increases from \$40 to \$52, raising equilibrium output through the multiplier effect from \$400 to \$460. Thus, a 10% rate of interest is consistent with a \$400 equilibrium output, and an 8% rate is consistent with a \$460 equilibrium output. The equilibrium outputs consistent with 10%, 8%, 6%, and 4% rates of interest are plotted in Fig. 5-3(*b*) with the schedule labeled *IS*.

EXAMPLE 5.3. $I = \$100 - 6i$ represents the investment behavior found in Fig. 5-1; we retain the saving equation $S = -\$40 + 0.20Y$ used in Example 5.2. An equation for *IS* is found by equating saving leakages and investment injections.

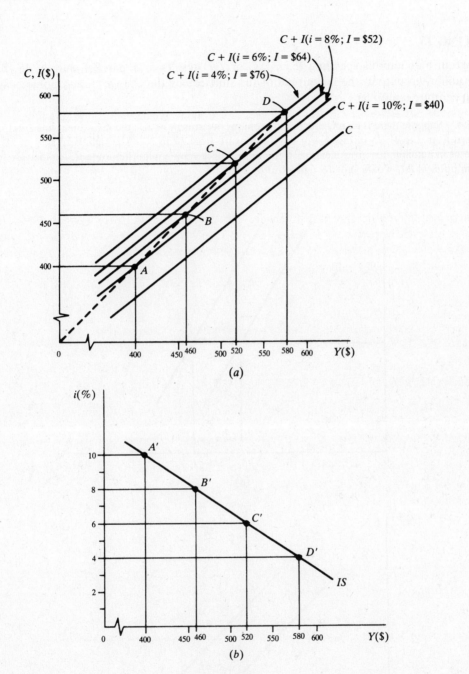

Fig. 5-3

$$S = I$$
$$-\$40 + 0.20Y = \$100 - 6i$$
$$0.20Y = \$140 - 6i$$
$$Y = \$700 - 30i$$

Since the *IS* equation is derived from the same behavior found in Example 5.2, 10%, 8%, 6%, and 4% rates of interest give us the same level of output. For example, when the rate of interest is 6%, $Y = \$700 - 30(6) = \$520$.

5.3   SHIFTING *IS*

A change in autonomous spending (e.g., $\Delta \bar{C}$ or $\Delta \bar{I}$) results in a parallel shift of *IS*. Since *IS* represents equilibrium output, the magnitude of the shift equals the change in autonomous spending times the expenditure multiplier.

EXAMPLE 5.4.   Suppose there is an increase in autonomous investment of $\Delta \bar{I}$; the investment line *I* in Fig. 5-4(*a*) shifts rightward from *I* to *I′*. *IS* in Fig. 5-4(*b*) shifts rightward from *IS* to *IS′*. The rightward shift of *IS* is $k_e \Delta \bar{I}$, since an increase in autonomous investment has a multiplier effect upon equilibrium output. An increase in autonomous consumption of $\Delta \bar{C}$ would shift *IS* rightward by $k_e \Delta \bar{C}$.

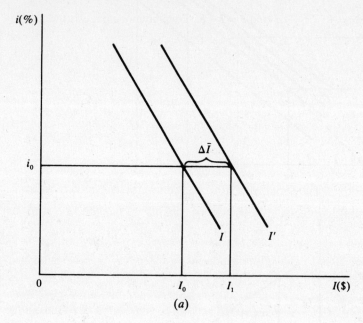

(*a*)

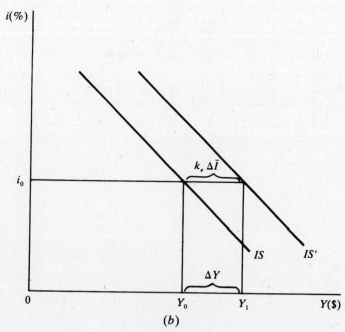

(*b*)

Fig. 5-4

5.4 THE SLOPE OF *IS*

The equation for *IS* can be presented as $Y = k_e(\bar{A} - bi)$ or when solving for the rate of interest $i = \bar{A}/b - (1/k_e b)Y$. $\bar{A}$ represents the sum of autonomous spending ($\bar{C} + \bar{I}$ in this model), k_e is the expenditure multiplier and b is a behavioral coefficient linking investment spending to the rate of interest. In Example 5.5, the slope for *IS* is $1/(k_e b)$; the slope for *IS* increases when b and/or k_e have lower values. Although both the interest sensitivity of investment spending and the marginal propensity to consume determine the slope of *IS*, a necessary condition for a negatively sloped *IS* schedule is a value for $b > 0$ (Example 5.7).

EXAMPLE 5.5. Suppose $C = \bar{C} + cY$ and $I = \bar{I} - bi$. Equilibrium output exists when

$$Y = \frac{\bar{C} + \bar{I} - bi}{1 - c}$$

or

$$Y = \frac{\bar{C} + \bar{I}}{1 - c} - \frac{bi}{1 - c}$$

Letting $\bar{A} = (\bar{C} + \bar{I})$, and $k_e = 1/(1 - c)$,

$$Y = k_e \bar{A} - k_e b i$$

We find the slope of *IS* by solving for i

$$i = \frac{\bar{A}}{b} - \frac{Y}{k_e b}$$

or

$$i = \bar{A}\left(\frac{1}{b}\right) - \left(\frac{1}{k_e b}\right)Y$$

Thus, the *IS* schedule's slope is $1/k_e b$; its location in space depends upon the multiplier effect of autonomous spending ($\bar{C} + \bar{I}$) as well as the schedule's slope.

EXAMPLE 5.6. When $C = \$10 + 0.75Y$ and $I = \$150 - 10i$, the *IS* equation is $Y = \$640 - 40i$. When the investment equation is $I = \$150 - 5i$, and the consumption equation remains $C = \$10 + 0.75Y$, the *IS* equation is $Y = \$640 - 20i$. As we can see from plotting the *IS* equations in Fig. 5-5, the slope of *IS* ($1/k_e b$) is greater (*IS* is steeper) when investment spending is less responsive to interest rate changes, i.e., when behavioral coefficient b has a smaller value.

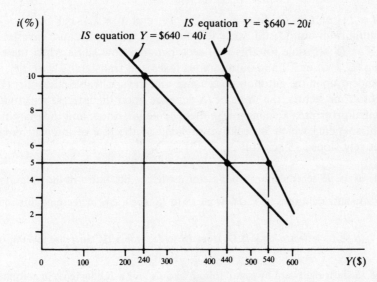

Fig. 5-5

EXAMPLE 5.7.   When $C = \$10 + 0.75Y$ and $I = \$150 - 10i$, the IS equation is $Y = \$640 - 40i$. When the investment equation remains $I = \$150 - 10i$, and a smaller MPC changes the consumption equation to $C = \$10 + 0.60Y$, the IS equation is $Y = \$400 - 25i$. Plotting these IS equations in Fig. 5-6, we find that the slope of IS increases (IS becomes steeper) as the MPC c and therefore k_e decreases, provided that investment spending is responsive to changes in the rate of interest.

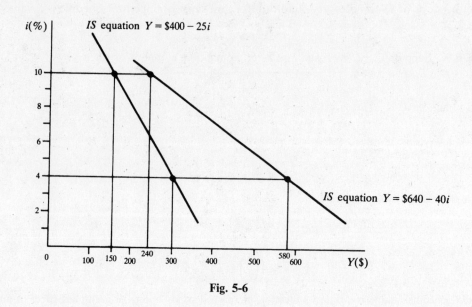

Fig. 5-6

5.5   GOODS EQUILIBRIUM FOR A FOUR-SECTOR MODEL

Equilibrium output is

$$Y = \frac{\bar{C} + \bar{I} + \bar{G} + \bar{X} - c\bar{T}x + c\bar{T}r - bi}{1 - c + ct + m}$$

when $C = \bar{C} + cY$, $I = \bar{I} - bi$, $G = \bar{G}$, $Tn = \bar{T}x + tY - \bar{T}r$, and $X = \bar{X} - mY$.

A schedule of equilibrium output still exists for the goods market because investment is related to the rate of interest. The IS schedule for this four-sector model now shifts when there are changes in autonomous spending ($\bar{C}, \bar{I}, \bar{G}$, or $\bar{X}$) and autonomous taxes and transfers ($\bar{T}x$ or $\bar{T}r$), with the magnitude of the shift dependent upon the autonomous change and the applicable multiplier (Example 5.8). In expanding the model to four sectors, the slope of IS depends upon the interest sensitivity of investment spending b, the marginal propensity to consume c, the income tax rate t, and the marginal propensity to import m. Investment spending which is negatively related to the rate of interest remains a necessary condition for a negatively sloped IS schedule.

EXAMPLE 5.8.   Shifts of the IS schedule for a four-sector model are illustrated in the situations below.

Situation I: In Fig. 5-7 IS shifts rightward by $k_e\Delta\bar{G}$ from IS to IS' for a $\Delta\bar{G}$ increase in autonomous government spending, *ceteris paribus*.

Situation II: In Fig. 5-7 IS shifts leftward by $k_t\Delta\bar{T}n$ from IS to IS'' for a $\Delta\bar{T}$ increase in lump-sum taxes, *ceteris paribus*.

Situation III: In Fig. 5-8 IS shifts rightward by $k_e\Delta\bar{X}$ from IS' to IS'' for a $\Delta\bar{X}$ increase in autonomous net exports, *ceteris paribus*.

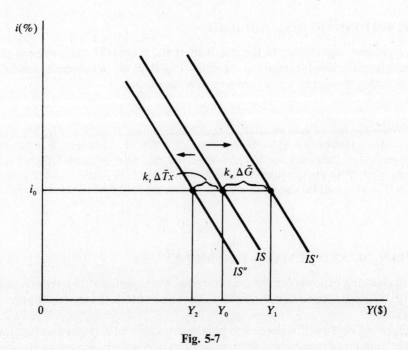

Fig. 5-7

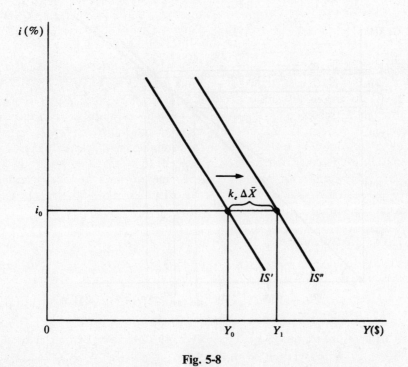

Fig. 5-8

5.6 *IS* AND POSITIONS OF DISEQUILIBRIUM

Because *IS* represents equilibrium in the goods markets, points off the curve are positions of disequilibrium. Excess output exists for points to the right of *IS* since output exceeds spending; points to the left represent production shortages, since spending exceeds output.

EXAMPLE 5.9. When the rate of interest is 10%, equilibrium output is $395 in Fig. 5-9(*a*) for a four-sector economy where $C = \$40 + 0.80Yd$, $I = \$55 - 2i$, $G = \$20$, $Tx = \$20$, $X = \$10$ and $M = \$10$. This equilibrium position appears as point *A* on the *IS* schedule in Fig. 5-9(*b*). Note that when output is $350 in Fig. 5-9(*a*), spending is $359 and excess demand exists. The existence of excess demand at the $350 output level is represented by point *B'* in Fig. 5-9(*b*). Point *C'* in Fig. 5-9(*b*) is a position of excess supply; the $450 level of output exceeds the $439 level of spending.

5.7 THE SUPPLY OF AND DEMAND FOR MONEY

Currency and checking deposits are the only financial assets included in a transactions definition of the money supply. We shall assume that the Federal Reserve controls the money supply; and the money supply equals $\bar{M}$.

Money is demanded because it is needed to purchase goods and services and because it serves as a store of value. The amount of money held for transactions is positively related to income and therefore spending; the transactions demand for money is presented as $L_t = f(Y)$. Money is a better store of value than financial instruments such as bonds and equity and real assets, since the value of money is unaffected by changes in the rate of interest. (We continue to assume that the price level is unchanged.) However, the amount of money held as a store of value is inversely related to the rate of interest because money provides no interest return; the store of value function of money is presented as $L_p = f(i)$. The combined demand for money balances is then

$$L = kY - hi$$

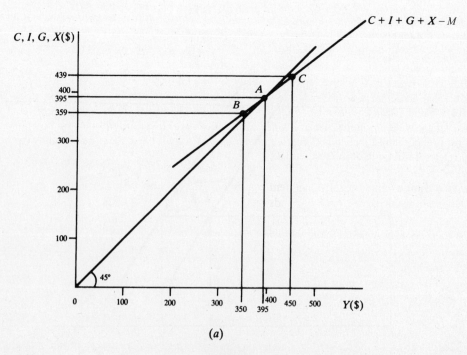

(*a*)

Fig. 5-9

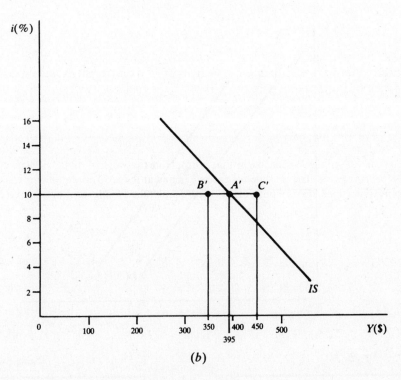

Fig. 5-9 (*continued*)

where k is the fraction of income held as an average transaction money balance and h is a behavioral coefficient indicating the interest sensitivity of the store of value demand for money.

EXAMPLE 5.10. Money receipts and disbursements rarely coincide; individuals and businesses normally hold money balances to meet disbursement needs. For example, an individual may be paid monthly; expenditures, however, may be continuous throughout the month. Thus, the monthly money income which an individual receives is budgeted—and money balances are held—to meet monthly expenditures. In doing so, an individual holds an average money balance which is related to his or her income. The transaction demand for money (L_t) equals kY.

EXAMPLE 5.11. There is an inverse relationship between the market rate of interest and the price of securities (bonds and stocks). Since the price of bonds and stocks falls as the rate of interest increases, bonds and stocks are an inferior store of value. (Bcause of this risk to capital value, bonds and stocks are classified as less liquid.) Bonds and stocks, however, provide an interest return, which money does not. Investors will thereby hold a smaller money balance as the rate of interest increases. Thus, with other variables unchanged, the store of value demand for money is inversely related to the rate of interest, and $L_p = -hi$.

On a two-dimensional graph, the demand for money appears as a series of demand schedules because the amount of money held depends upon both the rate of interest and the level of income. In Fig. 5-10, demand for money schedule $L_1(Y_1)$ relates the amount of money held at various rates of interest for income level Y_1. $L_2(Y_2)$ also represents the demand for money but at higher income level Y_2. The shift in the money demand schedule from $L_1(Y_1)$ to $L_2(Y_2)$ equals $k\Delta Y$, where ΔY is the difference between income levels Y_2 and Y_1.

EXAMPLE 5.12. Suppose the demand for money is specified as $L = kY - hi$, with $k = 0.20$ and $h = 5$. Tables 5-1 and 5-2 give values for kY and hi at various output levels and interest rates. The data from Tables 5-1 and 5-2 are plotted in Fig. 5-11 with L_1 representing the demand for money when output is \$500, L_2 when it is \$600, and L_3 when it is \$700. Note that L_1 is derived by subtracting values for hi at different rates of interest (Table 5-2) from \$100, the value for kY when output is \$500.

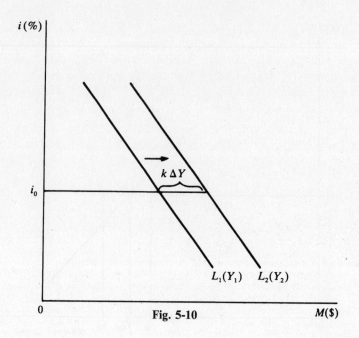

Fig. 5-10

Table 5-1

Output	kY (when $k = 0.20$)
$500	$100
600	120
700	140
800	160
900	180
1000	200

Table 5-2

Rate of interest (%)	hi (when $h = 5$)
10	$50
9	45
8	40
7	35
6	30
5	25

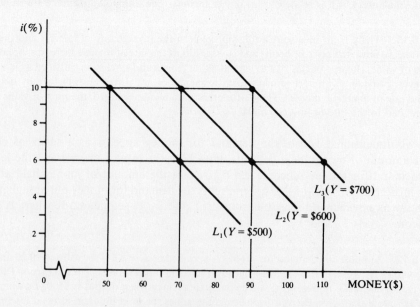

Fig. 5-11

5.8 THE *LM* SCHEDULE

Equilibrium exists in the money market when the demand for money equals the supply of money. The money supply is controlled by the Federal Reserve; we continue to assume an unchanged price level. Given demand for money schedules L_1, L_2, and L_3 in Fig. 5-12(a), there is a locus of points at which the demand for money equals the money supply, M. This locus of points is plotted in Fig. 5-12(b), with the positively sloped schedule labeled *LM*. When the demand for money is specified as $L = kY - hi$ and the money supply is $\bar{M}$, the equation for *LM* is

$$Y = \frac{\bar{M}}{k} + \left(\frac{h}{k}\right)i$$

or

$$i = \left(\frac{k}{h}\right)Y - \frac{\bar{M}}{h}$$

EXAMPLE 5.13. Suppose the demand for money is $kY - hi$ and the money supply is $\bar{M}$. Monetary equilibrium exists when the demand for money equals the supply of money.

$$L = M$$
$$kY - hi = \bar{M}$$

Solving for Y, $Y = \bar{M}/h + (h/k)i$, or solving for i, $i = 1/h(kY - \bar{M})$:

$$i = \left(\frac{k}{h}\right)Y - \frac{\bar{M}}{h}$$

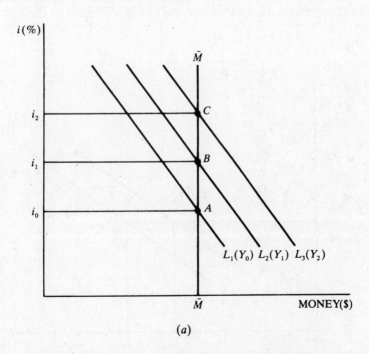

(a)

Fig. 5-12

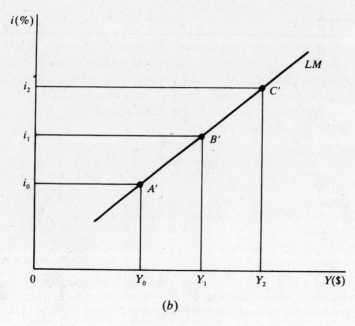

(b)

Fig. 5-12 (*continued*)

5.9   SHIFTING *LM*

Changes in either the demand for money or the supply of money shift *LM*. It is customary to assume no change in the demand for money so that a shift of *LM* is the result of a change in the money supply. An increase in the money supply shifts *LM* rightward by $\Delta \bar{M}(1/k)$ (see Fig. 5-13); a decrease in the money supply results in a similar leftward shift. Changes in behavioral coefficients h or k affect the location of *LM* as well as its slope. A decrease in k (a reduction in the transactions demand for money) results in a rightward movement as does an increase in h (an increase in the interest sensitivity of the demand for money).

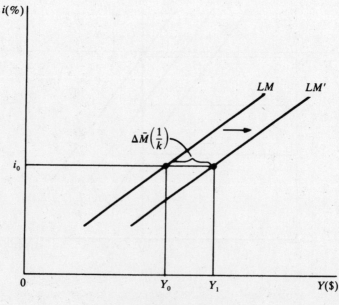

Fig. 5-13

EXAMPLE 5.14.   The equation for LM is $\bar{M} = kY - hi$ when the money supply is $\bar{M}$ and the demand for money is $kY - hi$. Holding the rate of interest constant as well as parameters k and h, $\Delta \bar{M} = k\Delta Y$. Money supply changes thereby shift LM by $(1/k)\Delta \bar{M}$.

5.10   THE SLOPE OF *LM*

The slope of LM is k/h when the money supply is exogenous, the demand for money is $kY - hi$, and the equation for LM is $i = (k/h)Y - \bar{M}/h$. Decreases in h increase the slope of LM, with the curve becoming vertical when $h = 0$. As h takes larger values, LM is less steeply sloped (LM is flatter).

EXAMPLE 5.15.   Suppose the money supply is \$200 and the demand for money is $kY - hi$. When $k = 0.20$ and $h = 5$, the LM equation is $i = 0.04Y - \$40$; the LM equation is $i = 0.02Y - \$20$ when $k = 0.20$ and $h = 10$. These LM equations are plotted in Fig. 5-14. Note that the LM schedule is less steeply sloped when $h = 10$ than when $h = 5$, i.e., LM is less steeply sloped when the demand for money is more sensitive to the rate of interest.

EXAMPLE 5.16.   Suppose the money supply is \$200 and the demand for money is $kY - hi$. When $k = 0.20$ and $h = 5$, the LM equation is $i = 0.04Y - \$40$; the LM equation is $i = 0.05Y - \$40$ when $k = 0.25$ and $h = 5$. These LM equations are plotted in Fig. 5-14. Note that the LM schedule is more steeply sloped when there is a larger transaction demand for money ($k = 0.25$).

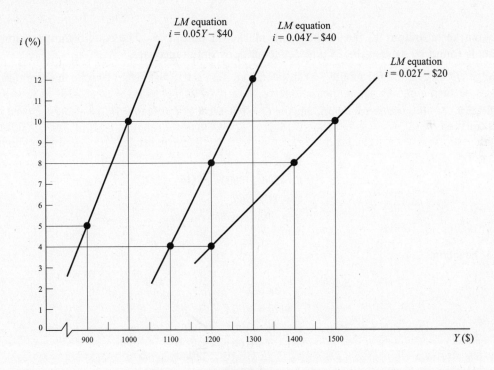

Fig. 5-14

5.11   SIMULTANEOUS EQUILIBRIUM IN THE MONEY AND GOODS MARKETS

Simultaneous equilibrium in the money and goods markets exists at only one output level and one rate of interest. In Fig. 5-15, i_0 is the only rate of interest and Y_0 the only level of output at which there is equilibrium in both the money and goods market. Other interest rates and output levels represent disequilibrium in one or both markets. For example, at interest rate i_1, there is equilibrium in the

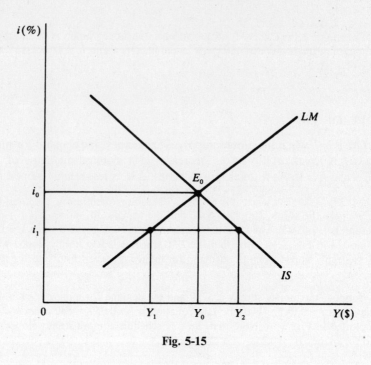

Fig. 5-15

money market at output Y_1 but in the goods market at output Y_2. The equilibrium position for both markets is found by solving the *IS* and *LM* equations simultaneously.

EXAMPLE 5.17. In a two-sector model, suppose $C = \$60 + 0.80Y$, $I = \$116 - 2i$, $L = 0.20Y - 5i$ and $M = \$120$. The *IS* equation:

$$Y = C + I$$
$$Y = \$60 + 0.80Y + \$116 - 2i$$
$$0.2Y = \$176 - 2i$$
$$i = -0.10Y + \$88$$

The *LM* equation:

$$M = L$$
$$\$120 = 0.20Y - 5i$$
$$5i = 0.20Y - \$120$$
$$i = 0.04Y - \$24$$

Simultaneous equilibrium for *IS* and *LM* is:

$$i = -0.10Y + \$88 \qquad IS \text{ equation}$$
$$\text{less } (i = 0.04Y - \$24) \qquad LM \text{ equation}$$
$$\overline{0 = -0.14Y + \$112}$$
$$Y = \$800$$
$$i = 8\%$$

Solved Problems

INVESTMENT AND THE RATE OF INTEREST

5.1　Suppose investment is $I = \bar{I} - bi$. (*a*) Find investment when $\bar{I} = \$250$, $b = 10$ and the rate of interest is 10%, 8%, and 6%. Plot the data and label the schedule I. (*b*) Find investment when $\bar{I} = \$250$, $b = 5$, and the rate of interest is 10%, 8%, and 6%. Plot the data and label the schedule I'. (*c*) Explain the effect that a decrease in behavioral coefficient b has upon the investment schedule.

(*a*)　When $I = \$250 - 10i$, investment is \$150 when the rate of interest is 10%, \$170 when the rate of interest is 8%, and \$190 when it is 6%. The data are plotted in Fig. 5-16 and labeled I.

(*b*)　When $I = \$250 - 5i$, investment is \$200 when the rate of interest is 10%, \$210 when it is 8%, and \$220 when it is 6%. The data are plotted in Fig. 5-16 and labeled I'.

(*c*)　A lower value for b indicates that a change in the rate of interest has a smaller effect upon the level of investment. Thus, a decrease in behavioral coefficient b causes the investment schedule to move right-ward and become more steeply sloped.

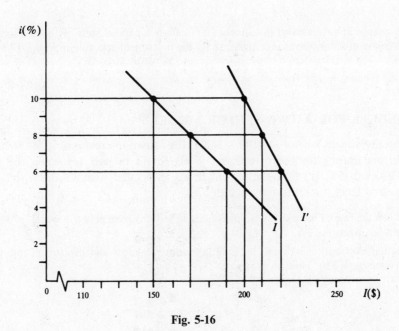

Fig. 5-16

5.2　(*a*) Plot in Fig. 5-17 the investment equation $I = \$250 - 5i$ [Problem 5-1(*b*)] and label the schedule I. (*b*) Find investment when $I = \$200 - 5i$ and the rate of interest is 10%, 8%, and 6%. Plot the data and label the schedule I'. (*c*) Explain the effect that a \$50 decrease in autonomous investment has on the investment demand schedule's location in space.

(*a*)　See Fig. 5-17.

(*b*)　Investment is \$150, \$160, and \$170 when the rate of interest is 10%, 8%, and 6%; the data are plotted in Fig. 5-17 with the schedule labeled I'.

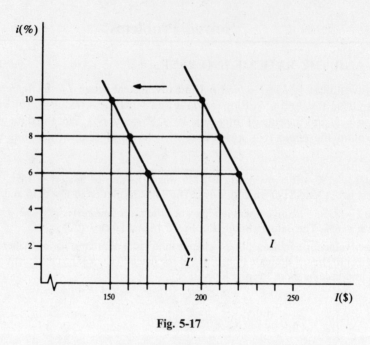

Fig. 5-17

(*c*)   A change in autonomous investment ($\Delta\bar{I}$) causes a parallel shift of the investment line. Thus, a \$50 decrease in autonomous investment shifts the investment schedule in Fig. 5-17 by \$50 from *I* to *I'*.

AN *IS* SCHEDULE FOR A TWO-SECTOR MODEL

5.3   (*a*) Find investment when $I = \$100 - 5i$ and the rate of interest is 4%, 5%, 6%, and 7%. (*b*) Find equilibrium output for the investment levels found in part (*a*) when the saving equation is $S = -\$40 + 0.25Y$. (*c*) Plot the output levels associated with 4%, 5%, 6%, and 7% rates of interest and label the resulting schedule *IS*.

(*a*)   When the rate of interest is 4%, investment is \$80. Investment is \$75 when $i = 5\%$, \$70 when $i = 6\%$, and \$65 when $i = 7\%$.

(*b*)   Equilibrium output is found by equating saving leakages and investment injections. When $i = 4\%$, investment is \$80. Thus,

$$S = I$$
$$-\$40 + 0.25Y = \$80$$
$$Y = \$480$$

When $i = 5\%$, $I = \$75$ and equilibrium output is \$460; when $i = 6\%$, $I = \$70$ and equilibrium output is \$440; when $i = 7\%$, $I = \$65$ and equilibrium output is \$420.

(*c*)   See Fig. 5-18.

5.4   (*a*) Use the saving and investment equations $S = -\$40 + 0.25Y$ and $I = \$100 - 5i$ from Problem 5.3 to find an equation that represents equilibrium in the goods market. (*b*) Find equilibrium output when the rate of interest is 4%, 5%, 6%, and 7%. Compare these answers to those found in Problem 5.3(*b*).

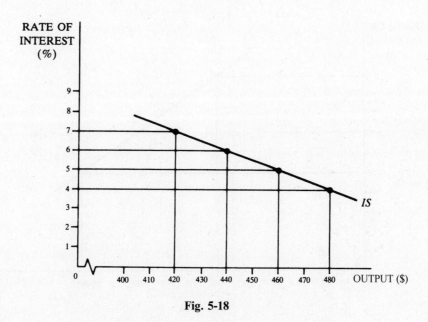

Fig. 5-18

(a)   Equating saving leakages and investment injections, we have

$$-\$40 + 0.25Y = \$100 - 5i$$
$$0.25Y = \$140 - 5i$$
$$Y = \$560 - 20i$$

or, solving for i, $i = \$28 - 0.05Y$

(b)   When the rate of interest is 4%, equilibrium output is \$480; $Y = \$460$ when $i = 5\%$; $Y = \$440$ when $i = 6\%$; and $Y = \$420$ when $i = 7\%$. The association of the rate of interest and equilibrium output is the same as that found in Problem 5.3(b).

5.5   Why is there a schedule of equilibrium output for the goods market?

In a two-sector model, equilibrium output varies directly with the level of investment, given a saving and consumption function. When investment in turn varies inversely with the rate of interest, so too will equilibrium output. For a family of interest rates, then, there is a schedule of equilibrium output, an *IS* schedule.

5.6   An *IS* equation is also found by equating output Y and spending $C + I$. (a) Find the *IS* equation when $C = \$40 + 0.80Y$ and $I = \$70 - 2i$. (b) Find equilibrium output when the rate of interest is 10% and 5%. (c) Plot the *IS* equation.

(a)   Equilibrium exists where $Y = C + I$:

$$Y = \$40 + 0.80Y + \$70 - 2i$$
$$0.20Y = \$110 - 2i$$
$$Y = \$550 - 10i$$

(b)   When $i = 10\%$, equilibrium output is \$450 $[Y = \$550 - 10(10)]$. Equilibrium output is \$500 when $i = 5\%$.

(c)   Fig. 5-19.

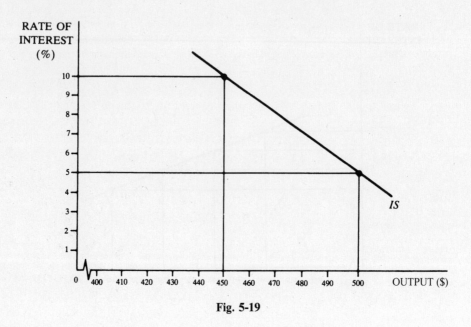

Fig. 5-19

5.7   Find an equation for equilibrium output when $C = \bar{C} + cY$ and $I = \bar{I} - bi$.

$$Y = C + I$$
$$Y = \bar{C} + cY + \bar{I} - bi$$
$$Y - cY = \bar{C} + \bar{I} - bi$$
$$Y(1 - c) = \bar{C} + \bar{I} - bi$$
$$Y = \frac{\bar{C} + \bar{I} - bi}{1 - c}$$

SHIFTING *IS*

5.8   (*a*) Find an equation for equilibrium output in the goods market when $C = \$40 + 0.80Y$ and investment spending is (1) $I = \$70 - 2i$; (2) $I = \$80 - 2i$; and (3) $I = \$90 - 2i$. (*b*) Find equilibrium output when the rate of interest is 10%. (*c*) What accounts for the change in equilibrium? (*d*) Plot the *IS* equations from part (*a*). (*e*) What happens to an *IS* schedule when there is a change in autonomous spending?

(*a*) Equilibrium exists where $Y = C + I$.

$$(1) \qquad\qquad Y = \$40 + 0.80Y + \$70 - 2i$$
$$Y - 0.80Y = \$110 - 2i$$
$$Y = \frac{\$110 - 2i}{0.20}$$
$$Y = \$550 - 10i$$
$$(2) \qquad\qquad Y = \$600 - 10i$$
$$(3) \qquad\qquad Y = \$650 - 10i$$

(*b*) When the rate of interest is 10%, equilibrium output is (1) \$450 $[Y = \$550 - 10(10) = \$450]$; (2) \$500; (3) \$550.

(c) Autonomous investment increases from (1) \$70 to (2) \$80 to (3) \$90; i.e., there is a \$10 change in autonomous spending from (1) to (2) and from (2) to (3). Holding the interest rate constant, equilibrium output should therefore change by $k_e \Delta \bar{I}$; since k_e is 5, equilibrium output increases \$50 for each situation.

(d) See Fig. 5-20.

(e) An *IS* schedule shifts by the multiplier times the change in autonomous spending; thus, *IS* shifts rightward \$50 in Fig. 5-20 for each \$10 increase in autonomous investment.

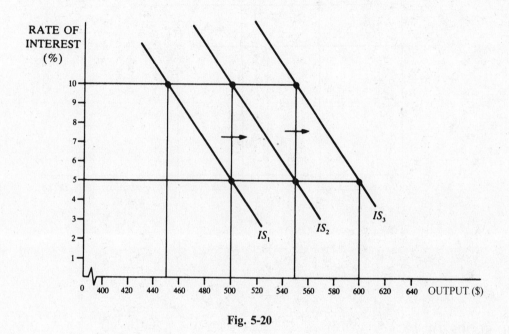

Fig. 5-20

5.9 Equilibrium output in the goods market is $Y = k_e(\bar{C} + \bar{I}) - k_e bi$. (a) Find an expression for ΔY when $\Delta \bar{C} > 0$, *ceteris paribus*, and when $\Delta \bar{I} > 0$, *ceteris paribus*. (b) Find the shift of *IS* due to $\Delta \bar{C}$ and $\Delta \bar{I}$.

(a) When $\Delta \bar{C} > 0$, *ceteris paribus* (i.e., autonomous consumption increases but there is no change in autonomous investment, the rate of interest or behavioral coefficients b or c), $\Delta Y = k_e \Delta \bar{C}$. When $\Delta \bar{I} > 0$, *ceteris paribus*, $\Delta Y = k_e \Delta \bar{I}$.

(b) The *IS* schedule shifts rightward by $k_e \Delta \bar{C}$ and $k_e \Delta \bar{I}$, respectively.

5.10 A change in autonomous spending shifts *IS* by the expenditure multiplier times the change in autonomous spending. What happens to *IS* when a behavioral coefficient such as the marginal propensity to consume changes?

In Fig. 5-21, *IS* is the goods equilibrium schedule for a two-sector model with behavioral equations $C = \$50 + 0.75Y$ and $I = \$150 - 5i$. When the *MPC* increases to 0.80, the *IS* schedule shifts rightward to *IS'*. The rightward shift of *IS* is \$150 at a 10% rate of interest and \$175 at a 5% rate of interest. Thus, a change in a behavioral coefficient causes a nonparallel shift of *IS* and a change in its slope.

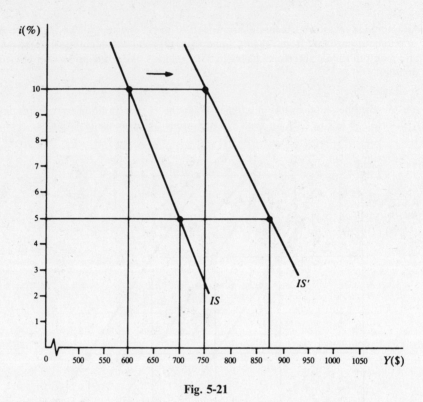

Fig. 5-21

THE SLOPE OF *IS*

5.11 The equation for equilibrium in the goods market is $Y = k_e(\bar{C} + \bar{I}) - k_ebi$. (*a*) Plot *IS* when $\bar{C} = \$50$; $\bar{I} = \$100$; $c = 0.80$; $b = 5$ and label the schedule *IS*. (*b*) Plot *IS* and label it *IS'* when $\bar{C} = \$50$; $\bar{I} = \$100$; $c = 0.80$; $b = 10$. (*c*) What happens to the slope of *IS* when the interest sensitivity of investment spending increases from $b = 5$ [part (*a*)] to $b = 10$ [part (*b*)]? (*d*) Plot *IS* and label it *IS''* when $\bar{C} = \$50$; $\bar{I} = \$100$; $c = 0.75$; $b = 10$. (*e*) Compare the slope of *IS'* and *IS''* when the marginal propensity to consume decreases from $c = 0.80$ (for *IS'*) to 0.75 (for *IS''*).

(*a*) The *IS* equation is $Y = 5(\$150) - 5(5i)$, which is plotted in Fig. 5-22, for 10%, 8%, and 6% rates of interest and labeled *IS*.

(*b*) The *IS* equation is $Y = 5(\$150) - 5(10)i$, which is plotted in Fig. 5-22 and labeled *IS'*.

(*c*) *IS* has a greater slope than *IS'* in Fig. 5-22. An increase in behavioral coefficient b decreases the slope of the *IS* schedule and shifts it leftward.

(*d*) The *IS* equation becomes $Y = 4(\$150) - 4(10)i$; it is plotted in Fig. 5-22 and labeled *IS''*.

(*e*) *IS''* is less steeply sloped than *IS'*. A reduction in the marginal propensity to consume reduces the expenditure multiplier, causing the *IS* schedule to shift to the left and become less steeply sloped.

5.12 The *IS* equation is $Y = k_e(\bar{C} + \bar{I}) - k_ebi$. (*a*) Solve the *IS* equation for i and find the slope of *IS*. (*b*) Find numerical values for and compare the slope of *IS* when $k_e = 5$ and $b = 10$; $k_e = 5$ and $b = 2$; $k_e = 2$ and $b = 5$. (*c*) What happens to the slope of *IS* as k_e and/or b increases?

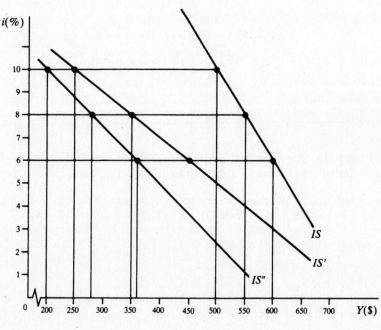

Fig. 5-22

(a)
$$Y = k_e(\bar{C} + \bar{I}) - k_e bi$$
$$k_e bi = k_e(\bar{C} + \bar{I}) - Y$$
$$i = \frac{k_e(\bar{C} + \bar{I})}{k_e b} - \frac{Y}{k_e b}$$
$$i = \frac{1}{b}(\bar{C} + \bar{I}) - \left(\frac{1}{k_e b}\right) \cdot Y$$

The slope of *IS* is $1/k_e b$.

(b)   The slope of *IS* is 0.02 when k_e is 5 and b is 10, 0.10 when k_e is 5 and b is 2, and 0.10 when k_e is 2 and b is 5.

(c)   The slope of *IS* decreases as k_e and/or b increases, i.e., the *IS* schedule is flatter for larger values of k_e and/or b.

GOODS EQUILIBRIUM FOR A FOUR-SECTOR MODEL

5.13   (a) Derive an *IS* equation when $C = \bar{C} + cYd$, $I = \bar{I} - bi$, $Tn = \bar{T}x + tY$, $G = \bar{G}$, $X = \bar{X} - mY$.
(b) Find the slope of *IS* by solving the *IS* equation for i.

(a)
$$Y = C + I + G + X$$
$$Y = \bar{C} + c(Y - \bar{T}x - tY) + \bar{I} - bi + \bar{G} + \bar{X} - mY$$
$$Y - cY + ctY + mY = \bar{C} - c\bar{T}x + \bar{I} - bi + \bar{G} + \bar{X}$$
$$Y = \frac{\bar{C} - c\bar{T}x + \bar{I} - bi + \bar{G} + \bar{X}}{1 - c + ct + m}$$

or
$$Y = k_e(\bar{C} - c\bar{T}x + \bar{I} + \bar{G} + \bar{X}) - k_e bi$$

where
$$k_e = 1/(1 - c + ct + m)$$

(b)   Solving the equation for i,

$$Y = k_e(\bar{C} - c\bar{T}x + \bar{I} + \bar{G} + \bar{X}) - k_e bi$$
$$k_e bi = k_e(\bar{C} - c\bar{T}x + \bar{I} + \bar{G} + \bar{X}) - Y$$
$$i = \frac{\bar{C} - c\bar{T}x + \bar{I} + \bar{G} + \bar{X}}{b} - \left(\frac{1}{k_e b}\right)Y$$

The slope of *IS* is $1/k_e b$.

5.14   Use the *IS* equation derived in part (*a*) of Problem 5.13 and find the shift of *IS* when there is a change in autonomous (1) taxes, (2) government spending, and (3) net exports, *ceteris paribus*.

When there is an autonomous change in the variables specified, the *IS* equation $Y = k_e(\bar{C} - c\bar{T}x + \bar{I} + \bar{G} + \bar{X}) - k_e bi$ becomes (1) $\Delta Y = k_e(-c\Delta \bar{T}x)$, (2) $\Delta Y = k_e \Delta \bar{G}$, and (3) $\Delta Y = k_e \Delta \bar{X}$. The shift of *IS* for a change (1) in autonomous taxes is $-ck_e(\Delta \bar{T}x)$, (2) in autonomous government spending is $k_e(\Delta \bar{G})$, and (3) in autonomous net exports is $k_e(\Delta \bar{X})$.

5.15   Use the *IS* equation found in part (*b*) of Problem 5.13 and establish what happens to the slope of *IS* when *c*, *t*, or *m* increases.

Behavioral coefficients *c* (marginal propensity to consume), *t* (personal income tax rate) and *m* (marginal propensity to import) determine the expenditure multiplier k_e. An increase in *c* increases k_e, and an increase in *t* and/or *m* decreases the expenditure multiplier. The *IS* slope thereby decreases (i.e., the schedule becomes flatter) when *c* increases; the slope increases when *t* and/or *m* increase.

5.16   Suppose $C = \$40 + 0.75(Y - tY)$, $t = 0.20$, $\bar{T}x = 0$, $\bar{G} = \$90$ and $I = \$150 - 5i$. (*a*) Find the equation for equilibrium in the goods market; plot the equation and label it *IS*. (*b*) Explain the direction and magnitude of the shift in *IS* when there is a \$40 increase in *G*, \$40 increase in $\bar{T}x$, or \$40 increase in $\bar{G}$ and $\bar{T}x$. (*c*) Plot the *IS* schedules associated with the shifts in part (*b*) and label them IS_1, IS_2, and IS_3.

(*a*)
$$Y = C + I + G$$
$$Y = \$40 + 0.75(Y - 0.20Y) + \$150 - 5i + \$90$$
$$Y - 0.60Y = \$280 - 5i$$
$$Y = \frac{\$280 - 5i}{1 - 0.60}$$
$$Y = \$700 - 12.5i$$

(*b*)   The expenditure multiplier is 2.5 $[k_e = 1/(1 - 0.75 + 0.15) = 2.5]$, and the lump-sum tax multiplier is -1.875 $[k_t = -0.75/(1 - 0.75 + 0.15) = -1.875]$. Therefore, a \$40 increase in $\bar{G}$ shifts *IS* rightward \$100, a \$40 increase in $\bar{T}x$ shifts *IS* leftward \$75, and a \$40 increase in $\bar{G}$ and $\bar{T}x$ shifts *IS* rightward by \$25.

(*c*)   See Fig. 5-23.

5.17   Find the *IS* equation when (1) $C = \$20 + 0.80Yd$, $Tx = 0.3Y$, $G = \$120$, $I = \$150 - 10i$ and $X = \$40 - 0.06Y$; (2) $C = \$20 + 0.80Yd$, $Tx = 0.22Y$, $G = \$120$, $I = \$150 - 10i$ and $X = \$40 - 0.024Y$. (*b*) Plot these *IS* schedules for 10% and 5% interest rates and label them IS_1 and IS_2. (*c*) What effect does a decrease in the income tax rate from 0.30 to 0.22 and a decrease in the marginal propensity to import from 0.06 to 0.024 have upon *IS*?

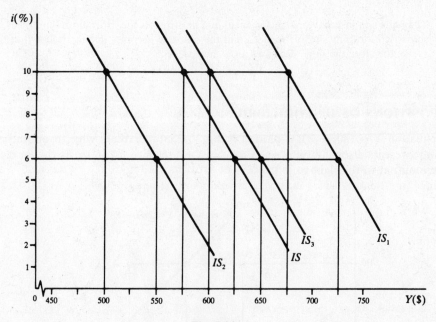

Fig. 5-23

(*a*)

$$(1) \quad Y = \$20 + 0.80(Y - 0.3Y) + \$150 - 10i + \$120 + \$40 - 0.06Y$$
$$Y - 0.8Y + 0.24Y + 0.06Y = \$330 - 10i$$
$$Y = \$660 - 20i$$
$$(2) \quad Y = \$20 + 0.80(Y - 0.22Y) + \$150 - 10i + \$120 + \$40 - 0.024Y$$
$$Y - 0.8Y + 0.176Y + 0.024Y = \$330 - 10i$$
$$Y = \$825 - 25i$$

(*b*) See Fig. 5-24.

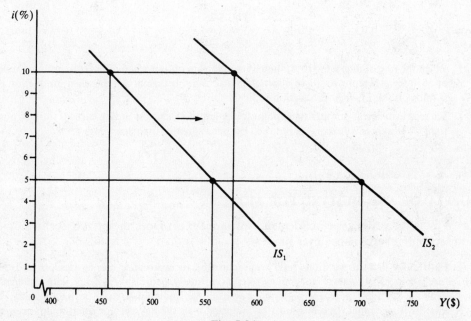

Fig. 5-24

(c) The reduction in behavioral coefficients t and m increases the expenditure multiplier. The *IS* schedule shifts rightward; its slope is reduced and the schedule becomes flatter. (Recall that the slope of *IS* is $1/k_e b$; therefore the slope decreases as k_e increases.)

IS AND POSITIONS OF DISEQUILIBRIUM

5.18   *IS* equation $Y = \$800 - 20i$ is plotted in Fig. 5-25. (a) Explain why an output level of \$550 or \$650 represents disequilibrium when the rate of interest is 10%. (b) Is there excess spending or excess output to the right or left of *IS*?

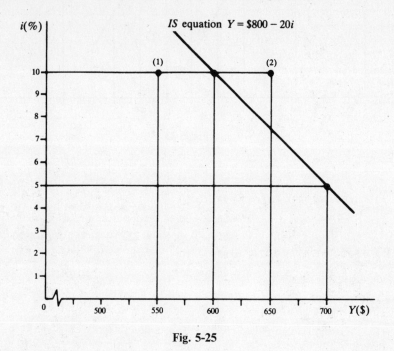

Fig. 5-25

(a) When the rate of interest is 10%, there is equilibrium output when $Y = \$600$; production levels of \$550 or \$650 thereby represent disequilibrium. There is a shortage of output when production is \$550 and a surplus of output when production is \$650.

(b) There is insufficient output at any point to the left of *IS* since spending exceeds output; positions to the right of *IS* represent excess output, i.e., output is greater than spending.

THE SUPPLY OF AND DEMAND FOR MONEY

5.19   (a) Why is there a transaction demand for money? (b) Does the private sector hold a constant transaction money balance over time?

(a) Individuals and corporations hold transaction balances because money receipts and disbursements rarely coincide. Private sector money receipts normally lead disbursements, with the lead time dependent on "typical" payment patterns. For example, individuals may be paid weekly, biweekly, or monthly; their money receipts must be budgeted over the pay period, resulting in an average holding of money balances for transactions.

(b)   The average money balance held for transactions depends on the length of the pay period, timing of expenditures, and the income level. Therefore, it is highly unlikely that the private sector will hold a constant money balance for transactions over time. In macroeconomic theory, it is customary to assume that pay periods and timing of expenditures do not change in the short run, with income the sole determinant of transaction money holdings. The transaction demand for money is presented as $L_t = f(Y)$.

5.20   (a) Why is there a store of value demand for money? (b) Is this portfolio demand constant over time?

(a)   Those who possess wealth allocate their accumulated savings among four asset categories: liquid assets (which include money), long-term bonds, equities, and real assets. Allocations among the four asset categories depend on the magnitude of accumulated savings, willingness to assume risk and market interest rates. For example, an investor whose portfolio of assets is relatively small or who is risk-averse may hold a large percentage of accumulated wealth as a money balance because of uncertainties about the future and a possible need to draw on this wealth. Individuals with a relatively large portfolio of assets may hold a combination of the four asset categories, with the actual percentage in each category influenced by market interest rates, i.e., the opportunity cost of holding liquid assets.

(b)   It is customary to assume that the distribution of wealth and willingness to assume risk are constant in the short run. Hence, the store of value demand for money is a stable function of market interest rates. Money balances held in portfolios do not change as long as the market rate of interest is unchanged; increases in market rates, however, decrease the quantity of money held in private sector portfolios, i.e., $L_p = f(i)$.

5.21   Tables 5-3 and 5-4 present the transaction and store of value demand for money. (a) Find the quantity of money demanded when output is $700 and the market rate of interest is 8% and 10%. (b) The total demand for money is found by summing the transaction and store of value demand for money. Present in a table a schedule of the total demand for money when output is $600, $700, and $800. (c) Plot the demand for money schedules derived in part (b) and label them L, L', and L'' respectively.

Table 5-3   Transaction Demand for Money

Output Level, $	Quantity of Money Demanded, $
500	100
600	120
700	140
800	160
900	180

Table 5-4   Store of Value Demand for Money

Market Rate of Interest, %	Quantity of Money Demanded, $
12	30
10	50
8	70
6	90
4	110

(a) The total demand for money is the sum of the balances demanded for transactions and those held in portfolios. When the output level is $700, transaction holdings are $140, and portfolio holdings are $70 at an 8% market rate of interest and $50 at a 10% rate. The total demand for money at a $700 output level and 8% market rate of interest is $210; total demand is $190 when output is $700 and the market rate is 10%.

(b)

Table 5-5   Total Demand for Money

Rate of Interest (%)	Quantity of Money Demanded When		
	$Y = \$600$	$Y = \$700$	$Y = \$800$
12	$150	$170	$190
10	170	190	210
8	190	210	230
6	210	230	250
4	230	250	270

(c)   See Fig. 5-26.

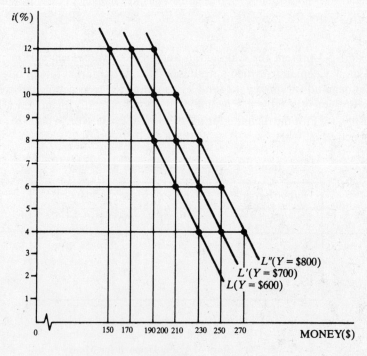

Fig. 5-26

5.22   Suppose the total demand for money is specified as $L = kY - hi$ and the value of behavioral coefficient k is 0.20 and $h = 5$. (a) Plot the demand for money schedule when output is $600 and the rate of interest is 12%, 10%, 8%, and 6%; label the demand schedule L. (b) Plot and label L' and L'' the demand for money schedules when output is $800 and $1000. (c) What happens to the demand for money schedules when output increases from $600 to $800 to $1000?

(*a*) and (*b*)   See Fig. 5-27.

(*c*)   The demand for money schedule shifts rightward $40 as a result of each $200 increase in output; the shift is equal to $k\Delta Y$.

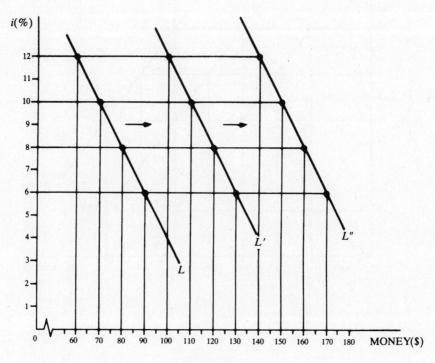

Fig. 5-27

THE *LM* SCHEDULE

5.23   Suppose $L = 0.20Y - 5i$. (*a*) Plot the demand for money when the rate of interest is 10%, 8%, and 6% and output is (1) $800, (2) $900, and (3) $1000. (*b*) Find equilibrium between the demand for money and the supply of money when the nominal money supply is $150. (*c*) Derive an *LM* schedule from the data plotted in part (*a*). (*d*) What is an *LM* schedule?

(*a*)   See Fig. 5-28(*a*).

(*b*)   Equilibrium between a $150 nominal money supply and demand for money schedules L, L', and L'' exists at a 10% rate of interest and a $1000 output level, a 6% rate of interest and a $900 output level, and a 2% rate of interest and an $800 output level.

(*c*)   See Fig. 5-28(*b*).

(*d*)   An *LM* schedule is a locus of points at which the demand for money is equal to the supply of money.

5.24   (*a*) Find an equation for equilibrium between the demand for money and the supply of money when the demand for money is $L = kY - hi$ and the money supply is $\bar{M}$. (*b*) Find a numerical equation for monetary equilibrium when $k = 0.20$, $h = 5$ and $\bar{M} = \$200$. (*c*) Find the output associated with interest rates 10%, 8%, and 6% when there is equilibrium in the money market.

(*a*)   Equilibrium in the money market exists where the demand for money equals the money supply.

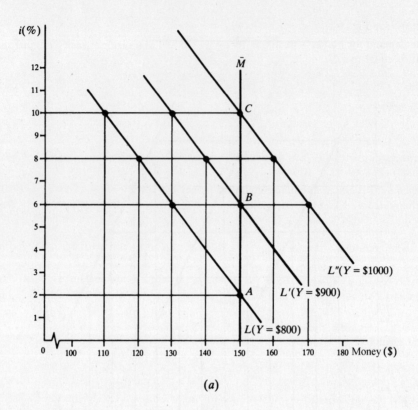

(a)

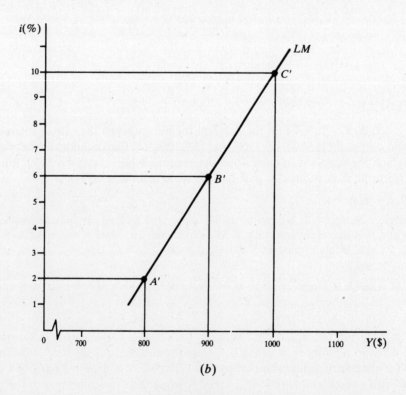

(b)

Fig. 5-28

$$L = M$$
$$kY - hi = \bar{M}$$
$$kY = \bar{M} + hi$$
$$Y = \frac{\bar{M} + hi}{k}$$

or
$$Y = \frac{\bar{M}}{k} + \frac{hi}{k}$$

(b) Substituting $k = 0.20$, $h = 5$, and $\bar{M} = \$200$ into the equation $Y = (\bar{M} + hi)/k$, we have $Y = \$1000 + 25i$.

(c) When $i = 10\%$, there is equilibrium in the money market when Y is \$1250. [$Y = (\$200 + 5(10))/0.20$.] When $i = 8\%$, Y is \$1200 at equilibrium; and Y must equal \$1150 when $i = 6\%$.

5.25 The *LM* schedule is $Y = \$1000 + 25i$ when $L = 0.20Y - 5i$ and $\bar{M} = \$200$. (a) Plot the *LM* schedule. (b) What is true of the supply of and demand for money at a 10% rate of interest and a \$1100 level of output? 10% rate of interest and a \$1350 level of output? (c) What generalizations can one make about positions to the right and to the left of the *LM* schedule?

(a) Fig. 5-29.

(b) L is \$170 when $i = 10\%$ and $Y = \$1100$; i.e., the demand for money is \$170, less than the \$200 money supply. L equals \$220 when $i = 10\%$ and $Y = \$1350$; a \$220 money demand exceeds a \$200 money supply.

(c) Positions to the left of *LM* represent positions where the demand for money is less than the money supply; there is therefore downward pressure on interest rates. Positions to the right of *LM* exist when money demand exceeds the money supply, and there is upward pressure on interest rates. Points on the *LM* schedule represent equilibrium between the supply of and demand for money.

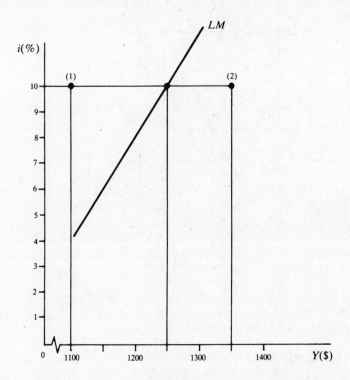

Fig. 5-29

SHIFTING *LM*

5.26   The equation for *LM* is $Y = \bar{M}/k + hi/k$. (*a*) Find the change in output associated with a $\Delta\bar{M}$ increase in money, holding behavioral coefficients k and h and the rate of interest constant. (*b*) What happens to the *LM* schedule when there is an increase in the money supply of $\Delta\bar{M}$?

(*a*)   With the rate of interest held constant, $\Delta Y = \Delta\bar{M}(1/k)$.

(*b*)   The $\Delta\bar{M}$ increase in the money supply shifts *LM* rightward by $\Delta\bar{M}(1/k)$.

5.27   (*a*) Find an equation for *LM* when the money supply is \$200 and the demand for money is specified as $L = 0.20Y - 4i$. (*b*) Plot the schedule and label it *LM*. (*c*) Find an equation for *LM* when the money supply increases from \$200 to \$210; plot the new *LM* schedule and label it *LM'*. (*d*) What happens to *LM* as a result of a \$10 increase in the money supply?

(*a*)
$$M = L$$
$$\$200 = 0.20Y - 4i$$
$$0.20Y = \$200 + 4i$$
$$Y = \$1000 + 20i$$

(*b*)   See Fig. 5-30.

(*c*)   The new *LM* equation is $Y = \$1050 + 20i$; the new schedule is *LM'* in Fig. 5-30.

(*d*)   The \$10 increase in the money supply shifts *LM* rightward \$50 from *LM* to *LM'*; the shift equals $\Delta\bar{M}(1/k)$, i.e., \$10/0.20.

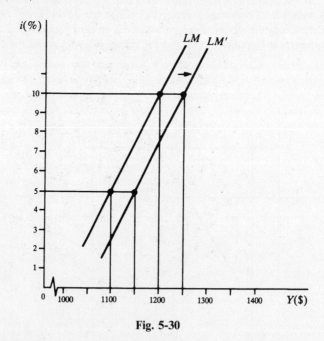

Fig. 5-30

5.28   Establish the direction and magnitude of the shift of *LM* when (*a*) $k = 0.20$ and there is a \$20 increase in the money supply, (*b*) $k = 0.50$ and there is a \$20 decrease in the money supply, (*c*) $k = 0.25$ and there is a \$20 increase in the money supply.

(*a*)   The *LM* schedule shifts rightward \$100; \$20/0.20 = \$100.

(*b*)   The *LM* schedule shifts leftward \$40; −\$20/0.50 = −\$40.

(*c*)   The *LM* schedule shifts rightward \$80; \$20/0.25 = \$80.

THE SLOPE OF *LM*

5.29 (*a*) Find an equation for *LM* in terms of the rate of interest *i* when the money supply equals $\bar{M}$ and the demand for money is $kY - hi$. (*b*) Find the slope of the *LM* equation. (*c*) Find the slope of *LM* when $k = 0.20$ and $h = 10$; $k = 0.20$ and $h = 20$; $k = 0.10$ and $h = 10$. (*d*) What happens to the slope of *LM* when the value for behavioral coefficient *k* decreases? What happens to the slope of *LM* when the value for behavioral coefficient *h* increases?

(*a*)
$$M = L$$
$$\bar{M} = kY - hi$$
$$hi = kY - \bar{M}$$
$$i = \left(\frac{k}{h}\right)Y - \frac{\bar{M}}{h}$$

(*b*) The slope of *LM* is k/h.

(*c*) When $k = 0.20$ and $h = 10$, the slope for *LM* is 0.02; when $k = 0.20$ and $h = 20$, the slope for *LM* is 0.01; when $k = 0.10$ and $h = 10$, the slope is 0.01.

(*d*) When the value for *k* decreases, the slope of *LM* decreases; the slope of *LM* also decreases when the value for *h* increases.

5.30 Suppose the money supply is \$200 and the demand for money is $kY - hi$. (*a*) Plot *LM* when (1) $k = 0.20$ and $h = 10$ and label it LM' and (2) $k = 0.20$ and $h = 20$ and label it LM''. (*b*) Explain why the slopes of LM' and LM'' differ.

(*a*) The *LM* equation is $Y = \$1000 + 50i$ for (1) and $Y = \$1000 + 100i$ for (2); they are plotted in Fig. 5-31.

(*b*) LM' is more steeply sloped than LM'' because the demand for money is more interest-sensitive in (2) (noted by the greater value for behavioral coefficient *h*) than in (1). The more interest-sensitive money demand is, the flatter the *LM* schedule (the lower the numerical value of the slope for *LM*).

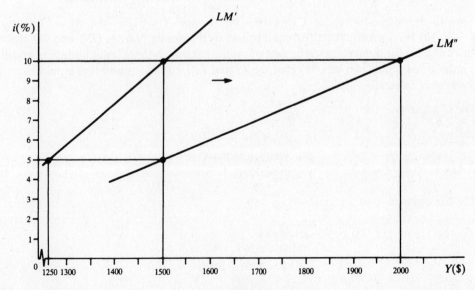

Fig. 5-31

5.31 Suppose the money supply is $200 and the demand for money is $kY - hi$. (*a*) Plot *LM* when k is 0.20 and h is zero. (*b*) Why is *LM* vertical?

(*a*) The *LM* equation is $Y = \$1000$ and is plotted in Fig. 5-32.

(*b*) *LM* has no relationship to the rate of interest because the demand for money is not influenced by the rate of interest. Hence, when h is zero or takes a very small value, the *LM* schedule is vertical or steeply sloped.

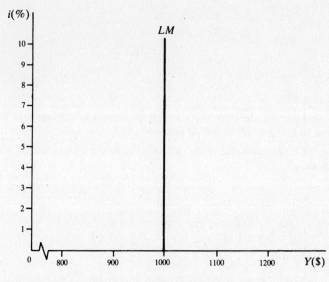

Fig. 5-32

SIMULTANEOUS EQUILIBRIUM IN THE MONEY AND GOODS MARKETS

5.32 Posit a two-sector model where $C = \$100 + 0.80Y$ and $I = \$150 - 6i$, $M = \$150$ and $L = 0.20Y - 4i$. (*a*) Find an equation for equilibrium in the goods market (*IS*) and for the money market (*LM*). (*b*) Find output and the rate of interest at which there is simultaneous equilibrium in the money and goods markets. (*c*) Plot the *IS* and *LM* equations and find equilibrium output and the rate of interest.

(*a*) The *IS* equation:

$$Y = C + I$$
$$Y = \$100 + 0.80Y + \$150 - 6i$$
$$Y = \$1250 - 30i$$

The *LM* equation:

$$M = L$$
$$\$150 = 0.20Y - 4i$$
$$Y = \$750 + 20i$$

(*b*) Simultaneous equilibrium occurs where $IS = LM$.

IS equation: $Y = \$1250 - 30i$

less LM equation: $-(Y = \$\ 750 + 20i)$
_____

                                          $0 = \$\ 500 - 50i$

                                          $i = 10\%$

                                          $Y = \$950$

(c) Simultaneous equilibrium exists at the intersecton of *IS* and *LM*. In Fig. 5-33, this occurs at a \$950 output level and a 10% rate of interest.

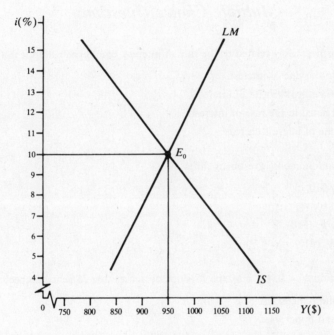

Fig. 5-33

5.33 Find simultaneous equilibrium for the goods and money market when $C = \$100 + 0.80Yd$, $I = \$150 - 6i$, $Tx = 0.25Y$, $G = \$100$, $L = 0.20Y - 2i$ and $M = \$150$.

The *IS* equation:

$$Y = C + I + G$$
$$Y = \$100 + 0.80(Y - 0.25Y) + \$150 - 6i + \$100$$
$$Y = \$350 + 0.6Y - 6i$$
$$Y = \$875 - 15i$$

The *LM* equation:

$$M = L$$
$$\$150 = 0.20Y - 2i$$
$$Y = \$750 + 10i$$

Simultaneous equilibrium for *IS* and *LM*:

$$IS = LM$$
$$\$875 - 15i = \$750 + 10i$$
$$25i = \$125$$
$$i = 5\%$$
$$Y = \$800$$

Multiple Choice Questions

1.   When investment is negatively related to the rate of interest, equilibrium output in the goods market

   (a)   Is unrelated to the rate of interest.

   (b)   Is inversely related to the rate of interest.

   (c)   Is positively related to the rate of interest.

   (d)   Falls as the rate of interest decreases.

2.   A \$10 increase in autonomous investment shifts *IS*

   (a)   Rightward by \$10.

   (b)   Leftward by \$10.

   (c)   Rightward by k_e (\$10).

   (d)   Leftward by k_e (\$10).

3.   Given the *IS* equation $Y = k_e \bar{A} - k_e bi$, the *IS* slope decreases (the *IS* schedule becomes flatter) when

   (a) k_e increases and b increases.

   (b) k_e decreases and b increases.

   (c) k_e increases and b decreases.

   (d) k_e decreases and b decreases.

4.   An increase in autonomous lump-sum taxes shifts *IS*

   (a)   Rightward by $k_t(\Delta \bar{T}x)$.

   (b)   Leftward by $k_t(\Delta \bar{T}x)$.

   (c)   Rightward by $k_e(\Delta \bar{T}x)$.

   (d)   Leftward by $k_e(\Delta \bar{T}x)$.

5.   The demand for money is

   (a)   Positively related to output and the rate of interest.

   (b)   Negatively related to output and the rate of interest.

   (c)   Negative related to output and positively related to the rate of interest.

   (d)   Positively related to output and negatively related to the rate of interest.

6.   Suppose the money supply and price level are constant, and the demand for money is a function of output and the rate of interest. When output increases, there is

Chapter 6

Monetary and Fiscal Policy in a Closed Economy

Chapter Summary

1. A change in autonomous domestic spending and/or a change in the supply or demand for money are the only possible causes of a change in output in a closed economy. The possibility exists that, in the absence of economic policy, output will remain below its full employment level in the short run.

2. An increase in the money supply shifts *LM* rightward, which results in a liquidity effect (a decrease in the rate of interest) and an output effect (an increase in the level of output). The magnitude of the liquidity and output effect depend upon the slopes of *IS* and *LM*, specifically upon the interest sensitivity of investment spending and the interest sensitivity of the demand for money. Special cases for monetary policy exist in which an increase in the money supply has no output effect and another where the output effect is fully realized.

3. The multiplier effect of a money supply change is evaluated using the formula for simultaneous equilibrium in the money and goods markets. A small value for *h* (the demand for money is interest-insensitive) and/or a large value for *b* (investment spending is highly interest-sensitive) are shown to be the conditions whereby a money supply change has a large effect upon output.

4. An increase in government spending shifts *IS* rightward and normally increases output and the rate of interest. The output effect of a fiscal action, however, depends upon the interest-sensitivity of investment spending and the interest-sensitivity of the demand for money. When investment spending is interest-sensitive, increased government spending crowds out interest-sensitive spending and there is a small output effect. The output effect from a fiscal stimulus is also small when the demand for money is not interest-sensitive.

5. The formula for simultaneous equilibrium in the money and capital markets demonstrates that fiscal policy has a small output effect when *b* is large and/or *h* is small. There is little crowding out and the output effect of a fiscal action is large when *b* is small and/or *h* is large.

Chapter Outline

6.1 EQUILIBRIUM OUTPUT IN A CLOSED ECONOMY

Equilibrium output in an IS–LM framework exists at the intersection of IS and LM, e.g., at Y_0 for IS' and LM' in Fig. 6-1. In a closed economy, this equilibrium is sustained unless there is a change in autonomous domestic spending and/or a change in the supply or demand for money. That is, equilibrium output will change only as a result of a shift of IS and/or LM. In this chapter we continue to assume that output is below its full-employment level, and analyze the extent to which monetary or fiscal policy will increase output.

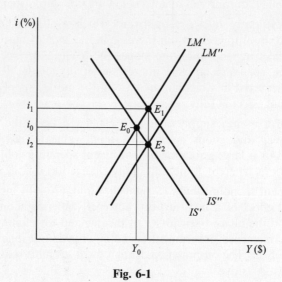

Fig. 6-1

EXAMPLE 6.1. IS' and LM' in Fig. 6-1 intersect at E_0, and equilibrium output is Y_0. An increase in autonomous consumption and/or investment shifts IS rightward from IS' to IS''; IS'' and LM' then intersect at E_1 and equilibrium output increases from Y_0 to Y_1. A decrease in the demand for money shifts LM from LM' to LM''; IS' and LM'' then intersect at E_2 and equilibrium output increases from Y_0 to Y_1. Output in the domestic economy changes as a result of autonomous changes in spending and/or the demand for money. In the absence of such changes, output is unchanged and the possibility exists that production remains below its full-employment level in the short run.

6.2 THE LIQUIDITY EFFECT FROM A CHANGE IN THE MONEY SUPPLY

The Federal Reserve increases the money supply by purchasing Treasury securities in the open market. An increase in the money supply creates a liquidity effect which results in a lower rate of interest. An output effect normally follows. A lower interest rate usually increases interest-sensitive spending, which raises output and the rate of interest. When the new equilibrium is reached, the increased money supply has lowered the rate of interest and increased equilibrium output.

EXAMPLE 6.2. IS and LM' intersect at A' in Fig. 6-2 and equilibrium output is Y_0. An increase in the money supply shifts LM by $\Delta \bar{M}/k$ from LM' to LM''. With no initial change in output, the rate of interest falls from i_0 to i_2. There is disequilibrium, however, at B', since there is no intersection of IS and LM'' at this point. Investment spending is induced by the lower interest rate; output increases from Y_0 to Y_1; the rate of interest increases from i_2 to i_1; and equilibrium is restored at C'. Thus, the increase in the money supply raises output from Y_0 to Y_1 and lowers the rate of interest from i_0 to i_1.

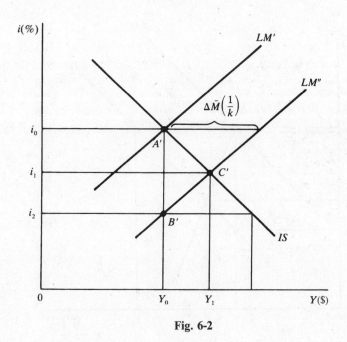

Fig. 6-2

EXAMPLE 6.3.   The equation for equilibrium in the goods market is $Y = \$1250 - 30i$ and in the money market is $Y = \$750 + 20i$, when $C = \$100 + 0.80Y$, $I = \$150 - 6i$, $M = \$150$, and $L = 0.20Y - 4i$. Simultaneous equilibrium in the money and goods markets exists at a 10% rate of interest and $950 output level. A $10 increase in the money supply, holding output constant at $950, lowers the rate of interest from 10 to 7.50%.

$$\$160 = 0.20(\$950) - 4i$$
$$4i = \$30 \qquad i = 7.50\%$$

However, a lower interest rate increases investment spending and through a multiplier effect equilibrium output. Simultaneous equilibrium in the money and goods markets is restored when output increases from $950 to $980 and the rate of interest is 9%.

the *IS* equation: $\qquad\qquad\qquad Y = \$1250 - 30i$

less the *LM* equation: $\qquad\qquad \underline{-(Y = \$\ 800 + 20i)}$

$$0 = \$\ 450 - 50i$$
$$i = 9\%$$
$$Y = \$\ 980$$

Thus, the $10 increase in the money supply causes a liquidity effect which reduces the rate of interest from 10 to 7.50%; the resulting output effect then increases the rate of interest from 7.50% to 9.00%.

6.3 THE OUTPUT EFFECT OF MONETARY POLICY

The slopes of *IS* and/or *LM* determine the output effect of monetary policy. *IS* is steeply sloped in Fig. 6-3. This occurs when investment spending is interest-insensitive and/or there is a low value for the expenditure multiplier. (The discussion here focuses upon the interest-sensitivity of investment spending as the primary determinant of the slope of *IS*.) The money supply increase of $\Delta\bar{M}$ in Fig. 6-3 shifts *LM* rightward from *LM'* to *LM"*, a shift equal to Y_0 to Y_3. At output Y_0, the rate of interest declines from i_0 to i_3 due to the liquidity effect. Investment spending increases as a result of a lower interest rate; however, the output effect is small. Output increases from Y_0 to only Y_1 because investment spending is insensitive to the rate of interest. There is an equal increase in the money supply of $\Delta\bar{M}$ in Fig. 6-4 with a similar liquidity effect, which lowers the rate of interest from i_0 to i_3. *IS* in Fig. 6-4, however, is less

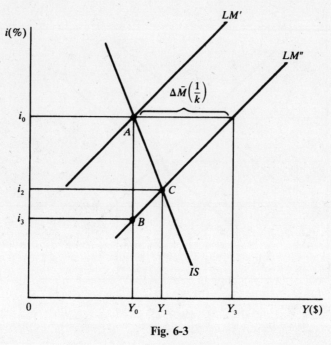

Fig. 6-3

steeply sloped, since investment spending is more interest-sensitive than in Fig. 6-3. Thus, the output effect is larger, from Y_0 to Y_2, because more investment spending is induced by the lower rate of interest. Note that the liquidity effect is the same in Fig. 6-3 and Fig. 6-4. Differences in the interest-sensitivity of investment spending result in a smaller output effect (Y_0 to Y_1) in Fig. 6-3 than the Y_0 to Y_2 output effect in Fig. 6-4. Examples 6.4 and 6.5 relate the effect that an increase in the money supply has upon output when there are differences in the slope of LM. We find that a money supply increase has a greater effect upon output when LM is steeply sloped, i.e., when the demand for money is relatively interest-insensitive. The analysis in this section shows that an increase in the money supply has its largest output effect when investment spending is highly interest-sensitive (the value of coefficient b is large) and/or the demand for money is interest-insensitive (the value of coefficient h is small).

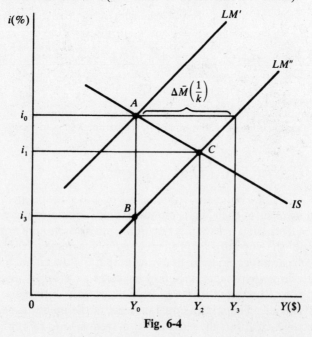

Fig. 6-4

EXAMPLE 6.4. Schedule LM' in Fig. 6-5 is steeply sloped because the demand for money is relatively insensitive to the rate of interest (the amount of money held in the private sector's portfolio of assets is little affected by interest rate levels). A $\Delta \bar{M}$ money supply increase results in a $\Delta \bar{M}(1/k)$ rightward shift of LM from LM' to LM'' (equivalent to a Y_0 to Y_3 shift at interest rate i_0). The liquidity effect is i_0 to i_4 at output Y_0. Equilibrium output increases from Y_0 to Y_2 which is slightly less than the $Y_0 Y_3$ LM shift.

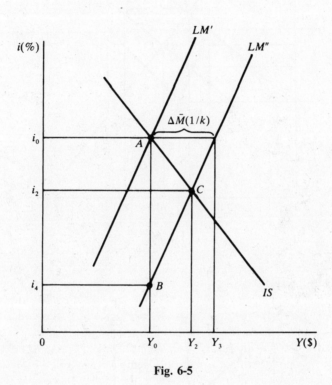

Fig. 6-5

EXAMPLE 6.5. In Fig. 6-6, LM' is not steeply sloped because the demand for money is interest-sensitive. A $\Delta \bar{M}$ increase in the money supply, equal to the money supply increase in Fig. 6-5, shifts LM from LM' to LM''. The liquidity effect at Y_0 is i_0 to i_3, which is smaller than the liquidity effect in Fig. 6-5. The weaker liquidity effect has a smaller effect upon interest-sensitive spending and therefore output; output in Fig. 6-6 increases from Y_0 to Y_1, which is less than the increase for the more steeply sloped LM schedule in Fig. 6-6. Thus, when the demand for money is interest-sensitive, a large portion of any increase in the money supply is held in private sector portfolios and there is a small decrease in the rate of interest (Fig. 6-6). A weak liquidity effect in turn has a smaller effect upon interest-sensitive spending and output.

6.4 MONETARY POLICY: SPECIAL CASES

Special cases exist for the output effect of monetary policy when LM is vertical, LM is horizontal, and IS is vertical. These special cases are depicted in Figs. 6-7, 6-8, and 6-9. A vertical LM exists when the demand for money is completely insensitive to the rate of interest, i.e., the portfolio demand for money is totally unrelated to the rate of interest. In the LM equation, $\bar{M} = kY - hi$; such a situation arises when $h = 0$ so that $\bar{M} = kY$. A money supply increase of $\Delta \bar{M}$ in Fig. 6-7 shifts LM from LM' to LM''; the Y_0 to Y_1 increase in output is equal to the $\Delta \bar{M}(1/k)$ shift, regardless of the slope of IS.

LM is horizontal (Fig. 6-8) when there is a liquidity trap. A liquidity trap arises when portfolio holders have an infinite demand for money because they do not want to hold bonds. The entirety of a money supply increase is held in portfolios; therefore there is no liquidity effect and no change in output.

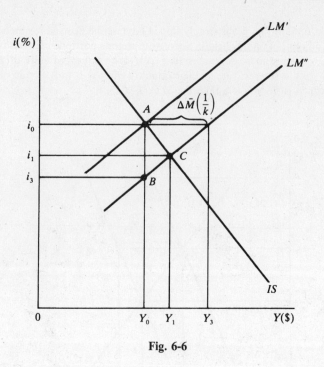

Fig. 6-6

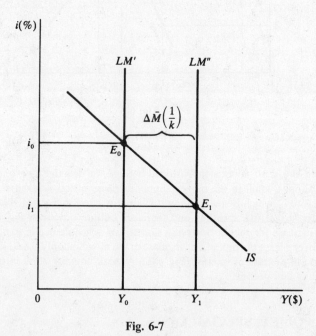

Fig. 6-7

Money supply changes do not affect the location of LM in space and therefore leave interest rates and output unchanged.

IS is vertical (Fig. 6-9) when investment spending is unrelated to the rate of interest. Suppose the IS equation for a two-sector model is $Y = (\bar{C} + \bar{I} - bi)/(1 - c)$. When behavioral coefficient b equals zero, the rate of interest has no effect on investment spending. The IS equation is then $Y = (\bar{C} + \bar{I})/(1 - c)$, and the IS schedule is vertical. Shifts of monetary equilibrium from LM' to LM'' in Fig. 6-9 have a liquidity effect of i_0 to i_1 but do not change output because investment is unrelated to the rate of interest.

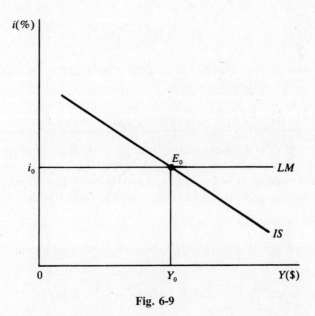

Fig. 6-9

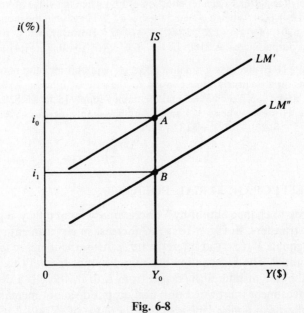

Fig. 6-8

6.5 THE MULTIPLIER EFFECT OF MONETARY POLICY IN AN *IS–LM* FRAMEWORK

Simultaneous equilibrium in the goods and money markets exists at the intersection of *IS* and *LM*. For a negatively sloped *IS* and positively sloped *LM*, this intersection is given by

$$Y = \bar{A}\left(\frac{hk_e}{h + kbk_e}\right) + \bar{M}\left(\frac{bk_e}{h + kbk_e}\right)$$

where $\bar{A}$ represents the sum of autonomous spending $(\bar{C} + \bar{I} - c\overline{Tn} + \bar{G} + \bar{X})$. (See Problem 6.13 for derivation.)

Assuming no change in autonomous spending $\bar{A}$ or behavioral coefficients h, k, b, and k_e, a change in the money supply is associated with the following change in equilibrium output.

$$\Delta Y = \Delta \bar{M} \left(\frac{bk_e}{h + kbk_e} \right)$$

The rate of change in output due to a change in the money supply—the multiplier effect of a money supply change, or $\Delta Y / \Delta \bar{M}$—is therefore written as

$$\frac{\Delta Y}{\Delta \bar{M}} = \frac{bk_e}{h + kbk_e}$$

Note that the multiplier effect of a money supply change increases as the value of h decreases. (Recall that small values for h are associated with a steeply sloped LM; and money supply changes have a greater effect on equilibrium output when LM is steeply sloped.) The larger the value of coefficients b and/or k_e (IS is less steeply sloped), the greater the multiplier effect of $\Delta \bar{M}$ on ΔY.

EXAMPLE 6.6. When there is a stable IS schedule, a change in equilibrium output due to a change in the money supply is written as

$$\Delta Y = \Delta \bar{M} \left(\frac{bk_e}{h + kbk_e} \right)$$

Situation I. A money supply change has a greater effect on output when the value of behavioral coefficient h is small. Suppose $b = 5$, $k_e = 4$ and $k = 0.20$. When $h = 5$ and there is a \$20 increase in the money supply, equilibrium output increases \$74.07. $[\Delta Y = \$20\{5(4)/[5 + (0.20)(5)(4)]\} = \$74.07.]$ However, when $h = 0$ and the money supply increases \$20, equilibrium output increases \$100. $[\Delta Y = \$20\{5(4)/[0 + (0.20)(5)(4)]\} = \$100.]$

Situation II. A money supply change has a smaller effect on equilibrium output when the value of behavioral coefficient b is small—spending is largely unresponsive to the rate of interest—than when b has a large value. Suppose $k_e = 4$, $k = 0.20$, and $h = 5$. When $b = 5$ and the money supply increases \$20, equilibrium output increases \$74.07 as calculated above. However, when $b = 1$ and the money supply increases \$20, equilibrium output increases \$13.79. $[\Delta Y = \$20\{1(4)/[5 + (0.20)(1)(4)]\} = \$13.79.]$

6.6   THE OUTPUT EFFECT OF FISCAL POLICY

Government can seek to change output by a discretionary fiscal policy, e.g., a change in government spending, taxes, and/or transfers. In Fig. 6-10, a $\Delta \bar{G}$ increase in government spending shifts IS by $k_e \Delta \bar{G}$ from IS' to IS'' which equals Y_0 to Y_3 at interest rate i_0. After the increase in government spending, IS and LM intersect at point B. The fiscal action has raised output from Y_0 to Y_2 and the rate of interest from i_0 to i_1. Because the rate of interest increases from i_0 to i_1, there is a decrease in interest-sensitive investment spending (investment is crowded out) and output does not increase by the $k_e \Delta \bar{G}$ shift of IS.

The output effect of a fiscal policy depends upon the slope of IS and LM. The LM schedule in Fig. 6-11(a) is steeply sloped because the demand for money is interest-insensitive. A $\Delta \bar{G}$ increase in government spending shifts IS rightward from IS' to IS''. Because the demand for money is relatively interest-insensitive, there must be a large increase in the rate of interest (from i_0 to i_2) to get people to hold smaller money balances in their portfolios so that more of the money supply is available to support a higher level of output. The large increase in the rate of interest, however, lowers interest-sensitive investment spending. Output increases from Y_0 to Y_1; output would have increased from Y_0 to Y_3 if there had been no increase in the rate of interest. Thus, private sector spending of Y_1 to Y_3 is crowded out by the i_0 to i_2 increase in the rate of interest. There is less crowding out in Fig. 6-11(b) from a similar $\Delta \bar{G}$ increase in government spending. LM is less steeply sloped in Fig. 6-11(b) because the demand for money is more interest-sensitive. That is, people hold smaller money balances in their portfolio at higher rates of interest. Thus, the shift from IS' to IS'' in Fig. 6-11(b) results in a smaller increase in the rate of interest, less crowding out, and a larger increase in output. The magnitude of crowding out is also influenced by the slope of IS. Examples 6.7 and 6.8 show that there is less crowding out when IS is

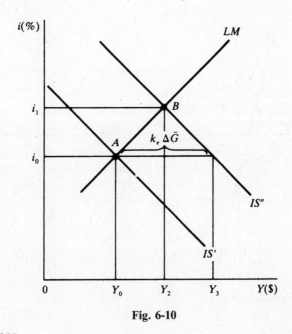

Fig. 6-10

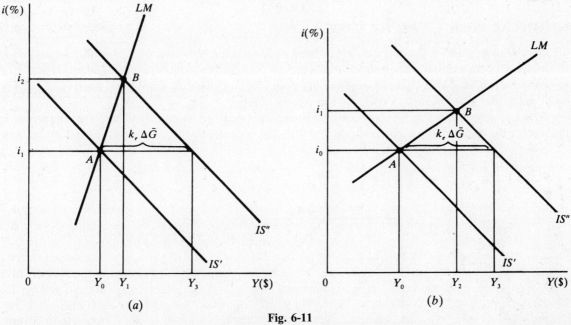

Fig. 6-11

steeply sloped (investment spending is less affected by a change in the rate of interest) than when IS is relatively flat and investment spending is highly sensitive to the rate of interest.

EXAMPLE 6.7.   Schedule IS' is steeply sloped in Fig. 6-12(a) because spending is largely unresponsive to the rate of interest. Increased government spending shifts IS from IS' to IS'' by $k_e \Delta \bar{G}$ which equals Y_0 to Y_3. Equilibrium output increases from Y_0 to Y_2 with a crowding out of private sector spending of Y_2 to Y_3.

EXAMPLE 6.8.   Schedule IS' is less steeply sloped in Fig. 6-12(b) because of the greater interest-sensitivity of investment spending. The shift from IS' to IS'', which is the same as the Y_0 to Y_3 shift in Fig. 6-12(a), increases output from Y_0 to Y_1. Because there is a larger decrease in private sector spending as the rate of interest increases from i_0 to i_1, crowding out is now Y_1 to Y_3.

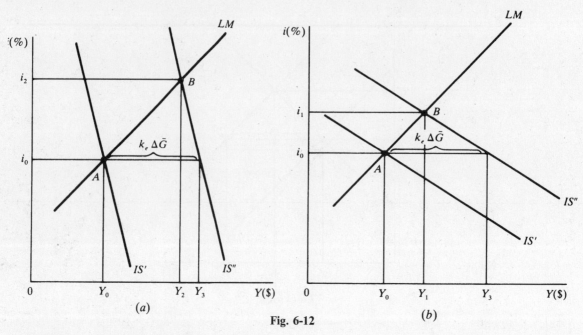

Fig. 6-12

6.7 FISCAL POLICY: SPECIAL CASES

Special cases exist for the output effect of fiscal policy when LM is vertical, LM is horizontal, and IS is vertical. In comparing this analysis with that in Section 6.5 on monetary policy, one finds that a fiscal action has a full multiplier effect when monetary policy has no effect on output and fiscal policy has no effect on output when monetary policy is completely effective.

The LM schedule in Fig. 6-13(a) is vertical because the demand for money is unrelated to the rate of interest (in the demand for money function $L = kY - hi$, h equals 0). The rightward shift of IS from IS'

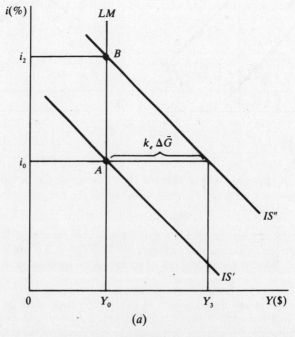

(a)

Fig. 6-13

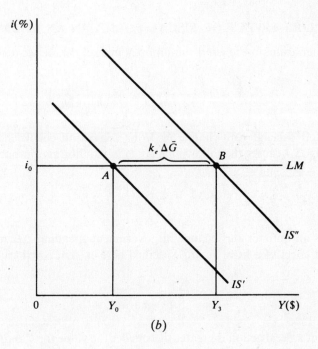

(b)

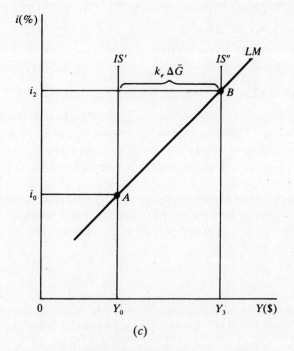

(c)

Fig. 6-13 (continued)

to IS'' raises the interest rate but does not change output; there is complete crowding out of Y_0 to Y_3, which is equal to the $k_e \Delta \bar{G}$ shift of IS. In Fig. 6-13(b), there is no crowding out because LM is horizontal; a $\Delta \bar{G}$ increase in government spending increases output by $k_e \Delta \bar{G}$ (Y_0 to Y_3) because investors have an infinite demand for money at interest rate i_0. The complete multiplier effect of a fiscal stimulus ($k_e \Delta \bar{G} = Y_0$ to Y_3) is also realized in the rightward shift of IS in Fig. 6-13(c). Increased government spending raises the rate of interest, but the higher rate has no crowding out effect because investment spending is unrelated to the rate of interest.

6.8   THE MULTIPLIER EFFECT OF FISCAL POLICY IN AN *IS–LM* FRAMEWORK

Simultaneous equilibrium in the goods and money market can be written as

$$Y = \bar{A}\left(\frac{hk_e}{h + kbk_e}\right) + \bar{M}\left(\frac{bk_e}{h + kbk_e}\right)$$

Assuming a stable *LM* schedule (no change in $\bar{M}$ or behavioral coefficients k_e and b), a change in autonomous spending $\Delta\bar{A}$ causes the following change in equilibrium output

$$\Delta Y = \Delta\bar{A}\left(\frac{hk_e}{h + kbk_e}\right)$$

where $\Delta\bar{A}$ represents an autonomous change in government spending $\Delta\bar{G}$, taxes $c\Delta\bar{T}x$ and transfers $c\Delta\bar{T}r$. The multiplier effect of a fiscal action, specified here as $\Delta\bar{A}$, is written as

$$\frac{\Delta Y}{\Delta\bar{A}} = \frac{hk_e}{h + kbk_e}$$

The multiplier effect of a fiscal action is greater the smaller the value for b and/or the larger the value for h. A small value for b makes *IS* steeply sloped, and a large value for h results in a relatively flat *LM* schedule.

6.9   THE MONETARY–FISCAL POLICY MIX

Except when special cases exist (Sections 6.5 and 6.7), fiscal and/or monetary policy can be used to increase equilibrium output. The economic policy chosen has a selective impact upon sector spending and therefore the composition of output. An easier monetary policy, in shifting *LM* rightward, lowers the rate of interest and stimulates spending, which is interest-sensitive. A reduction in household income taxes increases consumption spending, an investment tax credit increases the profitability of new plant and equipment expenditures and thereby investment, and increased government spending expands production of public sector goods. Because a fiscal stimulus results in higher interest rates, a reduction in household sector income taxes and/or an increase in government spending "crowds out" some private sector spending.

EXAMPLE 6.9.   Posit an economy where schedules IS' and LM' in Fig. 6-14 determine an 8% rate of interest and a $675 level of output. Sector spending behavior in the goods market is specified as $C = \$20 + 0.80(Y - 0.25Y)$, $I = \$130 - 5i$, and $G = \$160$. When output is $675 and the rate of interest is 8%, consumption is $425, investment is $90 and government spending is $160. A decrease in the income tax rate from 0.25 to 0.20 respecifies the consumption equation as $C = \$20 + 0.80(Y - 0.20Y)$, with *IS* shifting from IS''' to IS''''. IS'''' and LM' intersect at point B; the rate of interest rises from 8% to 10% and output increases from $675 to $722. At this higher output and interest rate level, consumption rises to $482 from $425; investment decreases from $90 to $80, and government spending remains at $160. An alternative fiscal action would be to increase government spending from $160 to $188.80. *IS* would shift from IS' to IS''; there would be simultaneous equilibrium in the money and goods market again at point B with output at $722 and the rate of interest at 10%. Consumption under this alternative action would be $453.20 rather than $482; investment would be $80, and government spending would increase from $160 to $188.80. The income tax cut primarily benefits consumers, while the expansion of government spending increases both consumer and public sector goods. Both fiscal actions lower investment.

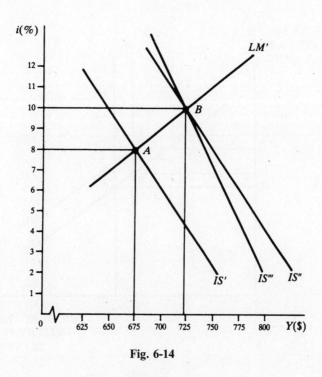

Fig. 6-14

Solved Problems

THE LIQUIDITY EFFECT FROM A CHANGE IN THE MONEY SUPPLY

6.1 Suppose the Federal Reserve purchases Treasury securities from the private sector. (*a*) Show in Fig. 6-15 what happens to the supply of Treasury securities held by the private sector and thereby the price of Treasury securities as a result of this purchase. What is happening to the yield on Treasury securities? (*b*) Show through a T-account for the banking system what has happened to the reserves of the banking system; assume the private sector deposits funds received from the sale of these securities in a checking account. (*c*) Assume that the banking system, as a result of holding excess reserves, purchases Treasury securities. Explain and show in Fig. 6-15 the effect additional purchases of Treasury securities by the banking system has upon the price of Treasury securities.

(*a*) When the Federal Reserve purchases Treasury securities from the private sector, it reduces the supply of Treasury securities held by the private sector; the supply of Treasury securities available to the private sector decreases from S_1 to S_2 in Fig. 6-15. The price of Treasury securities increases from P_0 to P_1; the yield on Treasury securities thereby falls.

(*b*) When the private sector places funds from the sale of Treasury securities in checking accounts, the reserve assets of the banking system increase, as does the bank's checking account liability to the private sector. The banking system has excess reserves because it is required to hold only a fraction of checking deposits as reserves.

Banking System

Δ Assets		Δ Liabilities	
Reserves	+	Checking deposits	+

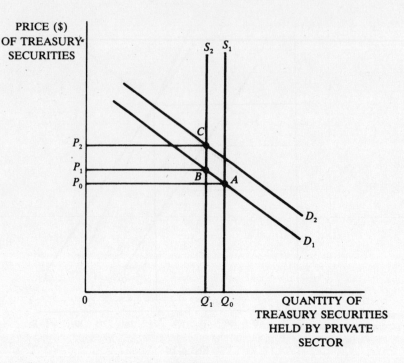

Fig. 6-15

(c)   The banking system reduces its excess reserve position by expanding checking deposits; the banking system pays for newly purchased Treasury securities by expanding checking deposit liabilities. The demand for Treasury securities would increase in Fig. 6-15 from D_1 to D_2, causing the price of Treasury securities to increase from P_1 to P_2. The yield on Treasury securities falls.

6.2   Why does an increase in the money supply result in a liquidity effect?

An increase in the money supply decreases the quantity of Treasury securities held by the private sector; at the existing rate of interest there is an imbalance in the amount of money and other financial assets held by the private sector. The private sector restores portfolio balance by increasing their demand for Treasury securities which increases the price of Treasury securities and lowers the rate of interest.

6.3   In Fig. 6-16(a), the money supply is initially M_0 and the demand for money is L_1, given a Y_0 output level. The equilibrium rate of interest is i_0. (a) In Fig. 6-16(a), show the effect that an M_0 to M_1 increase in the money supply has upon the rate of interest. (b) In Fig. 6-16(b), output is Y_0 and the rate of interest is i_0 for schedules IS and LM. What happens to LM and the rate of interest when the money supply increases from M_0 to M_1? (c) Does the liquidity effect result in a new equilibrium position?

(a)   The M_0 to M_1 increase in the money supply causes the rate of interest to decrease from i_0 to i_1 in Fig. 6-16(a).

(b)   The M_0 to M_1 increase in the money supply shifts LM rightward by $\Delta \bar{M}(1/k)$ to LM_1 in Fig. 6-16(b). With no change in output, the rate of interest falls from i_0 to i_1.

(c)   There is a production shortage at interest rate i_1 and output Y_0. Simultaneous equilibrium only exists at the intersection of IS and LM.

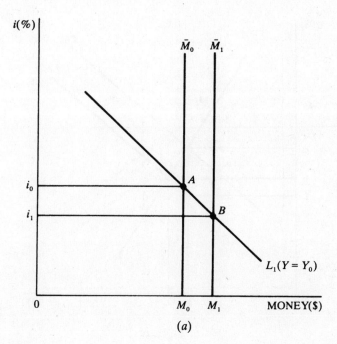

(a)

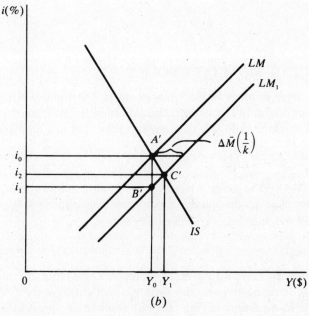

(b)

Fig. 6-16

6.4 Output is initially Y_0 and the rate of interest is i_0 in Fig. 6-17 for *IS* and *LM*. Find the liquidity effect and the output effect that results from a money supply increase which shifts *LM* from *LM* to LM_1.

The liquidity effect in Fig. 6-17 is the reduction in the rate of interest that occurs as a result of the rightward shift of *LM*, with output unchanged at Y_0. The liquidity effect is the reduction in the rate of interest from i_0 to i_1. There is disequilibrium in the goods market at output Y_0 and interest rate i_1. The output effect is the increase in output that occurs as simultaneous equilibrium in the money and goods markets is re-established. The output effect is the Y_0 to Y_1 increase in output.

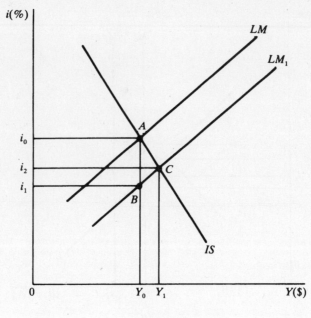

Fig. 6-17

THE OUTPUT EFFECT OF MONETARY POLICY

6.5 A money supply increase of $\Delta \bar{M}$ in Fig. 6-18 shifts LM rightward to LM_1. (a) Find the new equilibrium level of output in Fig. 6-18(a) and (b) which results from the Y_0 to Y_3 shift of LM. (b) Why is the output change in Fig. 6-18(a) greater than that in Fig. 6-18(b)?

   (a) The Y_0 to Y_3 shift of LM raises output from Y_0 to Y_2 in Fig. 6-18(a) and from Y_0 to Y_1 in Fig. 6-18(b).

   (b) There is a difference between the increase in output because of a difference in the interest sensitivity of investment. Investment spending is more interest-sensitive in Fig. 6-18(a), evidenced by the flatter IS schedule. Thus, although the liquidity effect is the same, there is a larger output effect because of investment's sensitivity to the lower rate of interest.

6.6 Suppose the LM equation for a two-sector model is $Y = \$750 + 20i$; money demand is specified as $L = 0.20Y - 4i$; the exogenous money supply is $150. (a) Plot the LM equation in Fig. 6-19(a) and (b); and the IS equation in Fig. 6-19(a) when it is specified as $Y = \$1250 - 30i$ with $C = \$100 + 0.80Y$ and $I = \$150 - 6i$ and in Fig. 6-19(b) when it is specified as $Y = \$1100 - 15i$ with $C = \$100 + 0.80Y$ and $I = \$120 - 3i$. (b) Find simultaneous equilibrium for the money and goods markets when the IS equation is specified as (1) $Y = \$1250 - 30i$ and (2) $Y = \$1100 - 15i$. (c) Plot the new LM equation in Fig. 6-19(a) and (b) and label it LM_1 for the $20 increase in the money supply. (d) Use the IS equations specified in part (a) and find output when the money supply increases from $150 to $170. For which IS equation is there a greater decrease in the rate of interest? Why is there a dissimilar output effect? (e) Find investment and consumption spending when the money supply is $150 [part (b)] and when the money supply is $170 [part (d)].

   (a) Fig. 6-19(a) and (b).

   (b) Equilibrium output is $950 for situation (1)

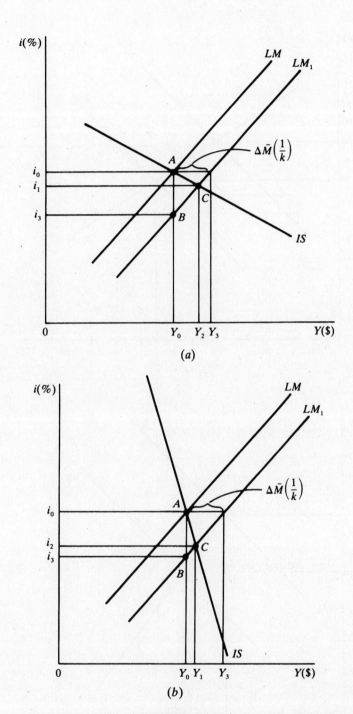

Fig. 6-18

the *IS* equation: $Y = \$1250 - 30i$
less the *LM* equation: $\underline{-(Y = \$\ 750 + 20i)}$
                                          $0 = \$500 - 50i$
                                          $i = 10\%$
                                          $Y = \$950$

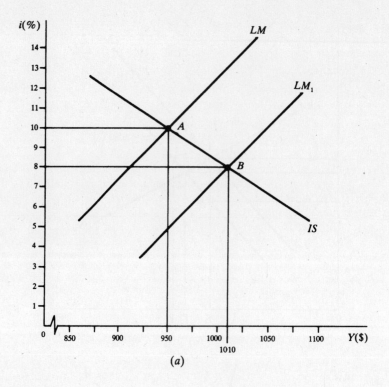

(a)

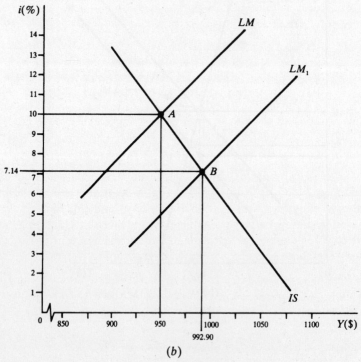

(b)

Fig. 6-19

Equilibrium output is also $950 for situation (2)

the *IS* equation: $\qquad\qquad\qquad Y = \$1100 - 15i$

less the *LM* equation: $\qquad\qquad -(Y = \$\ 750 + 20i)$

$$0 = \$350 - 35i$$
$$i = 10\%$$
$$Y = \$950$$

(c)   See Fig. 6-19.

(d)   The new *LM* schedule is $Y = \$850 + 20i$. The rate of interest falls from 10% to 8% for situation (1) and to 7.143% for situation (2). There is a greater output effect in situation (1). The investment equation, $I = \$150 - 6i$, in situation (1) is more interest-sensitive. Therefore, the liquidity effect from the $20 increase in the money supply has a larger output effect.

Equilibrium output for situation (1) is $1010 as a result of the $20 increase in the money supply:

the *IS* equation: $\qquad\qquad\qquad Y = \$1250 - 30i$

less the *LM* equation: $\qquad\qquad -(Y = \$\ 850 + 20i)$

$$0 = \$400 - 50i$$
$$i = 8\%$$
$$Y = \$1010$$

Equilibrium output is $992.50 for situation (2):

the *IS* equation: $\qquad\qquad\qquad Y = \$1100 - 15i$

less the *LM* equation: $\qquad\qquad -(Y = \$\ 850 + 20i)$

$$0 = \$250 - 35i$$
$$i = 7.143\%$$
$$Y = \$992.50$$

(e)   Investment is $90 for both (1) and (2) in part (b). The $20 money supply increase raises investment spending in situation (1) in part (d) to $102 ($I = \$150 - 6i$; $I = \$150 - 48$; $I = \$102$) and to $98.57 for (2): $I = \$120 - 3i$; $I = \$120 - 21.43$; $I = \$98.47$. Consumption in part (b) is $860 for both (1) and (2). As a result of the $20 money supply increase, consumption in (d) is $908 for (1) and $894.33 for (2).

6.7   The *IS* schedules in Fig. 6-20(a) and (b) have the same slope. Schedule LM_1 in Fig. 6-20(a) is more steeply sloped than LM_2 in Fig. 6-20(b). In Fig. 6-20(a) and (b) equilibrium output is initially Y_0 and the rate of interest is i_0. (a) In Fig. 6-20(a) and (b), find equilibrium output and the rate of interest resulting from a money expansion that shifts *LM* rightward from Y_0 to Y_3 at interest rate i_0. (b) Is there a greater change in equilibrium output in Fig. 6-20(a) or (b)? Why? (c) Why is there a smaller change in the rate of interest in Fig. 6-20(b) than in Fig. 6-20(a)?

(a)   Output increases from Y_0 to Y_2 and the rate of interest decreases from i_0 to i_2 in Fig. 6-20(a), whereas output increases from Y_0 to Y_1 in Fig. 6-20(b), with the rate of interest decreasing from i_0 to i_1.

(b)   Because of the greater decline in the rate of interest in Fig. 6-20(a), there is a greater response from interest-sensitive spending and therefore a larger increase in output.

(c)   The less steeply sloped *LM* schedule in Fig. 6-20(b) indicates that the demand for money is more interest-sensitive. Because larger money balances are held as the rate of interest falls, the money supply expansion has a smaller effect on the rate of interest and therefore on interest-sensitive investment spending.

6.8   Posit a two-sector economy where the *IS* equation is $Y = \$1250 - 30i$. (a) Given a $150 money supply, find equilibrium when the *LM* equation is (1) $Y = \$750 + 20i$ (where $L = 0.20Y - 4i$)

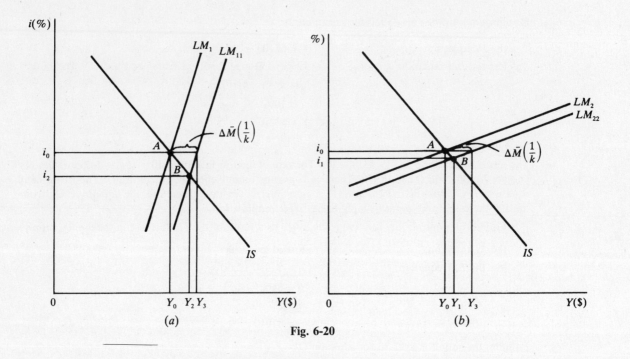

Fig. 6-20

and (2) $Y = \$600 + 35i$ (where $L = 0.25Y - 8.75i$). (b) What happens to equilibrium output and the rate of interest for situations (1) and (2) when the money supply increases $20? (c) What is responsible for the difference found in part (b)?

(a) Equilibrium output is $950, and the rate of interest is 10% for situations (1) and (2).

(b) For situation (1), the $20 money supply increase shifts LM rightward $100, that is, $\Delta \bar{M}(1/k) = \$20/(0.20)$. Output increases from $950 to $1010; the rate of interest falls from 10% to 8%.

$$
\begin{aligned}
\text{the } IS \text{ equation:} &\qquad Y = \$1250 - 30i \\
\text{less the } LM \text{ equation:} &\qquad \underline{-(Y = \$\ 850 + 20i)} \\
&\qquad 0 = \$400 - 50i \\
&\qquad i = 8\% \\
&\qquad Y = \$1010
\end{aligned}
$$

For situation (2), the $20 money supply increase shifts LM rightward $80 or $\Delta \bar{M}(1/k) = 20/0.25$. Output increases from $950 to $986.90; the rate of interest declines from 10 to 8.769%.

(c) The larger change in output in situation (1) is the result of a smaller transaction ratio, which causes LM to shift by $100 rather than $80, and the greater interest-sensitivity of the demand for money in situation (2), which allocates a larger portion of the money supply increase to portfolios rather than transactions.

6.9   What determines the effect of an increase in the money supply upon equilibrium output?

The effect of a money supply increase on equilibrium output depends on the transaction demand for money, the interest-sensitivity of the demand for money, the interest-sensitivity of investment spending, and the expenditure multiplier. When the transaction ratio is large, an increase in the money supply will support a smaller increase in output than when the ratio is small. For example, when $k = 0.50$, a $20 money supply increase can be associated with no more than a $40 increase in output $[\Delta Y = \Delta \bar{M}(1/k)]$. However, when $k = 0.20$, a $20 money supply increase can be associated with up to a $100 increase in output. The interest-sensitivity of the demand for money determines the extent to which money supply changes affect interest rates and thereby spending. For example, money demand which is highly interest-sensitive indicates that a money supply expansion is less successful in reducing interest rates than when money demand is interest-insensitive. The interest-sensitivity of investment spending determines the extent to which a change in the rate of interest affects investment spending. For example, a money supply increase has a greater effect upon output, *ceteris paribus*, the larger the value of behavioral coefficient b in the investment demand equation. And the value of k_e determines the extent to which investment spending has a multiplied effect upon output. A large value for k_e has a greater effect on output for a given increase in investment spending.

MONETARY POLICY: SPECIAL CASES

6.10 (*a*) Find the change in equilibrium output in Fig. 6-21(*a*), (*b*), and (*c*) when a $\Delta \bar{M}$ increase in the money supply shifts LM rightward to LM_1. (*b*) Explain the change in equilibrium output found in part (*a*).

   (*a*) The $\Delta \bar{M}$ money supply increase in Fig. 6-21(*a*) shifts LM rightward to LM_1. The rate of interest declines from i_0 to i_1 and output increases from Y_0 to Y_1. The change in output (Y_0 to Y_1) is equal to the LM shift. The $\Delta \bar{M}$ money supply increase in Fig. 6-21(*b*) shifts LM rightward to LM_1. The rate of interest declines from i_0 to i_2 with output remaining at its initial Y_0 level. The $\Delta \bar{M}$ money supply increase in Fig. 6-21(*c*) has no effect on the LM schedule, since it is horizontal at interest rate i_0. There is neither a change in the rate of interest nor output.

   (*b*) LM is vertical [Fig. 6-21(*a*)] when the demand for money is unrelated to the rate of interest. Because the demand for money is not affected by the rate of interest, a money expansion must be met by a $k\Delta Y$ increase in the transaction demand for money. Hence, ΔY must equal $\Delta \bar{M}(1/k)$. In contrast, the vertical IS schedule in Fig. 6-21(*b*) indicates that spending is unrelated to the rate of interest. The rightward shift of LM to LM_1, while lowering the rate of interest from i_0 to i_2, does not increase output because of the insensitivity of spending to the rate of interest. The horizontal LM schedule in Fig. 6-21(*c*) indicates that the private sector is willing to hold an infinite quantity of money without a change in the rate of interest. Thus, a money supply increase has no effect upon either the rate of interest or output.

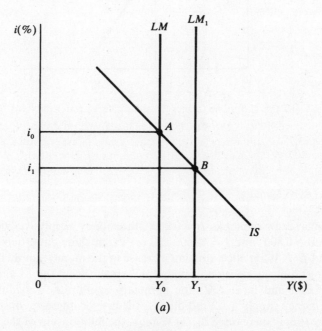

(*a*)

Fig. 6-21

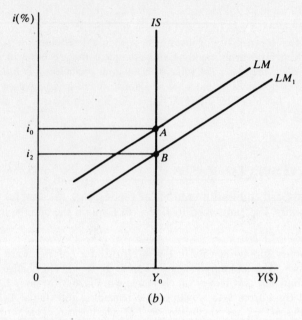

(b)

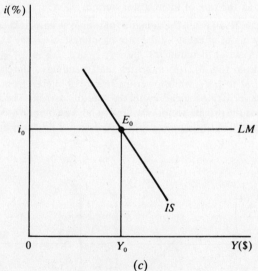

(c)

Fig. 6-21 (*continued*)

6.11 Suppose the demand for money is $L = 0.20Y$, the money supply is \$200, and, for a two-sector model, $C = \$100 + 0.80Y$ and $I = \$140 - 5i$. (*a*) From these data, derive an *IS* and *LM* equation; plot *IS* and *LM*. What effect does an increase in the money supply have on output? (*b*) Find the rate of interest, output, consumption and investment from the *IS* and *LM* equations derived in part (*a*). (*c*) Plot and label LM_1 the monetary equilibrium schedule resulting from a \$20 increase in the money supply. (*d*) Find output, the rate of interest, consumption and investment when the money supply increases \$20. (*e*) What is the relationship of the shift of *LM* in Fig. 6-22 and the change in output?

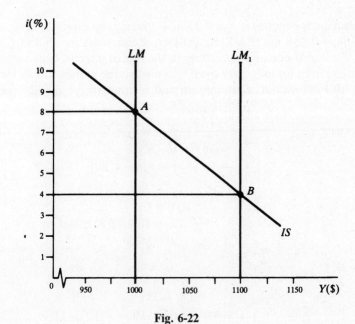

Fig. 6-22

(a)   The *LM* equation:

$$L = M$$
$$0.20Y = \$200$$
$$Y = \$1000$$

The *IS* equation:

$$Y = C + I$$
$$Y = \$100 + 0.80Y + \$140 - 5i$$
$$Y = \$1200 - 25i$$

Because the *LM* schedule is vertical (Fig. 6-22), we would expect output to change by $\Delta \bar{M}(1/k)$.

(b)   Simultaneous equilibrium $LM = IS$:

$$\$1000 = \$1200 - 25i$$
$$25i = \$200$$
$$i = 8\%$$
$$Y = \$1000$$
$$C = \$900$$
$$I = \$100$$

(c)   An increase in the money supply shifts *LM* rightward by $\Delta \bar{M}(1/k)$. Thus, *LM* shifts rightward $100 to LM_1; $\Delta \bar{M}(1/k) = \$20(1/0.20) = \$100$ (Fig. 6-22).

(d)   The *LM* equation is now $Y = \$1100$.

Simultaneous equilibrium

$$LM = IS$$
$$\$1100 = \$1200 - 25i$$
$$i = 4\%$$
$$Y = \$1100$$
$$C = \$980$$
$$I = \$120$$

(e)   The $100 increase in output equals the $100 rightward shift of *LM*.

6.12 Suppose the demand for money is $L = 0.2Y - 4i$, the money supply is \$200, and for a two-sector model, $C = \$100 + 0.80Y$ and $I = \$150$. (a) Derive equations for *IS* and *LM*; plot *IS* and *LM*. (b) From the *IS* and *LM* equations find output, the rate of interest, consumption, and investment. (c) Find a new equation for monetary equilibrium when the money supply increases \$20; plot and label it LM_1. (d) Find output, consumption and investment for the \$20 increase in the money supply.

(a) The *LM* equation:

$$L = M$$
$$0.20Y - 4i = \$200$$
$$Y = \$1000 + 20i$$

The *IS* equation:

$$Y = C + I$$
$$Y = \$100 + 0.80Y + \$1.50$$
$$Y = \$1250$$

See Fig. 6-23.

(b)

$$LM = IS$$
$$\$1000 + 20i = \$1250$$
$$20i = 250$$
$$i = 12.5\%$$
$$Y = \$1250$$
$$C = \$1100$$
$$I = \$150$$

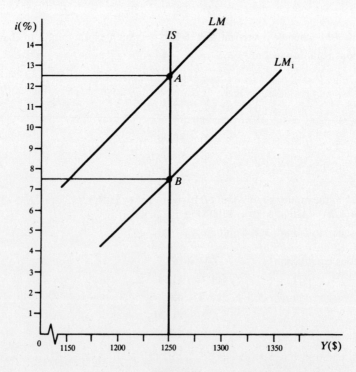

Fig. 6-23

(c)   *LM* equation for a \$220 money supply:

$$0.20Y - 4i = \$220$$
$$Y = \$1100 + 20i$$

See Fig. 6-23.

(d)   There is no change in output because consumption and investment spending are unrelated to the rate of interest. The \$20 money supply expansion lowers the rate of interest from 12.50 to 7.50% but has no effect upon output.

$$LM = IS$$
$$\$1100 + 20i = \$1250$$
$$20i = 150$$
$$i = 7.50\%$$
$$Y = \$1250$$
$$C = \$1100$$
$$I = \$150$$

THE MULTIPLIER EFFECT OF MONETARY POLICY IN AN *IS–LM* FRAMEWORK

6.13   Suppose spending is specified as $C = \bar{C} + cYd$, $I = \bar{I} - bi$, $Tx = \bar{T}x$, and $G = \bar{G}$. The demand for money is specified as $L = kY - hi$, and the money supply is $\bar{M}$. (*a*) Find an equation for equilibrium in the goods market. (*b*) Find an equation for equilibrium in the money market. (*c*) Find an equation that represents equilibrium output in the money and goods markets.

(a)   *LM* equation:

$$L = M$$

$$kY - hi = \bar{M}$$

$$Y = \frac{\bar{M}}{k} + \frac{hi}{k}$$

or,
$$i = \frac{kY}{h} - \frac{\bar{M}}{h}$$

(b)   *IS* equation:

$$Y = C + I + G$$
$$Y = \bar{C} + c(Y - \bar{T}x) + \bar{I} - bi + \bar{G}$$
$$Y - cY = \bar{C} - c\bar{T}x + \bar{I} - bi + \bar{G}$$
$$Y = \frac{\bar{C} + \bar{I} + \bar{G} - c\bar{T}x}{1 - c} - \frac{bi}{1 - c}$$

Letting $\bar{A} = \bar{C} + \bar{I} + \bar{G} - c\bar{T}x$ and $k_e = (1/(1 - c))$:

$$Y = k_e\bar{A} - k_ebi$$

(c)   We can find simultaneous equilibrium in the money and goods markets by substituting the *LM* equation $i = kY/h - \bar{M}/h$ into the *IS* equation. Thus,

$$Y = k_e\bar{A} - k_e b\left(\frac{kY}{h} - \frac{\bar{M}}{h}\right)$$

$$Y = k_e\bar{A} - \left(\frac{k_e bkY}{h} + \frac{k_e b\bar{M}}{h}\right)$$

$$hY = hk_e\bar{A} - k_e bkY + k_e b\bar{M}$$

$$hY + k_e bkY = hk_e\bar{A} + k_e b\bar{M}$$

$$Y = hk_e\bar{A}\left(\frac{1}{h + kbk_e}\right) + k_e b\bar{M}\left(\frac{1}{h + k_e bk}\right)$$

or

$$Y = \bar{A}\left(\frac{hk_e}{h + kbk_e}\right) + \bar{M}\left(\frac{bk_e}{h + kbk_e}\right)$$

6.14 (a) Holding variables constant other than Y and $\bar{M}$, find an expression that relates the change in output to a change in the money supply. (b) Find an expression for the multiplying effect μ that a change in the money supply has on output.

(a)

$$\Delta Y = k_e b\Delta\bar{M}\left(\frac{1}{h + k_e bk}\right)$$

$$\Delta Y = \Delta\bar{M}\left(\frac{k_e b}{h + k_e bk}\right)$$

(b)   Dividing both sides of the equation in part (a) by $\Delta\bar{M}$, we derive μ, the multiplying effect that a change in the money supply has on output.

$$\frac{\Delta Y}{\Delta\bar{M}} = \frac{k_e b}{h + k_e bk}$$

letting

$$\mu = \frac{\Delta Y}{\Delta\bar{M}}$$

$$\mu = \frac{k_e b}{h + k_e bk}$$

6.15 Find the value of $\mu(\Delta Y/\Delta\bar{M})$ for the values of k_e, b, h, and k given in situations (1) through (5) in Table 6-1. (b) What generalization can one make about the multiplying effect of a money supply change upon output when there is an increase in the value of k_e, b, h, or k? (c) Relate your answer in (b) to the slope of IS and/or LM and how the slope of these schedules influences the multiplying effect of a money supply change upon output.

Table 6-1

Situation	k_e	b	h	k
(1)	5	4	4	0.20
(2)	10	4	4	0.20
(3)	5	10	4	0.20
(4)	5	4	10	0.20
(5)	5	4	4	0.25

(a)   The values for μ are (1) 2.500, (2) 3.333, (3) 3.571, (4) 1.429, and (5) 2.222.

(b)   A large value for the expenditure multiplier k_e and the interest-sensitivity of investment spending b increases the multiplying effect of a money supply change on output. An increase in the interest-sensitivity of the demand for money h and the desire to hold transaction balances k reduces the multiplying effect of a money supply change on output.

(c) An increase in k_e and/or b reduces the slope of IS(IS becomes flatter), indicating that an interest rate change induced by a change in the money supply has a greater effect on output. That is, a money supply change has a greater multiplying effect on output when there is a small slope for IS. An increase in h or a decrease in k decreases the slope of LM (LM becomes flatter), indicating that a money supply change brings about a smaller change in the rate of interest. The multiplying effect of a money supply change on output is thereby lessened by a smaller-sloped LM.

THE OUTPUT EFFECT OF FISCAL POLICY

6.16 The LM equation is $Y = \$500 + 25i$; money demand is $L = 0.20Y - 5i$; the exogenous money supply is \$100. The IS equation is $Y = \$950 - 50i$; $C = \$40 + 0.80Yd$; $Tx = \$50$; $G = \$50$; $I = \$140 - 10i$. (a) Find equilibrium output, the rate of interest, consumption, and investment. (b) Find the IS equation when government spending increases from \$50 to \$80. (c) Find output, the rate of interest, consumption and investment when government spending is \$80 rather than \$50. (d) Why has output increased by less than $k_e\Delta\bar{G}$—an amount equal to the shift of IS?

(a) the IS equation:

$$Y = \$950 - 50i$$

less the LM equation:

$$-(Y = \$500 + 25i)$$

$$0 = \$450 - 75i$$
$$i = 6\%$$
$$Y = \$650$$
$$C = \$520$$
$$I = \$80$$

(b)

$$Y = C + I + G$$
$$Y = \$40 + 0.80(Y - \$50) + \$140 - 10i + \$80$$
$$Y = \$1100 - 50i$$

(c) the IS equation:

$$Y = \$1100 - 50i$$

less the LM equation:

$$-(Y = \$\ 500 + 25i)$$

$$0 = \$600 - 75i$$
$$i = 8\%$$
$$Y = \$700$$
$$C = \$560$$
$$I = \$60$$

(d) A \$30 increase in government spending has raised the rate of interest from 6% to 8% and crowded out private sector investment. As a result of this higher interest rate, investment falls from \$80 to \$60. Thus, the total net effect of increased government spending on output is \$50 rather than \$150 $[k_e\Delta\bar{G} = 5(\$30) = \$150]$.

6.17 (a) Explain the crowding-out effect. (b) What determines the magnitude of the crowding-out effect?

(a) A crowding-out effect occurs when increased government spending causes a higher interest rate which results in a lower level of investment spending, i.e., government spending "crowds out" interest-sensitive private sector spending.

(b) The magnitude of the crowding-out effect depends on (1) the increase in the interest rate due to the increase in government spending and (2) the interest-sensitivity of private sector spending. The interest-sensitivity of the demand for money determines the rise in the rate of interest, which results from an expansion in government spending. There is a smaller increase in the rate of interest from increased government spending when the demand for money is interest-sensitive. A given increase in the rate of interest has a larger crowding-out effect when private sector investment is highly sensitive to the rate of interest.

6.18   In Fig. 6-24(a) and (b), IS_1 is the initial IS schedule which shifts rightward by $k_e \Delta \bar{G}$ (Y_0 to Y_3) to IS_2 as a result of a $\Delta \bar{G}$ increase in government spending. (a) What is equilibrium output after the $\Delta \bar{G}$ increase in government spending? (b) Explain why the increase in equilibrium output in Fig. 6-24(a) and (b) differs.

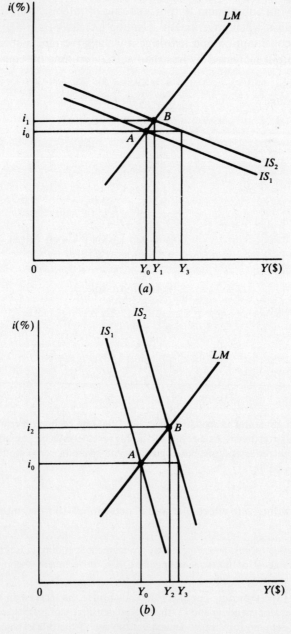

(a)

(b)

Fig. 6-24

(a)   Equilibrium output increases from Y_0 to Y_1 in Fig. 6-24(a) and Y_0 to Y_2 in Fig. 6-24(b).

(b)   There is a larger increase in output in Fig. 6-24(b) than in Fig. 6-24(a), although the rise in the rate of interest is greater in Fig. 6-24(b). Investment is more interest-sensitive in Fig. 6-24(a), indicated by a flatter IS schedule; thus, although the rise in the interest rate is smaller in (a), the $\Delta \bar{G}$ increase in government spending crowds out a larger amount of investment.

6.19   In Fig. 6-25, IS_1 shifts rightward to IS_2 when government spending increases by $\Delta \bar{G}$. (a) Find equilibrium output after the $\Delta \bar{G}$ increase in government spending for monetary equilibrium schedules LM_1 and LM_2. (b) Contrast the increase in output for monetary equilibrium schedule LM_1 and LM_2.

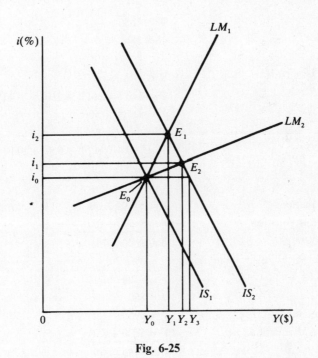

Fig. 6-25

(a)   Equilibrium output increases from Y_0 to Y_1 for LM_1 and from Y_0 to Y_2 for LM_2.

(b)   The demand for money is less interest-sensitive for monetary equilibrium schedule LM_1; hence, the rightward shift of IS causes a greater increase in the rate of interest (from i_0 to i_2) along LM_1. It therefore follows that increased government spending crowds out more investment along LM_1 than along LM_2.

6.20   The LM equation is $Y = \$500 + 25i$; money demand is $L = 0.20Y - 5i$; the money supply is $\$100$. (a) Find equilibrium output, the rate of interest and investment when the IS equation is (1) $Y = \$950 - 50i$, given $C = \$40 + 0.80Yd$, $I = \$140 - 10i$, $Tx = \$50$, $G = \$50$; (2) $Y = \$800 - 25i$, given $C = \$40 + 0.80Yd$, $I = \$110 - 5i$, $Tx = \$50$, $G = \$50$. (b) Recalculate the IS equation for part (a) when government spending increases from $\$50$ to $\$80$. (c) Find equilibrium output, the rate of interest and investment when government spending is $\$80$. (d) Explain why the increase in government spending from $\$50$ to $\$80$ has a different effect on output for situation (1) and situation (2). (Hint: look at the value for behavioral coefficient b.)

(a) (1) the IS equation:

$$Y = \$950 - 50i$$

less the LM equation:

$$-(Y = \$500 + 25i)$$

$$0 = \$450 - 75i$$

$$i = 6\%$$

$$Y = \$650$$

$$I = \$80$$

(2) the IS equation:

$$Y = \$800 - 25i$$

less the LM equation:

$$-(Y = \$500 + 25i)$$

$$0 = \$300 - 50i$$

$$i = 6\%$$

$$Y = \$650$$

$$I = \$80$$

(b) (1)

$$Y = C + I + G$$

$$Y = \$40 + 0.80(Y - \$50) + \$140 - 10i + \$80$$

$$Y = \$1100 - 50i$$

(2)

$$Y = C + I + G$$

$$Y = \$40 + 0.80(Y - \$50) + \$110 - 5i + \$80$$

$$Y = \$950 - 25i$$

(c) (1) the IS equation:

$$Y = \$1100 - 50i$$

less the LM equation:

$$-(Y = \$\ 500 + 25i)$$

$$0 = \$600 - 75i$$

$$i = 8\%$$

$$Y = \$700$$

$$I = \$60$$

(2) the IS equation:

$$Y = \$950 - 25i$$

less the LM equation:

$$-(Y = \$500 + 25i)$$

$$0 = \$450 - 50i$$

$$i = 9\%$$

$$Y = \$725$$

$$I = \$65$$

(d) Investment is more interest-sensitive in situation (1), where $I = \$140 - 10i$, than in situation (2), where $I = \$110 - 5i$. Thus, the stimulative effect of increased government spending has a larger crowding-out effect in (1) than (2) due to an increase in the rate of interest. The \$30 increase in government spending causes investment spending to decline from \$80 to \$60 in (1), whereas investment spending declines from \$80 to \$65 in (2).

FISCAL POLICY: SPECIAL CASES

6.21 Find the change in output in Fig. 6-26(a), (b), and (c) when government spending increases by $\Delta \bar{G}$ and shifts IS rightward by $k_e \Delta \bar{G}$.

In Fig. 6-26(a) the $\Delta \bar{G}$ increase in government spending shifts IS rightward from IS_1 to IS_2. The rate of interest increases from i_0 to i_2; however, output remains at Y_0. There is complete crowding out, i.e., the decline in investment equals the increase in government spending.

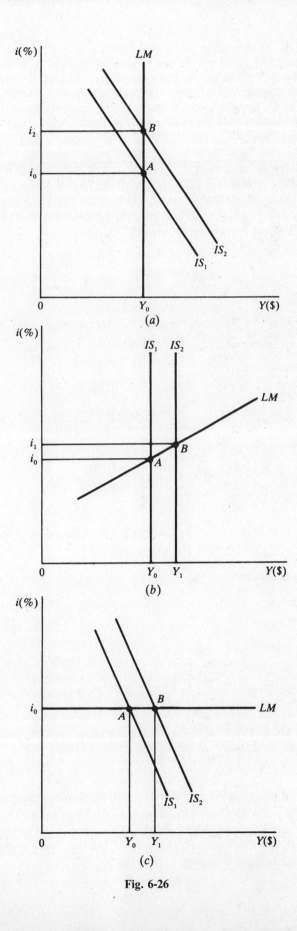

Fig. 6-26

In Fig. 6-26(b) the $\Delta\bar{G}$ increase in government spending shifts IS rightward from IS_1 to IS_2. Although the rate of interest increases from i_0 to i_1, output increases from Y_0 to Y_1, which equals the $k_e\Delta\bar{G}$ shift of IS. There is no crowding out because private sector spending is unrelated to the rate of interest.

There is no crowding out in Fig. 6-26(c) as IS shifts rightward from IS_1 to IS_2. The horizontal LM schedule indicates that the private sector is willing to supply additional money balances from their portfolios for transaction needs without a change in the rate of interest.

6.22 Suppose the demand for money is $L = 0.20Y$, the money supply is \$200, $C = \$90 + 0.80Yd$, $Tx = \$50$, $I = \$140 - 5i$, and $G = \$50$. (a) Derive the IS and LM equation. (b) Find equilibrium output, the rate of interest and investment. (c) Derive the IS equation when government spending increases \$20, *ceteris paribus*. (b) Find output, the rate of interest and investment when government spending is \$70. (e) Is there crowding-out?

  (a) *LM* equation:

$$L = M$$
$$0.20Y = \$200$$
$$Y = \$1000$$

       IS equation:

$$Y = C + I + G$$
$$Y = \$90 + 0.80(Y - \$50) + \$140 - 5i + \$50$$
$$Y = \$1200 - 25i$$

  (b) Simultaneous equilibrium:

      the *IS* equation:

      less the *LM* equation:

$$Y = \$1000$$
$$\underline{-(Y = \$1200 - 25i)}$$
$$0 = -\$200 + 25i$$
$$i = 8\%$$
$$Y = \$1000$$
$$I = \$100$$

  (c) *IS* equation:

$$Y = C + I + G$$
$$Y = \$90 + 0.80(Y - \$50) + \$140 - 5i + \$70$$
$$Y = \$1300 - 25i$$

  (d) Simultaneous equilibrium:

      the *IS* equation:

      less the *LM* equation:

$$Y = \$1000$$
$$\underline{-(Y = \$1300 - 25i)}$$
$$0 = -\$300 + 25i$$
$$i = 12\%$$
$$Y = \$1000$$
$$I = \$80$$

  (e) There is complete crowding-out; investment declines from \$100 to \$80 as government spending increases from \$50 to \$70. Complete crowding-out exists when the portfolio demand for money is unrelated to the rate of interest. When plotted, LM is a vertical line.

6.23 Suppose the demand for money is $L = 0.20Y - 10i$, the money supply is \$200, $C = \$60 + 0.8Yd$, $Tx = \$100$, $I = \$150$, $G = \$100$. (a) Find equations for IS and LM. (b) Find equilibrium output, the rate of interest, and investment. (c) Find the IS equation when government spending increases from \$100 to \$120. (d) Find output, the rate of interest, and investment when government spending is \$120. (e) Is there crowding-out?

(a) *LM* equation:
$$L = M$$
$$0.20Y - 10i = \$200$$
$$Y = \$1000 + 50i$$

IS equation:
$$Y = C + I + G$$
$$Y = \$60 + 0.80(Y - \$100) + \$150 + \$100$$
$$Y = \$1150$$

(b) Simultaneous equilibrium:

$$IS = LM$$
$$\$1150 = \$1000 + 50i$$
$$i = 3\%$$
$$Y = \$1150$$
$$I = \$150$$

(c) *IS* equation:
$$Y = C + I + G$$
$$Y = \$60 + 0.80(Y - \$100) + \$150 + \$120$$
$$Y = \$1250$$

(d) Simultaneous equilibrium:

$$IS = LM$$
$$\$1250 = \$1000 + 50i$$
$$i = 5\%$$
$$Y = \$1250$$
$$I = \$150$$

(e) There is no crowding-out. Although the interest rate increases from 3% to 5%, investment remains at $150, since it is not influenced by the rate of interest. Money balances are released from portfolios at the higher interest rate (3% to 5%) to meet the increased transaction need for money at the higher $1250 level of output.

THE MULTIPLIER EFFECT OF FISCAL POLICY IN AN *IS–LM* FRAMEWORK

6.24 Simultaneous equilibrium in the money and goods markets can be presented as

$$Y = \bar{A}\left(\frac{hk_e}{h + kbk_e}\right) + \bar{M}\left(\frac{k_e b}{h + k_e bk}\right)$$

(a) Holding variables constant other than Y and $\bar{G}$, find an expression that relates the change in equilibrium output to the change in government spending. (b) Find an expression for the multiplying effect γ that a change in government spending has upon output.

(a)
$$\Delta Y = \Delta \bar{G}\left(\frac{hk_e}{h + kbk_e}\right)$$

(b) Dividing both sides of the equation in part (a) by $\Delta \bar{G}$, we derive γ, the multiplying effect that a change in government spending has on output.

$$\frac{\Delta Y}{\Delta \bar{G}} = \frac{hk_e}{h + kbk_e}$$

Letting $\gamma = \Delta Y / \Delta \bar{G}$,

$$\gamma = \frac{hk_e}{h + kbk_e}$$

6.25 (a) Find the value of γ for the values of k_e, b, h, and k given in situations (1) through (5) in Table 6-2. (b) What multiplier effect would a change in government spending have on output in the simple $(C + I + G)$ model? (c) What generalizations can one make about the multiplying effect of a change in government spending on output where there is an increase in the value of k_e, b, h, and/or k?

Table 6-2

Situation	k_e	b	h	k
(1)	5	4	4	0.20
(2)	10	4	4	0.20
(3)	5	10	4	0.20
(4)	5	4	10	0.20
(5)	5	4	4	0.25

(a) The values for γ are (1) 2.500, (2) 3.333, (3) 1.429, (4) 3.571, and (5) 2.222.

(b) The multiplier effect associated with increased government spending in the simple $(C + I + G)$ model is k_e; hence, in the absence of a monetary sector, the value for the multiplying effect of government spending is 5 when $k_e = 5$ and 10 when k_e is 10.

(c) An increase in the expenditure multiplier k_e and the interest sensitivity of the demand for money h results in a larger value for γ; thus, larger values for k_e and/or h increase the multiplying effect that a change in government spending has on output. An increase in the interest-sensitivity of spending b and/ or in the desire to hold transaction balances k reduces the value of γ; increased values for b and/or k reduce the multiplying effect that a change in government spending has on output.

THE MONETARY–FISCAL POLICY MIX

6.26 Suppose output is initially Y_o for schedules IS_1 and LM_1 in Fig. 6-27; full employment exists at output Y_1. (a) Establish in Fig. 6-27 how monetary or fiscal policy can be used to reach full employment. (b) Explain how the choice of monetary or fiscal policy has a selective impact on sector spending and the composition of output.

(a) A money supply increase that shifts LM from LM_1 to LM_2 raises output to Y_1, with the interest rate decreasing to i_1. An alternative economic policy would be an expansion of government spending which shifts IS from IS_1 to IS_2, with output increasing to Y_1 and the interest rate increasing to i_2.

(b) A stimulative monetary policy lowers the rate of interest and increases interest-sensitive spending which in turn has a multiplier effect on output. Private sector goods and services become a larger percentage of output. However, when increased government spending is the policy choice, the interest rate increase crowds-out some interest-sensitive investment spending. The composition of output is weighted incrementally toward public sector goods and services as interest-sensitive private sector spending falls.

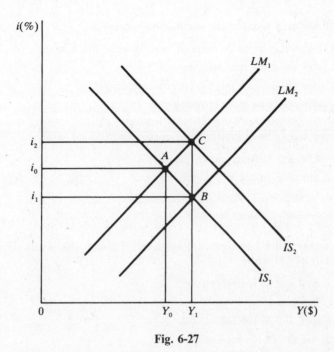

Fig. 6-27

6.27 The multiplying effect β of a money supply change upon output equals $k_e b/(h + k_e bk)$, whereas the multiplying effect α of a change in government spending on output is $hk_e/(h + kbk_e)$. In Problems 6.15 and 6.25 respectively, we find that β and α equal 2.5 when $k_e = 5$, $b = 4$, $h = 4$, and $k = 0.20$. (*a*) What increase in (1) the money supply or (2) government spending is needed to increase output \$100? (*b*) Find the change in investment as a result of policy (1) and policy (2) in part (*a*).

    (*a*) Policy (1)

$$\beta \Delta \bar{M} = \Delta Y$$
$$2.5 \Delta \bar{M} = \$100$$
$$\Delta \bar{M} = \$40$$

          Policy (2)

$$\alpha \Delta \bar{G} = \Delta Y$$
$$2.5 \Delta \bar{G} = \$100$$
$$\Delta \bar{G} = \$40$$

    (*b*) (1) The \$100 increase in output can be presented as $k_e \Delta \bar{I} = \$100$; since $k_e = 5$, the money supply expansion must lower the rate of interest to a level that causes investment to increase \$20. (2) In the absence of a monetary sector, a \$40 increase in government spending would increase output \$200. Since output expands only \$100, the interest rate increases to a level which results in a \$20 decrease in investment.

Multiple Choice Questions

1.   A liquidity effect occurs when

    (*a*) A reduction in government spending lowers the rate of interest.

    (*b*) A money supply increase lowers the rate of interest.

    (*c*) An increase in government spending increases the rate of interest.

    (*d*) A money supply increase raises the rate of interest.

2. A liquidity effect will normally result in an output effect because

(a) Lower interest rates will increase the store-of-value demand for money.
(b) Lower interest rates will cause less crowding-out.
(c) Lower interest rates will increase interest-sensitive spending.
(d) Lower interest rates will cause more crowding-out.

3. A change in the money supply has a greater effect upon output

(a) The more interest-sensitive private sector spending is.
(b) The less interest-sensitive private sector spending is.
(c) The smaller the expenditure multiplier is.
(d) The more interest-sensitive money holdings are to the rate of interest.

4. A money supply increase shifts LM rightward by $\Delta \bar{M}(1/k)$, with the actual change in output closely approximating the shift of LM when

(a) LM is steeply sloped and IS is steeply sloped.
(b) LM is relatively flat as is IS.
(c) LM is steeply sloped and IS is relatively flat.
(d) LM is relatively flat and IS is steeply sloped.

5. In which of the following situations will an increase in the money supply have no effect upon output?

(a) LM is steeply sloped and IS is relatively flat.
(b) LM is vertical and IS is steeply sloped.
(c) LM is steeply sloped and IS is vertical.
(d) LM is relatively flat as is IS.

6. k_e is the expenditure multiplier, b the interest sensitivity of private sector spending, h the interest sensitivity of the demand for money, and k is the transaction demand for money. From the following sets of values for k_e, b, h, and k, find the one in which a change in the money supply will have the largest multiplying effect on output.

(a) $k_e = 5$, $b = 5$, $h = 5$, $k = 0.20$
(b) $k_e = 4$, $b = 1$, $h = 5$, $k = 0.20$
(c) $k_e = 5$, $b = 10$, $h = 1$, $k = 0.20$
(d) $k_e = 4$, $b = 5$, $h = 10$, $k = 0.10$

7. An increase in government spending shifts IS rightward by $k_e \Delta \bar{G}$, with the actual change in output closely approximating the schedule's shift when

(a) The LM is relatively flat and IS is steeply sloped.
(b) The LM is vertical and IS is steeply sloped.
(c) The LM is relatively flat as is IS.
(d) The LM is steeply sloped and the IS is relatively flat.

8. Crowding-out is more likely to occur when

(a) The demand for money is interest-sensitive, and private sector spending is largely interest-insensitive.
(b) The demand for money is interest-sensitive, and private sector spending is interest-sensitive.
(c) The demand for money is interest-insensitive, and private sector spending is interest-insensitive.
(d) The demand for money is interest-insensitive, and private sector spending is interest-sensitive.

9.   Crowding-out occurs when

    (a)   A decrease in the money supply raises the rate of interest which crowds-out interest-sensitive private sector spending.

    (b)   An increase in taxes for the private sector reduces private sector disposable income and spending.

    (c)   A reduction in income taxes results in a higher interest rate, which crowds-out interest-sensitive private sector spending.

    (d)   A reduction in government spending induces less consumption spending.

10.   From the following sets of values for k_e, b, h, and k, find the set in which a change in government spending has the largest multiplier effect on output.

    (a) $k_e = 5$, $b = 5$, $h = 5$, $k = 0.20$.

    (b) $k_e = 10$, $b = 5$, $h = 10$, $k = 0.20$.

    (c) $k_e = 5$, $b = 10$, $h = 1$, $k = 0.20$.

    (d) $k_e = 5$, $b = 5$, $h = 1$, $k = 0.20$.

True or False Questions

11.   _____ There is a liquidity effect every time the Federal Reserve changes the money supply.

12.   _____ The liquidity effect is large when investment is interest-sensitive.

13.   _____ The output effect for a change in the money supply is large when investment is sensitive to the rate of interest and the demand for money is interest-insensitive.

14.   _____ An increase in the money supply has a small effect upon output when the store-of-value demand for money is interest-sensitive.

15.   _____ A large value for h and/or a small value for b are conditions whereby a change in the money supply has a small effect upon output.

16.   _____ An increase in government spending always crowds-out investment spending.

17.   _____ When investment is interest-sensitive, an increase in government spending has a weak crowding-out effect.

18.   _____ An increase in the money supply should have a large effect upon output when the value for coefficient b is large rather than when the value for b is small.

19.   _____ An increase in government spending should have a large effect upon output when the value for coefficient h is large rather than when the value for h is small.

20.   _____ An increase in the transaction demand for money ratio decreases the output effect of a change in the money supply.

Answers to Multiple Choice and True or False Questions

1. (*b*); **2**. (*c*); **3**. (*a*); **4**. (*c*); **5**. (*c*); **6**. (*c*); **7**. (*a*); **8**. (*d*); **9**. (*c*); **10**. (*b*); **11**. F; **12**. F; **13**. T; **14**. T; **15**. T; **16**. F; **17**. F; **18**. T; **19**. T; **20**. T.

Chapter 7

Monetary and Fiscal Policy in an Open Economy

Chapter Summary

1. In an open economy, trade flows affect the slope and location of *IS* in space. An increase in autonomous net exports shifts *IS* to the right while an increase in the economy's marginal propensity to import shifts *IS* leftward and increases its slope.

2. A market for foreign exchange exists because market participants either want to sell the domestic currency and purchase foreign currency or sell foreign exchange and purchase the domestic currency. Schedules of supply and demand for the domestic currency determine its exchange rate, the rate at which one unit of the domestic currency is exchanged for foreign currency. In a flexible exchange rate environment, a change in the supply and/or demand for the domestic currency affects its value. In a fixed exchange rate environment, a shift of supply and/or demand creates disequilibrium at the existing exchange rate. To remedy the disequilibrium, the monetary authority must buy or sell foreign exchange to maintain the fixed exchange rate. In the short run, the flow of financial capital is largely responsible for a change in the supply and demand for the domestic currency.

3. In the Mundell–Fleming model of perfect capital mobility, capital flows equate the domestic rate of interest with the world rate. In a flexible exchange rate environment, an increase in the world rate causes capital flows from the domestic economy into the world economies. As a result of the increased supply of the domestic currency in the foreign exchange markets, the exchange rate for the domestic economy depreciates, autonomous net exports increase, *IS* shifts rightward, and there is an increase in the domestic rate of interest. In a fixed exchange rate environment, an increase in the world rate forces the domestic central bank to sell foreign currency to support the fixed exchange rate; this action decreases the domestic money supply, *LM* shifts leftward, and the domestic rate of interest increases.

4. Monetary and fiscal policy are analyzed for an open economy in which there is perfect capital mobility and flexible exchange rates. A fiscal stimulus does not increase domestic output because any increase in the domestic rate of interest causes the domestic currency to appreciate, the domestic economy's exports to fall, and its *IS* schedule to shift back to its original position. Monetary policy is very effective, since an increase in the money supply shifts *LM* rightward, increases output, and lowers the domestic rate of interest. Capital outflows lower the value of the domestic currency, autonomous net exports increase, *IS* shifts to the right, and there is further increase in output.

5. Monetary policy is ineffective in a fixed exchange rate environment, while fiscal policy is effective. Monetary policy is ineffective since the monetary authority must support the fixed exchange rate. Thus, it cannot take any action which would cause the domestic rate to deviate from the world rate. Fiscal policy is very effective, since a fiscal stimulus which increases the domestic rate requires the monetary authority to expand the money supply to keep the domestic rate at parity with the world rate.

Chapter Outline

7.4 Monetary and Fiscal Policy in a Flexible Exchange Rate Environment

7.5 Monetary and Fiscal Policy in a Fixed Exchange Rate Environment

7.1 NET EXPORTS AND THE *IS* SCHEDULE

In an open economy, trade flows impact the slope and/or location of the *IS* schedule in space. The U.S. export function is presented as $X = \bar{X} - mY$, where $\bar{X}$ represents autonomous net exports (autonomous exports less autonomous imports) and m is the marginal propensity of the U.S.A. to import foreign-made goods and services. Autonomous net exports are largely influenced by the value of the dollar (the dollar's foreign exchange rate) and output in foreign countries. When the U.S. dollar devalues, *ceteris paribus*, autonomous exports increase as foreigners find that they can buy more U.S.-made goods with a given quantity of their currency. Autonomous exports also increase when the output level of U.S. trading partners increases and they purchase more U.S.-made goods. U.S. autonomous imports decline when the foreign exchange value of the dollar falls and there is an increased cost in purchasing foreign-made goods. In the export function, $X = \bar{X} - mY$, behavioral coefficient m measures the direct relationship of imports to output in the U.S.A. Behavioral coefficient m represents a leakage from the domestic spending flow, since m represents a demand for foreign rather than domestic-made goods and services. In an *IS–LM* framework, variable m, through the expenditure multiplier, affects the slope of *IS*; a change in autonomous net exports results in a parallel shift of *IS* equal to $k_e \Delta \bar{X}$.

EXAMPLE 7.1.   The export equation $X = \$50 - 0.10Y$ is plotted in Fig. 7-1 and labeled X. A decrease in the value of the dollar increases autonomous exports and decreases autonomous imports. This increase in autonomous net exports is noted by an increase in the constant of the export equation, e.g., from $X = \$50 - 0.10Y$ to $X = \$60 - 0.10Y$, and by a shift of the export function in Fig. 7-1 from X to X'. An appreciation of the dollar decreases net exports; this is noted in the export equation by a decrease in the constant of the export equation, e.g., from $X = \$50 - 0.10Y$ to $X = \$40 - 0.10Y$, and by a shift of the export function in Fig. 7-1 from X to X''.

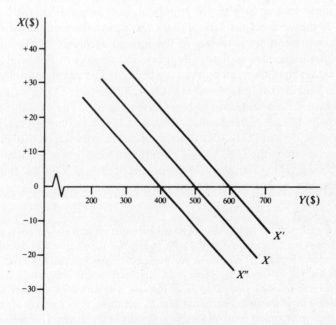

Fig. 7-1

148   MONETARY AND FISCAL POLICY IN AN OPEN ECONOMY   [CHAP. 7

EXAMPLE 7.2. When $C = \bar{C} + cYd$, $Yd = Y - Tx$, $Tx = tY$, $I = \bar{I} - bi$, $G = \bar{G}$, $X = \bar{X} - mY$, the IS equation is $Y = (\bar{C} + \bar{I} + \bar{G} + \bar{X} - bi)/(1 - c + ct + m)$ and is represented by schedule IS in Fig. 7-2. A $\Delta\bar{X}$ increase in autonomous net exports shifts the goods equilibrium schedule IS rightward by $k_e\Delta\bar{X}$ to IS'. An increase in m, *ceteris paribus*, reduces the expenditure multiplier; schedule IS shifts leftward to IS'' and becomes more steeply sloped.

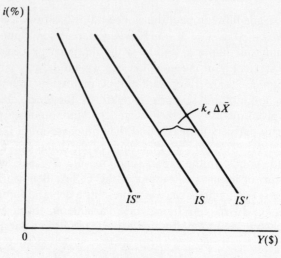

Fig. 7-2

7.2 FOREIGN EXCHANGE RATES

A foreign exchange rate is the price of one currency in terms of another, e.g., the German mark (DM) price of U.S. dollars ($). In the major industrialized countries, banks buy or sell foreign exchange, and thereby make a market in foreign exchange. In a flexible exchange rate environment, the exchange rate changes in response to a change in the supply and/or demand for the foreign and the domestic currency. In Fig. 7-3, the demand for U.S. dollars represents the number of dollars that individuals, corporations, and governments want to buy in the foreign exchange market in exchange for German marks. These dollars are demanded so that U.S. goods and services or financial assets may be purchased and/or U.S. dollars rather than German marks may be held. The supply of dollars in Fig. 7-3 represents the number of dollars that are being supplied at each exchange rate. Dollars are supplied, in Fig. 7-3, by those who currently own dollars and want to buy German marks. The equilibrium exchange rate in Fig. 7-3 is initially E_0 for supply and demand schedules S and D. This exchange rate changes when there is a shift in the supply and/or demand for dollars. Some of the factors which can shift these schedules are a change in (1) the interest rate in the U.S.A. ($i_{U.S.}$), (2) the interest rate in Germany (i_G), (3) the U.S. price level relative to the price level in Germany, (4) the preference for U.S. rather than German-made goods, (5) productivity in the U.S.A. relative to that in Germany.

EXAMPLE 7.3. In this example, the supply of dollars is held constant and exogenous forces affect only the demand for dollars. The equilibrium exchange rate is initially E_0 in Fig. 7-4 for supply and demand schedules S and D. An increase in the rate of interest in the U.S.A., *ceteris paribus*, encourages investors to invest more funds in the U.S.A. rather than in the German financial markets. There is an increased capital inflow into the U.S.A., evidenced by the rightward shift of the demand schedule from D to D' in Fig. 7-4. The exchange rate increases from E_0 to E_1, and the dollar appreciates. Starting from the initial exchange rate E_0, an increase in the rate of interest in Germany, *ceteris paribus*, makes investments in Germany more profitable and reduces the demand for dollars. The demand for dollars shifts downward from D to D'' and the exchange rate declines from E_0 to E_2.

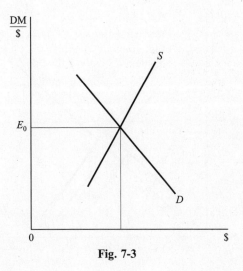

Fig. 7-3

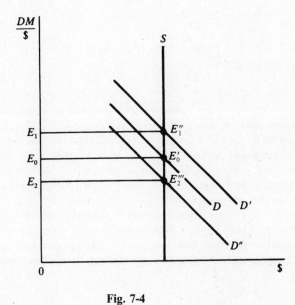

Fig. 7-4

In a fixed exchange rate environment, the exchange rate between two countries is officially set, with each country committed to taking whatever action is needed to maintain the agreed rate. For example, suppose the U.S.A. and Germany agree to set the exchange rate at E_0 in Fig. 7-5. For supply and demand schedules S and D in Fig. 7-5, E_0 is an equilibrium exchange rate. An increase in the German rate of interest, *ceteris paribus*, alters capital flows. German demand for U.S. securities decreases, while U.S. demand for German securities increases. This is evidenced by the decrease in the demand for dollars from D to D' in Fig. 7-5 and the increase in supply from S to S'. At exchange rate E_0, there is now a surplus of dollars equal to $Q_1 Q_2$, and therefore a shortage of marks in the foreign exchange market. The Federal Reserve, to support the exchange rate at E_0, sells marks and buys dollars to alleviate the imbalance. In doing so, bank reserves decrease, as does the U.S. money supply. In a fixed exchange rate environment, central banks hold foreign exchange (official reserves) which they use to support the country's exchange rate. [Note: revaluation of the official exchange rate or restriction of international transactions are other ways of addressing an imbalance of supply and demand. These means are not

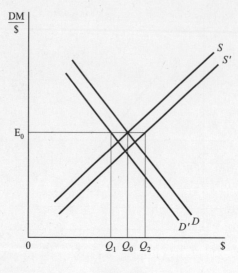

Fig. 7-5

considered here, since the focus is upon central bank intervention in the foreign exchange market as the means of overcoming disequilibrium.]

EXAMPLE 7.4. Suppose the U.S.A. and Germany have agreed to maintain an exchange rate of 1.5 between the German mark and the U.S. dollar, i.e., 1.5 German marks equal one U.S. dollar. In Fig. 7-6, for supply and demand schedules S and D, the 1.5 exchange rate is an equilibrium rate, since the quantity of dollars supplied ($300) is equal to the quantity of dollars demanded ($300). If the demand for dollars increases from D to D', a shortage of dollars develops at exchange rate 1.5, since the $400 demanded exceeds the $300 supplied. The shortage of $100 in the foreign exchange market means that there is a DM150 surplus of German marks at exchange rate 1.5. To support the exchange rate at 1.5, the Fed, as recorded in the T account below, buys the excess supply of marks (DM150) held by the banking system at the 1.5 exchange rate and credits the banking system's deposit account at the Fed $100. In doing so, the Fed has increased bank reserves $100, and with a 10% reserve requirement on checking deposits the U.S. money supply increases $1000. Note that Fed support of a fixed exchange rate affects the U.S. money supply. The money supply increases when the Fed buys foreign exchange and decreases when the Fed sells foreign exchange.

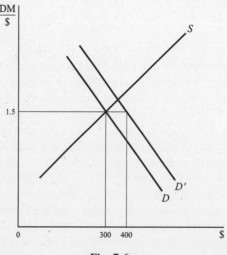

Fig. 7-6

ΔAssets	Federal Reserve System	ΔLiabilities
German marks	+ DM150	Dollar deposit of Banks	+ $100

ΔAssets	The Banking System	ΔLiabilities
German marks	− DM150		
Deposit at the Fed	+ $100		

7.3 CAPITAL MOBILITY AND THE LINKAGE OF MARKET ECONOMIES

The financial markets of the major industrialized countries are closely linked. In this chapter, we use the Mundell–Fleming model, in which the linkage is complete and there is perfect capital mobility. The presence of perfect capital mobility results in a uniformity of the rate of interest across national boundaries. If, for some reason, the rate of interest in a country rises above the world rate, capital flows into that country, lowering its rate to that of the world rate. For example, suppose the world rate of interest is 5% and the rate in the U.S.A. increases from 5% to 6%; the U.S.A. experiences capital inflows until its rate falls back to the 5% level. A small country model approach is assumed, where the world rate is unaffected by the rate in an individual country and the rate in an individual country is affected by the world rate. Examples 7.5 through 7.8 analyze what happens to output and the rate of interest in the U.S.A. when there is a shift of IS or a change in the world rate and exchange rates are (1) flexible or (2) fixed.

EXAMPLE 7.5.   Exchange rates are flexible. In Fig. 7-7(a), output in the U.S.A. is Y_0 for schedules IS' and LM'. The i_1 rate of interest in the U.S.A. is the same as the world rate. The exchange rate for the U.S.A. is E_0 for schedules D' and S' in Fig. 7-7(b). Suppose world rates increase to i_2. Seeking the higher i_2 rate, U.S. investors purchase German securities. U.S. investors supply additional dollars to the foreign exchange markets and shift the supply of dollar schedule in Fig. 7-7(b) rightward from S' to S''; the exchange rate decreases from E_0 to E_1. Capital flows from the U.S.A. to Germany depreciate the dollar. The depreciated dollar increases autonomous U.S. exports and decreases autonomous U.S. imports; autonomous net exports increase. There are increases in autonomous net exports until IS shifts rightward from IS' to IS''; for IS'' and LM' the rate of interest is i_2, and there is parity of the U.S. rate with the world rate. Output in the U.S.A increases from Y_0 to Y_2.

EXAMPLE 7.6.   The situation in Example 7.5 is analyzed in a fixed exchange rate environment. The increase in the world rate of interest from i_1 to i_2 shifts the supply of dollars in Fig. 7-7(b) from S' to S''. Because the U.S.A. is committed to keeping the exchange rate at E_0, there now exists at exchange rate E_0 a surplus of dollars. (The quantity of dollars demanded remains at Q_1 but the quantity supplied has increased to Q_2 as a result of the increased supply of dollars into the foreign exchange market.) The Fed sells German marks and buys U.S. dollars because of the shortage of marks and surplus of dollars. In doing so, U.S. bank reserves and the U.S. money supply decrease. LM' in Fig. 7-7(a) shifts leftward to LM''. IS' and LM'' intersect at output Y_1 and interest rate i_2, which is the same as the world rate. There is no longer an incentive for U.S. investors to invest in other countries and the supply of dollars in Fig. 7-7(b) shifts backward to S' and there is equilibrium in the foreign exchange market at exchange rate E_0. Note that with fixed exchange rates, output decreases to Y_1 as a result of the increase in the world rate of interest, whereas output increases to Y_2 (Example 7.5) when exchange rates are flexible.

EXAMPLE 7.7.   Exchange rates are flexible. In Fig. 7-8(a), output in the U.S.A. is Y_0 for schedules IS' and LM'. The i_1 rate of interest in the U.S.A. is the same as the world rate. The exchange rate for the U.S.A. is E_0 for schedules D' and S' in Fig. 7-8(b). Suppose autonomous investment increases in the U.S.A. due to a surge in new technology.

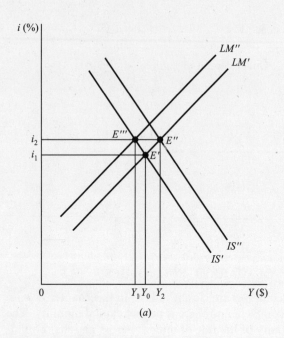

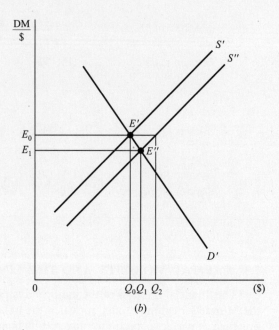

(a)   (b)

Fig. 7-7

Increased autonomous investment shifts the goods equilibrium schedule in Fig. 7-8(a) from IS' to IS'', and the rate of interest in the U.S.A. increases from i_1 to i_2. Because of the higher rate of interest in the U.S.A., there is a capital inflow from Germany; the demand for dollars schedule D' in Fig. 7-8(b) shifts rightward to D'', and the exchange rate increases from E_0 to E_1. The appreciation of the dollar decreases autonomous net exports and IS in Fig. 7-8(a) shifts leftward. The leftward shift of IS from IS'' continues until it returns to IS' and the U.S. rate of interest returns to its initial i_1 level. The autonomous increase in investment has no effect upon output, since the appreciation of the dollar causes a drop in autonomous net exports equal to the increase in autonomous investment.

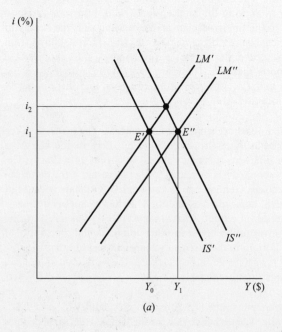

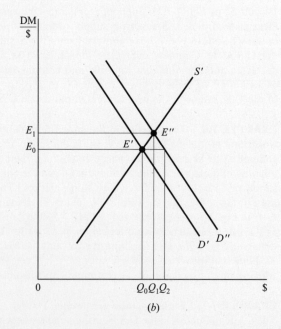

(a)   (b)

Fig. 7-8

EXAMPLE 7.8.   The situation in Example 7.7 is analyzed in a fixed exchange rate environment. The rate of interest has increased from i_1 to i_2 in Fig. 7-8(a) as a result of the rightward shift of IS from IS' to IS''. The increased demand for dollars in Fig. 7-8(b) shifts D' to D''. Since exchange rates are fixed, there is now a shortage of dollars (and therefore a surplus of DM) at exchange rate E_0. The Fed buys the excess supply of German marks, and in doing so increases bank reserves and the U.S. money supply. Monetary equilibrium schedule LM' in Fig. 7-8(a) shifts rightward until it reaches LM''; IS'' and LM'' intersect at output Y_1 and interest rate i_1, which is the same as the world rate. The demand for dollars in Fig. 7-8(b) returns to D', and there is equilibrium in the foreign exchange market at exchange rate E_0. Output in the U.S.A. increases from Y_0 to Y_1 in this fixed exchange rate environment, whereas output is unchanged in a flexible exchange rate environment.

7.4   MONETARY AND FISCAL POLICY IN A FLEXIBLE EXCHANGE RATE ENVIRONMENT

Fiscal policy is unable to change output in a flexible exchange rate environment, given the assumption of perfect capital mobility and a small country model. A fiscal action shifts IS and causes the domestic interest rate to rise above or fall below the world interest rate. When the domestic economy's interest rate is above the world rate, the value of the domestic currency rises, which reduces autonomous net exports. This decrease in autonomous net exports shifts IS leftward until IS and LM intersect at the world rate of interest. Thus, any fiscal change results in an offsetting change in autonomous net exports, making fiscal policy an ineffective policy tool.

EXAMPLE 7.9.   In Fig. 7-9(a), output in the U.S.A. is Y_0 for schedules IS' and LM'. The i_1 rate of interest in the U.S.A. is the same as the world rate. The exchange rate for the U.S.A. is E_0 for schedules D' and S' in Fig. 7-9(b). An increase in government spending in the U.S.A. shifts IS rightward from IS' to IS'', which pushes the U.S. interest rate upward from i_1 to i_2 for LM' and IS''. An increased capital inflow into the U.S.A. from Germany shifts the demand for dollars in Fig. 7-9(b) from D' to D''. The exchange rate for supply and demand schedules S' and D'' is E_1; the higher interest rate in the U.S.A. causes the exchange rate to increase from E_0 to E_1. This appreciation of the dollar decreases autonomous net exports, and IS shifts leftward. The leftward shift of IS continues until the goods equilibrium schedule returns to IS', and IS' and LM' intersect at interest rate i_1 which is equal to the world rate. The increase in government spending in the U.S.A. crowds out an offsetting amount of autonomous net exports, and output in the U.S.A. is unchanged.

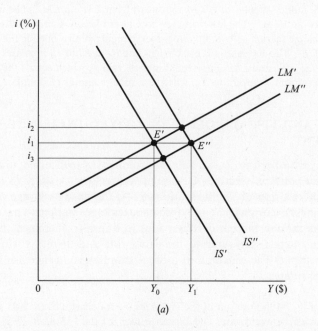

(a)

Fig. 7-9

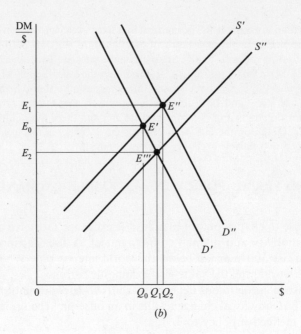

Fig. 7-9 (*continued*)

Monetary policy is extremely effective in a flexible exchange rate environment. An increase in the U.S. money supply, for example, lowers the U.S. rate of interest, which results in a depreciation of the dollar. This depreciation of the dollar increases autonomous net exports and the *IS* schedule shifts rightward until money market and goods market equilibria occur at an interest rate equal to the world rate.

EXAMPLE 7.10.   In Fig. 7-9(*a*), output in the U.S.A. is Y_0 for schedules IS' and LM'. The i_1 rate of interest in the U.S.A. is the same as the world rate. The exchange rate for the U.S.A. is E_0 for schedules D' and S' in Fig. 7-9(*b*). An increase in the U.S. money supply shifts LM rightward from LM' to LM''. The rate of interest in the U.S.A. is now i_3 for schedules IS' and LM''. The lower interest rate in the U.S.A. increases the supply of dollars (from S' to S'') in the foreign exchange market as U.S. investors seek a higher return outside the U.S.A. The exchange rate for schedules D' and S'' is E_2. The decrease in the exchange rate from E_0 to E_2 increases autonomous net exports, and IS shifts rightward to IS''. IS'' and LM'' intersect at interest rate i_1, which equals the world rate. An increase in the money supply increases output from Y_0 to Y_1, whereas a fiscal stimulus (Example 7.9) has no effect upon output.

7.5 MONETARY AND FISCAL POLICY IN A FIXED EXCHANGE RATE ENVIRONMENT

Monetary policy in a fixed exchange rate environment is ineffective, unable to change equilibrium output, whereas fiscal policy is effective. A stimulative fiscal policy shifts *IS* rightward and the domestic economy's rate of interest rises above the world rate. At the fixed exchange rate, capital inflows create a shortage of the domestic currency in the foreign exchange market. The central bank supports the exchange rate by purchasing foreign currency and in doing so increases the domestic money supply. The domestic rate of interest is lowered to the world rate and there is further increase in the domestic economy's level of output. The outcome of a fiscal stimulus is an increase in domestic output and no change in the rate of interest.

EXAMPLE 7.11.   In Fig. 7-10(*a*), output in the U.S.A. is Y_0 for schedules IS' and LM'. The i_1 rate of interest in the U.S.A. is the same as the world rate. The exchange rate for the U.S.A. is E_0 for schedules D' and S' in Fig. 7-10(*b*). An increase in government spending in the U.S.A. shifts IS rightward from IS' to IS''; for IS'' and LM', the

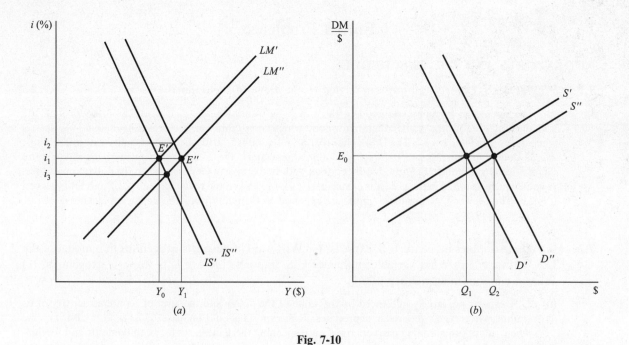

Fig. 7-10

U.S. interest rate is i_2. The demand for dollars in Fig. 7-10(b) shifts rightward from D' to D'' as a result of the higher U.S. interest rate and the capital flow into the U.S.A. At exchange rate E_0, there is now a $Q_1 Q_2$ shortage of dollars. (Recall that there is a surplus of foreign exchange when there is a shortage of dollars.) The Fed remedies the dollar shortage by purchasing the mark surplus in the foreign exchange market. As a result of these purchases, bank reserves increase, as does the U.S. money supply. The increase in the U.S. money supply shifts LM rightward in Fig. 7-10(a) until it eventually is located at LM''. IS'' and LM'' intersect at interest rate i_1; output increases from Y_0 to Y_1.

Monetary policy cannot be used in a fixed exchange rate environment, since any change in the money supply pushes the domestic interest rate above or below the world rate. A decrease in the domestic economy's money supply, for example, increases the domestic rate of interest. Capital inflows increase the demand for the domestic currency, and, at the fixed exchange rate, there is a shortage of the domestic currency. The domestic central bank sells foreign currency to support the domestic currency. In doing so, the domestic money supply increases, the LM shifts rightward to its initial location, and the domestic rate of interest returns to the world rate. Because the domestic central bank is committed to maintaining a fixed exchange rate, it cannot use a change in the money supply to change the domestic economy's rate of interest.

EXAMPLE 7.12. In Fig. 7-10(a), output in the U.S.A. is Y_0 for schedules IS' and LM'. The i_1 rate of interest in the U.S.A. is the same as the world rate. The exchange rate for the U.S.A. is E_0 for schedules D' and S' in Fig. 7-10(b). An increase in the U.S. money supply shifts LM rightward from LM' to LM''. The rate of interest in the U.S.A. is now i_3 for schedules IS' and LM''. The lower interest rate in the U.S.A. increases the supply of dollars (from S' to S'') in the foreign exchange market as U.S. investors seek a higher return outside the U.S.A. At exchange rate E_0, there is a surplus of dollars and a shortage of German marks. The Fed remedies the shortage of marks by selling marks to banks. In doing so, bank reserves and the U.S. money supply decrease. The LM shifts leftward from LM'' to LM', which returns the rate of interest to i_1. The Fed is unable to change output in a fixed exchange rate environment because of its inability to push the U.S. rate of interest below the world rate.

Solved Problems

NET EXPORTS AND THE *IS* SCHEDULE

7.1 Why are U.S. exports and imports related to the value of the dollar?

   The price of a foreign-made good in the U.S.A. is translated into a U.S. dollar price through the exchange rate. For example, a German-made good which costs DM45 in Germany costs $30 in U.S. dollars when the exchange rate is 1.5. The U.S. dollar cost of this good is $22.50 when the exchange rate is 2.0. Thus, as the dollar purchases more marks (the dollar appreciates), the U.S.A. is inclined to purchase more German-produced goods. U.S.-produced goods are more expensive in Germany when the dollar appreciates. A good which costs $20 in the U.S., for example, costs DM30 when the exchange rate is 1.5 and DM40 when it is 2.0. Thus, fewer U.S.-produced goods are exported to Germany when the dollar appreciates.

7.2 (*a*) What variables influence U.S. exports? (*b*) Why are U.S. exports exogenous in a model of the U.S. economy? (*c*) What variables influence U.S. imports? (*d*) Are U.S. imports exogenous? (*e*) What are autonomous net exports?

   (*a*) U.S. exports are largely influenced by the value of the dollar and the level of economic activity of its trading partners. As the dollar depreciates, U.S. exports should increase. U.S. exports also increase when output of its trading partners rises, since spending there increases for both domestic and foreign-produced goods.

   (*b*) Exports are exogenous in a model of the U.S. economy, since the model does not determine the exchange rate and does not determine the level of economic activity in foreign countries.

   (*c*) U.S. imports are largely explained by the value of the dollar and the level of economic activity in the U.S.A. An increase in the value of the dollar increases imports, as does an increase in U.S. output, since spending on U.S.- and foreign-produced goods increases along with GDP.

   (*d*) Imports which are tied to the value of the dollar are exogenous, while imports which are influenced by the U.S. level of output are endogenous.

   (*e*) Autonomous net exports equal exogenous exports less exogenous imports. In the export function, $X = \bar{X} - mY$, $\bar{X}$ represents autonomous net exports.

7.3 (*a*) Explain behavioral coefficient m in the export function $X = \bar{X} - mY$. (*b*) What happens to the *IS* schedule when there is an increase in m? (*c*) What happens to the *IS* schedule when there is an increase in $\bar{X}$?

   (*a*) Behavioral coefficient m relates the change in imports to a change in output; as such, m represents the marginal propensity to import foreign-made goods and services.

   (*b*) Behavioral coefficient m represents a leakage from the spending flow and has an effect on *IS* similar to that of a change in the marginal propensity to save. Hence, an increase in m causes *IS* to become more steeply sloped as it shifts leftward.

   (*c*) An increase in autonomous net exports shifts *IS* rightward by $k_e \Delta \bar{X}$.

FOREIGN EXCHANGE RATES

7.4 (*a*) What is a foreign exchange rate? (*b*) What happens to the U.S. dollar price of Japanese-made goods when the yen–dollar foreign exchange rate falls, *ceteris paribus*? (*c*) What happens to the price of U.S.-made goods in Japan when the yen–dollar foreign exchange rate falls, *ceteris paribus*? (*d*) What happens to U.S. autonomous net exports (autonomous U.S. exports less autonomous U.S. imports) when the yen–dollar foreign exchange rate falls? (*e*) What happens to the *IS* schedule when the yen–dollar foreign exchange rate falls?

(a) A foreign exchange rate is the rate at which one country's currency is exchanged for that of another. For example, $1 (U.S. currency) may purchase ¥130 (Japan's currency).

(b) Holding other variables constant, a decrease in the yen–dollar foreign exchange rate makes the price of Japanese-made goods more expensive in the U.S.A.

(c) The price of U.S.-made goods in Japan declines as the U.S. dollar falls in value relative to the Japanese yen.

(d) U.S. autonomous net exports increase when the yen–dollar exchange rate falls. This is because U.S. autonomous exports to Japan increase while U.S. autonomous imports from Japan fall.

(e) The increase in U.S. autonomous net exports causes the IS schedule to shift rightward by $k_e \Delta \bar{X}$.

7.5 What is the difference between a flexible exchange rate environment and a fixed exchange rate environment?

A shift of the supply and/or demand for foreign exchange changes the exchange rate in a flexible exchange rate environment. When the exchange rate is fixed, the central banks of the two countries agree to intervene in the foreign exchange market to maintain the agreed to exchange rate. Thus, a supply and/or demand shift in the foreign exchange market may create a surplus or shortage of foreign exchange. The central banks eliminate the surplus or shortage by buying or selling foreign exchange.

7.6 In Fig. 7-11, E_0 is the equilibrium exchange rate between the Japanese yen and the U.S. dollar for the supply of dollar S and the demand for dollar D schedules. (a) In a flexible exchange rate environment, what happens to the exchange rate when the demand schedule shifts upward from D to D' or downward from D to D''? (b) As a result of the shifts specified in part (a), what happens to U.S. autonomous net exports? (c) What happens to the IS or LM schedules?

(a) The exchange rate increases to E_1 when demand shifts upward from D to D'; the dollar appreciates relative to the Japanese yen. The exchange rate falls to E_2 when demand shifts downward from D to D''; the dollar depreciates relative to the Japanese yen.

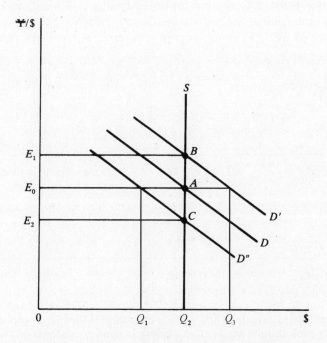

Fig. 7-11

(b) Autonomous net exports for the U.S.A. fall when demand shifts upward and the dollar appreciates. U.S.-made goods are more expensive in Japan, which decreases U.S. exports: and, since the U.S. price of Japanese-made goods is now lower, U.S. imports increase. The downward shift to D'' depreciates the dollar and increases autonomous net exports for the U.S.A.

(c) In a flexible exchange rate environment, a change in the exchange rate has no effect upon the LM schedule. When the dollar appreciates, the IS schedule shifts leftward by $k_e \Delta \bar{X}$ ($\Delta \bar{X}$ is negative since it represents a decrease in autonomous net exports). When the dollar depreciates, IS shifts rightward by $k_e \Delta \bar{X}$ ($\Delta \bar{X}$ is positive since autonomous net exports increase).

7.7   Would your answers to Problem 7.6 be different for a fixed exchange rate environment?

(a) The rightward shift of demand to D' would create a shortage of dollars of $Q_2 Q_3$ at exchange rate E_0, since the quantity of dollars supplied Q_2 is less than the quantity of dollars demanded Q_3 at exchange rate E_0. For demand schedule D'', there is a surplus of dollars of $Q_1 Q_2$ at exchange rate E_0.

(b) There is no change in autonomous net exports, since the exchange rate E_0 is maintained by the purchase or sale of yen by the Fed. When demand shifts rightward to D', the Fed remedies the dollar shortage by buying yen and thereby supplying dollars. When demand shifts leftward to D'', there is a dollar surplus and yen shortage. The Fed sells yen in exchange for dollars.

(c) Since the exchange rate is unchanged, there is no shift of IS. The LM schedule shifts as a result of the Fed's intervention in the foreign exchange market. For schedule D' and a dollar shortage, the money supply increases when the Fed buys yen; LM shifts rightward. For schedule D'', the dollar surplus requires the sale of yen; there is a decrease in the money supply and LM shifts leftward.

7.8   Suppose the exchange rate between the German mark and the U.S. dollar is 2.0, and at exchange rate 2.0 there is a $120 shortage of U.S. dollars. (a) What is the shortage or surplus of German marks? (b) Show, through T accounts for the Fed and a U.S. bank, how the Fed, through foreign exchange rate intervention, can remedy this disequilibrium. (c) If the reserve requirement is 10%, find the change in the U.S. money supply as a result of the Fed's foreign exchange rate intervention.

(a)   There is a DM240 surplus.

(b)

ΔAssets	Federal Reserve System	ΔLiabilities	
German marks	+ DM240	Dollar deposit of Bank	+ $120

ΔAssets	U.S. Bank		ΔLiabilities
German marks	− DM240		
Deposit at the Fed	+ $120		

(c) Bank reserves have increased $120, which is the change in the U.S. Bank's deposit at the Fed. This $120 increase in bank reserves supports an increase in checking deposits of $1200. The M1 money supply increases $1200.

CAPITAL MOBILITY AND THE LINKAGE OF MARKET ECONOMIES

7.9   (*a*) What is meant by perfect capital mobility? (*b*) Is there any difference in outcome when there is perfect capital mobility in a small country and a large country model?

(*a*)   Perfect capital mobility is a situation where there is free, unrestricted flow of financial capital among countries, such that the real rate of interest is the same in each country. Thus, whenever the rate of interest in one country deviates frrom the world rate, there is an unlimited capital inflow/outflow from that country which equates its rate with the world rate.

(*b*)   In a small country model, an interest rate deviation for a country is eliminated without a change in the world rate. For example, if Country A's rate of interest rises above the world rate, capital flows into A and this capital flow does not affect the world rate. In a large country model, an interest rate difference for a large country results in a capital flow which affects the world rate. For example, if Country B is a large country and its rate of interest rises above the world rate, the capital flows necessary to bring B's rate into parity with the world rate will increase the world rate. The small country model is used throughout this chapter.

7.10   In Fig. 7-12(*a*), equilibrium output for the U.S.A. is Y_0 and the rate of interest is i_0 for schedules IS' and LM'; the exchange rate in Fig. 7-12(*b*) is E_0 for schedules D' and S'. Suppose the world rate decreases from i_0 to i_1, *ceteris paribus*. (*a*) Use Fig. 7-12(*a*) and (*b*) to show and explain what happens as capital flows equate the U.S. rate with the world rate in a small country, flexible exchange rate model. (*b*) Now show and explain what happens in a fixed exchange rate environment. (*c*) Compare the change in output that results from a decrease in the world rate in flexible and fixed exchange rate environments.

(*a*)   The rate of interest is now higher in the U.S.A. than in other countries. Capital flows into the U.S.A. shift the demand for dollars schedule from D' to D''. In a flexible exchange rate environment, the dollar appreciates to E_1. The appreciation of the dollar reduces autonomous net exports and IS in Fig. 7-12(*a*) shifts leftward from IS' to IS''. The rate of interest in the U.S.A. for IS'' and LM' is i_1, which is equal to the world rate.

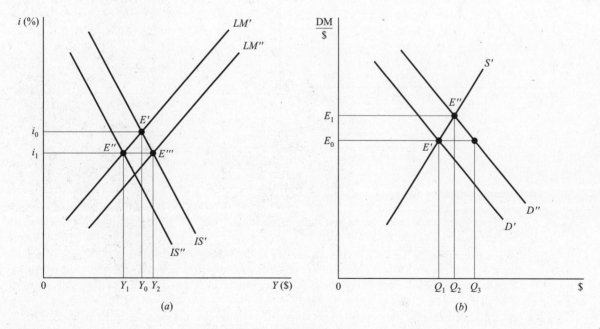

Fig. 7-12

(b) At exchange rate E_0 in Fig. 7-12(b), there is a dollar shortage of $Q_1 Q_3$ for schedules D'' and S'. The Fed purchases the surplus German marks, which increases bank reserves. The U.S. money supply increases and LM in Fig. 7-12(a) shifts rightward from LM' to LM''; the U.S. rate of interest for schedules IS' and LM'' is i_1, which is equal to the world rate.

(c) The decline in the world rate causes output in the U.S.A. to decline from Y_0 to Y_1 in a flexible exchange rate environment and to increase from Y_0 to Y_2 in a fixed exchange rate environment.

7.11 In Fig. 7-13(a), equilibrium output for the U.S.A. is Y_0 and the rate of interest is i_0 for schedules IS' and LM'; the exchange rate in Fig. 7-13(b) is E_0 for schedules D' and S'. Suppose autonomous consumption decreases, *ceteris paribus*, IS shifts leftward from IS' to IS'' and the U.S. rate of interest decreases to i_1. (a) Use Fig. 7-13(a) and (b) to show and explain how capital flows increase the U.S. rate so that it is at parity with the world rate in a small country, flexible exchange rate model. (b) Now show and explain what happens in a fixed exchange rate environment. (c) Compare the change in output that results from a decrease in autonomous consumption in a flexible and fixed exchange rate environment.

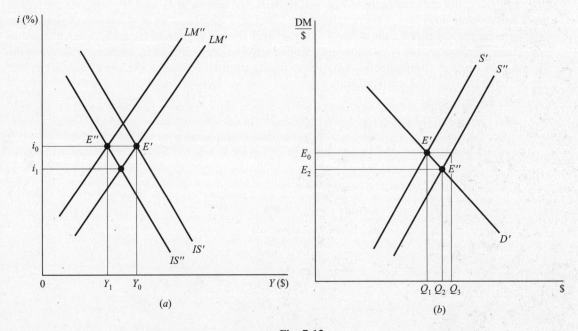

Fig. 7-13

(a) Because the rate of interest is now lower in the U.S.A., there is a capital outflow; the supply of dollars in the foreign exchange market shifts from S' to S'' in Fig. 7-13(b). The dollar depreciates to E_2, which increases autonomous net exports and shifts IS rightward from IS'' to IS'. IS' and LM' intersect at interest rate i_1, which is the world rate.

(b) At exchange rate E_0, there is a dollar surplus as a result of the rightward shift of the supply of dollars from S' to S'' in Fig. 7-13(b). The shortage of German marks is remedied by the Fed's sale of marks. This sale reduces bank reserves and the U.S. money supply decreases. The LM schedule shifs leftward from LM' to LM'' and IS'' and LM'' intersect at interest rate i_0, which is the world rate.

(c) In a flexible exchange rate environment, there is no change in output as a result of a decrease in autonomous consumption; output decreases from Y_0 to Y_1 in a fixed exchange rate environment.

MONETARY AND FISCAL POLICY IN A FLEXIBLE EXCHANGE RATE ENVIRONMENT

7.12   Suppose all market economies are below full-employment output; the world real rate of interest is i_0. In Fig. 7-14(a) output in the U.S.A. is Y_0 and the rate of interest is i_0. The U.S. exchange rate in Fig. 7-14(b) is E_0. (a) For a small country model, establish what happens to output in the U.S.A. when exchange rates are flexible and (1) the U.S.A. increases government spending, IS shifts rightward from IS' to IS'' in Fig. 7-14(a), and no policy action is taken by other countries; (2) the U.S.A. increases government spending, IS shifts rightward from IS' to IS'' and the world rate of interest increases from i_0 to i_1 as a result of fiscal stimuli in other market economies. (b) Explain the outcome in situations (1) and (2).

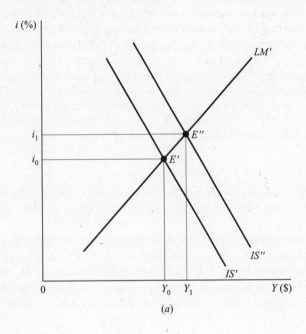

(a)

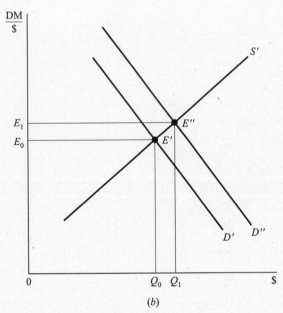

(b)

Fig. 7-14

(a) (1) The increase in government spending which shifts IS rightward from IS' to IS'' raises the rate of interest in the U.S.A. from i_0 to i_1. Because the U.S. rate exceeds the world rate, there is a flow of capital into the U.S.A. which shifts the demand for dollars in the foreign exchange market rightward from D' to D'' in Fig. 7-14(b). For schedules D'' and S', the value of the dollar increases to E_1. U.S. exports fall, IS shifts leftward from IS'' to IS', and the rate of interest in the U.S.A. returns to the i_0 world rate. The government spending stimulus in the U.S.A. does not increase U.S. output but crowds out U.S. exports.

     (2) IS shifts rightward from IS' to IS'' as a result of increased government spending in the U.S.A. The i_1 rate of interest in the U.S.A. does not result in an increase in the demand for dollars and an appreciation of the dollar, since the world rate of interest has also increased as a result of fiscal stimuli. Output in the U.S.A. increases from Y_0 to Y_1. Fiscal policy in the U.S.A. is successful only because the world rate of interest has increased. Thus, fiscal policy is successful in a flexible rate environment when there is coordination of fiscal stimuli among the world market economies.

(b) Output in the U.S.A. does not increase in situation (1), while it does in situation (2). In a small country model with flexible exchange rates, a domestic economy is constrained from following an independent fiscal policy [situation (1)] to change output, since any such action causes its rate of interest to move away from the world rate. Any increase or decrease in a country's rate of interest causes the economy's exchange rate to increase or decrease, which offsets the fiscal action. When the domestic economy's fiscal action is coordinated with fiscal stimuli in other market economies [situation (2)], the fiscal action is successful, since the world rate has increased.

7.13 Suppose all market economies are below full-employment output; the world real rate of interest is i_0. In Fig. 7-15(a) output in the U.S.A. is Y_0 and the rate of interest is i_0. The U.S. exchange rate in Fig. 7-15(b) is E_0. (a) For a small country model, establish what happens to output in the U.S.A. when exchange rates are flexible and (1) an increase in the U.S. money supply shifts LM in Fig. 7-15(a) rightward from LM' to LM'' and no policy action is taken by other countries; (2) the money supply increase in the U.S.A. shifts LM rightward from LM' to LM'' in Fig. 7-15(a), and the world rate of interest decreases from i_0 to i_2 as a result of an increase in the money supply in other market economies. (b) Explain the outcome in situations (1) and (2).

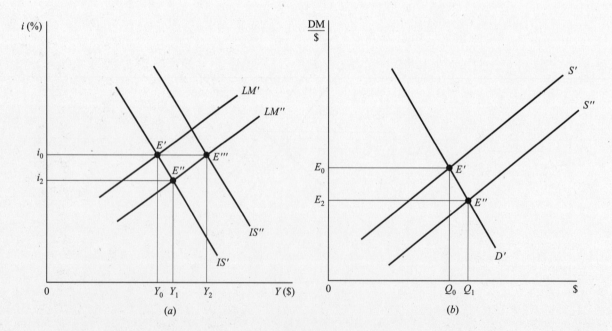

Fig. 7-15

(a)   (1) The increase in the money supply in the U.S.A. shifts LM in Fig. 7.15(a) from LM' to LM''; the intersection of IS' and LM'' determines an i_2 rate of interest. Since the rate of interest in the U.S.A. is now lower than the i_0 world rate, capital flows from the U.S.A. and there is an increase in the supply of dollars in the foreign exchange markets. The supply of dollars schedule in Fig. 7-15(b) shifts from S' to S'' and the exchange rate falls from E_0 to E_2. The depreciation of the dollar increases U.S. exports and IS shifts rightward. IS is eventually located at IS'', and the U.S. rate of interest, at the intersection of IS'' and LM'', equals the i_0 world rate. The increase in the U.S. money supply has increased U.S. output from Y_0 to Y_2.

(2) The increase in the U.S. money supply shifts LM from LM' to LM''; the rate of interest for LM'' and IS' is i_2. We shall assume that the increase in the money supply in other market economies lowers the world rate to i_2. Because there is a similar decrease in the U.S. and world rates, there is no change in the value of the dollar and therefore no shift of IS. Output in the U.S.A. increases from Y_0 to Y_1.

(b)   There is a larger increase in output for the U.S.A. in situation (1), when the U.S.A. lowers its rate of interest and there is no change in the world rate, than in (2), when both the U.S. and the world rates decline. The lower U.S. rate in situation (1) causes the dollar to depreciate, which induces U.S. exports and a rightward shift of IS. In situation (2), there is no change in the value of the dollar or shift of IS, since the U.S. and world rates are decreasing at the same time.

7.14   Suppose all market economies are below full-employment output; the world real rate of interest is i_0. In Fig. 7-16(a), output in the U.S.A. is Y_0 and the rate of interest is i_0. The U.S. exchange rate in Fig. 7-16(b) is E_0. For a small country model, establish what happens to output in the U.S.A. when exchange rates are flexible and the U.S.A. increases government spending, which shifts IS rightward from IS' to IS'' in Fig. 7-16(a); other market economies increase their money supply and the world rate of interest decreases from i_0 to i_2.

The increase in government spending in the U.S.A. shifts IS from IS' to IS'' in Fig. 7-16(a); the U.S. rate of interest increases from i_0 to i_1 at the same time that the world rate declines from i_0 to i_2. Because of the higher rate of interest in the U.S.A., capital flows into the U.S.A. and the demand for dollars in the foreign exchange market in Fig. 7-16(b) increases from D' to D''. The U.S. exchange rate for schedules D'' and S' is E_1. The dollar's appreciation lowers U.S. exports. The decrease of U.S. exports results in a leftward

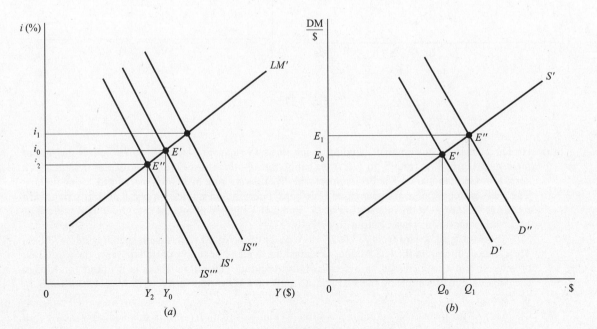

Fig. 7-16

shift of IS from IS'' to IS''', where the intersection of IS''' and LM' determines a U.S. rate of i_2, which is at parity with the lower world rate. The U.S. fiscal stimulus has no effect upon U.S. output; and U.S. output is lowered from Y_0 to Y_2 because of the decrease in the world rate.

MONETARY AND FISCAL POLICY IN A FIXED EXCHANGE RATE ENVIRONMENT

7.15 Suppose all market economies are below full-employment output; the world real rate of interest is i_0. In Fig. 7-17(a), output in the U.S.A. is Y_0 and the rate of interest is i_0. The U.S. exchange rate in Fig. 7-17(b) is E_0. (a) For a small country model, establish what happens to output in the U.S.A. when exchange rates are fixed and (1) the U.S.A. increases government spending, IS shifts rightward from IS' to IS'' in Fig. 7-17(a), and no policy action is taken by other countries; (2) the U.S.A. increases government spending, IS shifts rightward from IS' to IS'', and the world rate of interest increases from i_0 to i_1 as a result of fiscal stimuli in other market economies. (b) Explain the outcome in situations (1) and (2).

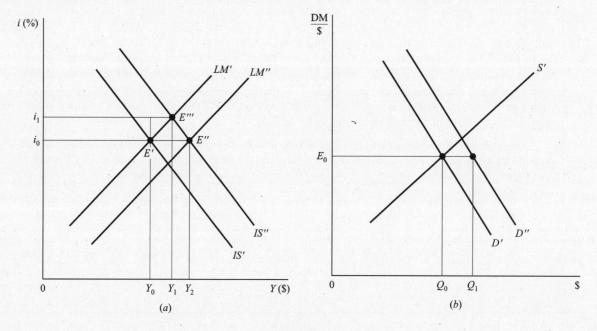

Fig. 7-17

(a) (1) The increase in government spending which shifts IS rightward from IS' to IS'' raises the rate of interest in the U.S.A. from i_0 to i_1. At exchange rate E_0 there is a $Q_0 Q_1$ shortage of dollars and a surplus of German marks. The Fed supports the E_0 exchange rate by buying marks and selling dollars. The Fed's purchase of marks increases U.S. bank reserves and money supply. LM shifts rightward from LM' to LM''. At the intersection of IS'' and LM'', the rate of interest is at the i_0 world rate. The U.S. fiscal stimulus increases output from Y_0 to Y_2.

(2) IS shifts rightward from IS' to IS'' as a result of increased government spending in the U.S.A. The i_1 rate of interest in the U.S.A. does not affect the demand or supply of dollars, since the world rate of interest has also increased as a result of fiscal stimuli. Therefore, there is no need for foreign exchange rate intervention by the Fed and no shift of LM. Output in the U.S.A. increases from Y_0 to Y_1.

(b) There is a larger increase in output in situation (1) than in situation (2). In a small country model with fixed exchange rates, the monetary authority must support the country's fixed exchange rate. Thus, a fiscal stimulus that puts upward pressure on the domestic rate of interest requires an increase in the domestic money supply to keep the domestic interest rate at parity with the world rate. When the domestic economy's fiscal stimulus coordinates with fiscal stimuli in other market economies [situation (2)], the fiscal stimulus has a smaller output effect, since it is not necessary to increase the domestic money supply to support the fixed exchange rate.

7.16 Suppose all market economies are below full-employment output; the world real rate of interest is i_0. In Fig. 7-18(a) output in the U.S.A. is Y_0 and the rate of interest is i_0. The U.S. exchange rate in Fig. 7-18(b) is E_0. (a) For a small country model, establish what happens to output in the U.S.A. when exchange rates are fixed and (1) an increase in the U.S. money supply shifts LM in Fig. 7-18(a) rightward from LM' to LM'' and no policy action is taken by other countries; (2) the money supply increase in the U.S.A. shifts LM rightward from LM' to LM'' in Fig. 7-18(a), and the world rate of interest decreases from i_0 to i_2 as a result of an increase in the money supply in other market economies. (b) Explain the outcome in situations (1) and (2).

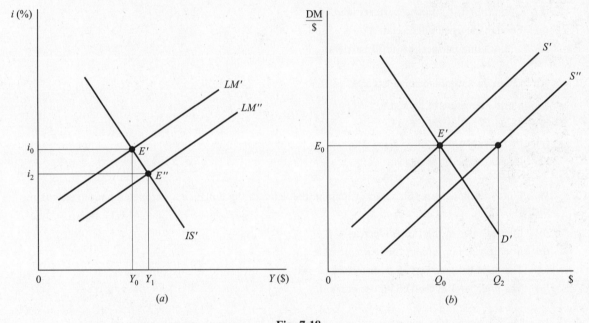

Fig. 7-18

(a)   (1) The increase in the money supply in the U.S.A. shifts LM in Fig. 7-18(a) rightward from LM' to LM''; the intersection of IS' and LM'' determines an i_2 rate of interest in the U.S.A. Since the rate of interest in the U.S.A. is now lower than the i_0 world rate, capital flows from the U.S.A. and there is an increase in the supply of dollars in the foreign exchange markets. The supply of dollars schedule in Fig. 7-18(b) shifts from S' to S'' and there is a dollar surplus of $Q_0 Q_2$ at exchange rate E_0. The Fed enters the foreign exchange market, exchanging dollars for marks. In selling, marks, U.S. bank reserves, and money supply decrease. LM shifts leftward from LM'' to LM' and the U.S. rate of interest returns to the i_0 world rate. Output in the U.S.A. remains at Y_0, since the Fed is unable to change the money supply to lower the U.S. rate of interest because it is committed to maintaining a fixed exchange rate.

   (2) The increase in the U.S. money supply shifts LM from LM' to LM''; the rate of interest for LM'' and IS' in Fig. 7-18(a) is i_2. We shall assume that the increase in the money supply in other market economies lowers the world rate to i_2. Because there is a similar decrease in the U.S. and world rates, there is no change in the supply and demand for dollars in the foreign exchange markets. Output in the U.S.A. increases from Y_0 to Y_1.

(*b*)   In a fixed exchange rate environment, a country can use monetary policy to increase output only when other market economies also expand their money supply to increase output. Thus, in situation (2), an increase in the money supply increases output only because other market economies are taking a similar action. Output in situation (1) does not increase because the monetary authority must support a fixed exchange rate. An independent monetary policy is not possible in a fixed exchange rate environment, since it creates disequilibrium in the foreign exchange markets.

Multiple Choice Questions

1.   Which of the following does not result in an increase in U.S. net exports?

(*a*)   The U.S. dollar depreciates.

(*b*)   Output for U.S. trading partners increases.

(*c*)   Foreign currencies depreciate.

(*d*)   U.S. trading partners lift tariff barriers.

2.   An increase in autonomous net exports.

(*a*)   Shifts *IS* rightward by $k_e \Delta \bar{X}$.

(*b*)   Shifts *IS* leftward by $k_e \Delta \bar{X}$.

(*c*)   Increases the slope of *IS*.

(*d*)   Decreases the slope of *IS*.

3.   Which of the following results in an increase in the value of the dollar in a flexible exchange rate environment?

(*a*)   Interest rates in the U.S.A. decrease.

(*b*)   Interest rates in foreign countries increase.

(*c*)   The price level in the U.S.A. increases.

(*d*)   The price level in the U.S.A. decreases.

4.   In a fixed exchange rate environment, an increase in the U.S. rate of interest results in

(*a*)   A depreciation of the dollar.

(*b*)   An appreciation of the dollar.

(*c*)   An increase in the U.S. money supply.

(*d*)   A decrease in the U.S. money supply.

5.   In the Mundell–Fleming model, an increase in the rate of interest in Country B

(*a*)   Increases the world rate.

(*b*)   Decreases the world rate.

(*c*)   Results in a depreciation of B's currency in a flexible exchange rate environment.

(*d*)   Results in an appreciation of B's currency in a flexible exchange rate environment.

6.   When Country B's rate of interest falls below the world rate in a fixed exchange rate environment,

(*a*)   B's exports decrease and *IS* shifts leftward.

(b) B's exports increase and *IS* shifts leftward.

(c) B's money supply increases and *LM* shifts rightward.

(d) B's money supply decreases and *LM* shifts leftward.

7. In the Mundell–Fleming model, an increase in Country B's money supply

(a) Increases B's exports in a flexible exchange rate environment.

(b) Decreases B's exports in a flexible exchange rate environment.

(c) Increases B's exports in a fixed exchange rate environment.

(d) Decreases B's exports in a fixed exchange rate environment.

8. When exchange rates are flexible, a decrease in Country B's taxes

(a) Has no effect upon output in Country B.

(b) Causes output in Country B to increase.

(c) Results in an increase in Country B's exports.

(d) Results in a decrease in the value of Country B's currency.

9. Which of the following does not increase output when exchange rates are fixed?

(a) There is an increase in the money supply.

(b) There is an increase in government spending.

(c) There is a decrease in taxes.

10. Which of the following increases output when exchange rates are flexible?

(a) There is an increase in the money supply.

(b) There is an increase in government spending.

(c) There is a decrease in taxes.

True or False Questions

11. _____ An increase in the marginal propensity to import decreases the slope of *IS*.

12. _____ An increase in U.S. exports shifts *IS* rightward.

13. _____ A decrease in the U.S. rate of interest in a flexible exchange rate environment causes the dollar to depreciate, exports to increase, and *IS* to shift rightward.

14. _____ Monetary policy in a fixed exchange rate environment is used to support the exchange rate; it cannot be used to change the rate of interest.

15. _____ In the Mundell–Fleming perfect capital mobility model, Country B's rate of interest must always equal the world rate.

16. _____ In the Mundell–Fleming model, a decrease in the world rate of interest will result in a decrease in the rate of interest in Country B in a flexible exchange rate environment.

17. _____ In the Mundell–Fleming model, an increase in the world rate of interest will not result in an increase in the rate of interest in Country B in a fixed exchange rate environment.

18. _____ Fiscal policy has no effect upon output in a flexible exchange rate environment.

19. _____ Country B's money supply must increase when B expands government spending in a fixed exchange rate environment.

20. _____ Monetary policy is ineffective in both a fixed and flexible exchange rate environment since the domestic rate of interest can not move away from the world rate.

Answers to Multiple Choice and True or False Questions

1. (*c*); **2.** (*a*); **3.** (*d*); **4.** (*c*); **5.** (*d*); **6.** (*d*); **7.** (*a*); **8.** (*a*); **9.** (*a*); **10.** (*a*); **11.** F; **12.** T; **13.** T; **14.** T; **15.** T; **16.** T; **17.** F; **18.** T; **19.** T; **20.** F.

Chapter 8

Schedules of Aggregate Demand and Aggregate Supply

Chapter Summary

1. The real money supply is presented as $\bar{M}/p$, indicating that the purchasing power of the nominal money supply ($\bar{M}$) depends upon the price level (p). An increase in the price level, *ceteris paribus*, decreases the real money supply, while a decrease increases it. Because the price level affects the real money supply, a change in the price level alters the equilibrium condition in the money markets and thereby the location of LM in space. An increase in the price level shifts LM leftward while a decrease in the price level shifts LM rightward.

2. Output is affected by each change in the price level, since LM shifts every time there is a change in the price level. An aggregate demand schedule is derived from the output effect of each change in the price level, with aggregate demand inversely related to the price level.

3. Chapter 6 demonstrates how IS shifts rightward when there is an increase in autonomous spending (e.g. $\Delta\bar{I}$, $\Delta\bar{G}$), while LM shifts rightward from an increase in the nominal money supply. Aggregate demand shifts rightward when there is a rightward shift of IS or LM and leftward when IS or LM shifts leftward.

4. In the short run it is reasonable to assume no change in productivity and/or the quantity of natural and capital resources. Thus, aggregate supply in the short run depends upon the number of workers employed in the labor markets.

5. The short-run neoclassical aggregate supply schedule is vertical, showing no relationship between the price level and output. This occurs because it is assumed that any price level change is incorporated immediately into both the supply of and demand for labor schedules. The nominal wage of labor thereby immediately mirrors any change in the price level. Since there is no change in the real wage from a change in the price level, output is also unaffected.

6. The short-run "sticky-wage" aggregate supply schedule displays a positive relationship between the price level and real output. In this model, a change in the price level affects the demand for labor schedule but has no effect upon the supply of labor schedule. An increase in the price level lowers the real wage, increases the number of workers employed, and thereby raises output.

7. The short-run, positively-sloped aggregate supply schedule shifts leftward in the long run when labor contracts expire, labor incorporates the price level increase into its wage demand, and the labor supply schedule shifts leftward.

Chapter Outline

8.1 The Price Level and Equilibrium Output

8.2 Deriving the Aggregate Demand Schedule

8.3 Shifting Aggregate Demand

8.4 Aggregate Supply in the Short and Long Run

8.5 The Short-Run Neoclassical Aggregate Supply Schedule

8.6 The Short-Run Sticky-Wage Aggregate Supply Schedule

8.1 THE PRICE LEVEL AND EQUILIBRIUM OUTPUT

An increase in the price level decreases the purchasing power of the nominal money supply. It therefore follows that the real money supply is inversely related to the price level, and is presented as $m = \bar{M}/p$, where m is the real money supply, $\bar{M}$ is the nominal money supply, and p is the price level (Example 8.1). A decrease in the price level, which increases the real money supply, shifts LM rightward. An increase in the price level, which decreases the real money supply, shifts LM leftward. A price level change, thereby, has the same effect on the location of LM in space as does a change in the nominal money supply. That is, a decrease in the nominal supply and/or an increase in the price level shifts LM leftward, whereas an increase in the nominal money supply and/or a decrease in the price level shifts LM rightward.

EXAMPLE 8.1.   The real money supply increases from \$100 to \$200 when the price level remains at 1.0 and the nominal money supply increases from \$100 to \$200: $m = \bar{M}/p$; \$100 = \$100/1.0 and \$200 = \$200/1.0. The real money supply also increases from \$100 to \$200 when the nominal money supply remains at \$100 and the price level falls from 1.0 to 0.5: $m = \bar{M}/p$; \$100 = \$100/1.0 and \$200 = \$100/0.5. Obviously, the real money supply is unchanged when there is an equal relative increase in the nominal money supply and the price level.

EXAMPLE 8.2.   Schedule LM in Fig. 8-1 is derived from schedules of the demand for real money balances and of the real money supply m_0, given price level p_0 and nominal supply $\bar{M}$. Equilibrium output is y_0 for schedules LM and IS. A doubling of the price level from p_0 to $2p_0$, *ceteris paribus*, reduces the real money supply from m_0 to $0.5\,m_0$; LM shifts leftward to LM', and equilibrium output declines from y_0 to y_1. Thus, a doubling of the price level, *ceteris paribus*, lowers equilibrium output from y_0 to y_1.

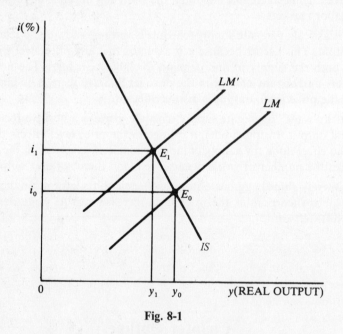

Fig. 8-1

8.2 DERIVING THE AGGREGATE DEMAND SCHEDULE

An aggregate demand schedule relates the price level to the output that exists when there is simultaneous equilibrium in the money and goods markets. In Fig. 8-2(a), the nominal money supply is constant; increases in the price level from p_0 to $1.1p_0$ to $1.2p_0$ shift monetary equilibrium leftward from LM to LM' to LM''. (LM is associated with price level p_0, LM' with price level $1.1p_0$, and LM'' with price level $1.2p_0$.) These leftward shifts of LM, due to a reduction in the real money supply, lower

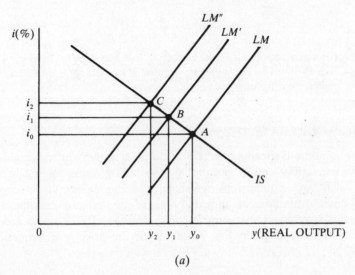

(a)

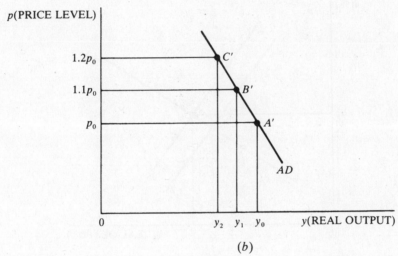

(b)

Fig. 8-2

equilibrium output and raise the rate of interest from i_0 to i_2. In Fig. 8-2(b) we derive an aggregate demand schedule by plotting equilibrium output y_0 with price level p_0, y_1 with price level $1.1p_0$, and y_2 with $1.2p_0$. The slope of aggregate demand depends on the value of behavioral coefficients b (the interest sensitivity of investment), k_e (the expenditure multiplier), h (the interest sensitivity of the demand for money), and k (the transaction demand for money-ratio).

EXAMPLE 8.3.   The equation for simultaneous equilibrium in the money and commodity markets is

$$y = \frac{hk_e}{h + kbk_e}(\bar{A}) + \frac{bk_e}{h + kbk_e}\left(\frac{\bar{M}}{p}\right)$$

where y represents real output, $\bar{A}$ autonomous spending, $\bar{M}$ the nominal money supply, p the price level, h the sensitivity of the demand for money to the rate of interest, k_e the spending multiplier, b the sensitivity of investment spending to the rate of interest, and k the transactions demand for money ratio. A change in the price level, *ceteris paribus*, has the following effect on equilibrium output:

$$\Delta y = \frac{bk_e}{h + kbk_e} \Delta\left(\frac{\bar{M}}{p}\right)$$

With price on the vertical axis and output on the horizontal axis, the slope of the derived aggregate demand schedule is $(h + kbk_e)/(bk_e)$. (See Problem 8.11.) Aggregate demand is less steeply sloped (flatter), the larger the value of b and k_e and/or the smaller the value of h and k.

8.3 SHIFTING AGGREGATE DEMAND

Changes in autonomous spending and/or the nominal money shift aggregate demand. An increase in the nominal money supply and/or autonomous spending shifts aggregate demand rightward, and decreases shift it leftward. Equilibrium output is y_0 in Fig. 8-3(a), given schedules LM, IS and price level p_0. This y_0 equilibrium position appears on aggregate demand schedule AD in Fig. 8-3(b) as point A'. An increase in government spending, *ceteris paribus*, shifts IS rightward to IS' with equilibrium output increasing from y_0 to y_1 in Fig. 8.3(a). With the price level remaining at p_0 in Fig. 8-3(b),

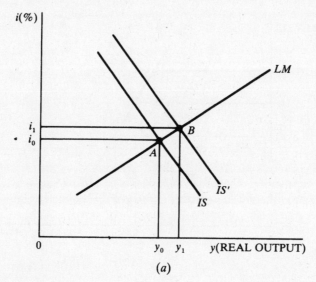

(a)

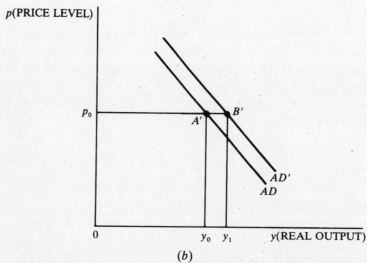

(b)

Fig. 8-3

equilibrium output y_1 is point B' on aggregate demand schedule AD'. Increases in autonomous spending $(\Delta \bar{A} > 0)$ shift aggregate demand rightward by $[hk_e/(h + kbk_e)]\Delta \bar{A}$, while increases in the nominal money supply shift aggregate demand rightward by $[bk_e/(h + kbk_e)](\Delta \bar{M}/\bar{p})$.

EXAMPLE 8.4.   The equation for simultaneous equilibrium in the money and commodity markets is

$$y = \frac{hk_e}{h + kbk_e}(\bar{A}) + \frac{bk_e}{h + kbk_e}\left(\frac{\bar{M}}{\bar{p}}\right)$$

Holding the price level and nominal money supply constant, a $\Delta \bar{A}$ increase in autonomous spending increases equilibrium output and shifts aggregate demand rightward by

$$\Delta y = \frac{hk_e}{h + kbk_e}(\Delta \bar{A})$$

Holding the price level and autonomous spending constant, a $\Delta \bar{M}$ increase in the nominal money supply increases equilibrium output and shifts aggregate demand rightward by

$$\Delta y = \frac{bk_e}{h + kbk_e}\left(\frac{\Delta \bar{M}}{\bar{p}}\right)$$

8.4   AGGREGATE SUPPLY IN THE SHORT AND LONG RUN

The economy's ability to supply in the long run depends upon human (L), capital (K), and natural (R) resources and productivity (T), i.e., $y = y(L, K, R; T)$. In the short run, productivity, capital, and natural resources are normally unchanged; therefore the economy's ability to produce depends upon the number of people employed. The dependency of short-run output upon the employment of labor is presented in Fig. 8-4 as a positive relationship between labor and output. Note that supply increases from y_1 to y_2 as the employment of labor increases from L_1 to L_2. Short-run supply thereby depends upon the supply of and demand for labor and therefore the number of workers hired.

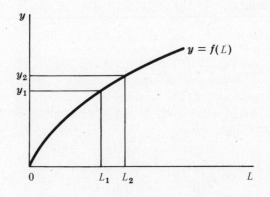

Fig. 8-4

8.5   THE SHORT-RUN NEOCLASSICAL AGGREGATE SUPPLY SCHEDULE

The Demand for Labor

The demand for labor depends upon the marginal revenue generated by each worker. As developed in Chapter 3, the incremental revenue associated with each worker depends upon the price at which output is sold and the marginal productivity of labor (MPL). When firms maximize profits, they hire additional labor until the marginal revenue product of the last worker hired equals the wage paid to that worker. That is, additional labor is employed until the marginal revenue product ($MPLp$) of the last worker hired equals the nominal wage (W) paid to that worker; i.e. $MPLp = W$ or $MPL = W/p$. The equation $MPL = W/p$ states that workers are hired until the value of their incremental output equals their real wage. The inverse relationship between labor units hired and the real wage is presented in Fig. 8-5 as L_d, which represents the demand for labor.

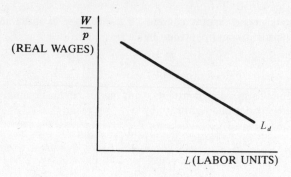

Fig. 8-5

EXAMPLE 8.5. Suppose the price level is 1 and the marginal physical productivity of labor is given by the equation $750 - 20L$. Labor's marginal revenue product is then $\$750 - 20L$ [$MPL\,p = (750{-}20L)(1)$]. A schedule for the marginal productivity of labor appears in Table 8-1.

Table 8-1

Labor Inputs	10	12	14	16	18	20
Marginal Revenue ($)	550	510	470	430	390	350

The Supply of Labor

Work competes with leisure. When workers attach a positive value to leisure, disutility is associated with working. It is normally assumed that the disutility of work is overcome by material reward. This behavior is presented in Fig. 8-6 as a positively sloped labor supply schedule, where more people are willing to work at a higher real wage.

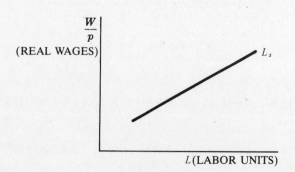

Fig. 8-6

Labor Market Equilibrium and Aggregate Supply

There is equilibrium in the labor markets when the demand for labor equals the supply of labor. In Fig. 8-7, this occurs when L_0 workers are employed and the real wage is W_0/p_0. The supply of labor shifts leftward and the demand for labor shifts rightward when there is an increase in the price level and the price level change is immediately incorporated into the supply and demand for labor schedules. Under such conditions, a change in the price level has no effect upon the real wage. Thus, in Fig. 8-8(a), L_0 workers continue to be employed when the price level increases from p_0 to $1.1p_0$ to $1.2p_0$. With the employment of labor unchanged, output remains at y^* in Fig. 8-8(b). The short-run neoclassical aggregate supply in Fig. 8-8(c) is vertical at output y^*, since a change in the price level has no effect upon labor market equilibrium and real output.

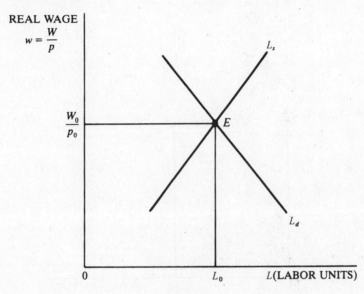

Fig. 8-7

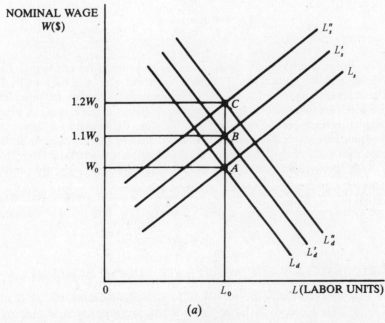

(a)

Fig. 8-8

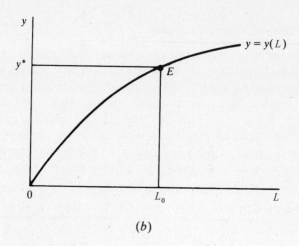

(b)

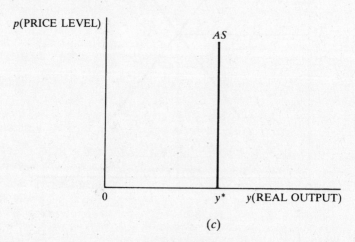

(c)

Fig. 8-8 (*continued*)

EXAMPLE 8.6. Suppose the price level is initially p_0, given the demand L_d for and supply L_s of labor in Fig. 8-8(a). Equilibrium in the labor markets occurs at a W_0 nominal wage. An increase in the price level to $1.1p_0$ or $1.2p_0$ shifts the demand for labor schedule rightward to L_d' and L_d'', respectively. (The marginal revenue product of labor equals the price at which goods are sold times the marginal physical product of labor; hence, a 10% or 20% increase in price causes the marginal revenue product of labor, and therefore the demand for labor, to shift rightward accordingly.) When the labor supply schedule also adjusts immediately to any increase (or decrease) in the price level, the labor supply schedule shifts leftward to L_s' when the price level increases 10% and to L_s'' for a 20% increase in the price level. Such proportional shifts of supply and demand keep the real wage intact—$W_0/p_0 = 1.1W_0/1.1p_0 = 1.2W_0/1.2p_0$—and the employment of labor remains at L_0. Labor market equilibrium with L_0 workers employed determines a y^* full employment level of output in Fig. 8-8(b). When labor market equilibrium is unaffected by the price level, aggregate supply is vertical [Fig. 8-8(c)] at a y^* full-employment level of output.

8.6   THE SHORT-RUN STICKY-WAGE AGGREGATE SUPPLY SCHEDULE

In the short run sticky-wage model, the supply of labor schedule does not shift in response to a change in the price level. This behavior is based upon a contract approach to employing labor. For example, the nominal wage for a unionized worker is fixed by the union's two- or three-year contract with a corporation. Even when a labor contract includes a cost of living adjustment (COLA) clause, wage adjustments are usually made annually or semiannually. In addition, most nonunionized workers have annual salary reviews; they thereby agree to work for a specific nominal wage for a one-year period. Thus, an increase in the price level in the short run, which shifts the demand for labor schedule rightward, results in an increase in the number of workers employed, since there is no shift of the labor supply schedule. An increase in the price level raises both employment and output. When employment is contractual, short-run supply is positively related to the price level. The labor supply schedule shifts leftward, however, when labor contracts expire and labor demands an increase in its nominal wage because of an increase in the price level. The number of workers employed and output decrease as a result of this shift of labor supply. A leftward shift of the supply of labor schedule thereby causes the positively sloped aggregate supply curve to also shift leftward. For example, aggregate supply AS_1 in Fig. 8-9 shifts leftward to AS_2 when the labor supply curve shifts leftward.

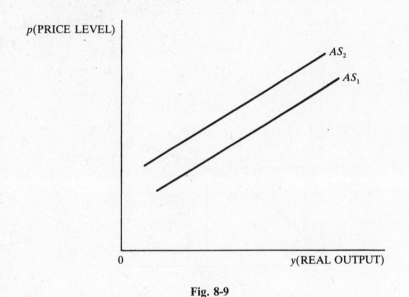

Fig. 8-9

EXAMPLE 8.7.   Aggregate demand and aggregate supply schedules AD and AS determine output y_0 and price level p_0 in Fig. 8-10(c). At price level p_0, L_0 workers are employed at nominal wage W_0 for schedules L_d and L_s in Fig. 8-10(a). In Fig. 8-10(b), real output is y_0 when L_0 workers are employed. Suppose aggregate demand in Fig. 8-10(c) shifts rightward from AD to AD' and the price level increases from p_0 to $1.1p_0$. This 10% increase in the price level shifts the demand for labor in Fig. 8-10(a) from L_d to L_d'; and L_1 workers are employed at a W_1 nominal wage. Because the 10% increase in the price level is greater than the W_0 to W_1 increase in the nominal wage, there is a decrease in the real wage and more workers are hired. The employment of L_1 workers raises output in Fig. 8-10(b) from y_0 to y_1, which is the output determined by the intersection of AD' and AS in Fig. 8-10(c).

EXAMPLE 8.8.   Example 8.7 shows that it is possible to increase output in the short run by moving along a positively sloped aggregate supply schedule. (Recall that aggregate supply is positively sloped and output is increased because the labor supply schedule does not shift as a result of a change in the price level.) When labor renegotiates its contract for the next period, it demands an increase in its nominal wage, since the price level rose faster than labor's nominal wage. For example, when labor contracts in Example 8.7 expire, labor demands an additional increase in its nominal wage, since the nominal wage increased by less than the 10% increase in the price level. Labor supply schedule L_s in Fig. 8-10(a) shifts leftward, which causes aggregate supply in Fig. 8-11 to shift leftward from AS to AS'. Output is y_0 for AS' at price level $1.1p_0$ and AS at p_0. Thus, in the longer run, when labor contracts can adjust for changes in the price level, output is unaffected by the price level.

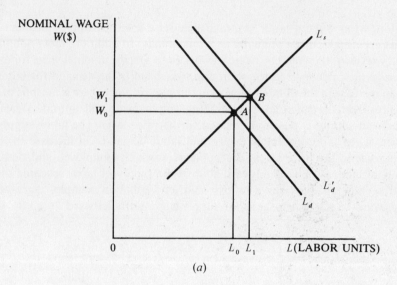

(a)

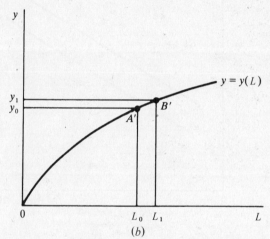

(b)

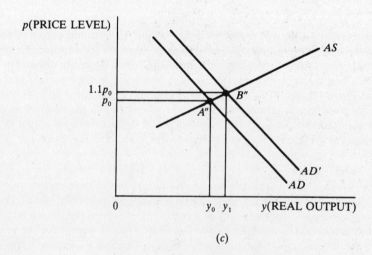

(c)

Fig. 8-10

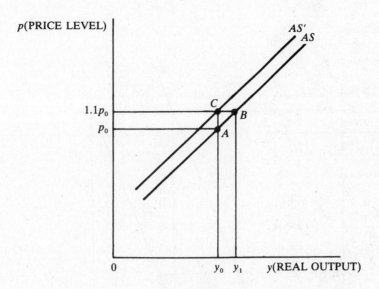

Fig. 8-11

Solved Problems

THE PRICE LEVEL AND EQUILIBRIUM OUTPUT

8.1   (a) What is the real money supply when the price level is 1, 1.5 and 2 and the nominal money supply is $450? (b) Explain why there is a negative relationship between the price level and the real money supply, *ceteris paribus*.

(a)   The real money supply equals the nominal money supply divided by the price level. When the nominal money supply is $450, the real money supply is $450 for a price level of 1, $300 for a price level of 1.5 and $225 for a price level of 2.

(b)   The nominal money supply is a stock of spending power whose value and therefore spending power falls as the price level increases. Thus, the spending power of the nominal money supply, and therefore the real money supply, is inversely related to the price level.

8.2   The money market is in equilibrium when the real money supply equals the demand for real money balances. (a) Find an equation for LM when the nominal money supply is $150, the price level is 1, and the demand for real money balances is given by the equation $0.20y - 4i$. (b) Plot and label LM the monetary equilibrium equation found in part (a). (c) Suppose the price level increases to 1.2, *ceteris paribus*. Find the new equation for LM, plot it and label it LM'. (d) What happens to LM when the price level increases, *ceteris paribus*?

(a)   Monetary equilibrium occurs where $\bar{M}/p = L$ or $m = L$:

$$\frac{\bar{M}}{p} = L$$

$$\$150/1 = 0.20y - 4i$$

$$y = \$750 + 20i \qquad (LM \text{ equation})$$

(b) See Fig. 8-12.

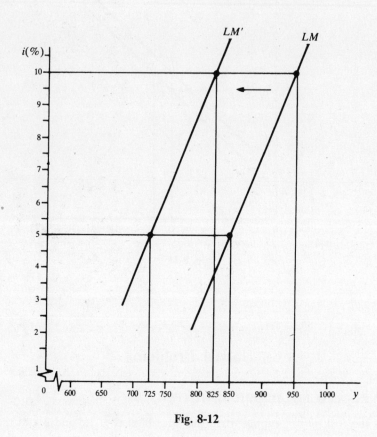

Fig. 8-12

(c)
$$\frac{\bar{M}}{p} = L$$
$$\$150/1.20 = 0.20y - 4i$$
$$\$125 = 0.20y - 4i$$
$$y = \$625 + 20i \quad (LM \text{ equation})$$

(d) An increase in the price level reduces the real money supply and shifts LM leftward.

8.3 In Fig. 8-13, the goods equilibrium schedule is IS' and the schedule for money market equilibrium is LM' for price level p_1. (a) Find output and the rate of interest for schedules IS' and LM'. (b) Find output and the rate of interest when the price level decreases from p_1 to p_2 and the monetary equilibrium schedule shifts rightward from LM' to LM''. (c) Why does the decrease in the price level from p_1 to p_2 increase output? (d) When there is no change in the price level might an increase in the nominal money supply result in a similar change in output and the rate of interest? Why?

(a) Simultaneous equilibrium in the money and goods market for LM' and IS' occurs at point A. The rate of interest is i_1 and output is y_1.

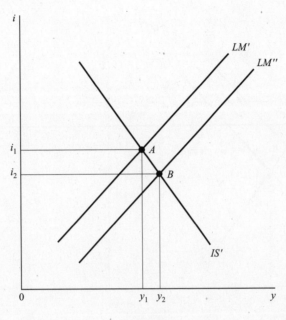

Fig. 8-13

(b) The decrease in the price level from p_1 to p_2 increases the real money supply and shifts LM rightward from LM' to LM''. Equilibrium for IS' and LM'' is at point B. The rate of interest decreases from i_1 to i_2, while output increases from y_1 to y_2.

(c) The decrease in the price level increases output because a fixed nominal money supply has greater purchasing power when prices are lower. Thus, the resulting increase in the real money supply lowers the rate of interest and raises interest-sensitive spending.

(d) An increase in the nominal money supply, with the price level unchanged, can also shift LM rightward from LM' to LM''. The location of LM'' is determined by the economy's real money supply. The economy's real money supply is increased by a decrease in the price level and/or by an increase in the nominal money supply.

DERIVING THE AGGREGATE DEMAND SCHEDULE

8.4 Suppose the nominal money supply is unchanged. In Fig. 8-14(a), curve LM' is associated with price level p_1 while LM'' is associated with price level $1.1p_1$. IS' is unaffected by a change in the price level. (a) Find output and the rate of interest in Fig. 8-14(a) when the price level is p_1 and $1.1p_1$. (b) Why is there an inverse relationship between the price level and output? (c) Plot the output associated with price level p_1 and $1.1p_1$ and label the aggregate demand schedule AD.

(a) In Fig. 8-14(a), output is y_1 for schedules IS' and LM' and the rate of interest is i_1. When the price level increases from p_1 to $1.1p_1$, LM shifts leftward from LM' to LM''. Output for IS' and LM'' is y_2, while the rate of interest is i_2.

(b) There is an inverse relationship between the price level and real output because an increase in the price level reduces the real money supply which results in an increase in the rate of interest. A higher rate of interest reduces interest-sensitive spending which decreases output.

(c) See Fig. 8-14(b).

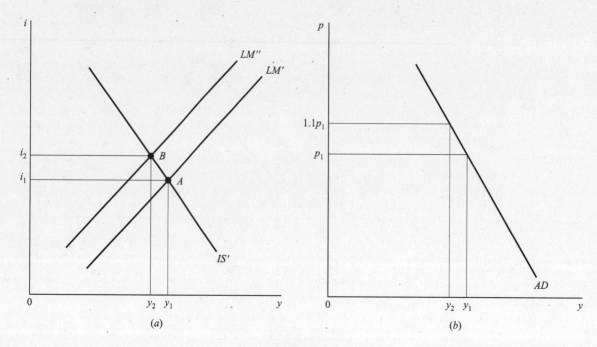

Fig. 8-14

8.5   Suppose the nominal money supply is unchanged. In Fig. 8-15(a), LM_1 is a schedule of monetary equilibrium for a model in which the demand for money is interest-sensitive, while the demand for money is less interest-sensitive for schedule LM_2. A decrease in the price level from p_1 to p_2 shifts schedules LM_1 and LM_2 rightward by $y_0\,y_3$ to LM_1' and LM_2'. (a) Find output and the rate of interest when a p_1 to p_2 decrease in the price level shifts LM_1 to LM_1' and LM_2 to LM_2'. (b) In Fig. 8-15(b), derive an aggregate demand curve from schedules LM_1 and LM_1' and from schedules

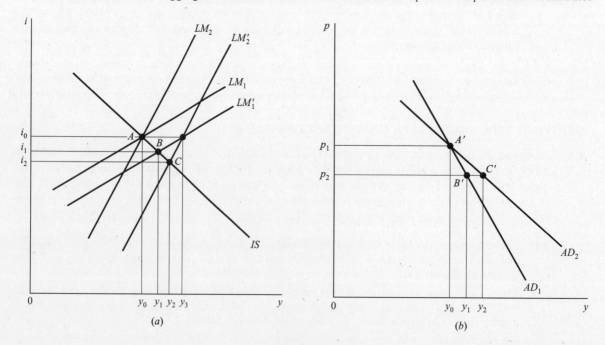

Fig. 8-15

LM_2 and LM_2'. (c) Explain why the aggregate demand curve derived from LM_1 and LM_1' is less steeply sloped than the aggregate demand curve derived from LM_2 and LM_2'.

(a) Simultaneous equilibrium for IS and LM_1 and for IS and LM_2 exists at point A, where the rate of interest is i_0 and output is y_0. Simultaneous equilibrium for IS and LM_1' occurs at point B, where the rate of interest is i_1 and output is y_1. Simultaneous equilibrium for IS and LM_2' occurs at point C, where the rate of interest is i_2 and output is y_2.

(b) Schedule AD_1, plotted in Fig. 8-15(b), is derived from LM_1, IS and LM_1', while AD_2 is derived from IS, LM_2 and LM_2'.

(c) AD_1 in Fig. 8-15(b) is more steeply sloped than AD_2. The same increase in the real money supply has a smaller effect upon the rate of interest for LM_1' than LM_2' because the demand for money is more interest-sensitive for schedule LM_1'. As LM_2 shifts rightward, the larger decrease in the rate of interest has a greater output effect, which results in a less steeply sloped aggregate demand schedule.

8.6   What factors are responsible for the negative slope of aggregate demand?

Aggregate demand is derived from the output effect that price level changes have upon the real money supply and therefore the intersection of IS and LM. The factors which influence the slope of aggregate demand are the same as those which affect the output effect of a change in the nominal supply. In Chapter 6 we found that the output effect of a change in the nominal money supply is greatest when investment spending is interest-sensitive, the expenditure multiplier is large, demand for money is not interest-sensitive, and the transactions demand for money ratio is small. A change in the real money supply through a change in the price level thereby has its greater output effect for similar behavior. It therefore follows that aggregate demand is less steeply sloped when the demand for money is interest-insensitive, the transactions demand ratio is small, the expenditure multiplier is large, and investment spending is interest-sensitive.

8.7   The IS equation is $y = \$1250 - 30i$ when $C = \$100 + 0.80Yd$, $I = \$150 - 6i$, $Tx = \$50$, and $G = \$40$. When the nominal money supply is $\$150$ and the demand for money is $0.20y - 4i$, the LM equation is $y = \$750 + 20i$ when the price level is 1.00; $y = \$625 + 20i$ when the price level is 1.20; $y = \$500 + 20i$ when the price level is 1.50. (a) Find simultaneous equilibrium for the money and goods market when the price level is 1.00, 1.20, and 1.50. (b) In Fig. 8-16, put the price level on the vertical axis and real output on the horizontal axis; from part (a) plot the equilibrium output associated with price levels 1.00, 1.20, and 1.50 and label the schedule AD. (c) Would simultaneous equilibrium in the money and goods market have differed if the price level remained at 1.00 and the central bank decreased the nominal money supply from $\$150$ to $\$125$ to $\$100$?

(a)   Equilibrium output is $\$950$ for price level 1.00:

$$y = \$1250 - 30i \qquad (IS \text{ equation})$$
$$\underline{-(y = \$\ 750 + 20i)} \qquad (LM \text{ equation})$$
$$0 = \$500 - 50i$$
$$i = 10\%$$
$$y = \$950$$

Equilibrium output is $\$875$ for price level 1.20:

$$y = \$1250 - 30i \qquad (IS \text{ equation})$$
$$\underline{-(y = \$\ 625 + 20i)} \qquad (LM \text{ equation})$$
$$0 = \$625 - 50i$$
$$i = 12.5\%$$
$$y = \$875$$

Equilibrium output is $800 for price level 1.50:

$$y = \$1250 - 30i \qquad (IS \text{ equation})$$
$$\underline{-(y = \$\ 500 + 20i)} \qquad (LM \text{ equation})$$
$$0 = \$750 - 50i$$
$$i = 15\%$$
$$y = \$800$$

(b) Fig. 8-16.

(c) The real money supply declines from $150 to $125 to $100 when the price level increases from 1.00 to
1.20 to 1.50 and the nominal money supply remains at $150. When the price level remains at 1.00, the
real money supply undergoes a similar decline if the monetary authority reduces the nominal money
supply from $150 to $125 to $100. A decrease in the real money supply from $150 to $125 to $100, due
to an increase in the price level and/or a reduction in the nominal money supply, lowers equilibrium
output from $950 to $875 to $800.

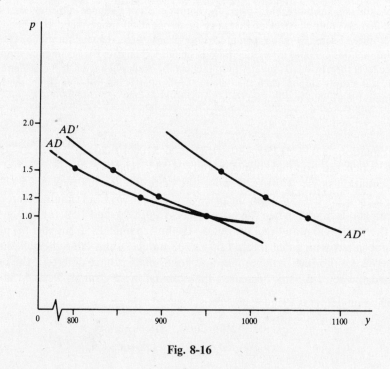

Fig. 8-16

8.8 Suppose investment spending is less interest-sensitive, with the investment equation now presented as $I = \$120 - 3i$ instead of $I = \$150 - 6i$ from Problem 8.7. The IS equation would
then be $y = \$1100 - 15i$ instead of $y = \$1250 - 30i$. We shall assume that the nominal money
supply remains at $150 and the demand for money is $0.20y - 4i$, as in Problem 8.7. (a) Find
simultaneous equilibrium for the money and goods market when the price level is 1.00, 1.20,
and 1.50. (b) Plot the relationship of real output and the price level and label the schedule
AD'.

(*a*)   Equilibrium output is $950 for price level 1.00:

$$
\begin{aligned}
y &= \$1100 - 15i \quad &(IS \text{ equation}) \\
-(y &= \$\ 750 + 20i) \quad &(LM \text{ equation}) \\
\hline
0 &= \$350 - 35i & \\
i &= 10\% & \\
y &= \$950 &
\end{aligned}
$$

Equilibrium output is $896.43 for price level 1.20:

$$
\begin{aligned}
y &= \$1100 - 15i \quad &(IS \text{ equation}) \\
-(y &= \$\ 625 + 20i) \quad &(LM \text{ equation}) \\
\hline
0 &= \$475 - 35i & \\
i &= 13.57\% & \\
y &= \$896.43 &
\end{aligned}
$$

Equilibrium output is $842.86 for price level 1.50:

$$
\begin{aligned}
y &= \$1100 - 15i \quad &(IS \text{ equation}) \\
-(y &= \$\ 500 + 20i) \quad &(LM \text{ equation}) \\
\hline
0 &= \$600 - 35i & \\
i &= 17.14\% & \\
y &= \$842.86 &
\end{aligned}
$$

(*b*)   See Fig. 8-16.

8.9   Suppose the demand for money becomes more interest-sensitive, changing from $0.20y - 4i$ to $0.20y - 10i$. When the nominal money supply is unchanged at $150, the *LM* equation is $y = \$750 + 50i$ when the price level is 1.0; $y = \$625 + 50i$ when the price level is 1.20; $y = \$500 + 50i$ when the price level is 1.50. The *IS* schedule is $y = \$1250 - 30i$ (Problem 8.7). (*a*) Find simultaneous equilibrium in the money and goods market when the price level is 1.00, 1.20, and 1.50. (*b*) Plot the relationship of the price level and real output and label the schedule AD''.

(*a*)   Equilibrium output is $1062.50 for price level 1.00:

$$
\begin{aligned}
y &= \$1250 - 30i \quad &(IS \text{ equation}) \\
-(y &= \$\ 750 + 50i) \quad &(LM \text{ equation}) \\
\hline
0 &= \$500 - 80i & \\
i &= 6.25\% & \\
y &= \$1062.50 &
\end{aligned}
$$

Equilibrium output is $1015.62 for price level 1.20:

$$
\begin{aligned}
y &= \$1250 - 30i \quad &(IS \text{ equation}) \\
-(y &= \$\ 625 + 50i) \quad &(LM \text{ equation}) \\
\hline
0 &= \$625 - 80i & \\
i &= 7.81\% & \\
y &= \$1015.62 &
\end{aligned}
$$

Equilibrium output is $968.75 for price level 1.50:

$$y = \$1250 - 30i \qquad (IS \text{ equation})$$
$$\underline{-(y = \$\ 500 + 50i)} \qquad (LM \text{ equation})$$
$$0 = \$750 - 80i$$
$$i = 9.375\%$$
$$y = \$968.75$$

(b)   See Fig. 8-16.

8.10   Compare the aggregate demand schedules AD, AD', and AD'' in Fig. 8-16. Why is there a difference in the slope of these aggregate demand schedules?

Changes in the price level affect the real money supply and thereby the rate of interest. LM shifts leftward, and the rate of interest increases when the price level increases and the real money supply declines; higher interest rates have a smaller effect on equilibrium output when investment spending is less sensitive to the rate of interest. Hence, a given increase in the price level (1.0 to 1.2) has a smaller effect upon output in Problem 8.8 (real output declines from \$950 to \$896) than in Problem 8.7 (real output falls from \$950 to \$875). Because investment spending is less interest-sensitive in Problem 8.7, AD' is more steeply sloped than AD. The interest sensitivity of the demand for money also affects the change in output for a given change in the price level. A 20% increase in the price level causes output to decline from \$1062.50 to \$1015.625 in Problem 8.9 and from \$950 to \$875 in Problem 8.7. AD'' is more steeply sloped than AD because the demand for money is more interest-sensitive for schedule AD''.

8.11   Simultaneous equilibrium in the money and goods markets is given by the equation

$$y = \frac{hk_e}{h + kbk_e}(\bar{A}) + \frac{bk_e}{h + kbk_e}\left(\frac{\bar{M}}{p}\right)$$

(a) Find an expression which relates the change in output to a change in the price level. (b) What does the equation in part (a) represent? (c) Find the slope of aggregate demand.

(a)   Holding the values of $\bar{A}$, $\bar{M}$, and the behavioral coefficients constant, $\Delta y = [bk_e/(h + kbk_e)]\Delta(\bar{M}/p)$, where $\Delta(\bar{M}/p)$ represents a change in the real money supply due to a change in the price level.

(b)   The equation in part (a) measures movement along an aggregate demand schedule for a change in the price level.

(c)   The slope of a straight line is $\Delta y/\Delta x$. With price p on the y-axis and output y on the x-axis, the slope of aggregate demand is $(h + kbk_e)/bk_e$.

8.12   What happens to the slope of the aggregate demand schedule when there is an increase in b, the interest sensitivity of investment; k_e, the expenditure multiplier; h, the interest sensitivity of the demand for money; and k, the transaction demand for money ratio?

The slope of aggregate demand decreases (the curve becomes flatter) when b, the interest sensitivity of investment, and k_e, the expenditure multiplier, increase; the slope increases (the curve is steeper) when h, the interest sensitivity of the demand for money, and k, the transaction ratio, increase.

SHIFTING AGGREGATE DEMAND

8.13   Suppose the nominal money supply is unchanged. In Fig. 8-17(a), LM' is associated with price level p_1, while LM'' is associated with higher price level $1.1p_1$. The goods equilibrium schedule is initially IS'. (a) Derive an aggregate demand curve from the equilibrium conditions for IS' and LM' and IS' and LM'' from Fig. 8-17(a) and plot it; label the derived aggregate demand schedule AD'. (b) Suppose an increase in government spending shifts IS rightward from IS' to IS''. Derive

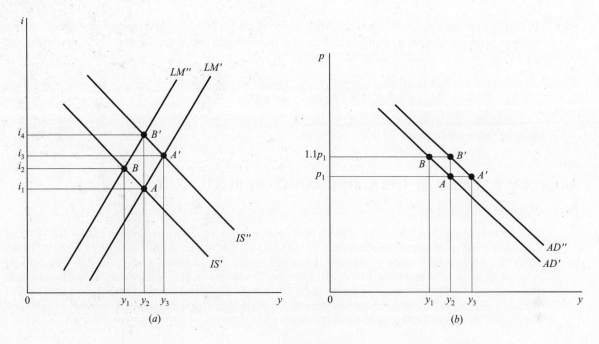

Fig. 8-17

an aggregate demand curve from the output associated with the new IS'' schedule, plot it, and label it AD''. (c) What effect does a rightward shift of IS have upon aggregate demand? What effect would an increase in the nominal money supply and therefore a rightward shift of LM have?

(a) There is simultaneous equilibrium in the goods and money markets for IS' and LM' (price level p_1) and IS' and LM'' (price level $1.1p_1$) at output y_2 and y_1. The price level p_1 which is associated with output y_2 and price level $1.1p_1$ with y_1 are plotted in Fig. 8-17(b) and the resulting schedule is labeled AD'.

(b) Simultaneous equilibrium for IS'' and LM' and IS'' and LM'' exists at levels y_3 and y_2. The association of price level p_1 with output y_3 and price level $1.1p_1$ with output y_2 are plotted in Fig. 8-17(b); the resulting schedule is labeled AD''.

(c) Aggregate demand shifts rightward when there is a rightward shift of IS. Aggregate demand also shifts rightward when there is an increase in the nominal money supply and therefore a rightward shift of LM.

8.14 Find the shift in aggregate demand when there is an increase in the nominal money supply, *ceteris paribus*, and simultaneous equilibrium in the money and commodity markets is given by the equation

$$y = \frac{hk_e}{h + kbk_e}(\bar{A}) + \frac{bk_e}{h + kbk_e}\left(\frac{\bar{M}}{p}\right)$$

An increase in the nominal money supply, holding other variables constant, shifts aggregate demand rightward by $\Delta y = [bk_e/(h + kbk_e)](\Delta\bar{M}/\bar{p})$, where $\Delta\bar{M}$ represents a change in the nominal money supply with the price level held constant.

8.15 Find the shift in aggregate demand when there is an increase in government spending, *ceteris paribus*, and simultaneous equilibrium in the money and commodity markets is given by the equation

$$y = \frac{hk_e}{h + kbk_e}(\bar{A}) + \frac{bk_e}{h + kbk_e}\left(\frac{\bar{M}}{p}\right)$$

Holding other variables constant, an increase in autonomous government spending shifts aggregate demand rightward by $\Delta y = [hk_e/(h + kbk_e)]\Delta \bar{G}$.

AGGREGATE SUPPLY IN THE SHORT AND LONG RUN

8.16 What is the difference between an economy's short-run and long-run supply curves?

An economy's long-run ability to produce depends upon the quantity of human (L), natural (R), and capital (K) resources and their productivity (T). Thus, long-run output is a function of L, R, K; T. In the short run, the quantity of natural and capital resources—factories, machines, tools, and land—are assumed to be unchanged, as is the productivity of all resources. The economy's ability to produce then depends upon the employment of labor. Thus, aggregate supply in the short run depends upon the supply of and demand for labor and thereby the equilibrium condition which exists in the labor markets. The analysis of aggregate supply in Chapters 8 and 9 focuses upon the short run.

THE SHORT-RUN NEOCLASSICAL AGGREGATE SUPPLY SCHEDULE

8.17 (*a*) From the short-run schedule of aggregate output in Table 8-2, find the incremental output associated with an additional worker. (*b*) Find the incremental revenue from each additional worker when the price level is 1.0, 1.1, and 1.2. (*c*) Plot the data from part (*b*). What happens to incremental revenue from each additional worker when there is an increase in the price level?

Table 8-2

Quantity of Labor	100	101	102	103	104	105	106
Aggregate Output	950	1000	1040	1075	1105	1130	1152

(*a*) The 101st worker increases output by 50. Thus, the incremental output for the 101st worker is 50, 40 for the 102nd, 35 for the 103rd, 30 for the 104th, 25 for the 105th, and 22 for the 106th.

(*b*) Incremental revenue from each additional worker equals *MPL* times p, where *MPL* (labor's marginal productivity) is the incremental output and p is the price level. When the price level is 1.0, incremental revenue of the 101st worker is $50, $40 for the 102nd, $35 for the 103rd, $30 for the 104th, $25 for the 105th, and $22 for the 106th. When the price level is 1.1, incremental revenue of the 101st through 106th labor input is, respectively, $55, $44, $38.50, $33, $27.50, and $24.20. When the price level is 1.2, incremental revenue of the 101st through 106th worker is, respectively, $60, $48, $42, $36, $30, and $26.40.

(*c*) The incremental revenue from each additional worker is plotted in Fig. 8-18. The schedule of incremental revenue shifts to the right when the price level increases from 1.0 to 1.1 to 1.2.

8.18 (*a*) Why is the labor supply schedule positively sloped? (*b*) What happens to the labor supply schedule when there is less disutility associated with work or there is an increase in the labor participation rates (a larger percentage of the working-age population seeks work)?

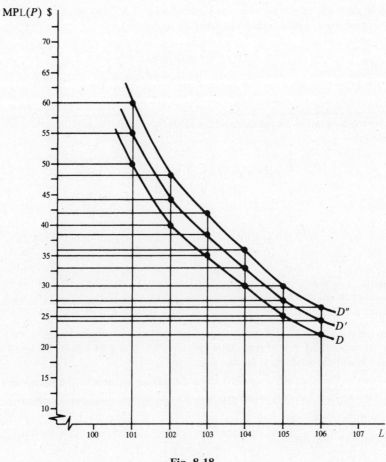

Fig. 8-18

(a) Work competes with leisure. It is believed that most people prefer leisure to work; a higher real wage, though, is sufficient incentive to encourage more people to work. Thus, the supply of labor is positively related to the real wage.

(b) The labor supply schedule shifts to the right when there is either a decrease in the disutility of work (labor is more willing to offer its services for a given real wage) or an increase in labor participation rates (a larger percentage of the working-age population seeks employment).

8.19   (a) Suppose the marginal physical production of labor is given by the equation $14 - 0.08L$, where L is the quantity of labor. How many workers are demanded when the price level is 1 and the nominal wage per labor unit is \$4, \$3, \$2, or \$1? (b) Find an expression for the demand for labor, given the equation for incremental revenue and incremental cost in part (a). (c). From the demand for labor schedule in part (b), find the number of workers hired when the price level is 1 and the nominal wage is \$4, \$3, \$2, and \$1. Plot the data and label the schedule L_d. (d) From the demand for labor schedule in part (b), find the number of workers hired when the price level is 2 and the nominal wage is \$4, \$3, \$2, and \$1. Plot the data and label the schedule L_d'. (e) What happens to the demand for labor when the price level increases, *ceteris paribus*?

(a) In a competitive market, workers are hired until the incremental revenue of the last worker hired equals the worker's incremental cost. The equation for incremental revenue is $p(14 - 0.08L)$. Incremental cost equals W, the nominal wage per worker. The number of people employed is found by solving the equation $p(14 - 0.08L) = W$ for L. When the price level is 1 and the nominal wage is \$4,

137.5 workers are employed when the nominal wage is $3, 150 when it is $2, and 162.5 when it is $1. [We assume a 0.5 worker equals one working half-time.]

$$1(14 - 0.08L) = \$4$$
$$0.08L = 14 - 4$$
$$L = 125$$

(b) We derive an equation for the demand for labor by solving the equation $p(14 - 0.08L) = W$ from part (a) for L:

$$p(14 - 0.08L) = W$$
$$0.08pL = 14p - W$$
$$L = 14/(0.08) - \left(\frac{W}{0.08p}\right)$$
$$L = 175 - 12.5\left(\frac{W}{p}\right)$$

(c) When the price level is 1, 125 workers are employed at a $4 nominal wage, 137.5 at a $3 nominal wage, 150 at a $2 nominal wage, and 162.5 at a $1 nominal wage. The data are plotted in Fig. 8-19, and the schedule is labeled L_d.

(d) When the price level is 2, 150 workers are employed at a $4 nominal wage, 156.25 are employed at a $3 nominal wage, 162.5 at a $2 nominal wage, and 168.75 at a $1 nominal wage. The data are plotted in Fig. 8-19, and the schedule is labeled L_d'.

(e) The demand for labor shifts upward when there is an increase in the price level, *ceteris paribus*.

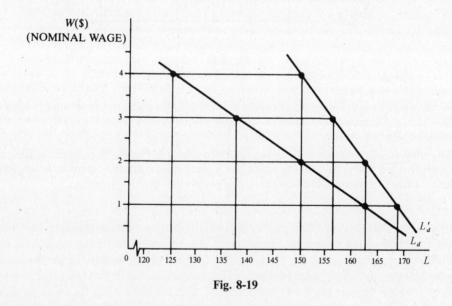

Fig. 8-19

8.20 Suppose the equation for the supply of labor is $140 + 5(W/p)$. (a) How many individuals are willing to work when the price level is 1 and the nominal wage is $4, $3, $2, $1? Plot the data and label the schedule L_s. (b) Find the number willing to work when the price level is 2 and the nominal wage is $4, $3, $2, and $1. Plot the data and label the schedule L_s'. (c) What happens to the labor supply schedule when the price level increases, *ceteris paribus*?

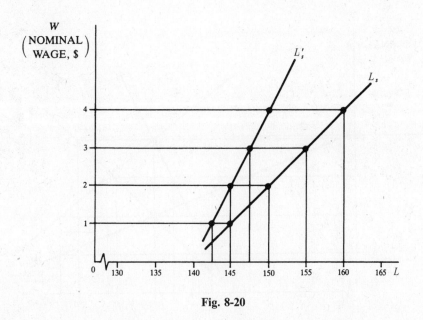

Fig. 8-20

(a) Substituting into the equation $L_s = 140 + 5(W/p)$, 160 individuals are willing to work when the price level is 1 and the nominal wage is $4: $140 + 5(4) = 160$. With the price level remaining at 1, 155 are willing to work at a $3 nominal wage, 150 at a $2 nominal wage and 145 at a $1 nominal wage. See Fig. 8-20.

(b) When the price level is 2 and the nominal wage is $4, 150 will work; 147.5 when the nominal wage is $3; 145 when the nominal wage is $2; 142.5 when the nominal wage is $1. See Fig. 8-20.

(c) The labor supply schedule shifts leftward when the price level increases, *ceteris paribus*.

8.21 (a) The demand for labor equation, $L = 125 - 12.5(W/p)$, and labor supply equation, $L_s = 140 + 5(W/p)$, are plotted in Fig. 8-21(a) when the price is 1 and 2. What happens to the number of workers employed (equilibrium in the labor markets) when the labor demand and labor supply schedules immediately incorporate a change in the price level? (b) Suppose a $600 output level is associated with the employment of 150 individuals. Put the price level on the vertical axis and real output on the horizontal axis; present and label *AS* the aggregate supply schedule. Why is it vertical?

(a) The equilibrium nominal wage is $2 when the price level is 1 and $4 when the price level is 2. The real wage (nominal wage/price level) is unaffected by an increase in the price level. One hundred and fifty individuals are employed before and after the increase in the price level.

(b) The aggregate supply schedule is vertical (Fig. 8-21(b)) because price level changes have no effect on the employment of labor and therefore output.

8.22 Why is the neoclassical aggregate supply schedule vertical?

Neoclassical analysis of the labor market assumes that any price-level change is incorporated immediately into the labor demand and labor supply schedules. Because of an immediate price-level adjustment, the number of workers employed is unaffected by the price level. Thus, the full employment condition in the labor markets, which is unrelated to the price level, results in an aggregate supply schedule which is also independent of the price level. Aggregate supply is therefore vertical.

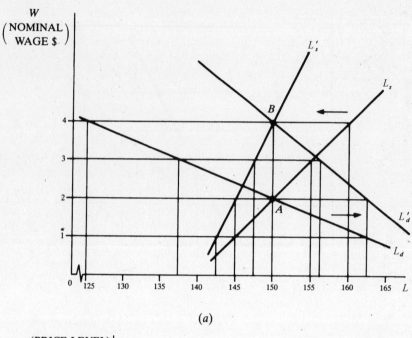

(a)

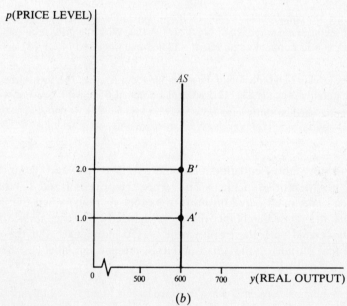

(b)

Fig. 8-21

THE SHORT RUN STICKY-WAGE AGGREGATE SUPPLY SCHEDULE

8.23   What does it mean that nominal wages are sticky in the short run?

Whether workers are unionized or nonunionized, labor's nominal wage is normally changed once a year in the U.S.A. Because of this practice, labor is unable to renegotiate its wage during the year in response to an unexpected increase in the price level, and its wage is fixed (stuck) for the year. This institutional behavior is presented in macroeconomics by a labor supply schedule that does not change in the short run. A sticky nominal wage does not mean, however, that the nominal wage paid to a new hire is also fixed. As the price level increases, the demand for labor shifts rightward and businesses pay a higher nominal wage to individuals who were unwilling to work at a lower nominal wage. The real wage of those under contract and those who are newly hired, however, falls in the short run; those who were employed prior to the price increase are obviously earning a lower real wage, since their nominal wage is unchanged; those who are newly hired also earn a lower real wage, since the increase in the nominal wage they receive is less than the increase in the price level.

8.24 Suppose labor agrees to work for a fixed nominal wage for one year. (*a*) Explain what happens to labor supply schedule L_s in Fig. 8-22 when the price level increases during the year from p_0 to $1.05p_0$ to $1.1p_0$. (*b*) Explain what happens to labor demand schedule L_d in Fig. 8-22 when the price level increases during the year from p_0 to $1.05p_0$ to $1.1p_0$. (*c*) What happens to the number of individuals employed when the price level increases from p_0 to $1.05p_0$ to $1.1p_0$?

(*a*) Labor is willing to work at the nominal wage rates depicted by L_s. There is therefore no shift of schedule L_s during the year, although the price level is increasing.

(*b*) Labor's marginal revenue product increases with the price level. Hence, labor demand schedule L_d shifts upward to L_d' when the price level increases to $1.05p_0$ and to L_d'' when the price level is $1.1p_0$.

(*c*) The number of individuals employed increases from L_0 to L_1 to L_2 as the price level rises from p_0 to $1.1p_0$.

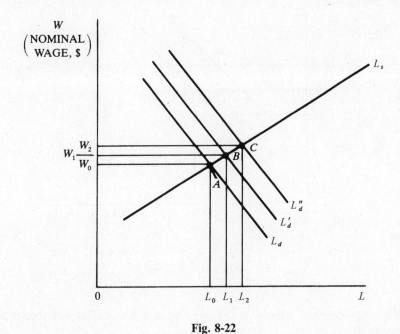

Fig. 8-22

8.25 Suppose labor renegotiates its nominal wage annually. In Fig. 8-23(*a*), the demand for labor schedule shifts upward when there is an increase in the price level, whereas the labor supply schedule remains unchanged. The productivity of labor is assumed constant. (*a*) Suppose labor demand schedules L_d, L_d', and L_d'' are associated with a p_0, $1.1p_0$, and $1.2p_0$ price level. From Fig. 8-23(*a*), find the number of workers employed when the price level is p_0, $1.1p_0$, and $1.2p_0$. (*b*) Suppose L_0, L_1, and L_2 are associated with output y_0, y_1, and y_2. With price level on the vertical axis and output on the horizontal axis, plot a short-run aggregate supply schedule and label it AS in Fig. 8-23(*b*) for price levels p_0, $1.1p_0$, and $1.2p_0$ and associated output levels y_0, y_1, and y_2.

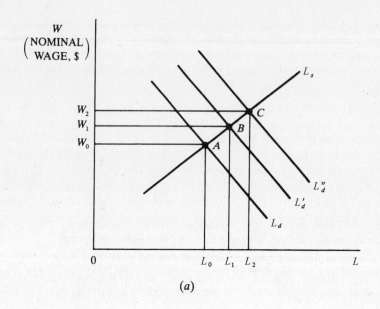

(a)

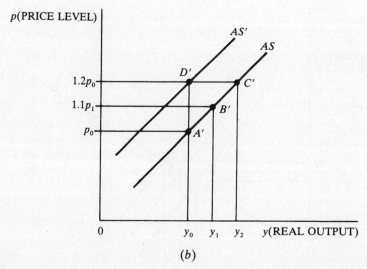

(b)

Fig. 8-23

(a) L_0 workers are employed at price level p_0; L_1 and L_2 workers are employed at price level $1.1p_0$ and $1.2p_0$, respectively.

(b) Aggregate supply schedule AS relates price level p_0 and output level y_0, $1.1p_0$, and y_1 and $1.2p_0$ and y_2. Because labor supply schedule is unchanged in the short run, aggregate supply is positively related to the price level.

8.26 What happens to aggregate supply schedule AS in Fig. 8-23(b) when one year later labor asks for a wage increase because the price level has increased from p_0 to $1.2p_0$?

Aggregate supply schedule AS in Fig. 8-23(b) shifts leftward to AS' one year later as labor demands a higher nominal wage because of the p_0 to $1.2p_0$ increase in the price level. Thus, along schedule AS' output y_0 is now associated with price level $1.2p_0$, whereas output y_0 was associated with price level p_0 one year earlier.

Multiple Choice Questions

1. Which of the following statements is not true?

    (*a*) When the relative increase in the price level is greater than the relative increase in the nominal money supply, the real money supply decreases.

    (*b*) When the relative increase in the nominal money supply is greater than the relative increase in the price level, the real money supply increases.

    (*c*) When the price level decreases, *ceteris paribus*, the real money supply decreases.

    (*d*) When the price level increases, *ceteris paribus*, the real money supply decreases.

2. An increase in the price level

    (*a*) Reduces the real money supply and shifts the *LM* schedule rightward.

    (*b*) Reduces the real money supply and shifts the *LM* schedule leftward.

    (*c*) Increases the real money supply and shifts the *LM* schedule rightward.

    (*d*) Increases the real money supply and shifts the *LM* schedule leftward.

3. The short-run labor supply function is

    (*a*) Positively sloped because of the disutility of work.

    (*b*) Negatively sloped because of the disutility of work.

    (*c*) Positively sloped because of the disutility of leisure.

    (*d*) Negatively sloped because of the disutility of leisure.

4. The demand for labor schedule

    (*a*) Shifts leftward when the price level rises.

    (*b*) Shifts rightward when the price level rises.

    (*c*) Shifts rightward when there is a proportionate increase in the price level and the nominal wage.

    (*d*) Shifts leftward when there is a proportionate increase in the price level and the nominal wage.

5. When the marginal physical product of labor is $800 - 2L$, the price of goods is \$2, and the cost of labor is \$4 per unit, the quantity of labor employed is

    (*a*) 20 units.

    (*b*) 399 units.

    (*c*) 800 units.

    (*d*) 80 units.

6. Aggregate demand is

    (*a*) Negatively related to the price level because a decline in the price level has a negative effect on the demand for output.

    (*b*) Negatively related to the price level because a decline in the price level has a positive effect on the demand for output.

    (*c*) Positively related to the price level because a decline in the price level has a negative effect on the demand for output.

    (*d*) Positively related to the price level because a decline in the price level has a positive effect on the demand for output.

7.   The slope of aggregate demand becomes flatter

    (*a*)   The more sensitive investment spending is to the rate of interest.

    (*b*)   The more sensitive the demand for money is to the rate of interest.

    (*c*)   The smaller the value of the expenditure multiplier.

    (*d*)   The larger the nominal money supply.

8.   Aggregate demand shifts

    (*a*)   Rightward when government spending decreases, *ceteris paribus*.

    (*b*)   Leftward when the price level increases, *ceteris paribus*.

    (*c*)   Leftward when there is a decrease in taxes, *ceteris paribus*.

    (*d*)   Rightward when the nominal money supply increases, *ceteris paribus*.

9.   A neoclassical aggregate supply schedule exists

    (*a*)   At an output level which is associated with zero rate of unemployment.

    (*b*)   At an output level determined by the supply of and demand for labor.

    (*c*)   When the demand-for-labor and supply-of-labor schedules adjust immediately to a change in the price level.

    (*d*)   When equilibrium in the labor markets is unaffected by a shift of the supply of labor schedule.

10.   Aggregate supply is positively related to the price level when

    (*a*)   Frictional and structural unemployment exists.

    (*b*)   The supply of labor schedule adjusts immediately to a change in the demand for labor.

    (*c*)   The demand for labor schedule adjusts immediately to the price level, and the labor supply schedule does not.

    (*d*)   The supply of labor schedule adjusts immediately to the price level, and the demand for labor does not.

True or False Questions

11.   _____ An increase in the nominal money supply, *ceteris paribus*, results in an increase in the real money supply.

12.   _____ The real money supply increases when there is an increase in the price level.

13.   _____ An increase in the price level, *ceteris paribus*, shifts *LM* leftward.

14.   _____ Aggregate demand is inversely related to the price level because an increase in the price level decreases the real money supply.

15.   _____ An increase in government spending, *ceteris paribus*, shifts aggregate demand rightward.

16.   _____ A neoclassical aggregate supply schedule is vertical because the supply of labor schedule does not adjust immediately to a change in the price level.

17.   _____ When there is a neoclassical aggregate supply schedule, a 10% increase in the price level results in a 10% increase in the nominal wage.

18. _____ Aggregate supply is positively sloped when labor supplies its services for a contractual wage for a specified period of time.

19. _____ A positively sloped aggregate supply schedule shifts rightward when there is an increase in the supply of labor.

20. _____ When there is a positively sloped aggregate supply schedule, a 10% increase in the price level does not result in a 10% increase in the nominal wage.

Answers to Multiple Choice and True or False Questions

1. (*c*); **2.** (*b*); **3.** (*a*); **4.** (*b*); **5.** (*b*); **6.** (*b*); **7.** (*a*); **8.** (*d*); **9.** (*c*); **10.** (*c*); **11.** T; **12.** F; **13.** T; **14.** T; **15.** T; **16.** F; **17.** T; **18.** T; **19.** T; **20.** T.

Chapter 9

Aggregate Supply and Aggregate Demand Analysis

Chapter Summary

1. The intersection of aggregate supply and aggregate demand determines output and the price level. The price level determines the location of *LM* in space, and *IS* and *LM* and aggregate supply and aggregate demand intersect at the same level of output. The price level also determines the location of the supply and demand for labor; their intersection determines the number of workers employed and the level of output, which is the same as that determined by the intersection of aggregate supply and aggregate demand.

2. A vertical aggregate supply schedule is a neoclassical aggregate supply schedule. Aggregate supply is vertical when a change in the price level immediately shifts the supply and demand for labor, and there is no change in the employment of labor and therefore output.

3. When aggregate supply is vertical, any shift of aggregate demand and/or aggregate supply changes the price level, and output remains at a full-employment level. A change in the price level caused by a shift of aggregate supply and/or aggregate demand may result in a redistribution of income and/or cause unwanted expenditure effects. Because of this, most economists support the use of economic policy to shift aggregate demand to a location where it intersects aggregate supply at the full employment level of output.

4. When aggregate supply is vertical and output is at its full-employment level, a change in the nominal money supply results in a proportional change in the price level. Money is neutral in this situation, since it does not change output or its composition. A fiscal action in a full-employment economy is not neutral because the output mix of public and private sector goods and services is affected by the resulting change in the rate of interest.

5. A positively sloped aggregate supply schedule exists when labor services are contracted, and the labor supply schedule does not shift in response to a change in the price level. When this exists, output may exceed its full-employment level. Once labor contracts expire and there has been an unexpected increase in the price level, the labor supply and aggregate supply schedules shift leftward, and output eventually returns to its full-employment level.

6. A supply shock occurs when the cost of labor or materials increases and aggregate supply shifts leftward. A supply shock results in a decrease in output and an increase in the price level.

7. The slope of aggregate supply is an unsettled topic in macroeconomics. In the new classical macroeconomics, a positively sloped aggregate supply schedule may develop as a result of imperfect knowledge and/or forecasting errors. Contemporary Keynesian macroeconomics suggests that labor contracts result in a positively sloped aggregate supply schedule for a period longer than is suggested by new classical macroeconomics.

Chapter Outline

9.5   Positively Sloped Aggregate Supply: Supply Shocks

9.6   The New Classical and Keynesian Macroeconomics

9.1   AGGREGATE SUPPLY, AGGREGATE DEMAND, AND THE PRICE LEVEL

The intersection of aggregate demand and aggregate supply determines output, the number of workers employed, the rate of interest, the composition of output, and the price level. In Fig. 9-1(a), aggregate demand and aggregate supply schedules AD and AS determine output y_0 and price level p_0. In Fig. 9-1(b), y_0 and p_0 are consistent with equilibrium in the money and goods markets at interest rate i_0 and a specific mix of public and private sector goods. The labor markets are in equilibrium [Fig. 9-1(c)] when L_0 workers are employed at a w_0 real wage ($w_0 = W_0/p_0$); the employment of L_0 workers in Fig. 9-1(d) is consistent with a y_0 level of output.

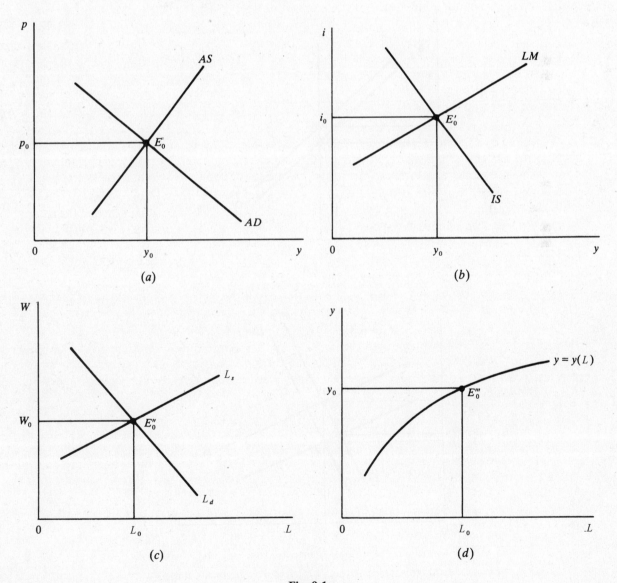

(a)

(b)

(c)

(d)

Fig. 9-1

9.2 NEOCLASSICAL AGGREGATE SUPPLY: DEMAND CHANGES

Aggregate supply is vertical when a change in the price level is incorporated immediately into the labor demand and labor supply schedules. Output remains at full employment along a vertical aggregate supply schedule when a shift of aggregate demand and/or aggregate supply is followed by a change in the price level. In Fig. 9-2(a), for example, output falls from output y_e to output y_1 when aggregate demand shifts leftward from AD to AD' and the price level remains at p_0. However, when the demand shift is followed by a decline in the price level from p_0 to p_1, output remains at its y_e full-employment level (see Example 9.1). Reliance upon a change in the price level to remedy a shift of aggregate demand and/or aggregate supply is likely to result in a redistribution and/or expectation effect. An unexpected change in the price level can redistribute income and wealth (see Problem 9.9). It is also possible that price expectations may influence spending decisions and contribute to a movement away from full-employment output (see Example 9.2). Because of possible negative expectation effects, most economists advocate intervention where an attempt is made to keep aggregate demand at a location where aggregate demand and aggregate supply intersect at the full employment level of output.

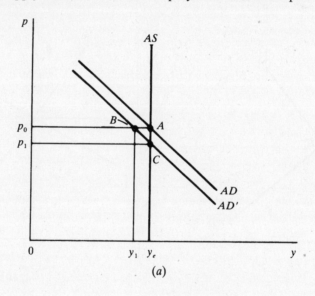

(a)

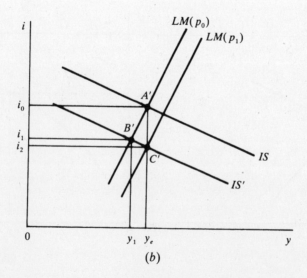

(b)

Fig. 9-2

EXAMPLE 9.1. Aggregate demand schedule AD and aggregate supply schedule AS intersect at point A in Fig. 9-2(a) and output is at its full-employment level y_e. Point A is represented in Fig. 9-2(b) by A' and the intersection of IS and $LM(p_0)$ with output at y_e and the rate of interest at i_0. A decrease in autonomous investment, *ceteris paribus*, shifts aggregate demand leftward from AD to AD'. When the price level remains at p_0, output falls to y_1. When the leftward shift of aggregate demand is accompanied by a decline in the price level from p_0 to p_1, output remains at its full-employment level y_e. The decrease in autonomous investment shifts IS leftward to IS' in Fig. 9-2(b). At price level p_0, IS' and $LM(p_0)$ intersect at B', and output and the rate of interest decrease to y_1 and i_1. When the price level falls to p_1 as a result of the decrease in autonomous investment, the real money supply increases, and LM shifts rightward to $LM(p_1)$. IS' and $LM(p_1)$ intersect at C', and output remains at full-employment level y_e.

EXAMPLE 9.2. Aggregate demand schedule AD and aggregate supply schedule AS intersect at point A in Fig. 9-3(a) and output is at its full-employment level y_e. Point A is represented in Fig. 9-3(b) by A' and the intersection of IS and $LM(p_0)$ with output at y_e and the rate of interest at i_0. A decrease in autonomous investment, *ceteris paribus*, shifts aggregate demand leftward from AD to AD'. When the private sector expects the price level to fall because of reduced spending, nonessential purchases are postponed; aggregate demand shifts further leftward to, say, AD'', and output declines to y_2 and not y_1 at price level p_0. These events are also presented in Fig. 9-3(b) by an initial shift of IS to IS' and then to IS'' due to the expectation of lower prices. Prior to a decrease in the price level, however, output decreases to y_2, determined by the intersection of IS'' and $LM(p_0)$. Eventually, output returns to its full-employment level y_e as analyzed in Example 9.1. Expectations push output to a lower level than would otherwise be the case. How long this lower level of output exists depends upon the amount of time needed for prices to fall to their new equilibrium level.

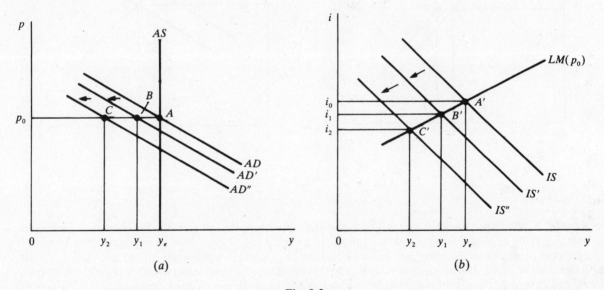

Fig. 9-3

9.3   NEOCLASSICAL AGGREGATE SUPPLY: MONETARY AND FISCAL POLICY

When monetary and/or fiscal policy stabilizes aggregate demand, there is no need for a change in the price level to keep output at its full-employment level. For example, the decrease in autonomous investment in Example 9.1 can be offset by an increase in government spending equal to the decrease in investment. Such an economic measure stabilizes aggregate demand in Fig. 9-2(a) at AD; and there is no change in price level p_0 or output y_e.

When output is at its full-employment level and there is an increase in government spending and/or the nominal supply, *ceteris paribus*, the price level increases and output is unchanged. An increase in the money supply causes a proportional increase in the price level, but has no effect upon either the rate of interest or output. Thus, a change in the nominal money supply is neutral, since it affects only the price level when output is at its full-employment level. A fiscal stimulus in a full-employment economy is not neutral. An increase in government spending, while not changing the level of output, increases both the price level and the rate of interest. In pushing up the rate of interest, some interest-sensitive investment spending is replaced by the higher level of government spending, and the economy's composition of output is changed.

EXAMPLE 9.3.   Output is y_e in Fig. 9-4(a) and the price level is p_0 for schedules AS and AD. A 10% increase in the nominal money supply shifts aggregate demand rightward from AD to AD'. Because there is at price level p_0 excess demand of $y_e y_1$, the price level increases from p_0 to $1.1 p_0$ to maintain equilibrium. In Fig. 9-4(b), LM shifts rightward from LM to LM' when the nominal money supply increases 10%. However, the resulting 10% increase in the price level returns the real money supply to its original level and LM' shifts rightward, back to LM. Thus, the 10% increase in the nominal money supply is neutral; it increases the price level 10%, but has no effect upon output and the rate of interest.

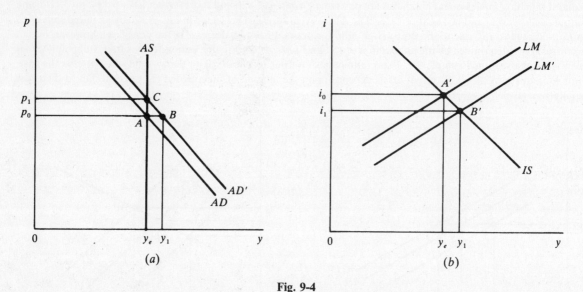

Fig. 9-4

EXAMPLE 9.4.   The price level is p_0 in Fig. 9-5(a) and output is y_e for AD and AS. An increase in government spending shifts aggregate demand rightward from AD to AD', and at price level p_0 aggregate demand exceeds aggregate supply. Once the price level increases from p_0 to p_1, there is equilibrium for AS and AD' at y_e. The intersection of IS and LM is initially at A' in Fig. 9-5(b). The increase in government spending shifts IS rightward to IS' and IS' and LM intersect beyond full employment at B'. The increase in the price level from p_0 to p_1 reduces the real money supply which shifts LM leftward to LM'. IS' and LM' intersect at C'. Real output is unchanged at y_e but the rate of interest increases from i_0 to i_2. The i_0 to i_2 increase in the rate of interest lowers interest-sensitive spending. The fiscal stimulus has changed the economy's composition of output since more goods and services are produced for the government sector while the production of investment goods is reduced. Fiscal policy is not neutral, since it has altered the types of goods and services produced.

9.4   POSITIVELY SLOPED AGGREGATE SUPPLY: DEMAND CHANGES

When aggregate supply is positively sloped, a change in aggregate demand impacts both output and the price level in the short run. In Fig. 9-6(a), for example, output is initially y_e and the price level p_0 for schedules AD and AS. An increase in government spending shifts aggregate demand rightward from AD to AD'. Schedules AD' and AS intersect at B, and output increases from y_e to y_1 while the price level rises from p_0 to p_1. Output y_1 is not a long-run equilibrium position, since aggregate supply eventually

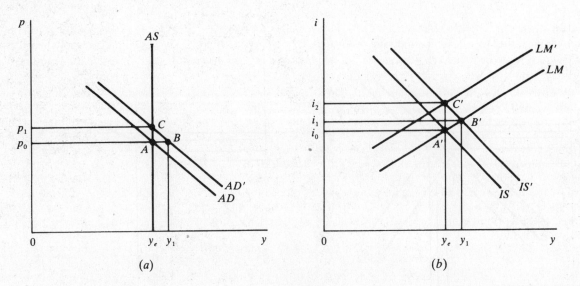

Fig. 9-5

shifts leftward. Upon the expiration of labor contracts, labor demands a higher nominal wage. This shifts aggregate supply leftward in successive periods until it comes to rest at AS''; AD' and AS'' intersect at D and output returns to full-employment level y_e.

EXAMPLE 9.5. The schedules of aggregate demand and aggregate supply AD and AS in Fig. 9-6(a) intersect at point A, with output at full-employment level y_e. An increase in government spending shifts aggregate demand

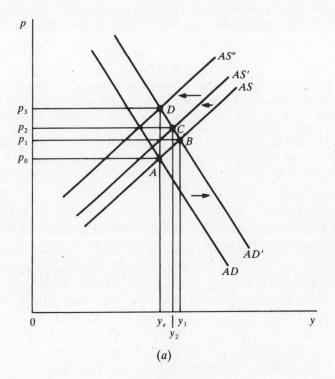

(a)

Fig. 9-6

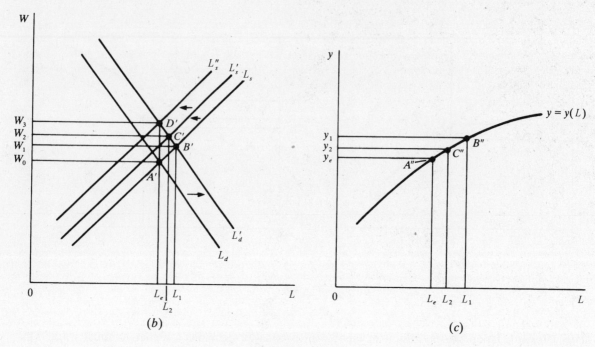

Fig. 9-6 (*continued*)

rightward from AD to AD'; the price level rises to p_1 and output increases to y_1. In the labor markets, the labor demand schedule is initially L_d and the labor supply schedule is L_s; L_e workers are hired at nominal wage W_0. The p_0 to p_1 increase in the price level in Fig. 9-6(*a*), caused by increased government spending, shifts the demand for labor schedule rightward from L_d to L_d'. Because contracts prevent the labor supply schedule from shifting, labor demand L_d' and labor supply L_s intersect at point B'; employment increases from L_e to L_1 workers and the nominal wage increases from W_0 to W_1. In Fig. 9-6(*c*), output is y_1 when L_1 workers are employed.

EXAMPLE 9.6. When the contract period in Example 9.5 ends, labor demands an increase in its nominal wage, since the increase in the price level exceeds the increase in the nominal wage. The labor supply schedule in Fig. 9-6(*b*) shifts leftward from L_s to L_s'. Labor market equilibrium for L_d' and L_s' is at point C'. The number of workers employed decreases from L_1 to L_2. Output in Fig. 9-6(*c*) is y_2 when L_2 workers are employed. In Fig. 9-6(*a*), the leftward shift of the labor supply schedule causes aggregate supply to shift leftward to AS'; AD' and AS' intersect at C. Because output is still above full-employment level y_e and the price level has increased again, labor demands a higher nominal wage upon expiration of its contract. Aggregate supply in successive periods shifts leftward until it reaches AS''; the intersection of AS'' and AD' at D returns output to full-employment level y_e.

9.5   POSITIVELY SLOPED AGGREGATE SUPPLY: SUPPLY SHOCKS

When labor is the only variable cost and firms utilize mark-up pricing in pricing output, per-unit supply price P equals $(1+\theta)W/a$, where θ is the mark-up on variable cost, W is the per-labor unit nominal wage, and a is the number of units produced by each labor input. The mark-up on labor cost covers the firm's fixed costs and provides it with a profit. When material costs are also variable in the short run, per-unit supply price P is written as $(1+\theta)W/a + P_n$, where P_n is the real per-unit cost of materials. There is a change in the supply cost of output when there is a change in W (the nominal wage), P_n (the real per-unit cost of materials), θ (the mark-up over variable cost) and/or a (the number of units produced per unit of labor input) alters the supply cost of output. A change in any of these variables shifts aggregate supply.

EXAMPLE 9.7.   The aggregate supply schedule AS in Fig. 9-7 is derived with the following variables held constant: the nominal wage W, the mark-up on variable cost θ, the productivity of labor a, and the real per-unit cost of materials P_n. An increase in nominal wages *or* mark-up on costs *or* real per-unit cost of materials, *ceteris paribus*, shifts aggregate supply leftward to AS'. An increase in labor productivity (the number of units produced per unit of labor input) lowers production costs and shifts aggregate supply rightward to AS''.

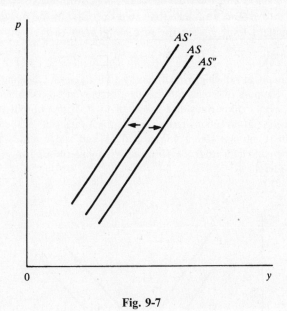

Fig. 9-7

OPEC's increase in oil prices in the 1970s raised the per-unit cost of materials. Because these oil price increases were permanent, aggregate supply shifted leftward, for example from AS to AS' in Fig. 9-8. The leftward movement of AS to AS' along aggregate demand schedule AD in Fig. 9-8 raised the price level from p_0 to p_1 and output fell from full-employment y_e to y_1. Because y_1 was less than full-employment output y_e, the actual rate of unemployment rose above the natural rate. (The association of rising

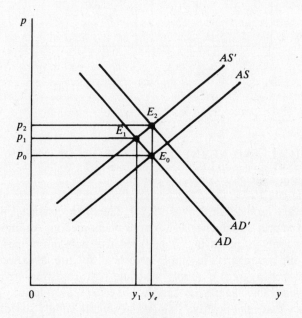

Fig. 9-8

prices and unemployment was classified as "stagflation" during the 1970s.) When government does not initiate an economic policy to alleviate the unemployment caused by higher material prices, the disequilibrium is remedied eventually by the labor markets. The nominal wage is reduced by a rightward shift of the labor supply schedule, which causes aggregate supply schedule AS' to shift rightward to AS; output returns to full-employment level y_e and the price level to p_0. A stimulative economic policy which shifts aggregate demand rightward to AD' is an alternative to a decrease in the nominal wage. Output returns more quickly to full-employment level y_e, but the price level rises to p_2.

EXAMPLE 9.8. Output is initially at full-employment level y_e, for aggregate demand and aggregate supply schedules AD and AS in Fig. 9-9. Suppose oil prices fall due to a surplus in oil production, i.e., the per-unit cost of materials declines. Aggregate supply shifts rightward from AS to AS'; real output rises to y_1 and exceeds full-employment output y_e. "Tightness" in the labor markets causes a leftward shift of the labor supply schedule and a higher nominal wage. Aggregate supply shifts from AS' back to AS, and output returns to y_e. A restrictive economic policy, which shifts aggregate demand leftward from AD to AD', is an alternative measure; the positive supply shock then results in a lower p_2 price level.

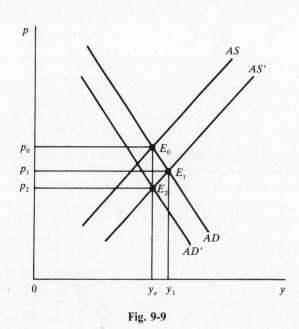

Fig. 9-9

9.6 THE NEW CLASSICAL AND KEYNESIAN MACROECONOMICS

The effect of a change in aggregate demand upon output depends upon the slope and location of aggregate supply. Since the late 1960s, there has been considerable discussion about and reformulation of Keynes' original rigid wage model (see Problem 9.20). The "new classical" macroeconomics views a positively sloped aggregate supply schedule as a short-run phenomenon. An imperfect knowledge model contends that aggregate supply is positively sloped because nominal wages "adapt" to price-level changes; however, in the long run, aggregate supply is vertical. A rational expectations model attributes the short-run positively sloped aggregate supply schedule to forecasting errors. Because forecasting errors have a zero expected value, aggregate supply is vertical over longer periods. Contemporary Keynesian macroeconomics bases the positively sloped aggregate supply schedule on institutional patterns such as wage contracts. Contemporary Keynesian analysis of the labor markets suggests that the positively sloped aggregate supply schedule persists for longer periods and is less steeply sloped than the one perceived by the new classical view.

Solved Problems

AGGREGATE SUPPLY, AGGREGATE DEMAND, AND THE PRICE LEVEL

9.1   The IS equation is $y = \$1300 - 30i$ when $C = \$90 + 0.80Yd$, $I = \$150 - 6i$, $Tx = \$100$, $G = \$100$; LM is $y = \$800 + 20i$ when the nominal money supply is \$160, the price level is 1, and the demand for money is $0.20y - 4i$; LM is $y = \$640 + 20i$ when the nominal money supply is \$160, the price level is 1.25, and the demand for money is $0.20y - 4i$. Find the output level at which there is simultaneous equilibrium in the money and goods markets for price level (*a*) 1.00, (*b*) 1.25.

(*a*)   When the price level is 1.00, simultaneous equilibrium in the money and goods markets exists when $y = \$1000$ and $i = 10\%$.

$$
\begin{aligned}
y &= \$1300 - 30i \quad &&(IS \text{ equation}) \\
-(y &= \$\ 800 + 20i) \quad &&(LM \text{ equation}) \\
\hline
0 &= \$500 - 50i \\
i &= 10\% \\
y &= \$1000
\end{aligned}
$$

(*b*)   When the price level is 1.25, simultaneous equilibrium in the money and goods markets exists when $y = \$904$ and $i = 13.2\%$.

$$
\begin{aligned}
y &= \$1300 - 30i \quad &&(IS \text{ equation}) \\
-(y &= \$\ 640 + 20i) \quad &&(LM \text{ equation}) \\
\hline
0 &= \$660 - 50i \\
i &= 13.2\% \\
y &= \$904
\end{aligned}
$$

9.2   Suppose the economy's short-run production equation is $y = 14L - 0.04L^2$, the demand for labor equation is $L_d = 175 - 12.5(W/p)$, and the labor supply equation is $L_s = 70 + 5(W/p)$. (*a*) Find labor market equilibrium when the price level is 1.00 and 1.25. (*b*) Find short-run supply when there is labor market equilibrium at price level 1.00 and 1.25.

(*a*)   When the price level is 1.00, labor market equilibrium exists when $L = 100$ and $W = \$6$.

$$
\begin{aligned}
L &= 175 - 12.5\left(\frac{W}{1.0}\right) \quad &&(\text{Labor demand}) \\
-\left(L &= \ 70 + \ \ 5\left(\frac{W}{1.0}\right)\right) \quad &&(\text{Labor supply}) \\
\hline
0 &= 105 - 17.5W \\
W &= \$6 \\
L &= 100
\end{aligned}
$$

When the price level is 1.25, and the equations for the supply and demand for labor adjust immediately to a price-level change, labor market equilibrium exists when $L = 100$ and $W = \$7.50$.

$$L = 175 - 12.5\left(\frac{W}{1.25}\right) \quad \text{(Labor demand)}$$

$$-\left(L = 70 + 5\left(\frac{W}{1.25}\right)\right) \quad \text{(Labor supply)}$$

$$0 = 105 - 17.5\left(\frac{W}{1.25}\right)$$

$$W = \$7.50$$

$$L = 100$$

(b)   Labor market equilibrium is unaffected by the price level; 100 workers are employed when the price level is 1.00 or 1.25. Hence, short-run supply is $1000 at both price levels:

$$y = 14L - 0.04L^2$$
$$y = 1400 - 400 = 1000$$

9.3   Utilize the solutions in Problems 9.1 and 9.2 to explain why there is equilibrium in the money, goods, and labor markets at only one price level.

Because the labor demand and supply equations in Problem 9.2 are immediately affected by a change in the price level, labor market equilibrium is unaffected by the price level. However, the price level affects the real money supply in Problem 9.1; money and goods market equilibrium exists at $y = \$1000$ when the price level is 1.00 and at $y = \$904$ when the price level is 1.25. When the price level is 1.00, aggregate demand ($y = \$1000$) equals aggregate supply ($y = \$1000$); however, when the price level is 1.25, aggregate demand ($y = \$904$) is less than aggregate supply ($y = \$1000$). When the price level affects the real money supply (and therefore the location of the LM schedule in space), there is only one price level at which there is equilibrium in the money, goods, and labor markets.

9.4   Aggregate demand AD in Fig. 9-10(a) is derived from the money and goods market equilibrium schedules in Fig. 9-10(b). Explain why equilibrium does not exist at price level p_0. What must happen to the price level?

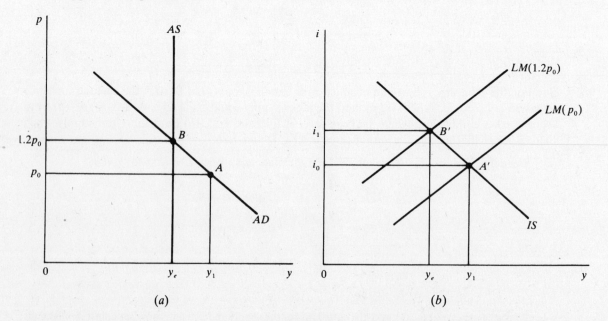

Fig. 9-10

Point A in Fig. 9-10(a) is the counterpart of A' in Fig. 9-10(b). At point A there is disequilibrium, since aggregate demand exceeds aggregate supply. As a result of this shortage of output, the price level increases from p_0 to $1.2p_0$ in Fig. 9-10(a); at point B, aggregate demand equals aggregate supply at output y_e. The 20% increase in the price level causes LM to shift leftward from $LM(p_0)$ to $LM(1.2p_0)$ in Fig. 9-10(b); there is equilibrium in the money and goods market at B', with output at y_e and the rate of interest at i_1.

NEOCLASSICAL AGGREGATE SUPPLY: DEMAND CHANGES

9.5   Schedules AD and AS in Fig. 9-11(a) are in equilibrium at full-employment output y_e and price level p_0. This equilibrium condition is also depicted in Fig. 9-11(b) for goods and money market schedules IS and $LM(p_0)$. (a) Explain what happens to the IS, LM, and AD schedules and the equilibrium condition when taxes are increased, *ceteris paribus*. (b) Explain how the price level corrects for the disequilibrium caused by a tax increase.

(a)   Increased taxes shift IS leftward to IS' in Fig. 9-11(b) and aggregate demand leftward to AD' in Fig. 9-11(a). Spending is y_1 at price level p_0, which is below full-employment supply y_e. Unless the price level declines to p_1, output remains below its full-employment level.

(b)   When prices are flexible, the price level declines when aggregate spending is less than full-employment output. In Fig. 9-11(a) the price level falls from p_0 to p_1; there is movement along schedule AD' from B to C until full-employment output y_e is reached. In Fig. 9-11(b), the decline in the price level increases the real money supply which shifts LM rightward to $LM(p_1)$; there is movement down IS' until IS' and $LM(p_1)$ intersect at full-employment output y_e.

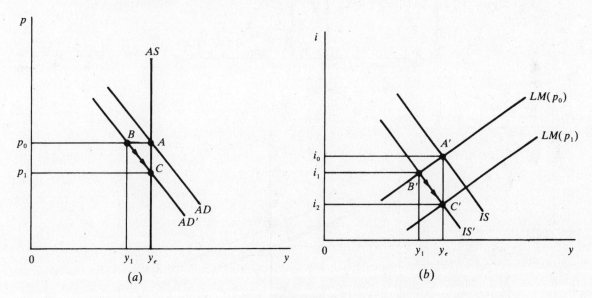

Fig. 9-11

9.6   The goods market equation, plotted and labeled IS in Fig. 9-12(a), is $y = \$1300 - 30i$ when $C = \$90 + 0.80Yd$, $I = \$150 - 6i$, $Tx = \$100$, and $G = \$100$. The money market equation, plotted and labeled LM in Fig. 9-12(a), is $y = \$800 + 20i$ when the nominal money supply is $\$160$, the price level is 1.00 and the demand for money is $0.20y - 4i$. The neoclassical aggregate supply schedule AS in Fig. 9-12(b) is derived from the short-run production function

$y = 14L - 0.04L^2$ and the supply and demand for labor equations $L_s = 70 + 5(W/p)$ and $L_d = 175 - 12.5(W/p)$. Equilibrium output is initially $1000, the price level 1.00, and rate of interest 10%. (a) Find simultaneous equilibrium in the money and goods market when taxes increase $20 and there is no change in the price level. (b) A $20 increase in taxes shifts aggregate demand leftward to AD'; the price level at equilibrium is 0.9374. What happens to the real money supply when the price level declines from 1.00 to 0.9374? Find the new LM equation. (c) Find the rate of interest when the price level is 0.9374. (d) Compare C, I, and G when the price level is 1.00 and 0.9374. (e) Find the nominal and real wage when the price level is 1.00 and 0.9374.

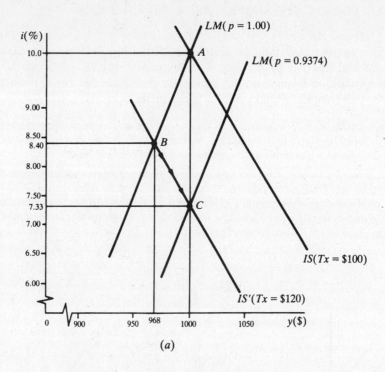

(a)

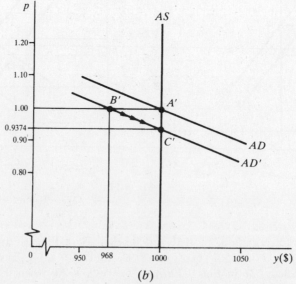

(b)

Fig. 9-12

(a)   When taxes increase $20, the *IS* equation becomes $y = \$1220 - 30i$.

$$y = \$90 + 0.80(y - \$120) + \$150 - 6i + \$100$$
$$y = \$1220 - 30i$$

Simultaneous equilibrium in the money and goods markets exists when output is $968.

$$
\begin{aligned}
y &= \$1220 - 30i \qquad &(\textit{IS equation when } Tx = \$120) \\
-(y &= \$\ 800 + 20i) \qquad &(\textit{LM when price level is } 1.00) \\
\hline
0 &= \$420 - 50i \\
i &= 8.40\% \\
y &= \$968
\end{aligned}
$$

(b)   The real money supply increases from $160, or $160/1.00, to $170.68, or $160/0.9374. The *LM* equation is $y = \$853.40 + 20i$. ($\$170.68 = 0.20y - 4i$; $\$853.40 = y - 20i$.)

(c)   When the price level is 0.9374, simultaneous equilibrium in the money and goods markets exists at a $1000 output and 7.33% rate of interest:

$$
\begin{aligned}
y &= \$1220.00 - 30i \qquad &(\textit{IS equation when } Tx = \$120) \\
-(y &= \$\ 853.40 + 20i) \qquad &(\textit{LM when price level is } 0.9374) \\
\hline
0 &= \$366.60 - 50i \\
i &= 7.33\% \\
y &= \$1000
\end{aligned}
$$

(d)   When the price level is 1.00, the rate of interest is 10%, taxes equal $100, and output is $1000, $C = \$90 + 0.80(\$1000 - \$100) = \$810$; $I = \$90$; and $G = \$100$. When the price level is 0.9374, the rate of interest is 7.33%, taxes equal $120, and output is $1000, $C = \$90 + 0.80(\$1000 - \$120) = \$794$; $I = \$106$; $G = \$100$. The $20 tax increase causes consumption to decline from $810 to $794 and investment to increase from $90 to $106 as the decrease in the price level expands the real money supply and lowers the rate of interest from 10% to 7.33%.

(e)   When the price level is 1.00, the equilibrium nominal wage is $6.

$$
\begin{aligned}
L &= 175 - 12.5\left(\frac{W}{1.00}\right) \qquad &\text{(Demand for labor)} \\
-\left(L &= \ \ 70 + 5.0\left(\frac{W}{1.00}\right)\right) \qquad &\text{(Supply of labor)} \\
\hline
0 &= 105 - 17.5\left(\frac{W}{1.00}\right) \\
W &= \$6
\end{aligned}
$$

When the price level is 0.9374, the equilibrium nominal wage is $5.62.

$$
\begin{aligned}
L &= 175 - 12.5\left(\frac{W}{0.9374}\right) \qquad &\text{(Demand for labor)} \\
-\left(L &= \ \ 70 + 5.0\left(\frac{W}{0.9374}\right)\right) \qquad &\text{(Supply of labor)} \\
\hline
0 &= 105 - 17.5\left(\frac{W}{0.9374}\right) \\
0 &= 98.427 - 17.5W \\
W &= \$5.62
\end{aligned}
$$

The real wage is unaffected by the change in the price level and remains at $6, since $\$6/1 = \dfrac{\$5.62}{0.9374}$.

9.7   Full-employment equilibrium is initially y_e in Fig. 9-13, for schedules AD and AS. Suppose new technology shifts aggregate supply rightward to AS'. (*a*) Explain how the economy adjusts to its increased capacity through a change in the price level. (*b*) What happens to the components of aggregate output?

(*a*)   With increased capacity, full-employment output y_1 exceeds y_e spending at price level p_0. The price level declines from p_0 to p_1; the real money supply increases; LM shifts to the right; the rate of interest falls; and interest-sensitive private sector spending increases.

(*b*)   When taxes are unrelated to output and there is no change in government spending, interest-sensitive private sector spending expands, as does consumption.

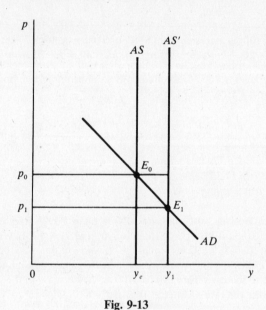

Fig. 9-13

9.8   Full-employment output is initially y_e in Fig. 9-14, for schedules AD and AS. A decrease in government spending shifts AD leftward to AD'. At price level p_0, full-employment output y_e now exceeds spending; the price level is expected to fall. (*a*) Explain why the expectation that the price level will fall shifts aggregate demand further to the left, e.g., to AD''. (*b*) What disadvantages are there to relying on a decrease in the price level to correct a situation in which there is insufficient demand? (*c*) What economic policy might the government implement to avert the destabilizing effect of a decrease in the price level?

(*a*)   Deflation (a decline in the price level) means that goods and services can be purchased at lower prices in the future. When the price level is expected to fall, the private sector postpones nonessential expenditures. Decreases in $(C + I)$ further depress aggregate demand (shift it to AD''), and output falls to y_2 rather than to y_1 in Fig. 9-14.

(*b*)   The disadvantages include not only the likelihood of postponed spending but less responsiveness from interest-sensitive private sector spending to increases in the real money supply. Recall that a decrease in the price level increases the real money supply, which lowers the rate of interest. In a period of declining output, private sector spending may become less interest-sensitive. Aggregate demand would not only shift to the left due to expected deflation, but would become steeper as well. The required decrease in the price level to reach full employment might be substantial, which would further feed deflationary expectations, deepen the contraction and prolong the recession.

(c) Rather than rely on deflation, government can initiate a stimulative economic policy (increase the nominal money supply, expand government spending, and/or decrease taxes), which shifts aggregate demand back to AD in Fig. 9-14. Economic contractions would be moderated and also shortened.

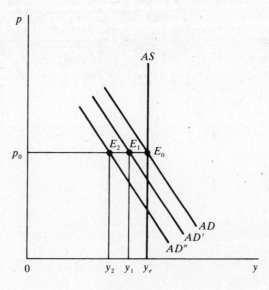

Fig. 9-14

9.9 Explain why unexpected deflation might have redistribution effects which could further dampen aggregate demand.

Unexpected deflation increases the real indebtedness of borrowers (debtors) and the real wealth of lenders (creditors). Since debtors are more likely to have a higher marginal propensity to consume than creditors, unexpected deflation is likely to reduce consumption and shift aggregate demand to the left, further contracting output.

NEOCLASSICAL AGGREGATE SUPPLY: MONETARY AND FISCAL POLICY

9.10 An economy is initially at full-employment output y_e, for schedules AD and AS in Fig. 9-15(a) and IS and $LM(p_0)$ in Fig. 9-15(b). (a) What effect does an increase in government spending have on equilibrium output, the price level, and the rate of interest, *ceteris paribus*? (b) What effect does increased government spending have on sector output in this full-employment economy?

(a) IS shifts rightward from IS to IS' in Fig. 9-15(b) with aggregate demand shifting from AD to AD' in Fig. 9-15(a). Because at points B and B' output y_1 exceeds full employment output y_e, the price level increases from p_0 to p_1, and LM shifts leftward from $LM(p_0)$ to $LM(p_1)$. Output remains at full-employment output y_e, the price level increases from p_0 to p_1, and the rate of interest increases from i_0 to i_1.

(b) With output remaining at y_e and the rate of interest increasing from i_0 to i_1, increased government spending crowds out interest-sensitive investment. Thus, the expansion of public sector output is achieved by an equal decrease in interest-sensitive private sector output.

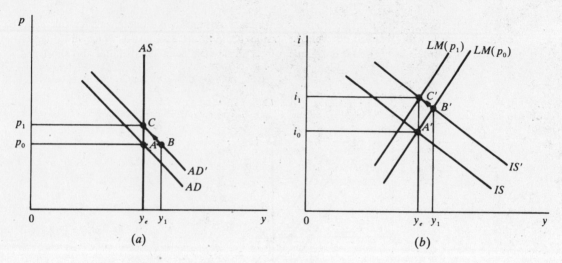

Fig. 9-15

9.11 Output is at the $700 full-employment output level, and the price level is 2.00 in Fig. 9-16 for schedules *AD* and *AS*. The equation for *IS* is $y = \$1000 - 30i$ with $C = \$30 + 0.80yd$, $I = \$150 - 6i$, $Tx = \$100$, and $G = \$100$. The *LM* equation is $y = \$500 + 20i$ when the nominal money supply is $200; the price level is 2.00, and the demand for money is $0.20y - 4i$. (*a*) Find equations for *IS* and *LM* when a $15 increase in government spending shifts aggregate demand rightward in Fig. 9-16 to AD' and the price level increases to 2.22. (*b*) Find the rate of interest, *C*, and *I* when the price level is 2.00 and 2.22. (*c*) What effect does the $15 increase in government spending have on the composition of output?

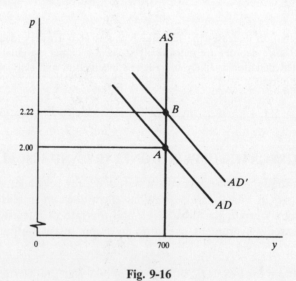

Fig. 9-16

(*a*)   The *IS* equation is $y = \$1075 - 30i$ when government spending increases from $100 to $115.

$$y = \$30 + 0.8(y - \$100) + \$150 - 6i + \$115$$
$$y = \$1075 - 30i$$

The LM equation is $y = \$450.45 + 20i$ when the price level is 2.22.

$$\frac{\$200}{2.22} = 0.20y - 4i$$
$$\$90.09 = 0.20y - 4i$$
$$y = \$450.45 + 20i$$

(b)   Output remains at the \$700 full-employment level; the rate of interest increases from 10 to 12.5%.

$$y = \$1075.00 - 30i \qquad (IS \text{ equation when } G \text{ is } \$115)$$
$$\underline{-(y = \$\ 450.45 + 20i)} \qquad (LM \text{ equation when price level is } 2.22)$$
$$0 = \$624.55 - 50i$$
$$i = 12.50\%$$
$$y = \$700$$

Consumption remains at \$510. Investment is \$90 when the price level is 2.00 and government spending is \$100; investment declines to \$75 when government spending increases \$15 and the price level rises to 2.22.

(c)   The \$15 increase in government sector spending crowds out \$15 of investment spending.

9.12   The initial parameters of Problem 9.11 are retained, but we now assume that aggregate demand AD in Fig. 9-16 shifts rightward to AD' because the nominal money supply increases from \$200 to \$222. (a) What effect does the \$22 increase in the nominal money supply have on the real money supply when the rightward shift of aggregate demand raises the price level from 2.00 to 2.22? (b) What has happened to the composition of sector output in this full employment economy?

(a)   There is no change in the real money supply. The real money supply is \$100 when the nominal money supply is \$200 and the price level is 2.00, and \$100 when the nominal money supply is \$222 and the price level is 2.22.

(b)   With the real money supply constant, the rate of interest is unchanged as is the composition of sector output.

9.13   Why is a change in the nominal money supply neutral when aggregate supply is vertical and output is at its full employment level?

When aggregate supply is vertical, changes in the nominal money supply cause proportional changes in the price level. Because the real money supply remains unchanged, a nominal money supply change has no effect on the rate of interest or the composition of output. Thus, a nominal money change is neutral in its effect on the composition and level of real output.

POSITIVELY SLOPED AGGREGATE SUPPLY: DEMAND CHANGES

9.14   Suppose the money, goods, and labor markets are in equilibrium at full-employment output y_e: schedules AD and AS in Fig. 9-17(a) determine output y_e and price level p_0; schedules IS and $LM(p_0)$ in Fig. 9-17(b) determine output y_e and interest rate i_0; and L_e labor units are employed for schedules L_d and L_s in Fig. 9-17(c) at nominal wage W_0. Assume that the labor supply schedule does not immediately incorporate a change in the price level. (a) What happens to the price level, real output, and number of workers employed when the nominal money supply increases, *ceteris paribus*? (b) Is output at an equilibrium level after the money supply expansion?

(a)   In Fig. 9-17(a) aggregate demand shifts rightward to AD', the price level and output increase to p_1 and y_2 respectively. $LM(p_0)$ in Fig. 9-17(b) shifts rightward to $LM'(p_0)$ initially, but the rise in the price

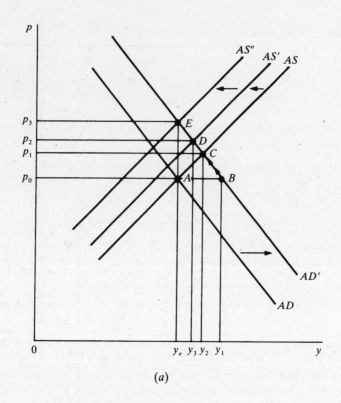

(a)

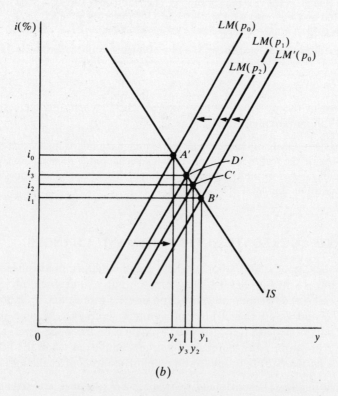

(b)

Fig. 9-17

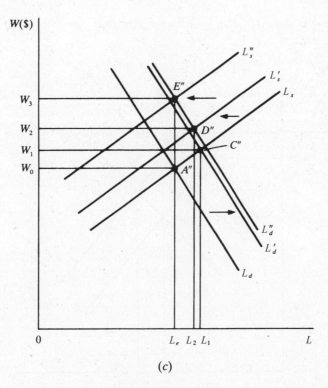

(c)

Fig. 9-17 (*continued*)

level to p_1 shifts LM leftward to $LM(p_1)$; the rate of interest declines to i_2 and output expands to y_2. The p_0 to p_1 increase in the price level shifts labor demand rightward to L'_d in Fig. 9-17(c) with the labor supply schedule remaining at L_s; the nominal wage increases to W_1 with employment increasing from L_e to L_1.

(b) The economy is not in equilibrium. Schedule AS in Fig. 9-17(a) is derived from labor market equilibrium, where price level p_0 is expected to continue and the nominal wage is W_0; output y_2 and employment of L_1 exceed the level associated with full employment. Because the price level is above p_0 and L_1 exceeds L_e, labor is able to demand and receive a higher nominal wage upon the expiration of its contract, which shifts the labor supply schedule L_s in Fig. 9-17(c) leftward to L'_s. Aggregate supply in Fig. 9-17(a) shifts leftward to AS', the price level rises to p_2, and real output declines to y_3. Money equilibrium schedule $LM(p_1)$ in Fig. 9-17(b) shifts leftward to $LM(p_2)$ with the rate of interest rising to i_3. And in Fig. 9-17(c), the labor demand schedule shifts rightward to L''_d, and schedules L'_s and L''_d determine a W_2 nominal wage and L_2 workers are employed. Labor continues to demand a higher nominal wage, which shifts aggregate supply leftward, as long as the number of workers employed and real output exceeds L_e and y_e, respectively. The economy returns to equilibrium when AD' and AS'' determine full-employment output y_e and price level p_3.

9.15 In Fig. 9-18, output is at its full-employment level y_e for schedules AS and AD, and the price level is p_0. An increase in the nominal money supply shifts aggregate rightward to AD' and real output increases to y_1. Explain and show what happens to output as output returns to its equilibrium level.

Because price level p_1 is higher than the expected p_0 level and output y_1 exceeds full-employment output y_e, labor demands a higher nominal wage, which shifts aggregate supply to the left. Higher nominal wage demands persist until aggregate supply and aggregate demand intersect at output y_e and price level p_2. Hence, output increases from y_e to y_1 and then declines over successive periods as aggregate supply shifts to the left and moves along AD' until price level p_2 is reached. The path of real output is indicated by the arrows in Fig. 9-18.

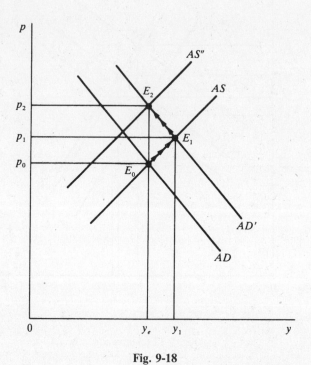

Fig. 9-18

9.16 Suppose the equation for short-run supply is $y = 14L - 0.04L^2$, and the demand for labor equation is $L_d = 175 - 12.5(W/p)$. The labor supply equation is $L_s = 70 + 5W$; labor expects the 1.00 price level to continue. Output is initially at the $1000 full-employment level; the price level is 1.00; the nominal wage is $6; the real wage is $6; and 100 workers are employed. (*a*) What happens to the number of workers employed, the nominal wage and the real wage when increased government spending shifts aggregate demand rightward, real output expands to $1011.40, and the price level increases to 1.10? (*b*) What happens to the nominal wage, the real wage and workers employed when labor's demand for a 10% increase in the nominal wage (because of the 10% increase in the price level) shifts aggregate supply leftward, which causes output to decline to $1005.96 and the price level to increase to 1.15? (*c*) What output, real wage, and labor employment prevail in the long run? (*d*) Why did output exceed the $1000 full-employment level?

(*a*) The number of workers employed increases from 100 to 102, the nominal wage increases from $6.00 to $6.42, and the real wage declines from $6.00 to $5.84 [the real wage w equals W/p; when $W = \$6.42$ and $p = 1.10$, $w = (\$6.42/1.10) = \$5.84$].

$$L = 175 - 12.5\left(\frac{W}{1.10}\right) \qquad \text{(Demand for labor)}$$

$$\underline{-(L = 70 + 5.0W)} \qquad \text{(Supply of labor)}$$

$$0 = 105 - 12.5\left(\frac{W}{1.10}\right) - 5W$$

$$W = \$6.42$$

$$L = 102.08$$

(b)   The number of workers employed decreases from 102 to 101, the nominal wage increases from \$6.42 to \$6.81, and the real wage increases from \$5.84 to \$5.92.

$$L = 175 - 12.5\left(\frac{W}{1.15}\right) \qquad \text{(Demand for labor)}$$

$$- \left(L = 70 + 5.0\left(\frac{W}{1.10}\right)\right) \qquad \text{(Supply of labor)}$$

$$\overline{0 = 105 - 12.5\left(\frac{W}{1.15}\right) - 5\left(\frac{W}{1.10}\right)}$$

$$W = \$6.81$$

$$L = 101$$

(c)   Labor demands a higher nominal wage as long as the real wage is below its initial equilibrium level and workers employed exceed the 100 employed at the \$1000 full-employment level of output. Thus, in the long run, output returns to \$1000, employment to 100 and the real wage to \$6.

(d)   Since labor did not expect the initial increase in the price level, it did not include a cost of living adjustment in its nominal wage contract. The result is a decline in labor's real wage, an increase in employment and an increase in output beyond the full employment level.

POSITIVELY SLOPED AGGREGATE SUPPLY: SUPPLY SHOCKS

9.17   Explain how an increase in variable W, θ, a, and Pn in the mark-up pricing formula $P = W/a(1 + \theta) + Pn$ affects the supply cost of output and the aggregate supply schedule.

W is the nominal wage; an increase in the nominal wage increases per-unit supply cost and therefore shifts aggregate supply to the left. θ is the mark-up on variable cost; an increase in mark-up increases per-unit supply cost and shifts aggregate supply to the left. Variable a represents the productivity of labor; an increase in labor productivity, the number of units produced per labor input, decreases per-unit supply cost and shifts aggregate supply to the right. An increase in the per-unit cost of materials, Pn, increases per-unit supply cost and shifts aggregate supply to the left.

9.18   Output is initially at full-employment level y_e in Fig. 9-19 for schedules AD and AS. (a) What happens to output and the price level when the per-unit cost of materials increases, *ceteris paribus*? (b) What happens to output in part (a) when nominal wages are "sticky" downward? Is labor able to bargain for a higher nominal wage because of the p_0 to p_1 increase in the price level? (c) When prices and wages are flexible and there is no demand-stabilizing economic policy, what eventually happens to the nominal wage and/or the price level? (d) What demand-stabilizing economic policies could the government implement to eliminate the disequilibrium in (a)? (e) What is true of the disequilibrium in (a) when the increase in the per-unit cost of materials is temporary?

(a)   Aggregate supply in Fig. 9-19 shifts leftward from AS to AS'. There is movement along schedule AD with output declining from y_e to y_1 and the price level increasing from p_0 to p_1.

(b)   When the nominal wage remains at its initial W_0 level and there is no demand-stabilizing economic policy, output remains at y_1, which is below full-employment output. Although the price level has increased from p_0 to p_1 and the real wage has fallen, labor is unable to bargain for a higher nominal wage because employment and real output is below the full-employment level.

(c)   When labor markets are competitive and nominal wages are flexible, the nominal wage should decline, since output and employment are below full employment. The decline in the nominal wage reduces the per-unit cost of output and shifts aggregate supply rightward from AS' to AS. There is a return to output y_e and price level p_0.

(d)   Rather than rely on the labor markets to correct the disequilibrium, government could increase its expenditures, reduce taxes, and/or increase the nominal money supply and shift aggregate demand rightward to AD'. At AD' and AS' demand-stimulating policies return output to the y_e full-employment level but cause a further increase in the price level to p_2.

(e)   When material cost increases are temporary, aggregate supply shifts leftward to AS' in Fig. 9-19 but returns to AS in a future period. The decline in real output is temporary, as is the increase in the price level.

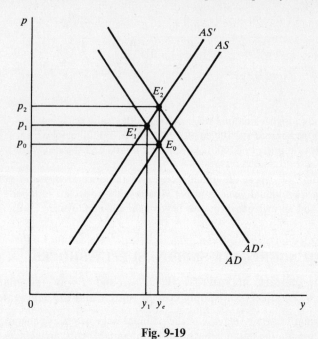

Fig. 9-19

9.19   Output is initially at full-employment level y_e in Fig. 9-20 for schedules AD and AS. Suppose there is a decrease in the per-unit cost of materials. (a) In the absence of a demand-stabilizing economic policy, what eventually happens to the nominal wage and/or the price level to reestab-

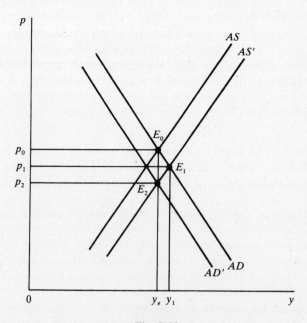

Fig. 9-20

lish equilibrium? (*b*) What demand-stabilizing policies could government utilize to correct the disequilibrium caused by a decrease in the cost of materials?

(*a*)   The decrease in the per-unit cost of materials shifts aggregate supply in Fig. 9-20 rightward from AS to AS'. Movement along AD causes output to expand from y_e to y_1 with the price level decreasing from p_0 to p_1 because of a lower per-unit production cost. Since output y_1 exceeds full-employment output y_e, labor's bargaining power is enhanced. The nominal wage increases; aggregate supply shifts back to AS with output and the price level returning to y_e and p_0.

(*b*)   The government could shift aggregate demand leftward from AD to AD' in Fig. 9-20 by reducing government spending, increasing taxes, and/or decreasing the nominal money supply. Output would return to y_e at a lower p_2 price level.

THE NEW CLASSICAL AND KEYNESIAN MACROECONOMICS

9.20   Explain the original Keynesian analysis of labor market equilibrium and aggregate supply.

Early Keynesian analysis contended that a nominal wage floor existed; the nominal wage would not fall and remained constant until real output reached its full-employment level. The nominal wage was thereby presented as fixed, for example, at W_0 in Fig. 9-21(*a*), and remained at that level until L_e workers were

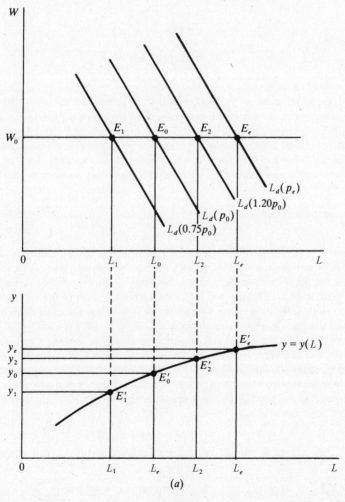

Fig. 9-21

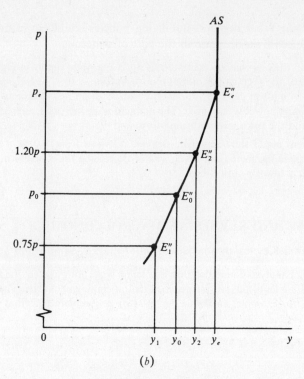

Fig. 9-21   (*Continued*)

employed at full employment output y_e. In Fig. 9-21(*a*), L_0 labor units are employed, and real output is y_0 at price level p_0; L_1 labor units are employed, and real output is y_1 for price level $0.75p_0$; and L_2 labor units are employed, and real output is y_2 for price level $1.20p_0$. Upon reaching L_e, the nominal wage increases at the same rate as the price level, and real output remains at y_e. Aggregate supply schedule *AS* in Fig. 9-12(*b*) presents the effect of labor's money illusion with respect to the nominal wage in Fig. 9-21(*a*); aggregate supply is positively sloped until output y_e, where aggregate supply becomes vertical.

9.21   How does contemporary Keynesian analysis of the labor markets differ from earlier Keynesian analysis?

Contemporary Keynesian analysis rejects the contention of a wage floor but views nominal wages as "sticky" in the short run because workers sign a contract and agree to work for a specific nominal wage for the term of the contract. For example, in the labor supply schedule $L_s(p_0)$ in Fig. 9-22(*a*), labor expects continuance of price level p_0. The demand for labor during the term of the contract depends on the actual price level. Thus, an increase in the price level shifts the labor demand schedule rightward to L_d $(1.20p_0)$ in Fig. 9.22(*a*), when the price level increases from p_0 to $1.20p_0$, or leftward to $L_d(0.80p_0)$ when the price level falls to $0.80p_0$. Aggregate supply is therefore positively sloped in the short run, but its location in space depends on the price level expected when labor contracts its services. We note this dependency by appending p_0 to the aggregate supply schedule in Fig. 9-22(*b*). When labor contracts expect the higher $1.20p_0$ price level, aggregate supply is located to the left of $AS(p_0)$ at $AS(1.20p_0)$. When the price level included in labor contracts is the same as the price level which exists during the period of the contract, aggregate supply is vertical at full-employment output y_e.

9.22   How does the new classical theory of aggregate supply differ from contemporary Keynesian theory?

Both recognize that aggregate supply may be positively sloped in the short run. In the new classical aggregate supply models, the nominal wage adapts to a change in the price level and, in more recent models,

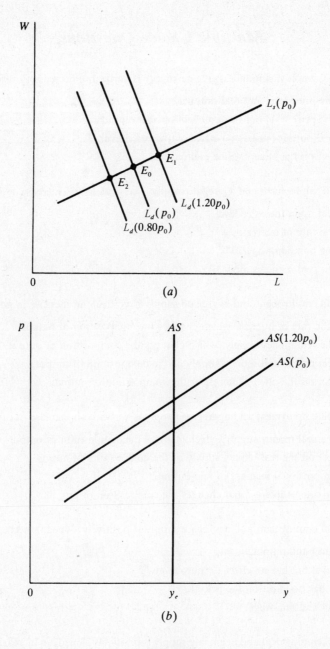

Fig. 9-22

uses information which may be incomplete in setting the nominal wage. Hence, the nominal wage may be above or below the market-clearing real wage for a time, but the period is shorter than the one assumed in contemporary Keynesian models. As more complete information becomes available, aggregate supply becomes more steeply sloped and is vertical over longer periods.

Multiple Choice Questions

1. When there is full employment and aggregate supply is vertical, a decrease in taxes

    (a) Increases the price level and real output.

    (b) Increases the price level but has no effect on real output.

    (c) Increases real output but has no effect on the price level.

    (d) Has no effect on the price level or real output.

2. When there is full employment and aggregate supply is vertical, a 10% increase in the nominal money supply

    (a) Has no effect upon the price level.

    (b) Increases the rate of interest.

    (c) Increases the nominal wage 10%.

    (d) Increases the real money supply 10%.

3. When there is full employment and aggregate supply is vertical, an increase in government spending

    (a) Pushes up the rate of interest, which changes the composition of output.

    (b) Increases the real money supply, which changes the composition of output.

    (c) Has no effect on the real money supply or the composition of output.

    (d) Has no effect on the rate of interest or the composition of output.

4. When there is full employment and aggregate supply is vertical, an increase in the nominal money supply

    (a) Increases the real money supply, which changes the composition of output.

    (b) Has no effect on the real money supply or the composition of output.

    (c) Causes a proportional increase in real output.

    (d) Reduces the rate of interest and changes the composition of output.

5. When there is full employment and aggregate supply is positively sloped, a decrease in taxes increases

    (a) The price level and output.

    (b) The price level but has no effect on output.

    (c) Output but has no effect on the price level.

    (d) The nominal and real wage.

6. When there is full employment and aggregate supply is positively sloped, an increase in government spending

    (a) Decreases output and the price level.

    (b) Decreases output and the real wage.

    (c) Increases output and the real wage.

    (d) Increases output and the price level.

7. When there is full employment and aggregate supply is positively sloped, a rightward shift of aggregate demand increases

    (a) The real wage, the employment of labor, and real output.

    (b) The nominal wage, the employment of labor, and real output.

    (c) The productivity of labor and real output.

    (d) The demand for labor, the employment of labor, and the real wage.

8.   When aggregate supply is positively sloped and there is an increase in the per-unit cost of materials, aggregate supply shifts

   (a)   Rightward, the price level falls, and output increases.

   (b)   Leftward, the price level falls, and output increases.

   (c)   Rightward, the price level increases, and output decreases.

   (d)   Leftward, the price level increases, and output decreases.

9.   When aggregate supply is positively sloped and there is a decrease in the mark-up on variable cost, aggregate supply shifts

   (a)   Leftward, the price level falls, and real output increases.

   (b)   Rightward, the price level falls, and real output increases.

   (c)   Leftward, the price level increases, the real output decreases.

   (d)   Rightward, the price level increases, and real output decreases.

10.   Which of the following statements about the labor markets is false?

   (a)   The imperfect knowledge model contends that nominal wages adapt to changes in the price level.

   (b)   In a rational expectations model, aggregate supply may be positively sloped in the short run because of forecasting errors.

   (c)   In the "new classical" macroeconomics, aggregate supply is positively sloped in the long run.

   (d)   Contemporary Keynesian macroeconomics attributes the positively sloped aggregate supply schedule to nominal wage contracts.

True or False Questions

11.   _____ When there is full employment and aggregate supply is vertical, an increase in taxes, *ceteris paribus*, has no effect upon output but increases the price level.

12.   _____ When there is full employment and aggregate supply is vertical, an increase in productivity, *ceteris paribus*, increases output and decreases the price level.

13.   _____ Output and the price level increase when there is neoclassical aggregate supply schedule and aggregate demand shifts rightward.

14.   _____ When there is full employment and aggregate supply is vertical, an increase in the nominal money supply has no effect upon output, the composition of output, or the price level.

15.   _____ When there is full employment and aggregate supply is vertical, a decrease in taxes increases interest-sensitive spending, decreases the price level, and has no effect upon output.

16.   _____ Output may exceed its full-employment level when aggregate supply is positively sloped.

17.   _____ When aggregate supply is positively sloped, an increase in government spending increases output and the price level in the short run.

18.   _____ When output exceeds its full-employment level, the supply of labor schedule shifts leftward when labor contracts expire.

19. _____ An increase in the cost of materials shifts a positively sloped aggregate supply schedule leftward.

20. _____ When labor demands a higher nominal wage, *ceteris paribus*, output decreases and the price level increases.

Answers to Multiple Choice and True or False Questions

1. (*b*); **2.** (*c*); **3.** (*a*); **4.** (*b*); **5.** (*a*); **6.** (*d*); **7.** (*b*); **8.** (*d*); **9.** (*b*); **10.** (*c*); **11.** F; **12.** T; **13.** F; **14.** F; **15.** F; **16.** T; **17.** T; **18.** T; **19.** T; **20.** T.

Chapter 10

Aggregate Supply, Aggregate Demand, and Inflation

Chapter Summary

1. When aggregate supply is vertical, the price level increases over time only when there are repeated increases in aggregate demand.

2. The Phillips curve displays an inverse relationship between the rate of inflation and the rate of unemployment when aggregate supply is positively sloped and there are repeated increases in aggregate demand. A negatively sloped Phillips curve shifts rightward when a positively sloped aggregate supply schedule shifts leftward. The Phillips curve is vertical and displays no relationship between inflation and unemployment when aggregate supply is vertical.

3. A dynamic aggregate demand (*DAD*) schedule displays an inverse relationship between the rate of inflation and output. When money supply growth and fiscal expansion are the sources of demand growth, increases in the growth rate of the nominal money supply and/or additional fiscal stimuli shift dynamic aggregate demand rightward, while decreases shift it leftward.

4. The dynamic aggregate supply schedule displays a positive relationship between the rate of inflation and output; it exists when the growth rate of the nominal wage is less than that of inflation. Wages can increase at a slower rate than inflation when labor's inflationary expectations lag the actual rate of inflation. When labor expects a higher rate of inflation, dynamic aggregate supply shifts leftward; dynamic aggregate supply shifts rightward when labor expects a lower rate of inflation.

5. An economy can be in a state of inflationary equilibrium, where output remains at its full-employment level and the inflation rate is unchanged. An increase in nominal money supply growth and/or an additional fiscal stimulus shift dynamic aggregate demand rightward, and output is pushed beyond its full-employment level for a number of periods when dynamic aggregate supply is positively sloped. Output returns to its full-employment level over time as a result of further shifts of dynamic aggregate demand and dynamic aggregate supply. An increase in the growth rate of the nominal money supply results in a higher rate of inflation when output returns to its full-employment level. Inflation and output return to their initial position when the rightward shift of *DAD* is caused by a fiscal stimulus.

6. Output falls below its full-employment level when dynamic aggregate supply is positively sloped and policy-makers implement measures that will lower the rate of inflation. A large decrease in nominal money supply growth results in a large decrease in inflation and output in the short run. A slowdown of nominal money supply growth over time results in a less severe decrease in output but output remains below its full-employment level for a longer period of time, and the inflation rate falls more slowly.

Chapter Outline

10.1 AGGREGATE DEMAND AND INFLATION

When output is initially at its full-employment level and aggregate supply is vertical, an increase in aggregate demand has no effect upon output; and, the increase in the price level is proportional to the increase in aggregate demand. Thus, when output is at its full-employment level, the price level increases over time only when there are repeated increases in aggregate demand. For example, when aggregate supply is vertical and output is $100, 5% increases in aggregate demand from $100 to $105 to $110.25 to $115.76 cause the price level to rise 5% in successive periods, and there is a 5% rate of inflation.

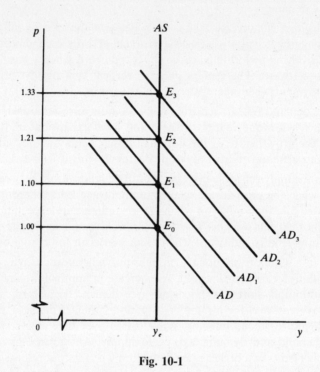

Fig. 10-1

EXAMPLE 10.1. Output is y_e and the price level is 1.0 for schedules AS and AD in Fig. 10-1. 10% increases in aggregate demand in successive periods, which shift aggregate demand from AD to AD_1 to AD_2 to AD_3, increase the price level from 1.00 to 1.10 to 1.21 to 1.33. The inflation rate (π) for each period is found by the formula $\pi = [(p - p_{-1})/p_{-1}]100$, where p is the current period price level and p_{-1} is the price level in the previous period. In the situation depicted, the inflation rate for each period is 10%: $(0.10/1.00)(100) = 10\%$; $(0.11/1.00)(100) = 10\%$; $(0.12/1.21)(100) = 10\%$.

EXAMPLE 10.2. LM is vertical when the demand for money is unrelated to the rate of interest; fiscal policy is ineffective and shifts of aggregate demand are solely the result of changes in the nominal money supply. The central bank controls aggregate demand's location in space and thereby inflation through its management of the nominal money supply.

10.2 INFLATION AND UNEMPLOYMENT: THE PHILLIPS CURVE

When aggregate supply is positively sloped, rightward shifts of aggregate demand increase both the price level and output (see Section 9.4). The rate of unemployment decreases when increased aggregate demand raises output and the price level. This inverse relationship between the rate of inflation and the rate of unemployment is presented by the Phillips curve; its slope and location in space depend upon the inflationary expectations of labor. When labor underestimates the inflation rate, the Phillips curve is negatively sloped. When labor expects a higher inflation rate, the negatively sloped short-run Phillips curve shifts rightward. When labor correctly anticipates inflation, aggregate supply is vertical at the full-employment level of output. Over long periods, the Phillips curve is vertical, since errors in inflationary expectations should have a zero value.

EXAMPLE 10.3. Output is y_e in Fig. 10-2(a) for schedules AD and AS. Increases in the nominal money supply shift aggregate demand rightward from AD to AD_1, AD_2, and AD_3; output and the price level increase from y_e to y_1, y_2, and y_3 and from p_0 to p_1, p_2, and p_3, respectively. Suppose the price level increases of p_0 to p_3 are associated with π_1, π_2, and π_3 inflation rates, and output increases y_e to y_3 are associated with unemployment rates of 6%, 5%, and 4%. Inflation rate π_1 is thereby associated with a 6% unemployment rate, π_2 with 5%, and π_3 with 4%. This association is depicted in Fig. 10-2(b) by the negatively sloped Phillips curve SPC.

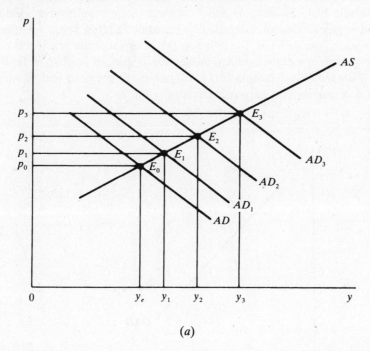

(a)

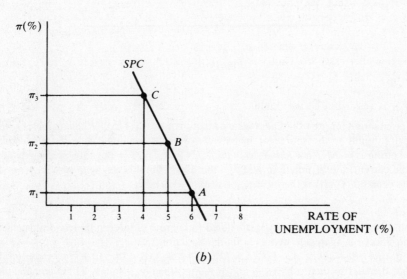

(b)

Fig. 10-2

10.3 SCHEDULE OF DYNAMIC AGGREGATE DEMAND

The equation for aggregate demand derived in Section 8.2 is $y = [hk_e/(h + kbk_e)](\bar{A}) + [bk_e/(h + kbk_e)](\bar{M}/p)$. An increase in autonomous spending and/or the nominal money supply, with the price level held constant, shifts aggregate demand rightward by $\Delta y = [hk_e/(h + kbk_e)]\Delta\bar{A} + [bk_e/(h + kbk_e)](\Delta\bar{M}/\bar{p})$. Growth in the level of aggregate demand (the dynamic aggregate demand schedule) is $y = y_{-1} + \Delta y$, where y is current period aggregate demand, y_{-1} is the previous period aggregate demand, and Δy is the change in aggregate demand between the current and previous period. When growth in aggregate demand is due to an increase in the nominal money supply and/or a fiscal expansion, the equation for dynamic aggregate demand is $y = y_{-1} + \beta(\dot{M} - \pi) + \alpha f$, where β is the multiplier for an increase in the money supply and α for fiscal expansion, $\dot{M}$ is the growth rate of the nominal money supply, π is the current inflation rate, $(\dot{M} - \pi)$ is the rate of increase in the real money supply, and f is the fiscal stimulus. (See Example 10.4.) Holding $\dot{M}$ and f constant, there is an inverse relationship between the rate of inflation and aggregate demand, depicted by schedule DAD in Fig. 10-3. (Since we are now analyzing the growth of aggregate demand, the inflation rate π replaces the price level p on the vertical axis.) An increase in the growth rate of the nominal money supply, *ceteris paribus*, shifts DAD rightward, and a decrease shifts it leftward. (See Example 10.5.) An increase in previous period output (y_{-1}) shifts DAD rightward, and a decrease shifts it leftwards (Example 10.6).

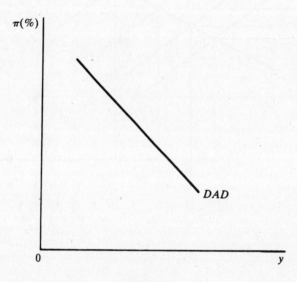

Fig. 10-3

EXAMPLE 10.4. The equation for growth of aggregate demand is $y = y_{-1} + \Delta y$. When an increase in the monthly supply and/or a fiscal stimulus is the source of increased aggregate demand, $\Delta y = [bk_e/(h + kbk_e)](\Delta\bar{M}/p) + [hk_e/(h + kbk_e)]\Delta\bar{G}$. Letting $\beta = [bk_e/(h + kbk_e)]$, $\alpha = [hk_e/(h + kbk_e)]$, $\dot{M} =$ the rate of growth of the nominal money supply, $\pi =$ the current rate of inflation, and $f =$ the fiscal stimulus, $\Delta y = \beta(\dot{M} - \pi) + \alpha f$. The equation for dynamic aggregate demand (DAD) is then $y = y_{-1} + \beta(\dot{M} - \pi) + \alpha f$.

EXAMPLE 10.5. When the demand for money is unrelated to the rate of interest (behavioral coefficient $h = 0$), a fiscal stimulus has no effect on aggregate demand. In the equation $\Delta y = \beta(\dot{M} - \pi) + \alpha f$, $\beta = 1/k$ and $\alpha = 0$. $[\beta = bk_e/(h + kbk_e);\ \beta = bk_e/(0 + kbk_e);\ \beta = 1/k.\ \alpha = hk_e/(h + kbk_e);\ \alpha = 0k_e/(0 + kbk_e);\ \alpha = 0.]$ The equation for dynamic aggregate demand is then $y = y_{-1} + 1/k(\dot{M} - \pi)$. When y_{-1} equals \$100, nominal money supply growth is 10%, and $k = 0.20$, current period aggregate demand is \$100 when the inflation rate is 10%

$[y = \$100 + 5(10\% - 10\%) = \$100]$, \$115 when the inflation rate is 7%, and \$125 when the inflation rate is 5%. The association of a 10%, 7%, and 5% rate of inflation with aggregate demand of \$100, \$115, and \$125 is plotted in Fig. 10-4 with the schedule labeled DAD. When nominal money supply growth is 7% instead of 10%, aggregate demand levels \$85, \$100, and \$110 are associated with inflation rates of 10%, 7%, and 5%. These data are plotted in Fig. 10-4 with the schedule labeled DAD'. When nominal money supply growth is 13%, inflation rates 10%, 7%, and 5% are associated with aggregate demand levels \$115, \$130, and \$140. These data are plotted in Fig. 10-4 with the schedule labeled DAD''. Holding the inflation rate constant, an increase in nominal money supply growth shifts DAD rightward, and a decrease in nominal money supply growth shifts DAD leftward.

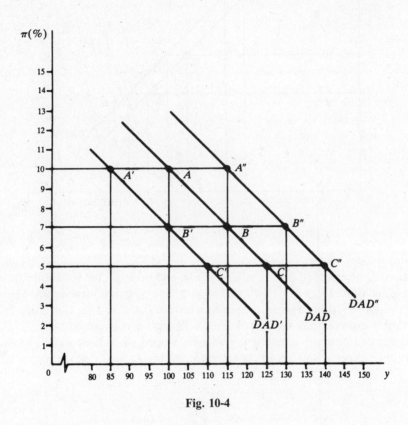

Fig. 10-4

EXAMPLE 10.6.   The dynamic aggregate demand schedule also shifts when there is a change in the previous period output y_{-1}. In Fig. 10-5, schedule DAD is reproduced from Fig. 10-4. When y_{-1} is \$105 rather than \$100, the level of aggregate demand is \$105 when the inflation rate is 10%, \$120 when it is 7%, and \$130 when it is 5%. These data are plotted in Fig. 10-5 with the schedule labeled DAD'. The dynamic aggregate demand schedule shifts rightward when previous period output is higher and leftward when the previous period output is lower, *ceteris paribus*.

10.4 SCHEDULE OF DYNAMIC AGGREGATE SUPPLY

When the percentage change in the nominal wage always equals that of the price level, equilibrium in the labor markets is unaffected by the price level, as is output, and aggregate supply is vertical. (See Section 8.5.) When the nominal wage lags a change in the price level, the real wage deviates from the market-clearing real wage, and aggregate supply can be higher or lower than full-employment output. (See Section 8.7.) In a dynamic setting, it therefore follows that dynamic aggregate supply is vertical (DAS in Fig. 10-6) when the growth rate of the nominal wage (gW) is the same as the rate of inflation (π). However, dynamic aggregate supply is positively sloped (DAS' in Fig. 10-6) when nominal wage

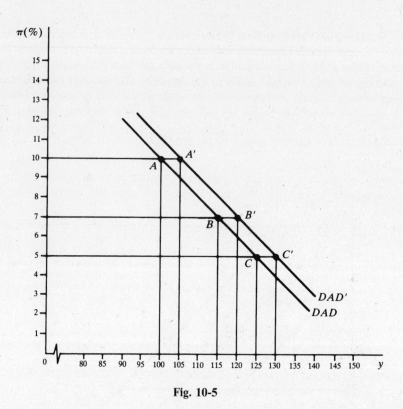

Fig. 10-5

growth is a function of the expected rate of inflation (π^e), and the expected inflation rate is not the same as the actual rate of inflation, i.e., $gW = f(\pi^e)$ and $\pi^e \neq \pi$. The equation for dynamic aggregate supply is then $\pi = \pi^e + \lambda(y - y_e)$. Dynamic aggregate supply schedule DAS' in Fig. 10-6 shifts leftward when a higher inflation rate is expected and rightward when a lower one is expected.

The dynamic aggregate supply schedule is positively sloped when the location of the labor supply schedule depends upon expectations about the rate of inflation [$L_s = f(\pi^e)$], the location of the demand

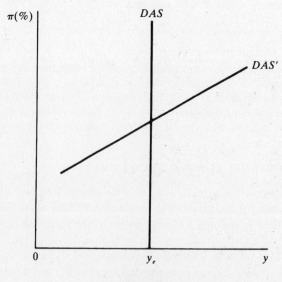

Fig. 10-6

for labor schedule depends on the actual rate of inflation $[L_d = f(\pi)]$, and the actual rate of inflation is not the same as the expected rate of inflation. Economists disagree on how labor arrives at inflationary expectations. The adaptive expectations hypothesis is a backward-looking approach, contending that π^e is derived from past economic behavior. In its most simplified form, inflationary expectations lag the actual inflation rate $\pi^e = \pi_{-1}$; inflationary expectations are a function of the previous period's rate of inflation. A rational expectations approach suggests that inflationary expectations are formed from all current, available information. The adaptive expectations approach $(\pi^e = \pi_{-1})$ is used in this chapter.

EXAMPLE 10.7. Suppose there is no inflation and the labor markets are in equilibrium in Fig. 10-7(a) when L_e workers are employed for labor supply and demand schedules $L_s(\pi^e = 0)$ and $L_d(\pi = 0)$. Labor's expectation of a 5% rate of inflation shifts the labor supply schedule leftward to $L_s(\pi^e = 5\%)$. When the actual inflation rate is 3%, 5%, or 7%, the labor demand schedule shifts rightward to $L_d(\pi = 3\%)$, $L_d(\pi = 5\%)$, or $L_d(\pi = 7\%)$, respectively. At a current inflation rate of 3%, 5%, or 7%, L_1, L_e, and L_2 workers are employed, which are associated in Fig. 10-7(b) with output levels y_1, y_e, and y_2. Along dynamic aggregate supply schedule $DAS(\pi^e = 5\%)$ in Fig. 10-7(c), inflation rates 3%, 5%, and 7% are associated with output levels y_1, y_e, and y_2.

EXAMPLE 10.8. The equation for dynamic aggregate supply is $\pi = \pi^e + \lambda(y - y_e)$. Suppose $\lambda = 0.50$, $\pi^e = 5\%$, and $y_e = \$100$. When the actual inflation rate is 3%, 6%, or 7%, output is $96 [3\% = 5\% + 0.5(y - 100);$ $3\% = 5\% + 0.50(\$96 - \$100)]$, $102, or $104, respectively. The data are plotted in Fig. 10-8 with the schedule labeled $DAS\ (\pi^e = 5\%)$. When $\pi^e = 3\%$ and actual inflation is 3%, 6%, or 7%, output is $100, $106, or $108. Labor's expectation of a 3% inflation rate produces dynamic aggregate supply schedule $DAS(\pi^e = 3\%)$ in Fig. 10-8. The dynamic aggregate supply schedule shifts leftward when labor expects a higher rate of inflation and rightward when labor expects a lower inflation rate.

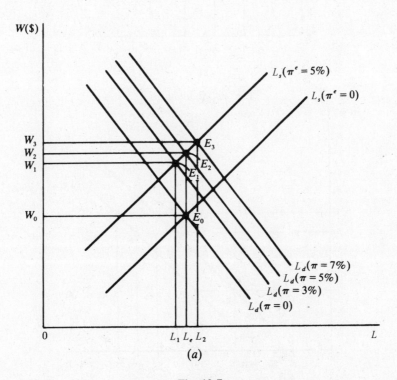

(a)

Fig. 10-7

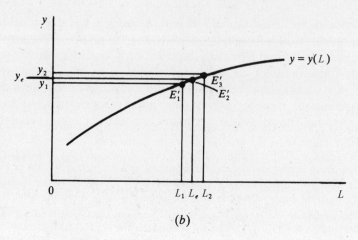

(b)

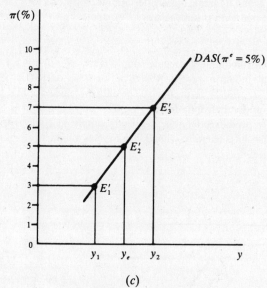

(c)

Fig. 10-7 (continued)

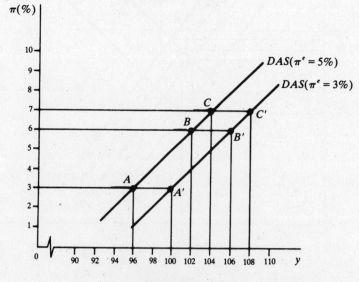

Fig. 10-8

10.5 INFLATION AND OUTPUT

An economy can be in inflationary equilibrium at full employment. For example, output is at full-employment level y_e at a 5% inflation rate for schedules DAD and $DAS(\pi^e = 5\%)$ in Fig. 10-9. The 5% inflation rate continues into successive periods when the variables affecting DAD and DAS are unchanged. A change in the rate of money supply growth and/or fiscal stimulus shifts the dynamic aggregate demand schedule, impacting output and inflation in successive periods. (See Examples 10.9 and 10.10.) Equilibrium is restored over time as changing inflation rates are incorporated into the dynamic aggregate supply schedule. Fig. 10-10 traces the path of inflation and output which results from an increase in the growth rate of the nominal money supply; there is an eventual return to full-employment output, but at a higher inflation rate. Fig. 10-11 traces the path of inflation and output due to a fiscal stimulus; note that both output and inflation return to their initial levels.

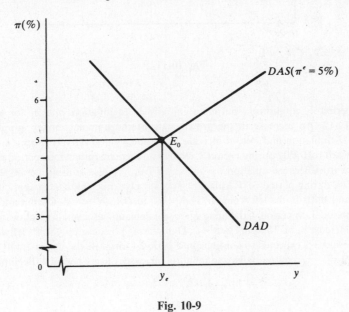

Fig. 10-9

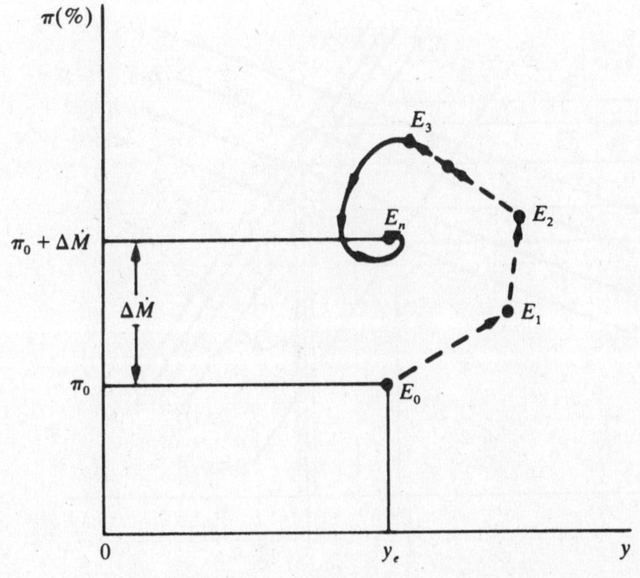

Fig. 10-10

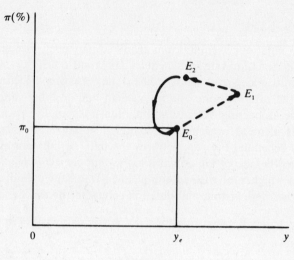

Fig. 10-11

EXAMPLE 10.9. In period 1, equilibrium output is initially y_e at inflation rate π_1 for schedules DAD_1 and $DAS(\pi^e = \pi_1)$ in Fig. 10-12. An increase in the growth rate of the nominal money supply in period 2 shifts DAD_1 rightward to DAD_2; inflation and output increase to π_2 and y_2, respectively. Because output has increased to y_2, DAD_2 shifts rightward to DAD_3 during period 3. (Recall an increase in previous period output shifts dynamic aggregate demand rightward.) Because inflation has increased from π_1 to π_2 during period 2, labor's inflationary expectations increase to π_2 during period 3. [Recall $\pi^e = f(\pi_{-1})$.] Dynamic aggregate supply incorporates inflation rate π_2 during period 3 and shifts to the left from $DAS(\pi^e = \pi_1)$ to $DAS(\pi^e = \pi_2)$. Output and inflation increase to y_3 and π_3 by the end of period 3. In period 4, dynamic aggregate demand has a smaller rightward shift than in period 3 because of the smaller increase in real output (y_2 to y_3). Dynamic aggregate supply shifts leftward to $DAS(\pi^e = \pi_3)$ as the inflation rate of period 3 is expected to continue into period 4. Because the upward shift of DAD_4 is less than the leftward shift of $DAS(\pi^e = \pi_3)$, output falls, and inflation increases during period 4. Beginning in period 5, DAD

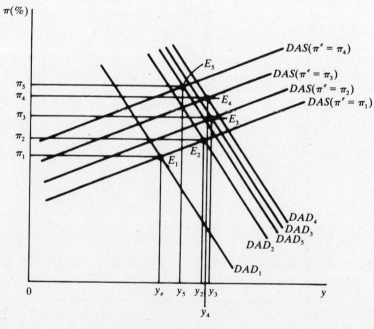

Fig. 10-12

begins shifting leftward with output and inflation following the path traced out in Fig. 10-10. When output returns to full-employment level y_e, inflation has increased from π_1 to π_n, which is equal to the change in the growth rate of the nominal money supply.

EXAMPLE 10.10. Equilibrium output is y_e at inflation rate π_1 for schedules DAD_1 and $DAS(\pi^e = \pi_1)$ in Fig. 10-13. A fiscal stimulus during period 2 shifts DAD_1 rightward to DAD_2. Output and inflation increase to y_2 and π_2. Although the fiscal expansion is permanent, it is not continuous. Hence, dynamic aggregate demand begins shifting leftward during period 3; however, it does not return to DAD_1 immediately because output during period 2 (y_2) is greater than that in period 1 (y_e). Hence, DAD_2 shifts leftward during period 3 to DAD_3; dynamic aggregate supply shifts leftward to $DAS(\pi^e = \pi_2)$, since labor expects inflation rate π_2 to continue. By the end of period 3, output has fallen to y_3, and inflation has increased to π_3. In successive periods, DAD and DAS shift leftward; the path of inflation and output are traced out in Fig. 10-11. Note that equilibrium is reestablished at full-employment output y_e at the initial π_1 rate of inflation.

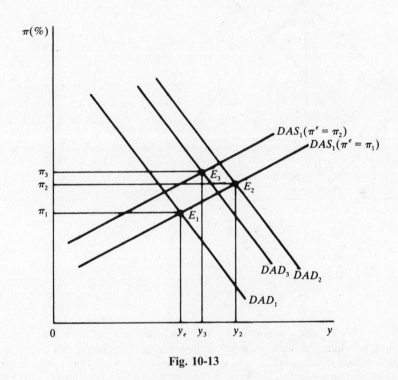

Fig. 10-13

10.6 DISINFLATION AND OUTPUT

Because labor's nominal wage demands lag the inflation rate $[\pi^e = f(\pi_{-1})]$, disinflation (reducing the rate of inflation) causes output to fall below full-employment. (See Examples 10.11 and 10.12.) How rapidly the inflation rate declines depends on the magnitude of the initial reduction in aggregate demand. A "cold turkey" strategy calls for a substantial, initial reduction in aggregate demand, which causes a sharp drop in output. (See Example 10.11.) In a policy of "gradualism," the decrease in aggregate demand is initially moderate. The decline in output is less pronounced; however, output remains below its full-employment level for a longer period of time, and a greater number of periods are needed to reduce the inflation rate. (See Example 10.12.) The actual number of periods needed to achieve full employment output at a lower inflation rate is also influenced by labor's formation of inflationary expectations and the length of labor contracts. The adjustment process is lengthy when three-year labor contracts are the norm and inflationary expectations adjust to past inflation rates; adjustment is much quicker when expectations are rational and labor contracts do not exceed one year.

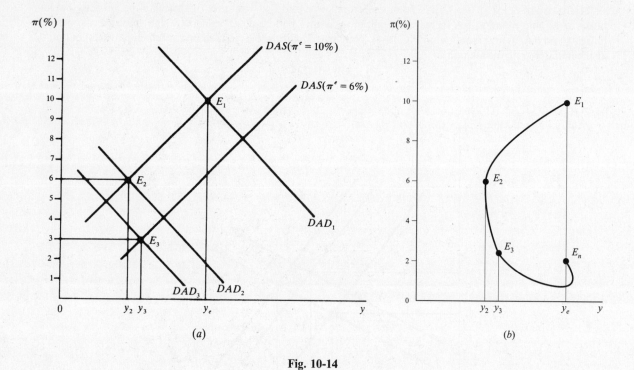

Fig. 10-14

EXAMPLE 10.11. In Fig. 10-14(a), output is y_e and the inflation rate is 10% for schedules DAD_1 and $DAS(\pi^e = 10\%)$. Suppose the central bank is committed to lowering the inflation rate to 2% as soon as possible, nominal money supply growth is reduced from 10% to 2% during period 2, and DAD_1 shifts leftward to DAD_2. The inflation rate falls to 6% during period 2, and output declines to y_2. DAD_2 shifts leftward to DAD_3 during period 3, since output fell from y_e to y_2; dynamic aggregate supply shifts rightward to $DAS(\pi^e = 6\%)$, since the inflation rate in period 2 is lowered to 6%. By the end of period 3, output has increased to y_3 and the inflation rate is 3%. DAD shifts rightward in future periods, eventually returning to DAD_2, and DAS shifts rightward until it intersects DAD_2 at output y_e and there is a 2% inflation rate. The path to full-employment output at a lower rate of inflation is traced out in Fig. 10-14(b).

EXAMPLE 10.12. Output is y_e and inflation is 10% in Fig. 10-15(a) for schedules DAD_1 and $DAS(\pi^e = 10\%)$. A policy of gradualism consists of a 2% decrease in nominal money supply growth during the next four periods, lowering nominal money growth from 10% to 2%. During period 2, DAD_1 shifts leftward to DAD_2, and the inflation rate declines to 9%. In successive periods dynamic aggregate demand continues to shift leftward as nominal money supply growth is further reduced. Dynamic aggregate supply shifts rightward as the inflation rate falls. The path of adjustment from a 10% to a 2% inflation rate is traced out in Fig. 10-15(b).

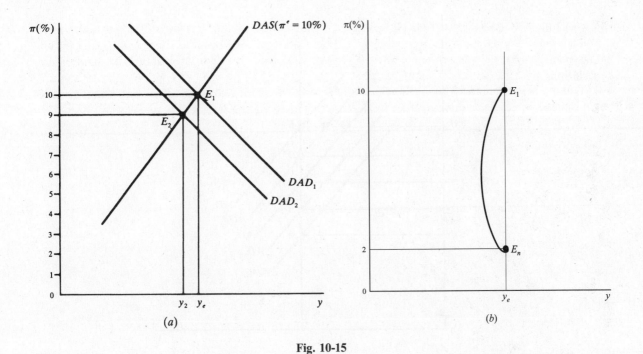

Fig. 10-15

Solved Problems

AGGREGATE DEMAND AND INFLATION

10.1 Define the terms *inflation*, *disinflation*, and *deflation*.

Inflation exists when there are continuous increases in the price level over time; the rate of inflation is found from the formula $\pi = [(p - p_{-1})/p_{-1}](100)$, where π is the inflation rate, p is the price level in the current period and p_{-1} is the price level in the previous period. When the rate of inflation is declining, there is disinflation. Deflation occurs when there are continuous decreases in the price level.

10.2 In period 1 schedules AS_1 and AD_1 in Fig. 10-16 determine price level 2.00 and full-employment output y_e. Suppose increases in aggregate demand shift schedule AD_1 upward to AD_2 in period 2, AD_3 in period 3, AD_4 in period 4, and AD_5 in period 5, with the price level increasing from 2.00 to 2.12, 2.25, 2.38, and 2.52 respectively. Find the economy's inflation rate for each period.

The rate of inflation π is found by solving the equation $\pi = [(p - p_{-1})/p_{-1}](100)$ for π. The rate of inflation between period 1 and period 2 is 6% or $[(2.12 - 2.00)/2.00](100)$; the rate is 6% for each successive period.

10.3 The equation for aggregate demand is $y = \alpha(\bar{A}) + \beta(\bar{M}/p)$, where α is the multiplying effect of autonomous spending $\bar{A}$ and β is the multiplying effect of the real money supply $\bar{M}/p$. Suppose output is $1000 in period 1; investment spending is $200; $\alpha = 2$ and $\beta = 3$. (a) Find the level of aggregate demand in period 2 and in period 3 when autonomous investment increases 5% each period. (b) If full-employment output is $1000, what government spending and/or money supply change is necessary to keep output at the full employment level?

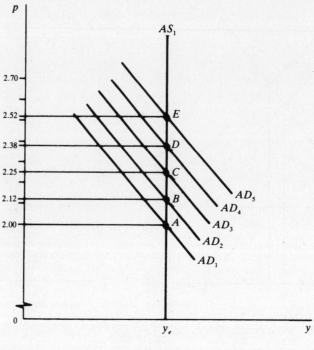

Fig. 10-16

(a) Investment spending increases from \$200 in period 1 to \$210 in period 2 to \$220.50 in period 3. The multiplier effect on the level of aggregate demand is $\alpha \Delta \bar{I}$. The level of aggregate demand increases \$20 during period 2 to \$1020 and \$21 during period 3 to \$1041.

(b) Since a change in autonomous government spending has the same multiplying effect as a change in autonomous investment, government spending must decrease \$10 during period 2 and \$10.50 during period 3 to keep output at \$1000. An alternative economic policy is a reduction in the nominal money supply. With β equal to 3, the nominal money supply must decrease \$6.67 during period 1 and \$7.00 during period 2 to keep output at \$1000.

INFLATION AND UNEMPLOYMENT: THE PHILLIPS CURVE

10.4   What is a Phillips curve?

In studying the relationship between the rate of unemployment and inflation, A.W. Phillips found that a low rate of unemployment was associated with a high rate of inflation, whereas a high rate of unemployment was associated with a low rate of inflation. The curve tracing out this relationship is presented in Fig. 10-17 and labeled *PC*. Some economists used this relationship to support expansive economic policies which increased the rate of inflation and lowered the rate of unemployment. A debate followed regarding the stability and long-run location and shape of the Phillips curve; some economists suggested that the curve shifted over time and/or was vertical in the long run.

10.5   In period 1, schedules AS_1 and AD_1 in Fig. 10-18(a) determine price level 2.00 and full employment output y_1. Continuous increases in aggregate demand shift AD_1 rightward in periods 2 through 5; the price level increases from 2.00 in the initial period to 2.04, 2.12, 2.25, and 2.43 in successive periods with associated output at y_e, y_2, y_3, y_4, and y_5. Outputs y_e through y_5 are

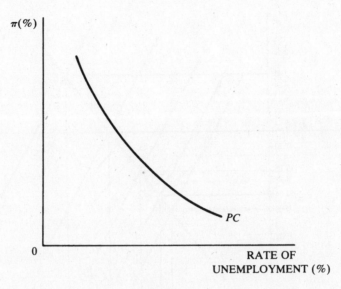

Fig. 10-17

associated with unemployment rates of 7%, 6%, 5%, 4%, and 3%. (*a*) Find the rate of inflation associated with aggregate demand schedules AD_1 through AD_5 in Fig. 10-18(*a*). (*b*) What rate of unemployment is associated with each rate of inflation? Plot this association and label the curve *PC*. (*c*) Does aggregate supply schedule AS_1 remain stable over time?

(*a*) Increases in the price level from 2.00 in period 1 to 2.43 in period 5 result in the following inflation rates: 2% in period 2, 4% in period 3, 6% in period 4, and 8% in period 5.

(*b*) A zero inflation rate in period 1 is associated with output y_e and a 7% rate of unemployment; 2% inflation is associated with a 6% unemployment rate in period 2; 4% with 5% in period 3; 6% with 4% in period 4, and 8% with 3% in period 5. The data are plotted in Fig. 10-18(*b*); the Phillips curve is labeled *PC*.

(*c*) The location of schedule AS_1 in space depends on the price level expected by labor when it contracted to supply its services. If AS_1 is associated with a 2.00 price level, we can expect AS_1 to shift leftward during some future period. When this occurs, the Phillips curve shifts rightward; with a specific unemployment rate associated with a higher rate of inflation.

10.6 Is there an inverse relationship between the rate of unemployment and the rate of inflation in the long run?

The relationship of the rate of unemployment and inflation depends on labor's ability to demand a higher nominal wage when there is an increase in the price level. Recall that aggregate supply is vertical when the nominal wage adjusts immediately to a change in the price level. Under such circumstances, a change in aggregate demand has no effect on real output; there is no relationship between inflation and unemployment, and the Phillips curve is vertical at the natural rate of unemployment. However, when labor contracts and/or incorrect inflationary expectations result in a growth of the nominal wage which is greater or less than the rate of inflation, aggregate supply is positively sloped, and the Phillips curve shows an inverse relationship between inflation and the rate of unemployment. It is unlikely that nominal wage growth will consistently differ from inflation over long periods. Hence, the Phillips curve is vertical at the natural rate of unemployment in the long run.

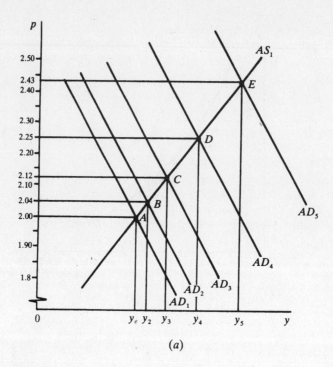

(a)

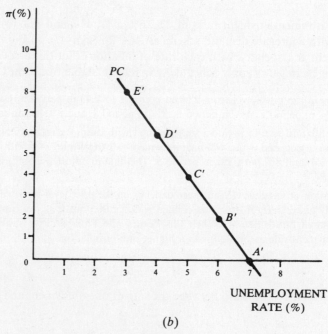

(b)

Fig. 10-18

SCHEDULE OF DYNAMIC AGGREGATE DEMAND

10.7 Suppose aggregate demand in period 1 is $y_1 = [hk_e/(h + kbk_e)]\bar{A} + [bk_e/h + kbk_e)]\bar{M}/p$. (*a*) Find an expression for aggregate demand in period 2 when there is a $\Delta\bar{G}$ increase in government spending, *ceteris paribus*. (*b*) Find an expression for aggregate demand in period 3 when the nominal money supply increases by $\Delta \bar{M}$, *ceteris paribus*. (*c*) Find a generalized equation for aggregate demand when there are changes in autonomous spending and/or the nominal money supply. (*d*) Why is the equation in part (*c*) an equation for dynamic aggregate demand?

(*a*) Aggregate demand in period 2 (y_2) equals the level of aggregate demand in period 1 (y_1) plus the increase in aggregate demand (Δy) due to increased government spending. Hence, $y_2 = y_1 + [hk_e/(h + kbk_e)]\Delta \bar{G}$.

(*b*) Aggregate demand in period 3 (y_3) equals the level of aggregate demand in period 2 (y_2) plus the increase in aggregate demand (Δy) due to an increase in the nominal money supply. Hence, $y_3 = y_2 + [bk_e/(h + kbk_e)](\Delta \bar{M}/p)$.

(*c*) A generalized equation for aggregate demand is $y = y_{-1} + \Delta y$; current period aggregate demand is the sum of aggregate demand in the previous period plus the increase in aggregate demand due to an increase in autonomous spending and/or an increase in the nominal money supply. Hence, $y = y_{-1} + [hk_e/(h + kbk_e)](\Delta \bar{A}) + [bk_e/(h + kbk_e)](\Delta \bar{M}/p)$.

(*d*) A dynamic aggregate demand schedule represents continuous growth in the level of aggregate spending over time. Growth of the nominal money supply shifts LM and aggregate demand rightward over successive periods. Such continuous increases in aggregate demand are captured by the equation $y = y_{-1} + [hk_e/(h + kbk_e)(\Delta \bar{A}) + [bk_e/(h + kbk_e)](\Delta \bar{M}/p)$.

10.8 (*a*) Find an equation for dynamic aggregate demand when the sources of incremental spending are permanent increases in government spending and/or growth rate for the nominal money supply. (*b*) Let $\dot{M}$ = the growth rate for the nominal money supply and π = the inflation rate. Explain why $(\dot{M} - \pi)$ can be substituted for $(\Delta \bar{M}/p)$ in the dynamic aggregate demand equation in part (*a*). (*c*) When $\alpha = hk_e/(h + kbk_e)$ and $\beta = bk_e/(h + kbk_e)$, the dynamic aggregate demand equation is $y = y_{-1} + \beta(\dot{M} - \pi) + \alpha(\Delta \bar{G})$. Find α and β when $h = 0$, $k_e = 5$, $b = 5$, and $k = 0.25$.

(*a*) When a permanent expansion of government spending is the only source of increased autonomous spending, and growth of the nominal money supply is the cause of a larger real money supply, the dynamic aggregate demand equation is $y = y_{-1} + [hk_e/(h + kbk_e)](\Delta \bar{G}) + [bk_e/(h + kbk_e)](\Delta \bar{M}/p)$.

(*b*) A change in the real money supply depends upon the change in the nominal money supply and the price level. For example, the real money supply is unchanged when the nominal money supply increases from \$100 to \$110 and the price level increases from 1.00 to 1.10; or restated, the real money supply is unchanged when the nominal money supply and price level increase 10%. Hence, a change in the real money supply can be presented as $(\Delta \bar{M}/p)$ or as $(\dot{M} - \pi)$, where $\dot{M}$ is the growth rate of the nominal money supply and π is the inflation rate.

(*c*) Substituting into the equation, we find that $\alpha = 0$ and $\beta = 4$:

$$\alpha = \frac{hk_e}{h + kbk_e}$$

$$\alpha = \frac{0(5)}{0 + 0.25(5)5} = 0$$

$$\beta = \frac{bk_e}{h + kbk_e}$$

$$\beta = \frac{5(5)}{0 + 0.25(5)5} = 4$$

10.9 The equation for dynamic aggregate demand is $y = y_{-1} + \beta(\dot{M} - \pi) + \alpha(\Delta \bar{G})$. Suppose $y_{-1} = \$800$, $\alpha = 2$, $\beta = 3$, $\dot{M} = 9\%$, and $\Delta \bar{G} = \$5$. (*a*) Find the level of aggregate demand when the inflation rate is 7%, 5%, or 3%. Plot and label the schedule DAD. (*b*) Find the level of aggregate demand when $\dot{M} = 9\%$ but $\Delta \bar{G} = \$10$ and the inflation rate is 7%, 5%, and 3%. Plot and label the schedule DAD'. (*c*) Find the level of aggregate demand when $\Delta \bar{G} = \$5$ but $\dot{M} = 5\%$ and the inflation rate is 7%, 5%, and 3%. Plot and label the schedule DAD''. (*d*) What happens to the dynamic aggregate demand schedule when there is a permanent increase in government spending [part (a) compared with part (b)] or a decrease in the growth rate of the nominal money supply [part (a) compared with part (c)]? (e) Are the shifts in dynamic aggregate demand due to changes in $\bar{G}$ and/or $\bar{M}$, sustained over time?

(a)   The level of aggregate demand is $816 when $\pi = 7\%$:

$$y = y_{-1} + \beta(\dot{M} - \pi) + \alpha(\Delta\bar{G})$$
$$y = \$800 + 3(9 - 7) + 2(5) = \$816$$

The level of aggregate demand is $822 when $\pi = 5\%$; it is $828 when the inflation rate is 3%. The data are plotted and the schedule is labeled DAD in Fig. 10-19.

(b)   The level of aggregate demand is $826 when the inflation rate is 7%, $\Delta\bar{G} = \$10$ and $\dot{M} = 9\%$; aggregate demand is $832 when $\pi = 5\%$ and $838 when $\pi = 3\%$. The data are plotted and the schedule is labeled DAD' in Fig. 10-19.

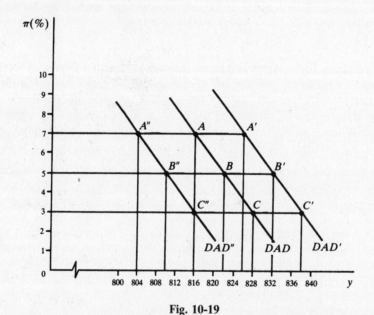

Fig. 10-19

(c)   The level of aggregate demand is $804 when $\pi = 7\%$, $\dot{M} = 5\%$, and $\Delta\bar{G} = \$5$; it is $810 when $\pi = 5\%$ and $816 when $\pi = 3\%$. The data are plotted and the schedule is labeled DAD'' in Fig. 10-19.

(d)   An increase in government spending shifts the dynamic aggregate demand schedule rightward. A decrease in the growth rate of the nominal supply shifts the dynamic aggregate demand schedule leftward.

(e)   An increase in government spending causes a one-period upward shift of DAD. For the shift to be sustained, government spending must continue to increase in successive periods. An increase in the growth rate of the nominal money supply results in a permanent shift of the dynamic aggregate demand schedule.

10.10   The equation for dynamic aggregate demand is $y = y_{-1} + \beta(\dot{M} - \pi) + \alpha(\Delta\bar{G})$. Suppose $\alpha = 2$, $\beta = 3$, $\dot{M} = 9\%$, and $\Delta\bar{G} = \$5$. (a) Find the level of aggregate demand when the inflation rate is 3%, 5%, and 7% and previous period output is $800, $830, or $710. Plot the data and label the schedule DAD when $y_{-1} = \$800$, DAD' when $y_{-1} = \$830$, and DAD'' when $y_{-1} = \$710$. (b) What happens to the dynamic aggregate demand schedule when there is a higher or lower level of aggregate demand in the previous period?

(a)   When previous output is $800 and $\pi = 3\%$, the level of aggregate demand is $828; it is $822 when $\pi = 5\%$ and $816 when $\pi = 7\%$. The data are plotted in Fig. 10-20; the schedule is labeled DAD. When previous period output is $830 and $\pi = 3\%$, the level of aggregate demand is $858; it is $852 when $\pi = 5\%$ and $846 when $\pi = 7\%$. The data are plotted in Fig. 10-20; the schedule is labeled DAD'. The level of aggregate demand is $798 when previous period output is $770 and $\pi = 3\%$. It is $792 when $\pi = 5\%$ and $786 when $\pi = 7\%$. The data are plotted in Fig. 10-20; the schedule is labeled DAD''.

(b)   The dynamic aggregate demand schedule shifts rightward when previous period output is increased and leftward when previous period output is reduced.

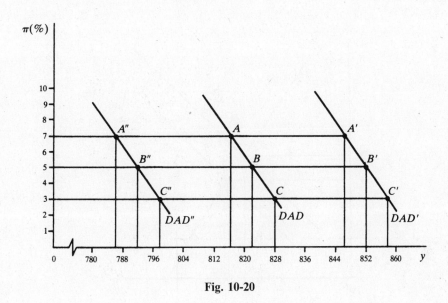

Fig. 10-20

SCHEDULE OF DYNAMIC AGGREGATE SUPPLY

10.11   (a) Explain the difference between the functions $W = f(p)$, the nominal wage as a function of the price level, and $gW = f(\pi)$, the growth of the nominal wage is a function of the inflation rate. (b) What is the difference between an aggregate supply and a dynamic aggregate supply schedule?

(a)   The function $W = f(p)$ ties the nominal wage to the price level; hence, the nominal wage increases 5% when the price level increases 5%. In the function $gW = f(\pi)$, we move from one-time changes in the price level to a continuous change. Labor asks for increases in the nominal wage because of inflation.

(b)   An aggregate supply schedule is derived from a labor supply function which links the nominal wage to the price level. Price-level changes are continuous for a dynamic aggregate supply schedule where labor's demand for nominal wage growth is tied to the inflation rate.

10.12   (a) Explain the function $\pi^e = f(\pi_{-1})$. (b) Are labor markets in equilibrium when $gW = f(\pi^e)$, $\pi^e = f(\pi_{-1})$, and the current inflation rate differs from the previous period's inflation rate?

(a)   The function $\pi^e = f(\pi_{-1})$ is an adaptive approach to inflationary expectations; it specifies that inflation is expected to continue at the rate which existed in the previous period.

(b) $gW = f(\pi^e)$ specifies that labor's demand for an increase in its nominal wage is a function of the expected rate of inflation. When $\pi^e = f(\pi_{-1})$, $gW = f(\pi_{-1})$. Hence, the labor markets are not in equilibrium when current period inflation differs from the inflation rate in the previous period. When $\pi > \pi_{-1}$, the real wage is below the equilibrium real wage, and output exceeds full-employment output. The real wage is above the market-clearing real wage when $\pi < \pi_{-1}$.

10.13 Suppose labor market equilibrium exists when L_e workers are employed in Fig. 10-21. The demand for labor schedule is $L_d(\pi = 10\%)$ when the current inflation rate is 10%; the labor supply schedule is $L_s(\pi^e = 5\%)$ when labor expects a 5% inflation rate and $L_s(\pi^e = 10\%)$ when it expects a 10% inflation rate. Compare the number of workers employed when current inflation exceeds expected inflation with the workers employed when current inflation equals expected inflation.

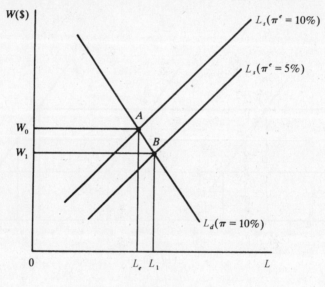

Fig. 10-21

L_1 workers are employed for schedules $L_d(\pi = 10\%)$ and $L_s(\pi^e = 5\%)$; L_e workers are employed for schedules $L_d(\pi = 10\%)$ and $L_s(\pi^e = 10\%)$. The labor markets are in equilibrium when the expected inflation rate is the same as the current inflation rate. When labor's inflationary expectations are below the current inflation rate, the labor markets are in disequilibrium since employment exceeds the market-clearing full-employment level.

10.14 The equation for dynamic aggregate supply is $\pi = \pi^e + \lambda(y - y_e)$. Suppose $y_e = \$200$ and $\lambda = 0.50$ (a) Find y when π^e is 6% and the current inflation rate is 4%, 6%, or 8%. Plot the dynamic aggregate supply schedule and label it $DAS(\pi^e = 6\%)$. (b) Compare the amount supplied to the $200 full-employment level of output when $\pi^e > \pi$ and $\pi^e < \pi$. (c) Find y when $\pi^e = 4\%$ and the current inflation rate is 4%, 6%, and 8%. Plot the dynamic aggregate supply schedule and label it $DAS(\pi^e = 4\%)$. (d) What happens to the dynamic aggregate supply schedule when inflationary expectations decline from 6% to 4%? (e) When $\pi^e = f(\pi_{-1})$, what happens to the DAS schedule in the next period when current inflation differs from previous period inflation?

(a) When π^e is 6% and $\pi = 4\%$, y is $196 [4\% = 6\% + 0.5(y - \$200); y = \$196]$. y is $200 when $\pi = 6\%$; $y = \$204$ when $\pi = 8\%$. The association of inflation and output is plotted in Fig. 10-22 with the schedule labeled $DAS(\pi^e = 6\%)$.

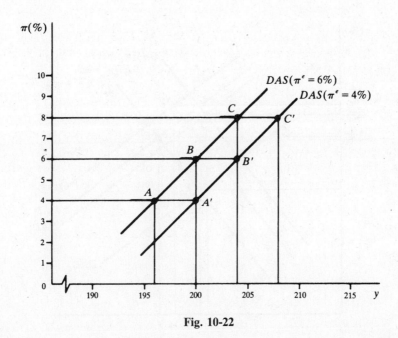

Fig. 10-22

(b) When $\pi^e > \pi$, the \$196 supplied is less than the \$200 full-employment level. Aggregate supply is at the \$200 full-employment level when $\pi^e = \pi$ and exceeds the full-employment level when $\pi^e < \pi$.

(c) When π^e is 4% and $\pi = 4\%$, y equals \$200; y is \$204 when $\pi = 6\%$ and equals \$208 when $\pi = 8\%$. The association of inflation and output is plotted in Fig. 10-22 with the schedule labeled $DAS(\pi^e = 4\%)$.

(d) The dynamic aggregate supply schedule shifts rightward from $DAS(\pi^e = 6\%)$ to $DAS(\pi^e = 4\%)$ when inflationary expectations decline from 6% to 4%.

(e) When $\pi^e = \pi_{-1}$, the DAS schedule shifts leftward in the next period if $\pi > \pi_{-1}$. DAS shifts rightward in the next period when current inflation is less than previous period inflation.

INFLATION AND OUTPUT

10.15 Output is at full-employment level y_e during period 0 for schedules DAD_0 and $DAS(\pi^e = \pi_0)$ in Fig. 10-23. During period 1, the nominal money supply increases $X\%$. What happens to the DAD and DAS schedules during periods 1, 2, and 3? Find output and inflation at the end of periods 1, 2, and 3.

> *Period 1*: Because of an $X\%$ increase in the nominal money supply, the DAD schedule shifts rightward from DAD_0 to DAD_1. Because $\pi^e = f(\pi_{-1})$, there is no shift of DAS. Output expands from y_e to y_1, and the inflation rate increases from π_0 to π_1.
>
> *Period 2*: Increased output in period 1 (y_e to y_1) causes DAD_1 to shift rightward to DAD_2. Because inflation increased during period 1 to π_1, dynamic aggregate supply shifts leftward to $DAS(\pi^e = \pi_1)$. Output declines to y_2 and inflation increases to π_2.
>
> *Period 3*: The decrease in output during period 2 (y_1 to y_2) causes DAD_2 to shift leftward to DAD_3. DAS shifts leftward to $DAS(\pi^e = \pi_2)$ due to increased inflation during period 2. Output falls to y_3 and inflation declines to π_3.

10.16 The equations for dynamic aggregate demand and dynamic aggregate supply are $y = y_{-1} + \beta(\dot{M} - \pi) + \alpha f$ and $\pi = \pi^e + \lambda(y - y_e)$, respectively. Output is initially at the \$500 full-employment level, the inflation rate is 4%, $\beta = 3$, $\alpha = 2$, $f = 0$, and $\lambda = 0.5$. Suppose the growth

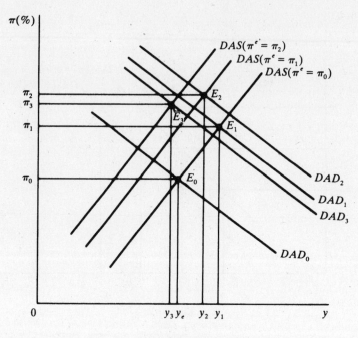

Fig. 10-23

rate of the nominal money supply increases from 4 to 10%, *ceteris paribus*. (*a*) Find inflation and output for periods 1 through 6 which result from the more rapid growth of the nominal money supply. (*b*) Plot the output levels and inflation rates found in part (*a*). (*c*) What is the rate of inflation when the economy eventually returns to full-employment output?

(*a*)   *Period 1*:

$$y = y_{-1} + \beta(\dot{M} - \pi) + \alpha f \qquad (DAD \text{ equation})$$
$$y = \$500 + 3(10 - \pi) + 0$$
$$\pi = \pi^e + \lambda(y - y_e) \qquad (DAS \text{ equation})$$
$$\pi = 4 + 0.5(y - \$500)$$

Substituting the *DAS* equation into the *DAD* equation, we have

$$y = \$500 + 3(10) - 3[4 + 0.5(y - \$500)]$$
$$y = \$500 + 30 - 12 - 1.5y + \$750$$
$$y = \$507.20$$
$$\pi = 7.60\%$$

Period 2:

$$y = y_{-1} + \beta(\dot{M} - \pi) + \alpha f \qquad (DAD \text{ equation})$$
$$y = \$507.20 + 3(10 - \pi) + 0$$
$$\pi = \pi^e + \lambda(y - y_e) \qquad (DAS \text{ equation})$$
$$\pi = 7.60 + 0.5(y - \$500)$$

Substituting the *DAS* equation into the *DAD* equation, we have

$$y = \$507.20 + 3(10) - 3[7.6 + 0.5(y - \$500)]$$
$$y = \$505.76$$
$$\pi = 10.48\%$$

Period 3: Substituting the *DAS* equation into the *DAD* equation, we have

$$y = \$505.76 + 3(10) - 3[10.48 + 0.5(y - \$500)]$$
$$y = \$501.73$$
$$\pi = 11.345\%$$

Period 4: Substituting the *DAS* equation into the *DAD* equation, we have

$$y = \$501.73 + 3(10) - 3[11.345 + 0.5(y - \$500)]$$
$$y = \$499.08$$
$$\pi = 10.88\%$$

Period 5:

$$y = \$498.58$$
$$\pi = 10.17\%$$

Period 6:

$$y = \$499.23$$
$$y = 9.79\%$$

(b)   See Fig. 10-24.

(c)   At equilibrium $y = y_{-1}$, $\pi = \pi_{-1}$ and $\dot{M} = \pi$ so that there are no further shifts of *DAD* or *DAS*. At equilibrium the rate of inflation must be 10%, which equals the 10% growth rate of the nominal money supply.

10.17   Output is at full-employment level y_e during period 0 for schedules DAD_0 and $DAS(\pi^e = \pi_0)$ in Fig. 10-25. During period 1, there is an increase in the level of government spending, *ceteris paribus*. What happens to the *DAD* and *DAS* schedules during periods 1, 2, and 3? Find output and inflation at the end of periods 1, 2, and 3.

Period 1: The *DAD* schedule shifts rightward to DAD_1. There is no shift of *DAS*, since inflationary expectations are based on the inflation rate in period 0. Output expands from y_e to y_1, and the inflation rate increases from π_0 to π_1 at the end of period 1.

Period 2: The leftward shift of DAD_1 to DAD_2 is the net result of no further additions to the level of government spending in period 2 (a negative influence on further demand growth) and the y_e to y_1 increase in output in period 1 (a positive factor expanding demand growth). *DAS* shifts leftward to $DAS(\pi^e = \pi_1)$. As a·result of the leftward shift of *DAD* and *DAS*, output and inflation are y_2 and π_2 at the end of period 2.

Period 3: Dynamic aggregate demand schedule shifts leftward to DAD_3 due to decline in output between period 1 and 2. Dynamic aggregate supply shifts leftward to $DAS(\pi^e = \pi_2)$ due to the increase in inflation during the previous period. Output and inflation fall to y_3 and π_3 at the end of period 3.

10.18   The equations for *DAD* and *DAS* are $y = y_{-1} + \beta(\dot{M} - \pi) + \alpha f$ and $\pi = \pi^e + \lambda(y - y_e)$, respectively. The economy is initially at the $500 full-employment level, the inflation rate is 4%, nominal money supply growth is 4%, $\beta = 3$, $\alpha = 2$, and $\lambda = 0.5$. Suppose there is a $10 increase in the level of government spending, *ceteris paribus*. (a) Find inflation and output for periods 1

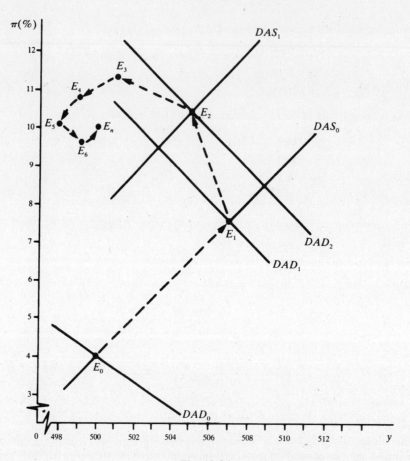

Fig. 10-24

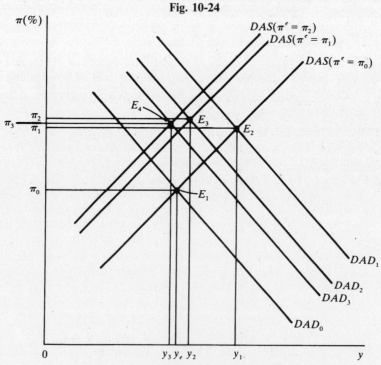

Fig. 10-25

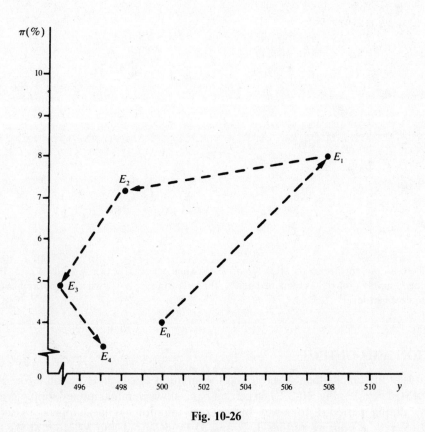

Fig. 10-26

through 4 which result from the $10 fiscal stimulus. (*b*) Plot the output levels and inflation rates found in part (*a*). (*c*) What is the rate of inflation when the economy returns to the $500 full employment level?

(*a*)   *Period 1*:

$$y = y_{-1} + \beta(\dot{M} - \pi) + \alpha f \qquad (DAD \text{ equation})$$
$$y = \$500 + 3(4 - \pi) + 2(10)$$
$$\pi = \pi^e + \lambda(y - y_e) \qquad (DAS \text{ equation})$$
$$\pi = 4 + 0.5(y - \$500)$$

Substituting the *DAS* equation into the *DAD* equation, we have

$$y = \$500 + 3(4) - 3[4 + 0.5(y - \$500)] + 2(10)$$
$$y = \$508$$
$$\pi = 8\%$$

Period 2:

$$y = \$508 + 3(4 - \pi) + 0 \qquad (DAD \text{ equation})$$
$$\pi = 8 + 0.5(y - \$500) \qquad (DAS \text{ equation})$$

(*b*)   See Fig. 10-26.

Substituting the *DAS* equation into the *DAD* equation, we have

$$y = \$508 + 3(4) - 3[8 + 0.5(y - \$500)] + 0$$
$$y = \$498.40$$
$$\pi = 7.20\%$$

Period 3:

$$y = \$498.40 + 3(4) - 3[7.20 + 0.5(y - \$500)]$$
$$y = \$495.52$$
$$\pi = 4.96\%$$

Period 4:

$$y = \$495.52 + 3(4) - 3[4.96 + 0.5(y - \$500)]$$
$$y = \$497.06$$
$$\pi = 3.49\%$$

(c)   There are no further shifts of *DAD* or *DAS* when $y = y_{-1}$, $\pi = \pi_{-1}$, and $\dot{M} = \pi$. Because nominal money supply growth has remained at 4%, the inflation rate is 4% when output returns to the \$500 full-employment level.

DISINFLATION AND OUTPUT

10.19   Output is at full-employment level y_e and the inflation rate is π_0 in period 0 for schedules DAD_0 and $DAS(\pi^e = \pi_0)$ in Fig. 10-27. The central bank slows nominal money supply growth from $Y\%$ to $X\%$ during period 1 to lower the rate of inflation. What happens to schedules DAD_0 and $DAS(\pi^e = \pi_0)$ during periods 1, 2, and 3? Find output and inflation at the end of periods 1, 2, and 3.

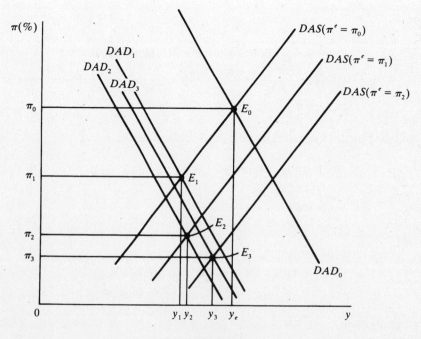

Fig. 10-27

Period 1: The DAD schedule shifts leftward from DAD_0 to DAD_1 because of slower growth of the nominal money supply. Since inflationary expectations lag current inflation by one period, there is no change in the DAS schedule. Output and inflation decline from y_e to y_1 and from π_0 to π_1 at the end of period 1.

Period 2: The DAD schedule continues to shift leftward because of the decline in previous period output; DAD_1 shifts leftward to DAD_2. The DAS schedule shifts rightward from $DAS(\pi^e = \pi_0)$ to $DAS(\pi^e = \pi_1)$ as a result of lower inflation during period 1. When we assume that the DAS shift is greater than that of DAD, output increases to y_2 while inflation falls to π_2.

Period 3: DAD_2 shifts rightward to DAD_3 because output increased in period 2. The lower inflation rate shifts DAS rightward to $DAS(\pi^e = \pi_2)$. Output increases to y_3 and inflation decreases to π_3.

10.20 The equation for dynamic aggregate demand and dynamic aggregate supply are $y = y_{-1} + \beta(\dot{M} - \pi) + \alpha f$ and $\pi = \pi^e + \lambda(y - y_e)$, respectively. The inflation rate is 10%, full-employment output is \$1000, nominal money supply growth is 10%, $\beta = 3$, $\alpha = 2$, $f = 0$, and $\lambda = 0.5$. The central bank lowers nominal money supply growth from 10% to 2% during period 1 to reduce inflation. (*a*) Find inflation and output at the end of periods 1 through 5 which result from slower growth of the nominal money supply. (*b*) Plot the output and inflation rates found in part (*a*).

(*a*)   *Period 1*:

$$y = y_{-1} + \beta(\dot{M} - \pi) + \alpha f \qquad (DAD \text{ equation})$$
$$y = \$1000 + 3(2 - \pi) + 0$$
$$\pi = \pi^e + \lambda(y - y_e) \qquad (DAS \text{ equation})$$
$$\pi = 10 + 0.5(y - 1000)$$

Substituting the DAS equation into the DAD equation, we have

$$y = \$1000 + 3(2) - 3[10 + 0.5(y - 1000)]$$
$$y = \$990.40$$
$$\pi = 5.20\%$$

Period 2:

$$y = \$992.32$$
$$\pi = 1.36\%$$

Period 3:

$$y = \$997.70$$
$$\pi = 0.21\%$$

Period 4:

$$y = \$1001.23$$
$$\pi = 0.83\%$$

Period 5:

$$y = \$1001.90$$
$$\pi = 1.78\%$$

(*b*)   See Fig. 10-28.

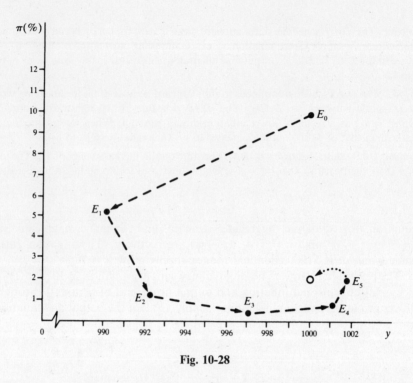

Fig. 10-28

10.21 The equations for dynamic aggregate demand and dynamic aggregate supply are $y = y_{-1} + \beta(\dot{M} - \pi) + \alpha f$ and $\pi = \pi^e + \lambda(y - y_e)$, respectively. The inflation rate is 10%, full-employment output is $1000, nominal money supply growth is 10%, $\beta = 3$, $\alpha = 2$, $f = 0$, and $\lambda = 0.5$. Concerned about the recessionary effect of a reduction in the inflation rate, the central bank introduces a policy of "gradualism" where nominal money supply growth is lowered 2% in each of the next four periods. (Note: nominal money supply growth is reduced 8% as in Problem 10.20, but over four quarters rather than entirely in period 1.) (a) Find inflation and output for periods 1 through 5, which result from slower money supply. (b) Plot the output and inflation rates found in part (a). (c) Compare the "cold turkey" (Problem 10.20) and "gradualism" (Problem 10.21) approaches to reducing inflation.

(a)   *Period 1*:

$$y = y_{-1} + \beta(\dot{M} - \pi) + \alpha f \qquad (DAD \text{ equation})$$
$$y = \$1000 + 3(8 - \pi) + 0$$
$$\pi = \pi^e + \lambda(y - y_e) \qquad (DAD \text{ equation})$$
$$\pi = 10 + 0.5(y - \$1000)$$

Substituting the *DAS* equation into the *DAD* equation, we have

$$y = \$1000 + 3(8) - 3[10 - 0.5(y - 1000)]$$
$$y = \$997.60$$
$$\pi = 8.80\%$$

Period 2: Substituting the *DAS* equation into the *DAD* equation, we have

$$y = \$997.60 + 3(6) - 3[8.80 + 0.5(y - 1000)]$$
$$y = \$995.68$$
$$\pi = 6.64\%$$

Period 3:

$$y = \$995.10$$
$$\pi = 4.19\%$$

Period 4:

$$y = \$995.41$$
$$\pi = 1.89\%$$

Period 5:

$$y = \$998.29$$
$$\pi = 1.04\%$$

(*b*)   See Fig. 10-29.

(*c*)   When nominal money growth is lowered to 8% in one period (Problem 10.20), output and inflation experience a dramatic decline during the first two periods; by the third period output is rapidly approaching full-employment output. The decline in output with the gradualism approach is less severe; however, output remains below full employment for more periods. Policy-makers have the choice of a sharp recession followed by rapid recovery or a mild but prolonged recession in lowering the inflation rate.

10.22   Suppose $\pi^e = f(\pi_{-2})$, inflationary expectations lag actual inflation by two periods. (*a*) Use the parameters of Problem 10.21 and a two-period lag structure for inflationary expectations to find output and inflation for periods 1 through 5. (*b*) What effect does a longer lag structure have upon the adjustment path?

(*a*)   *Period 1*: Output and inflation are the same as in Problem 10.21; $y = \$997.60$ and $\pi = 8.80\%$.

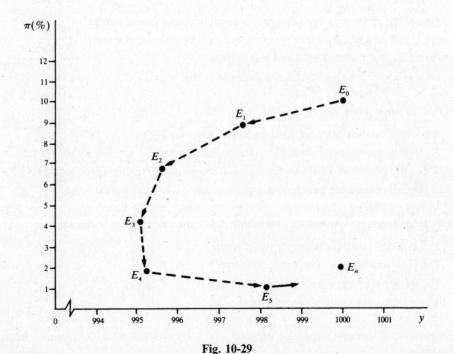

Fig. 10-29

Period 2:

$$y = \$994.25$$
$$\pi = 7.13\%$$

Period 3:

$$y = \$990.50$$
$$\pi = 5.25\%$$

Period 4:

$$y = \$990.05$$
$$\pi = 2.15\%$$

Period 5:

$$y = 992.12$$
$$\pi = 1.31\%$$

(b) The decline in output is more severe and prolonged when aggregate supply reacts slowly to changing inflation. Thus, long-term contracts make it difficult for policy-makers to lower the economy's inflation rate.

Multiple Choice Questions

1. When the aggregate supply schedule is positively sloped, continuous increases in the nominal money supply, *ceteris paribus*, result in

    (a) No change in the price level and proportional increases in real output.

    (b) No change in real output and proportional increases in the price level.

    (c) An increase in the price level and real output.

    (d) An increase in the price level and a decrease in real output.

2. The Phillips curve shows

    (a) An inverse relationship between the real and nominal wage.

    (b) An inverse relationship between the rate of inflation and the rate of unemployment.

    (c) A positive relationship between the nominal wage and the rate of unemployment.

    (d) A positive relationship between the rate of inflation and the nominal wage.

3. The dynamic aggregate demand schedule shifts rightward when there is an increase in

    (a) The expected rate of inflation, *ceteris paribus*.

    (b) The growth rate of the nominal money supply, *ceteris paribus*.

    (c) The income tax rate, *ceteris paribus*.

    (d) The current inflation rate, *ceteris paribus*.

4. The equation for dynamic aggregate demand is $y = y_{-1} + \beta(\dot{M} - \pi) + \alpha f$. Dynamic aggregate demand shifts to the

    (a)   Right when y_{-1} increases, *ceteris paribus*.

    (b)   Right when π increases, *ceteris paribus*.

    (c)   Right when $\dot{M}$ decreases, *ceteris paribus*.

    (d)   Left when π decreases, *ceteris paribus*.

5.   Dynamic aggregate supply is

    (a)   Positively sloped when $\pi^e = f(\pi_{-1})$.

    (b)   Positively sloped when $gW = f(\pi)$.

    (c)   Vertical when $gW = f(\pi_{-1})$.

    (d)   Vertical when $gW = f(\pi^e)$.

6.   The equation for dynamic aggregate supply is $\pi = \pi^e + \lambda(y - y_e)$. Dynamic aggregate supply shifts leftward, when

    (a)   There is an increase in y, *ceteris paribus*.

    (b)   There is an increase in π^e, *ceteris paribus*.

    (c)   There is an increase in π, *ceteris paribus*.

    (d)   There is a decrease in λ, *ceteris paribus*.

7.   An economy is in inflationary equilibrium. An increase in the growth rate of the nominal money supply shifts

    (a)   *DAD* rightward, establishing equilibrium at a higher rate of inflation and level of output.

    (b)   *DAD* and *DAS* rightward, establishing equilibrium at a higher rate of inflation and level of output.

    (c)   *DAD* and *DAS* leftward with a new equilibrium established at a future period at a higher rate of inflation and level of output.

    (d)   *DAD* to the right and *DAS* to the left with a new equilibrium established at a future period at a higher rate of inflation and no change in output.

8.   An economy is in inflationary equilibrium. A sustained increase in government spending shifts

    (a)   *DAD* rightward for one period.

    (b)   *DAD* rightward permanently.

    (c)   *DAD* and *DAS* rightward permanently.

    (d)   *DAD* rightward, and a new equilibrium is established after successive periods at a higher rate of inflation.

9.   Disinflationary demand-management policies:

    (a)   Achieve a lower rate of inflation without causing a decrease in output.

    (b)   Reduce output but have no initial effect on the inflation rate.

    (c)   Require an increase in government spending.

    (d)   Require a reduction in the growth rate of the nominal money supply.

10.   The economy is in inflationary equilibrium. A reduction in

    (a)   Government spending permanently lowers the economy's rate of inflation.

    (b)   Nominal money supply growth lowers the inflation rate with no effect on output in the short run.

    (c)   Nominal money supply growth lowers the inflation rate and the level of output in the short run.

    (d)   Government spending lowers the rate of inflation with no effect on output in the short run.

True or False Questions

11. _____ When output is at its full-employment level and aggregate supply is positively sloped, an increase in the nominal money supply results in an increase in the price level and output in the short run.

12. _____ The economy's rate of inflation is 3% when the price level increases from 100 to 103 to 106 to 109.

13. _____ The Phillips curve displays no relationship between output and the rate of inflation when aggregate supply is vertical.

14. _____ The dynamic aggregate demand schedule shifts rightward when there is an increase in the growth rate of the nominal money supply, *ceteris paribus*.

15. _____ The dynamic aggregate demand schedule shifts leftward when output during the past period decreases, *ceteris paribus*.

16. _____ Dynamic aggregate supply is positively sloped when increases in the nominal wage are a function of the inflation rate during the current period.

17. _____ A positively sloped dynamic aggregate supply schedule shifts leftward when there is a decrease in the current rate of inflation.

18. _____ An economy can be in equilibrium with a 5% rate of inflation.

19. _____ An attempt to lower the economy's rate of inflation will result in a decrease in output when the dynamic aggregate supply schedule is positively sloped.

20. _____ An increase in the level of government spending has no effect upon the economy's level of output or rate of inflation in the long run.

Answers to Multiple Choice and True or False Questions

1. (*c*); **2.** (*b*); **3.** (*b*); **4.** (*a*); **5.** (*a*); **6.** (*b*); **7.** (*d*); **8.** (*a*); **9.** (*d*); **10.** (*c*); **11.** T; **12.** F; **13.** T; **14.** T; **15.** T; **16.** F; **17.** F; **18.** T; **19.** T; **20.** T.

Chapter 11

Economic Growth

Chapter Summary

1. The sources of economic growth are the productivity of resources, the stock of capital, and the labor supply. In the absence of technological change, output per worker increases only when there is an increase in the capital–labor ratio, i.e., capital increases at a faster rate than labor.

2. In the Solow growth model with a constant labor supply, an economy reaches a steady state when saving per worker equals depreciation investment per worker, and there are no further increases in the capital–labor ratio. An increase in the economy's rate of saving increases the steady state capital–labor ratio and output per worker.

3. When there is growth of the labor supply, steady state growth is reached when saving per worker equals investment per worker for depreciation and labor supply growth. An economy moves to a higher capital–labor ratio and output per worker when the labor supply grows at a slower rate.

4. A neutral technological change makes capital and labor more productive, and increases the capital–labor ratio as well as output per worker.

5. A labor augmenting technological change increases only the productivity of labor. Such a technological improvement increases the effective labor supply and leaves the capital–effective labor supply ratio unchanged; output per worker increases.

6. The equation $\Delta Y/Y = \Delta A/A + \alpha \Delta K/K + (1-\alpha)\Delta L/L$ is used to measure the sources of economic growth.

Chapter Outline

11.1 SOURCES OF ECONOMIC GROWTH

The goal of economic growth is improvement in people's economic well-being, i.e., an increase in their standard of living. This is achieved for the majority of individuals when output per worker increases over time. The Cobb–Douglas production function $Y = A(K^\alpha L^{1-\alpha})$, presented in Section 3.1, relates potential output to A, the productivity of resources, K, the economy's stock of capital, and L, its labor supply. When the labor supply is a subset of the total population, an increase in the labor participation rate (percentage of the population in the labor supply), raises output as does an increase in the economy's stock of capital, and/or improved technology. While an increase in the labor supply, in the absence of technological change and capital accumulation, raises total output, output per worker is reduced because of the law of diminishing returns.

EXAMPLE 11.1. Suppose an economy's production function is $Y = A(K^{0.5}L^{0.5})$. When $A = 1$, $K = 36$, and $L = 9$, potential output is $18.00 [$Y = 1(\sqrt{36}\sqrt{9})$; $Y = 6(3) = \$18.00$] and output per worker is $2.00 [$Y = Y/L$; $Y = \$18.00/9 = \$2.00$]. When the labor supply increases from 9 to 12, *ceteris paribus*, potential output increases from \$18.00 to \$20.78, but output per worker decreases from \$2.00 to \$1.73.

In the absence of technological change, capital per worker (the capital–labor ratio) increases only when capital increases at a faster rate than the labor supply. Output per worker decreases when the labor supply increases at a faster rate than capital. Output per worker is unchanged when labor and capital increases at the same rate; output per worker increases when capital grows at a faster rate than the labor supply. Fig. 11-1 relates output per worker to the capital–labor ratio. When the capital–labor ratio is k_0, output per worker is y_0. A decrease in the capital–labor ratio below k_0 reduces output per worker, while an increase raises it. In the absence of technological change, an increase in the economy's capital–labor ratio is the only source of a higher standard of living.

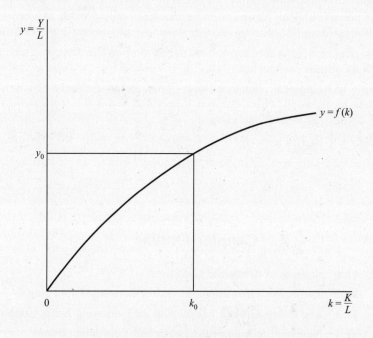

Fig. 11-1

EXAMPLE 11.2. Suppose an economy's production function is $Y = A(K^{0.5}L^{0.5})$. When $A = 1$, $K = 36$, and $L = 9$, potential output is \$18.00, and output per worker is \$2.00. The capital–labor ratio is 4 [$k = K/L$; $k = 36/9 = 4$].

Situation 1: Capital increases by 50% and the labor supply increases by 100%.

    The stock of capital increases from 36 to 54 while the labor supply increases from 9 to 18. The capital–labor ratio decreases from 4 to 3. Although potential output increases from \$18.00 to \$31.18, output per worker decreases from \$2.00 to \$1.73. A decrease in the capital–labor results in a decrease in output per worker.

Situation 2: The supplies of capital and labor double.

    Capital increases from 36 to 72 while labor increases from 9 to 18. The capital–labor ratio is unchanged at 4. Output increases from \$18.00 to \$36.00, and output per worker remains at \$2.00. When capital and labor grow at the same rate, the capital–labor ratio is unchanged, as is output per worker.

Situation 3: Capital increases 50% from 36 to 54 while the labor supply increases 33% from 9 to 12.

The capital–labor ratio rises from 4 to 4.5. Output increases from $18.00 to $25.46 and output per worker from $2.00 to $2.12. An increase in the capital–labor ratio raises output per worker.

11.2   THE SOLOW GROWTH MODEL WITH A CONSTANT LABOR SUPPLY

Robert Solow's model of economic growth can be used to analyze how the saving rate, growth rate of the labor supply, and improved technology affect output per worker. In this section, we show the linkage between saving and the economy's capital–labor ratio and output per worker. A steady state is eventually reached where there is no further increase in the capital–labor ratio and output per worker.

Fig. 11-1 shows the linkage between output per worker and the capital–labor ratio. In a closed economy with no government, the capital–labor ratio increases, as does output per worker, as long as savings per worker (and therefore gross investment per worker) exceeds depreciation investment per worker. With s representing the rate of saving, $s[f(k)]$ saving per worker, d the rate of depreciation, and $d \cdot k$ depreciation investment per worker, the capital–labor ratio and output per worker increase as long as

$$s[f(k)] - d \cdot k > 0$$

A steady state exists and there is no further increase in the capital–labor ratio and output per worker when

$$s[f(k)] = d \cdot k$$

For depreciation rate d and saving rate s, the capital–labor ratio at the steady state is

$$k^* = A^2[(s^2/d^2)]$$

and output per worker is

$$y^* = A\sqrt{k^*}$$

(See Problem 11.3 for derivation of k^* and y^*.) It therefore follows that an increase in the economy's rate of saving raises the steady state capital–labor ratio k^* and output per worker y^* (Example 11.5). There is, however, a saving rate at which consumption per worker is maximized. The steady state capital–labor ratio which maximizes consumption per worker is called the Golden Rule of Capital Accumulation (Example 11.6).

EXAMPLE 11.3.   In Fig. 11-2, line $d \cdot k$ is the depreciation investment line. A fixed percentage d of existing capital per worker k wears out and must be replaced. The output curve $f(k)$ related output per worker y to the capital–labor ratio k. For example, in Fig. 11-2 output per worker is AF when the capital–labor ratio is k_0. In this no-government closed economy, AF also represents income per worker. Saving curve $s[f(k)]$ represents saving per worker at each capital–labor ratio. At capital–labor ratio k_0, saving per worker is AC. Since income is either saved or consumed, CF at k_0 is consumption per worker. Since saving equals investment in this no-government closed economy, saving per worker always equals gross investment per worker. At k_0, saving and therefore gross investment per worker is AC; depreciation investment per worker is AB. Since gross investment per worker AC is greater than depreciation investment per worker AB, the capital–labor ratio increases. When the capital–labor ratio reaches k^*, saving per worker DE equals depreciation investment per worker DE. The economy reaches a steady state in which there is no further increase in the capital–labor ratio k^* or output per worker DG.

EXAMPLE 11.4.   Suppose $A = 1$, $K = 36$, $L = 9$, the saving rate s is 0.30, and the depreciation rate d is 0.10. As calculated in Example 11.1, output per worker is $2.00 and the capital–labor ratio is 4. At this output level, saving per worker is $0.60, as is gross investment per worker. Since 10% of the existing capital per worker is depreciating, depreciation investment per worker is $0.40. Gross investment per worker exceeds depreciation investment per worker ($0.60 − $0.40 = $0.20), and the capital–labor ratio increases to 4.20 in the next time period. When the capital–labor ratio is 9 and output per worker is $3.00, saving and gross investment per worker of $0.90

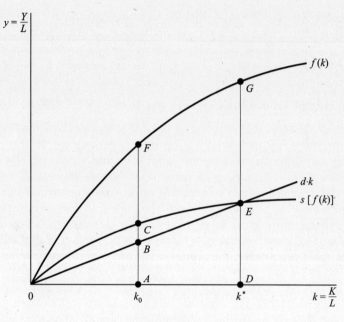

Fig. 11-2

$[0.30(\$3.00) = \$0.90]$ equals depreciation investment per worker of $\$0.90$ $[0.10(9) = \$0.90]$. The economy has reached a steady state, since there is no further increase in the capital–labor ratio and output per worker.

EXAMPLE 11.5. In Fig. 11-3, k^* is the steady state capital–labor ratio and y^* is output per worker for depreciation line $d \cdot k$, saving curve $s[f(k)]$, and output curve $f(k)$. An increase in the saving rate from s to s_1 shifts the saving curve upward from $s[f(k)]$ to $s_1[f(k)]$. Gross investment per worker now exceeds depreciation investment per worker at k^* and the capital–labor ratio increases. The economy eventually reaches a new steady state at k_1^*. The higher saving rate raises the steady state capital–labor ratio from k^* to k_1^* and output per worker from y^* to y_1^*.

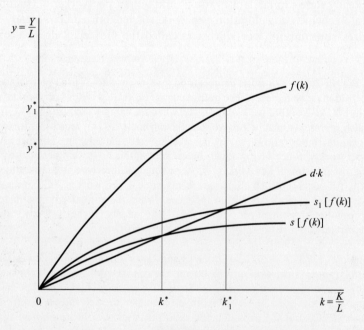

Fig. 11-3

EXAMPLE 11.6. Table 11-1 presents the steady state capital–labor ratio (column 2) and output per worker (column 3) for various saving rates (column 1) when $A = 2$ and $d = 0.10$. [The steady state capital–labor ratio is found from the equation $k^* = A^2[(s^2/d^2)]$ and steady state output per worker from $y^* = A\sqrt{k^*}$.] Consumption per worker is calculated in column 4 by multiplying one minus the saving rate $(1 - s)$ by output per worker, found in column 3. For example, the consumption rate is 0.90 and consumption per worker is $3.60 when the saving rate is 0.10 and output per worker is $4.00. The golden rule of capital accumulation exists at a 0.50 saving rate, and consumption per worker is maximized at $10.00.

Table 11-1

(1)	(2)	(3)	(4)
s	k^*	y^*	c
0.10	4.00	$4.00	$3.60
0.20	16.00	$8.00	$6.40
0.30	36.00	$12.00	$8.40
0.40	64.00	$16.00	$9.60
0.45	81.00	$18.00	$9.90
0.50	100.00	$20.00	$10.00
0.55	121.00	$22.00	$9.90
0.60	144.00	$24.00	$9.60
0.70	196.00	$28.00	$8.40

11.3 THE SOLOW GROWTH MODEL WITH AN INCREASING LABOR SUPPLY

When the labor supply increases over time, capital must increase at the same rate to maintain the capital–labor ratio and output per worker. For example, when the labor supply increases from 9 to 18, capital must increase from 18 to 36 to maintain a capital–labor ratio of 2. The steady state capital–labor ratio therefore depends upon the saving rate s, the depreciation rate d, and the growth rate of the labor supply n. The capital–labor ratio increases when saving per worker exceeds the sum of investment per worker for depreciation and labor supply growth. With $s[f(k)]$ representing saving per worker, $d \cdot k$ depreciation investment per worker, and $n \cdot k$ investment per worker to maintain the capital–labor ratio due to labor supply growth, the capital–labor ratio increases when

$$s[f(k)] - [d \cdot k + n \cdot k] > 0$$

or
$$s[f(k)] - (d + n)k > 0$$

There is no further increase in the capital–labor ratio and the economy reaches a steady state when

$$s[f(k)] = (d + n)k$$

For depreciation rate d, labor supply growth rate n, and saving rate s, the capital–labor ratio at the steady state is

$$k^* = A^2[s^2/(n + d)^2]$$

and output per worker is

$$y^* = A\sqrt{k^*}$$

An economy has a larger steady state capital–labor ratio and a higher level of output per worker when there is a slower rather than faster rate of growth of the labor supply.

EXAMPLE 11.7. Suppose $A = 2$, $L = 10$, $K = 40$, the saving rate s is 0.30 and the depreciation rate d is 0.10. The capital–labor ratio is 4 and outut per worker is \$4.00. Saving and gross investment per worker are \$1.20.

Situation 1: There is no growth of the labor supply.

> Depreciation investment per worker is \$0.40. Gross investment per worker less depreciation investment per worker is \$0.80. The capital–labor ratio during the next time period increases from 4.00 to 4.80.

Situation 2: The labor supply increases at a 10% rate.

> Depreciation investment per worker is \$0.40 and investment per worker of \$0.40 is needed to maintain a 4.00 capital–labor ratio due to the 10% increase in the labor supply. Gross investment per worker less investment per worker for depreciation and labor supply growth is \$0.40. The capital–labor ratio during the next time period increases from 4.00 to 4.40.

Situation 3: The labor supply increases at a 20% rate.

> Depreciation investment per worker is \$0.40 and investment per worker for labor supply growth is \$0.80. Gross investment per worker equals investment per worker for depreciation and labor supply growth. There is no change in the capital–labor ratio in the next time period, since the economy is at steady state growth.

EXAMPLE 11.8. In Fig. 11-4, line $n \cdot k$ represents investment per worker needed to maintain the capital–labor ratio due to labor supply growth. Depreciation investment per worker is added to line $n \cdot k$ to obtain steady state investment line $(n + d)k$. At capital–labor ratio k_0, output per worker is y_0, saving per worker is AD, and consumption per worker is DE. Gross investment per worker is AD, since saving per worker equals investment per worker. The need for additional capital per worker due to labor supply growth is AB; depreciation investment per worker is BC. There is an increase in the capital–labor ratio, since gross investment per worker exceeds investment per worker for depreciation and labor supply growth. When the capital–labor ratio reaches k^* and output per worker is y^*, saving per worker is FH. Gross investment per worker FH equals the sum of investment per worker for depreciation and labor supply growth.

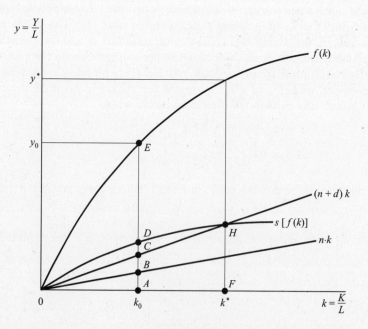

Fig. 11-4

EXAMPLE 11.9.   As in Example 11.7, $A = 2$, $L = 10$, $K = 40$, the saving rate s is 0.30 and the depreciation rate d is 0.10. The capital–labor ratio is 4 and output per worker is $4.00. Saving and gross investment per worker is $1.20. Situations 1 through 3 demonstrate that there is a lower capital–labor ratio and less output per worker when the labor supply grows at a faster rate.

Situation 1: There is no growth of the labor supply; $n = 0$.

When $n = 0$, $k^* = A^2[s^2/(n+d)^2]$; $k^* = 2^2[0.3^2/(0+0.10)^2]$; $k^* = 36$.

At steady state growth, output per worker y^* is $12.00

Situation 2: The labor supply grows at a 10% rate; $n = 0.10$.

When $n = 0.10$, $k^* = 9$ and, at steady state growth, output per worker y^* is $6.00.

Situation 3: The labor supply grows at a 20% rate; $n = 0.20$.

When $n = 0.20$, $k^* = 4$ and, at steady state growth, $y^* = 4.00.

11.4   NEUTRAL TECHNOLOGICAL CHANGE AND ECONOMIC GROWTH

Neutral technological change exists when a technological advance makes capital and labor more productive. Such a technological improvement increases the value of A for production function $Y = A\sqrt{K}\sqrt{L}$. A neutral technological advance shifts the output curve and the saving curve upward, and there is an increase in the steady state capital–labor ratio and output per worker.

EXAMPLE 11.10.   In Fig. 11-5, the economy is at steady state growth when the capital–labor ratio is k^* and output per worker is y^* for output curve $f(k)$, saving curve $s[f(k)]$, and depreciation line $d \cdot k$. A technological improvement, which increases the productivity of capital and labor shifts the output curve $f(k)$ upward to $f(k)'$. Since a fixed percentage of income is saved, the saving curve also shifts upward from $s[f(k)]$ to $s[f(k)']$. At each capital–labor ratio, saving per worker is larger. Since there is no change in the rate of depreciation, and therefore no shift of the depreciation line $d(k)$, steady state growth exists at capital–labor ratio k_1^* and output per worker y_1^*. Technological improvement has increased the capital–labor ratio and output per worker.

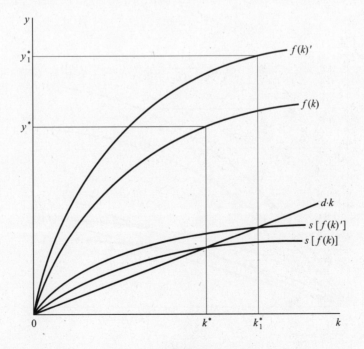

Fig. 11-5

EXAMPLE 11.11. Suppose $A = 1$, $L = 9$, $K = 36$, $s = 0.30$, $d = 0.10$ and there is no growth of the labor supply. At steady state growth, $k^* = 9$ and output per worker is $3.00. A 10% increase in the productivity of capital and labor raises the value of A from 1.00 to 1.10. The capital–labor ratio at the steady state increases from 9.00 to 10.89 and output per worker increases from $3.00 to $3.63. A 10% increase in capital and labor productivity increases output per worker 20%.

11.5   LABOR-AUGMENTING TECHNOLOGICAL CHANGE

Technological change is labor-augmenting when a technological improvement affects only the productivity of labor. Thus, while there may be no change in the labor supply, the greater productivity of labor is viewed as an increase in the effective labor supply. For example, when a worker's productivity doubles, the output generated by that worker is the same as two workers whose productivity is unchanged. Accumulation of knowledge, improved education, and better organization of labor are all factors which increase the productivity of labor and therefore the effective labor supply. When there is a labor-augmenting technological change, the capital–effective labor supply ratio is unchanged and output per worker increases by the rate of increase in the effective labor supply.

EXAMPLE 11.12. Suppose there is no growth of the labor supply. For investment line $d \cdot k$, saving curve $s[f(k)]$, and output curve $f(k)$ in Fig. 11-6, steady state capital is k^* and output per worker is y^*. Now suppose there is a labor-augmenting technological change, and the effective labor supply increases at rate g. Since a larger number of workers needs additional capital to maintain a capital–labor ratio, an increased effective labor supply needs additional capital to maintain a capital–effective labor supply ratio. Hence growth of the effective labor supply pivots depreciation line $d \cdot k$ leftward to $(d + g)k$. The increased effective labor supply raises output per worker; output curve $f(k)$ shifts upwards to $f(k)'$; and saving curve $s[f(k)]$ shifts upward to $s[f(k)']$. There is no change in the steady state capital–effective labor supply ratio; output per worker increases from y^* to y_1^* at a rate equal to the rate of increase in the effective labor supply.

EXAMPLE 11.13. For the production function $Y = A \sqrt{K}\sqrt{LE}$, E is a measure of the efficiency of labor. When $A = 1.00$, $K = 81.00$, $L = 9$, the efficiency of labor $E = 1.00$, $s = 0.30$, and $d = 0.10$, the steady state capital–effective labor supply ratio $k^* = 9.00$ and output per worker $y^* = 3.00$. A 10% increase in the efficiency of labor

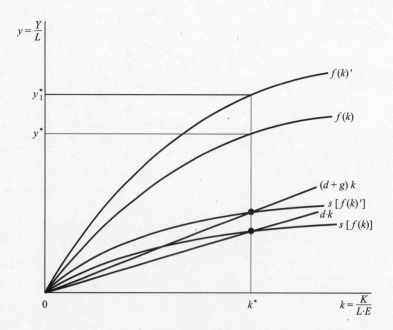

Fig. 11-6

raises the efficiency factor E from 1.00 to 1.10. The capital–effective labor supply ratio k^* remains at 9.00 and output per worker y^* increases to \$3.30. Proof: since $Y = A\sqrt{K}\sqrt{LE}$, $k^* = A^2(s^2/d^2)$ with $k^* = K/L\,E$ and $y^* = A\sqrt{E}\sqrt{k}$ with $y^* = Y/L$. $k^* = 1^2[0.3^2/0.1^2] = 9.0$. $y^* = 1(\sqrt{1.1})(\sqrt{9.9}) = \$3.30$. A 10% increase in the effective labor supply has no effect upon the steady state capital–effective labor supply ratio and increases output per worker 10%.

11.6 ACCOUNTING FOR ECONOMIC GROWTH

The following equation is used to account for the sources of economic growth

$$\Delta Y/Y = \Delta A/A + \alpha\Delta K/K + (1 - \alpha)\Delta L/L$$

where $\Delta Y/Y$ is the growth in output, $\alpha\Delta K/K$ is the contribution of capital to the growth of output, $(1 - \alpha)\Delta L/L$ is the contribution of labor to the growth of output, $\Delta A/A$ is the contribution of increased productivity, α represents a weight for capital's share of output, and $(1 - \alpha)$ a weight for labor's share of output. When capital's share of output is 0.30 and labor's share is 0.70, the growth equation is

$$\Delta Y/Y = \Delta A/A + 0.30\Delta K/K + 0.70\Delta L/L$$

The growth of factor productivity is a residual since it is not measurable as is the growth of output, capital, and labor. Frequently called Solow's residual, the equation for growth is

$$\Delta A/A = \Delta Y/Y - \alpha\Delta K/K - (1 - \alpha)\Delta L/L$$

EXAMPLE 11.14. Suppose the share of income going to capital is 0.25 and the share going to labor is 0.75; productivity of resources increases 1.5%, labor supply growth is 2%, and capital increases 6%. The growth of output is 4.5% since $\Delta Y/Y = \Delta A/A + \alpha\Delta K/K + (1 - \alpha)\Delta L/L$, and $\Delta Y/Y = 1.50\% + 0.75(2.00\%) + 0.25(6.00\%) = 4.5\%$.

EXAMPLE 11.15. Suppose the growth of the labor supply is 3%, capital is 4%, and output is 5%. The share of income going to capital is 0.25 while the share going to labor is 0.75. The growth of factor productivity is 1.75% since $\Delta A/A = \Delta Y/Y - \alpha\Delta K/K - (1 - \alpha)\Delta L/L$, and $\Delta A/A = 5.00\% - 0.25(4.00\%) - 0.75(3.00\%) = 1.75\%$.

Solved Problems

SOURCES OF ECONOMIC GROWTH

11.1 (a) Find Y when the economy's production function is $Y = A(K^\alpha L^{1-\alpha})$, and the productivity of resources $A = 2.00$, $K = 16$, and $L = 9$. (b) Find Y when (1) productivity increases 5% and the value of A increases from 2.00 to 2.10, *ceteris paribus*; (2) the capital stock K increases to 20, *ceteris paribus*; (3) the labor supply L increases to 12, *ceteris paribus*. (c) Find output per worker y for the output levels calculated in parts (a) and (b). (d) What are the sources of increased economic-well being for the labor supply?

(a) $Y = 2.00\sqrt{16}\sqrt{9}$; $Y = \$24.00$.

(b) (1) $Y = 2.10\sqrt{16}\sqrt{9}$; $Y = \$25.20$. (2) $Y = 2.00\sqrt{20}\sqrt{9}$; $Y = \$26.83$; (3) $Y = 2.00\sqrt{16}\sqrt{12}$; $Y = \$27.71$.

(c) Output per worker equals output divided by the labor supply, i.e., Y/L. Output per worker is as follows: (a) \$2.67; (b) (1) \$2.80; (2) \$2.98; (3) \$2.31.

(d) Economic well-being is indicated by output per worker. Output per worker increases when there is an increase in factor productivity and/or capital. Economic well-being decreases when there is an increase in the labor supply and no increase in factor productivity or the supply of capital.

11.2 (a) Find Y and the capital–labor ratio k when the economy's production function is $Y = A\sqrt{K}\sqrt{L}$; $A = 2.00$; $K = 40$, and $L = 10$. (b) (1) Find Y and k when there is a 10% increase in capital and labor, *ceteris paribus*. (2) Find Y and k when there is a 20% increase in capital and a 10% increase in labor, *ceteris paribus*. (3) Find Y and k when there is a 10% increase in capital and a 20% increase in labor, *ceteris paribus*. (c) Find output per worker y for the output levels calculated in parts (a) and (b). (d) What do your calculations from (a) through (c) indicate about aggregate output, capital–labor ratio and economic well-being?

(a)   Output $Y = \$40.00$ [$Y = 2.00\sqrt{40}\sqrt{10} = \$40.00$]. The capital–labor ratio $k = 4.00$.

(b)   (1) Capital increases from 40 to 44 while labor increases from 10 to 11. $Y = \$44.00$ [$Y = 2.00\sqrt{44}\sqrt{11} = \$44.00$]. The capital–labor ratio $k = 4.00$. (2) Capital increases from 40 to 48 while labor increases from 10 to 11. $Y = \$45.96$ [$Y = 2.00\sqrt{48}\sqrt{12} = \$45.96$]. The capital–labor ratio $k = 4.36$. (3) Capital increases from 40 to 44 while labor increases from 10 to 11. $Y = \$45.96$ [$Y = 2.00\sqrt{44}\sqrt{12} = \$45.96$]. The capital–labor ratio $k = 3.67$.

(c)   Output per worker y is \$4.00 in part (a); in part (b) output per worker is \$4.00 for situation (1); \$4.18 for situation (2); and \$3.83 for situation (3).

(d)   Output increases in part (b) due to increases in capital and labor. Economic well-being increases only in situation (2), when there is an increase in the capital–labor ratio, i.e., labor has more capital to work with.

THE SOLOW GROWTH MODEL WITH A CONSTANT LABOR SUPPLY

11.3 (a) Derive $y = A\sqrt{k}$ from the Cobb–Douglas production function $Y = AK^{0.5}L^{0.5}$. (b) Prove that the equation for the steady state capital–labor ratio is $k^* = A^2(s^2/d^2)$ when there is no growth of the labor supply, the saving rate is s, and the depreciation rate is d.

(a)   To derive output per worker, divide both sides of the production function $Y = AK^{0.5}L^{0.5}$ by L. Thus,

$$Y/L = [AK^{0.5}L^{0.5}]/L$$

or
$$Y/L = A[K/L]^{0.5}$$

letting $y = Y/L$ and $k = K/L$
$$y = Ak^{0.5}$$

$$y = A\sqrt{k}$$

(b)   A steady state exists when saving per worker equals depreciation investment per worker.

saving per worker = depreciation per worker

Since a fixed percent d of capital per worker k depreciates, depreciation investment per worker is $d \cdot k$; and since a fixed percent s of the income earned from output y is saved, saving per worker is $s \cdot y$:

$$s \cdot y = d \cdot k$$

since $y = A\sqrt{k}$
$$s[A\sqrt{k}] = d \cdot k$$

rearranging terms
$$s(A)/d = k/\sqrt{k}$$

and squaring both
sides of the equation

$$s^2 A^2/d^2 = k^2/k$$

or
$$k^* = A^2(s^2/d^2)$$

11.4 (a) Find output Y, saving S, gross investment I, and depreciation investment D when the production function is $Y = AK^{0.5}L^{0.5}$, $A = 2.00$, $K = 16$, $L = 4$, the saving rate $s = 0.30$, and the depreciation rate d is 0.10. (b) Is there net investment in this economy? (Recall that net investment adds to an economy's stock of capital.) (c) Use the calculations from (a) to find output per worker, saving per worker, gross investment per worker, depreciation investment per worker, and capital per worker. (d) From your calculations in (c), establish whether the economy has reached a steady state.

(a) $Y = \$16.00$. Saving S equals $\$4.80$ $[S = 0.30(Y)]$. Since saving equals gross investment, gross investment is $\$4.80$. Depreciation investment is 10% of the capital stock; depreciation investment is $\$1.60$.

(b)   Net investment equals gross investment less depreciation investment. Net investment is $\$3.20$, i.e., there is a $\$3.20$ addition to the economy's stock of capital.

(c) $y = \$4.00$; saving per worker $= \$1.20$; gross investment per worker is $\$1.20$; depreciation investment per worker is $\$0.40$; net investment per worker is $\$0.80$; capital per worker (the capital–labor ratio) is 4.00.

(d)   The economy has not reached a steady state since there is net investment per worker of $\$0.80$. The capital–labor ratio increases from 4.00 to 4.80.

11.5   Line $d \cdot k$ is the depreciation line in Fig. 11-7, $s[f(k)]$ is the saving curve and $f(k)$ the output curve. (a) Use the notation in Fig. 11-7 and find output per worker, saving per worker, gross investment per worker, depreciation investment per worker, and consumption per worker when the capital–labor ratio is k_0. (b) Is this economy at a steady state when the capital–labor ratio is k_0?

(a)   When the capital–labor ratio is k_0, output per worker is AD, saving per worker is BD, as is gross investment per worker, depreciation investment per worker is CD, and consumption per worker is AB.

(b)   This economy is not at a steady state when the capital–labor ratio is k_0 since gross investment per worker exceeds depreciation investment per worker. The steady state exists at capital–labor ratio k_1, where gross investment per worker FG equals depreciation investment per worker FG.

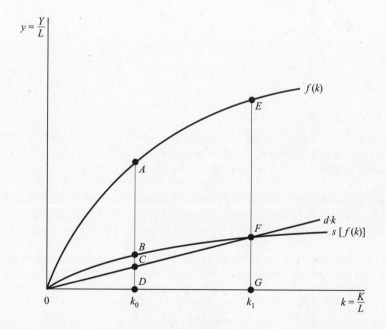

Fig. 11-7

11.6 Suppose Country A and Country B have the same Cobb–Douglas production function and resources are equally productive. Each country has the same depreciation rate d, and the depreciation line for each country is $d \cdot k$ in Fig. 11-8. The output curve for each country is $f(k)$. The saving rate s_A is lower in Country A than Country B's higher saving rate s_B. Country A's saving curve is $s_A[f(k)]$ and B's is $s_B[f(k)]$ in Fig. 11-8. (a) From Fig. 11-8, find the steady state capital–labor ratio and output per worker for Country A and Country B. (b) Why is output per worker higher in Country B than in Country A?

(a) The steady state capital–labor ratio occurs at the intersection of the saving curve and the depreciation line. For Country A, the steady state capital–labor ratio is k_1 and output per worker is y_1. For Country B, the steady state capital–labor ratio is k_2 and output per worker is y_2.

(b) Output per worker is higher for B than A because B's higher saving rate allows it to accumulate more capital and therefore have a higher capital–labor ratio.

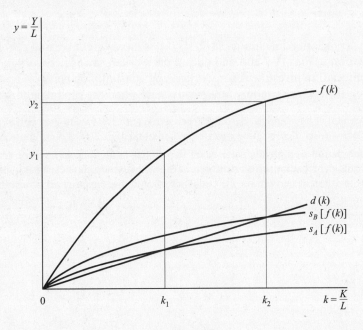

Fig. 11-8

11.7 Suppose an economy's labor supply is unchanged and its rate of depreciation is 10%. The capital–labor ratio is 4 and output per worker is $4.00 since $K = 16$, $L = 4$, and $A = 2.00$. (a) Find net investment per worker when the saving rate is (1) 0.20 or (2) 0.30. (b) What is the capital–labor ratio in the next time period when the saving rate is (1) 0.20 or (2) 0.30? (c) What is output per worker in the next time period for each saving rate? (d) From (b) and (c) find the rate of change in the capital–labor ratio and output per worker for each saving rate. (e) What effect does an increase in the saving rate have upon the rate of economic growth in the short run?

(a) Depreciation investment per worker is $0.40 when the capital–labor ratio is 4.00 and the depreciation rate is 10%. (1) When the saving rate is 20%, saving and gross investment per worker is $0.80 and there is net investment per worker of $0.40. (2) Saving and gross investment per worker is $1.20 and net investment per worker is $0.80 when the saving rate is 30%.

(b) In the next time period the capital–labor ratio increases to 4.40 when the saving rate is 20% and to 4.80 when the saving rate is 30%.

(c) Output per capita in the next time period increases from $4.00 to $4.20 for a 20% saving rate and $4.00 to $4.38 for a 30% saving rate.

(d) The capital–labor ratio increases 10% and output per capita increases 5% when the saving rate is 20%. At a 30% saving rate, the capital–labor ratio increases 20% and output per worker 9.5%.

(e) In the short run, an economy which is not at its steady state experiences a faster rate of growth in output per worker the higher its rate of saving.

11.8 What is meant by "the golden rule steady state?"

The objective of economic growth is increased economic well-being, which is measured by consumption per worker. Hence individuals are encouraged to save, and therefore postpone consumption in the short run, to enhance their future standard of living. Thus, the objective of saving in the short run is maximization of consumption in the long run. The golden rule steady state holds that an economy's saving rate should be one which maximizes consumption per worker at the steady state.

11.9 Use Fig. 11-9 to prove that the golden rule steady state exists when a saving curve intersects the depreciation line at point F rather than E or J and the capital–labor ratio is k_2 rather than k_1 or k_3.

Line AB is parallel to depreciation line $d \cdot k$ and tangent to output curve $f(k)$ at point G. Since two parallel lines are equidistant, CE at k_1, GF at k_2, and HJ at k_3 are equal. The distance between the output curve and the depreciation line at capital–labor ratio k_1 is DE, at k_2 GF and at k_3 IJ. Since DE and IJ are less than GF, consumption per worker is increased by a capital–labor ratio which is greater than k_1 and less than k_3. By selecting other capital–labor ratios, we find that k_2 is the only capital–labor ratio which produces the highest consumption per worker. Thus, a saving rate which results in a saving curve which intersects the depreciation line at F is an optimum saving rate; the resulting capital–labor ratio is identified as the golden rule steady state.

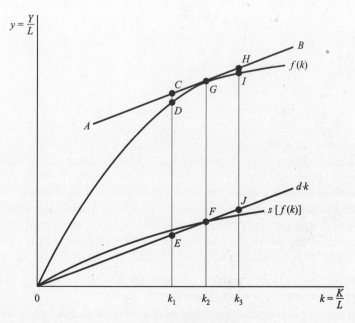

Fig. 11-9

THE SOLOW GROWTH MODEL WITH AN INCREASING LABOR SUPPLY

11.10 Suppose for Country A and Country B the rate of depreciation is 10%, rate of saving is 20%, $K = 40$, $L = 10$, and $A = 2.00$. The capital–labor ratio is 4.00 for each country. Country A's labor supply is unchanged; B's labor supply grows at a 10% rate. (*a*) Find output and saving per worker for Country A and Country B. (*b*) Since B's labor supply is increasing at a 10% rate, what must Country B do to maintain a capital–labor ratio of 4.00? (*c*) What is gross investment per worker for Country A and Country B? What is net investment per worker for each country? (*d*) Has either country reached a steady state?

(*a*) Output per worker for each country is $4.00; saving per worker is $0.80.

(*b*) During the next time period, B's labor supply increases by one worker, from 10 to 11. Capital must increase by 4 to maintain the 4.00 capital–labor ratio.

(*c*) Gross investment per worker is $0.80 in each country, an amount equal to saving per worker. Depreciation investment per worker is $0.40 in each country since 10% of the existing capital per worker wears out. Because of its increasing labor supply, Country B needs investment per worker of $0.40 to maintain the capital–labor ratio at 4.00. Net investment per worker is $0.40 for Country A and 0 for Country B.

(*d*) Country A is below its steady state capital–labor ratio since net investment is greater than zero. Country B is at its steady state.

11.11 Prove that the steady state capital–labor ratio is $k^* = A^2[s^2/(n+d)^2]$ when the labor supply growth rate is n.

A steady state exists when saving per worker = investment per worker for depreciation and labor supply growth:

saving per worker = investment per worker for depreciation + labor supply growth

When n is the growth rate of labor, $n \cdot k$ is the investment per worker which is necessary to maintain the capital–labor ratio. The depreciation rate is d and $d \cdot k$ the investment per worker needed to replace worn-out capital. The saving rate is s and saving per worker is $s[f(k)]$. Thus,

$$s \cdot y = [n+d]k$$

since $y = A\sqrt{k}$
$$s[A\sqrt{k}] = [n+d]k$$

rearranging terms
$$s[A]/[n+d] = k/\sqrt{k}$$

and squaring both
sides of the equation

$$s^2 A^2/[n+d]^2 = k^2/k$$

or
$$k^* = A^2\{s^2/[n+d]^2\}$$

11.12 For Fig. 11-10, the saving rate is s, depreciation is d, and the labor supply grows at a rate n. Curve $s[f(k)]$ represents saving per worker at each capital–labor ratio, $d \cdot k$ the depreciation line, and $[d+n]k$ the investment line for depreciation and growth of the labor supply. (*a*) For capital–labor ratio k_0 in Fig. 11-10, find output per worker, saving per worker, depreciation investment per worker, and investment per worker for growth of the labor supply. (*b*) What happens to the economy's capital–labor ratio in the next time period? (*c*) Find the steady state for this economy. (*d*) Find the steady state for this economy when the labor supply is unchanged.

(*a*) Output per worker at k_1 is AE; saving per worker is AD; depreciation investment per worker is AB; and BC investment per worker for labor supply growth.

(*b*) The capital–labor ratio increases by DC, the amount of net investment per worker during the current production period.

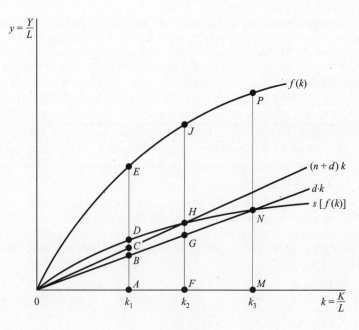

Fig. 11-10

(c)   When the rate of labor supply growth is n, steady state growth exists at k_2 capital–labor ratio, and output per worker is FJ.

(d)   When there is no labor supply growth, the steady state capital–labor ratio is k_3 and output per worker is MP.

11.13 Suppose the saving rate is 0.30, the depreciation rate is 0.08, and the productivity of resources A is 2.00. (a) Find the capital–labor ratio and output per worker at the steady state when labor supply growth is (1) 2%, (2) 4%, (3) 7%. (b) What happens to the economic well-being of individuals when there is faster growth of the labor supply?

(a)   The equation $k^* = A^2\{s^2/[n+d]^2\}$ is used to find the steady state capital–labor ratio. (1) When labor supply growth is 2%, $k^* = 36$ $[k^* = 2^2\{0.3^2/(0.02+0.08)^2\}]$. (2) The steady state capital–labor ratio is 25 when labor supply growth is 4%, and (3) $k^* = 16$ when it is 7%. Output per worker for each rate of growth of the labor supply is (1) \$12.00; (2) \$10.00; (3) \$8.00. Faster labor supply growth lowers the capital–labor ratio and reduces output per worker.

(b)   Economic well-being is indicated by consumption per worker. Consumption per worker decreases from \$8.40 to \$7.00 to \$5.60 as the rate of labor supply growth increases from 2% to 4% to 7%.

NEUTRAL TECHNOLOGICAL CHANGE AND ECONOMIC CHANGE

11.14 (a) What is meant by a neutral technological change? (b) What is a labor-augmenting technological change?

(a)   A neutral technological change makes capital and labor more productive. This is noted in the Cobb–Douglas production function $Y = A(K^\alpha L^{1-\alpha})$ as an increase in the value of A which represents the productivity of capital and labor.

(b) A labor-augmenting technological change affects only the productivity of labor. The increased efficiency of labor is noted by multiplying the labor supply by an efficiency factor E; $L \cdot E$ is termed the effective labor supply. Hence the effective labor supply doubles when there is no change in the productivity of labor and the supply of labor doubles or when the number of workers is unchanged and the productivity of labor doubles.

11.15 The steady state capital–labor ratio is k_1 and output per worker is y_1 in Fig. 11-11 for output curve $f(k)$, saving curve $s[f(k)]$, and depreciation line $d \cdot k$. What happens to the steady state capital–labor ratio and output per worker when a technological improvement increases the productivity of capital and labor?

A neutral technological change shifts output curve $f(k)$ upward to $f(k)'$ in Fig. 11-11. Output per worker is now greater for each capital–labor ratio. Since the saving rate s is a fixed percentage of income (output), saving per worker is also higher at each capital–labor ratio. Thus, saving curve $s[f(k)]$ shifts upward to $s[f(k)']$. The steady state capital–labor ratio increases to k_2 and output per worker increases to y_2.

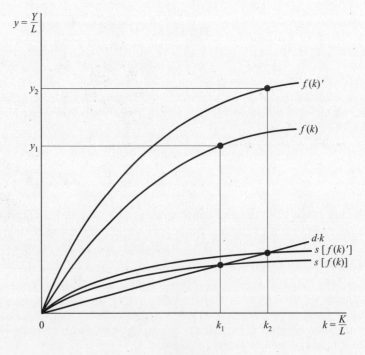

Fig. 11-11

11.16 The saving rate is 0.30, the depreciation rate is 0.10, there is no growth of the labor supply, and the productivity of labor and capital A is 3.00. (a) Find the steady state capital–labor ratio and output per worker at the steady state. (b) Find the steady state capital–labor ratio and output per worker at the steady state when the productivity of labor and capital increases 10% and the value of A increases from 3.00 to 3.30. (c) What is the growth rate of output per worker when there is a 10% increase in the productivity of capital and labor?

(a) The steady state capital–labor ratio is 81 $\{k^* = A^2[s^2/d^2]; k^* = 3^2[0.3^2/0.1^2] = 81\}$. Output per worker is \$27.00 $\{y^* = A\sqrt{k^*}; y = 3\sqrt{81} = 27\}$.

(b) The steady state capital–labor ratio is 98; output per worker is \$32.67.

(c) The 10% increase in the productivity of capital and labor has increased output per worker 21%.

LABOR-AUGMENTING TECHNOLOGICAL CHANGE

11.17 (a) Find output, saving, and depreciation investment when $L = 10$, $K = 90$, $A = 1.00$, the saving rate is 0.30, the depreciation rate is 0.10, and there is no growth of the labor supply. Is the economy at a steady state? (b) Suppose there is a labor-augmenting technological change which increases the effective labor supply 10%. Does this increase in the effective labor supply require additional capital? If so, what is the necessary change in the stock of capital? (c) Find output, saving, depreciation investment and investment for growth of the effective labor supply when the effective labor supply increases at a 10% rate. (d) From your calculations in (a) and (c), find output per worker, output per effective worker, capital per effective worker, and capital per worker. Is the economy at a steady state? (e) What happens to the steady state capital–effective labor supply ratio when there is labor-augmenting technological change? What happens to output per worker?

(a) Output is \$30.00 $[Y = A(K^\alpha L^{1-\alpha}); Y = 1(\sqrt{90}\sqrt{10}) = 30]$ saving is \$9.00 and depreciation investment is \$9.00. The economy is at a steady state since gross investment equals depreciation investment.

(b) There is need for additional capital to maintain the capital–effective labor supply ratio. Hence, a 10% increase in the effective labor supply (from 10 to 11) necessitates a 10% increase in capital (from 90 to 99) to keep the capital–effective labor supply ratio at 9.

(c) The effective labor supply $[LE]$ increases from 10 to 11 when E increases 10%. The stock of capital increases from 90 to 99 to keep the capital–effective labor supply ratio at 9. Output thereby increases to \$33.00 $[Y = 1(\sqrt{99}\sqrt{11}) = 33]$. Saving per worker is \$9.90 and depreciation investment is \$9.90. The economy is in a steady state.

(d) Before the increase in the effective labor supply, output per worker is \$3.00, output per effective worker is \$3.00, capital per effective worker is 9, and capital per worker is 9. After the 10% increase in the effective labor supply, output per worker increases to \$3.30, output per effective worker remains at \$3.00, capital per effective worker remains at 9, and capital per worker increases from 9 to 9.9.

(e) The capital–effective labor supply ratio is unchanged when there is an increase in the effective labor supply. Output per worker increases by the rate of increase in the effective labor supply, as does capital per worker.

11.18 The capital–effective labor supply ratio is k^* in Fig. 11-12 for depreciation line $d \cdot k$, saving curve $s[f(k)]$ and output curve $f(k)$. Now suppose the effective labor supply increases at a rate g. (a) What effect does this growth in the effective labor supply have upon the depreciation line, saving curve, and output curve? (b) What happens to the capital–effective labor supply ratio and output per worker?

(a) The depreciation line pivots upward to $(d + g)k$ since additional capital is needed for the increase in the effective labor supply. The output curve shifts upward to $f(k)'$, by the rate of increase in the effective labor supply. Because of the shift of the output curve, the saving curve shifts upward to $s[f(k)']$.

(b) Because the shift of $(d + g)k$, $s[f(k)']$, and $f(k)'$ are at a rate g, the capital–effective labor supply ratio is unchanged at k^*. Output per worker increases from y_1 to y_2.

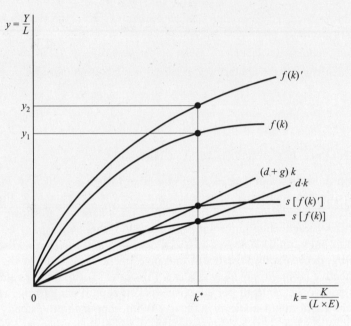

Fig. 11-12

ACCOUNTING FOR ECONOMIC GROWTH

11.19 Suppose capital's share of output is 0.25 and labor's share of output is 0.75. (*a*) Find the rate of growth of output $\Delta Y/Y$ when the labor supply increases at a 1% rate, capital increases at a 4% rate, and factor productivity increases at a 2% rate. (*b*) Find the rate of growth of output $\Delta Y/Y$ when the labor supply increases at a 4% rate, capital increases at a 1% rate, and factor productivity increases at a 2% rate. (*c*) Explain the difference in the rate of growth in part (*a*) and (*b*).

    (*a*) $\Delta Y/Y$ equals $\Delta A/A + \alpha \Delta K/K + (1-\alpha)\Delta L/L$, where $\alpha = 0.25$ (capital's share of output) and $1 - \alpha = 0.75$ (labor's share of output). Thus, $\Delta Y/Y = 2\% + 0.25(4\%) + 0.75(1\%) = 3.75\%$; output is increasing at a 3.75% rate.

    (*b*) $\Delta Y/Y = 2\% + 0.25(1\%) + 0.75(4\%) = 5.25\%$; output is increasing at a 5.25% rate.

    (*c*)   The impact of the growth of capital and labor upon the growth of output depends upon their relative importance in producing output as measured by their weighted share of income. Since labor's share is three times that of capital, a 4% growth rate for labor contributes 3% to output growth, whereas a 4% growth rate for capital contributes 1% to output growth.

11.20 Suppose capital's share of output is 0.25 and labor's share of output is 0.75. (*a*) Find the growth of factor productivity $\Delta A/A$ when the labor supply increases 1%, capital increases 4%, and output growth is 4%. (*b*) Find the growth of factor productivity $\Delta A/A$ when the labor supply increases 3%, capital increases 3%, and output growth is 4%. (*c*) Why is the growth of factor productivity a residual?

    (*a*) $\Delta A/A$ equals $\Delta Y/Y - \alpha \Delta K/K - (1-\alpha)\Delta L/L$, where $\alpha = 0.25$ and $1-\alpha = 0.75$. Thus, $\Delta A/A = 4\% - 0.25(4\%) - 0.75(1\%) = 2.25\%$; productivity growth is 2.25%.

    (*b*) $\Delta A/A = 4\% - 0.25(3\%) - 0.75(3\%) = 1.00\%$; productivity growth is 1.00%.

    (*c*)   Capital, labor and output are directly measured; factor productivity is not. Productivity is a residual since its contribution to output is inferred from the output change unexplained by labor and capital.

Multiple Choice Questions

1.   Which of the following will not result in an increase in output per worker?

   (*a*)   An increase in the capital stock, *ceteris paribus*.

   (*b*)   The capital stock increases at a faster rate than the labor supply, *ceteris paribus*.

   (*c*)   The capital stock and labor supply increase at the same rate, *ceteris paribus*.

   (*d*)   There is a labor-augmenting technological change, *ceteris paribus*.

2.   A steady state exists when there is no growth of the labor supply and

   (*a*)   Saving per worker is greater than depreciation investment per worker.

   (*b*)   Depreciation investment per worker is greater than saving per worker.

   (*c*)   Saving per worker less depreciation investment per worker is zero.

   (*d*)   Depreciation per worker is zero.

3.   When $A = 2$, $K = 80$, $L = 20$, and the Cobb–Douglas production function is $Y = K^{0.5}L^{0.5}$,

   (*a*)   The capital–labor ratio is 4 and output per worker is \$4.00.

   (*b*)   The capital–labor ratio is 0.25 and output per worker is \$4.00.

   (*c*)   The capital–labor ratio is 4 and output per worker is \$2.00.

   (*d*)   The capital–labor ratio is 0.25 and output per worker is \$2.00.

4.   When $A = 3$, the saving rate is 0.40, the depreciation rate is 0.10, and there is no labor supply growth,

   (*a*)   The steady state capital–labor ratio is 48 and output per worker is \$36.00.

   (*b*)   The steady state capital–labor ratio is 144 and output per worker is \$36.00.

   (*c*)   The steady state capital–labor ratio is 16 and output per worker is \$12.00.

   (*d*)   The steady state capital–labor ratio is 36 and output per worker is \$18.00.

5.   When an economy is at steady state growth and there is an increase in the saving rate,

   (*a*)   The saving curve shifts upward and there is no change in output curve.

   (*b*)   Saving per worker exceeds depreciation investment per worker and the economy is below the steady state capital–labor ratio.

   (*c*)   The saving curve shifts upward and there is no shift of the depreciation line.

   (*d*)   All of the above.

   (*e*)   None of the above.

6.   The golden rule steady state exists when

   (*a*)   Saving per worker is maximized at a steady state capital–labor ratio.

   (*b*)   Depreciation investment per worker at a steady state capital–labor ratio is maximized.

   (*c*)   The distance between the output curve and depreciation line is maximized at a steady state capital–labor ratio.

   (*d*)   The depreciation rate is zero.

7.   An increase in the rate of labor supply growth

   (*a*)   Has no effect upon the steady state capital–labor ratio.

   (*b*)   Increases the steady state capital–labor ratio.

  (*c*) Decreases the steady state capital–labor ratio.

  (*d*) Increases output per worker at the steady state.

8. A neutral technological change

  (*a*) Shifts the depreciation line leftward.

  (*b*) Increases the effective labor supply.

  (*c*) Has no effect upon the capital–labor ratio.

  (*d*) Shifts the saving and output curve upward.

9. A labor-augmenting technological change has no effect upon the

  (*a*) Depreciation investment line.

  (*b*) Saving curve.

  (*c*) Output curve.

  (*d*) Capital–effective labor ratio.

10. When the share of output going to capital is 0.25, the share going to labor is 0.75, output increases 4%, labor increases 1%, and capital increases 2%, the increase in productivity is

  (*a*) 0.75%.

  (*b*) 1%.

  (*c*) 1.25%.

  (*d*) 2.75%.

True or False Questions

11. _____ Output increases when there is an increase in the labor supply, *ceteris paribus*.

12. _____ Output per worker increases when there is an increase in the capital–labor ratio, *ceteris paribus*.

13. _____ Output per worker increases when there is an increase in the labor supply, *ceteris paribus*.

14. _____ When there is labor supply growth and no technological change, steady state grows exists when saving per worker equals depreciation investment per worker.

15. _____ An increase in the saving rate always increases consumption per worker.

16. _____ A neutral technological change increases the steady state capital–labor ratio.

17. _____ A labor-augmenting technological change increases the effective labor supply.

18. _____ When there is no labor supply growth and no technological change, steady state growth exists when saving per worker equals depreciation investment per worker.

19. _____ An increase in the saving rate, *ceteris paribus*, increases the steady state capital–labor ratio.

20. _____ There is no output growth unless there is growth of capital and/or labor.

Answers to Multiple Choice and True or False Questions

1. (*c*); **2.** (*c*); **3.** (*a*); **4.** (*b*); **5.** (*d*); **6.** (*c*); **7.** (*c*); **8.** (*d*); **9.** (*d*); **10.** (*d*); **11.** T; **12.** T; **13.** F; **14.** F; **15.** F; **16.** T; **17.** T; **18.** T; **19.** T; **20.** F

Chapter 12

The Supply of and Demand for Money

Chapter Summary

1. Money is the economy's unit of account and standard of deferred payment; money is demanded because of its medium of exchange and store of value function.

2. Three measures of the money supply, $M1$, $M2$, and $M3$, are frequently published by the Federal Reserve. The $M2$ and $M3$ measures of money include financial assets which are store of value substitutes for $M1$ balances, although they cannot be used as a medium of exchange.

3. The $M1$ money supply equals $m1 \cdot B$, where the $m1$ money multiplier equals $(1+k)/(r+k+e)$ and the monetary base B consists of bank reserves plus currency outside banks. The Federal Reserve increases the $M1$ money supply by increasing the monetary base through open market operations: the purchase and sale of Treasury securities.

4. There are two versions of the equation of exchange. $MV = py$ focuses upon V, the velocity of money, and the transaction function of money. The Cambridge k version $M = kpy$ focuses upon the demand for money, where k is the proportion of nominal income (py) which is held as a money balance.

5. The transaction demand for money is a function of the rate of interest, nominal income, and the number of days in a pay period. The average $M1$ balance held is positively related to the number of days in a pay period and nominal income and inversely related to the rate of interest.

6. There is a precautionary demand for money because of uncertainty about the receipt and expenditure of future income. Money held as a precautionary balance is inversely related to the rate of interest and positively related to income and uncertainty.

7. Money is held in a portfolio because it is a better store of value than interest or dividend-paying financial instruments. The portfolio demand for money is inversely related to the expected return from interest and dividend-yielding financial instruments.

8. A money supply monetary policy should be used when the location of IS is uncertain, whereas an interest rate monetary policy should be used when the location of LM is uncertain.

Chapter Outline

12.1 THE FUNCTIONS OF MONEY

Money serves the following functions: medium of exchange, unit of account, standard of deferred payment, and store of value. As a medium of exchange, money provides a transaction function, facilitating the allocation of economic resources and the exchange of goods and services. For example, labor works for a money wage and then uses its money income to purchase goods and services. The unit of account function provides a system of measurement; in the U.S.A., units are measured in dollars and cents, which are specified as prices, revenues, costs, and incomes. As a standard of deferred payment, savings are loaned to borrowers and repayment is in dollars, the unit of account. Debt instruments in the U.S.A. are therefore dollar-denominated, i.e., the debt instrument specifies the dollar sum which is payable in the future. Money is a liquid store of value; it is always available for the purchase of goods or services or other transactions unlike debt instruments which must be converted into money first.

12.2 DEFINITIONS OF MONEY

In the U.S.A., several financial instruments fulfill one or more of the functions of money. Currently, the Federal Reserve compiles and releases data on the $M1$, $M2$, and $M3$ money supply. $M1$ is a transactions definition which consists of currency outside banks, checking accounts, and travelers' checks. $M2$ includes $M1$ and other financial assets which are store of value substitutes for $M1$ balances but cannot be used for transactions. In addition to $M1$, $M2$ includes small-denomination time deposits (certificates of deposits), savings deposits, and noninstitutional money market mutual fund balances. $M3$ includes store-of-value substitutes for $M1$ balances which are primarily owned by businesses. $M3$ adds the following financial assets to $M2$: large-denomination time deposits, overnight and term RPs at deposit institutions, overnight and term Eurodollar deposits owned by U.S. residents at foreign branches of U.S. banks and at all banking offices in the U.K. and Canada and institution-only money market mutual funds.

EXAMPLE 12.1. The $M1$, $M2$, and $M3$ measures of the money supply appear in Table 12-1. The currency total excludes the amount of currency held by the Treasury, Federal Reserve Banks, and private banks. The total for

Table 12-1   Money Stock Measures December 1996 (In Billion Dollars)

$M1$		1076.9
Currency	395.7	
Traveler's checks of nonbank issuers	8.6	
Demand deposits adjusted	400.7	
Other checkable deposits	271.8	
$M2$		3825.8
$M1$	1076.9	
Money market and savings deposit accounts	1271.4	
Small-denomination time deposits	948.6	
Noninstitution money market funds	528.9	
$M3$		4894.5
$M2$	3825.8	
Large-denomination time deposits	494.2	
Overnight and term RPs and Eurodollars	300.6	
Institution-only money market funds	273.9	

Source: *Federal Reserve Bulletin*, March 1997.

checking deposits does not include checking deposits held by the U.S. government, foreign banks, official institutions and interbank checking deposits. Other checking deposits consist of automatic transfer serve (ATS) balances, NOW accounts, and credit union share draft accounts (CUSD). Small-denomination time deposits are certificates of deposit whose balance is $100,000 or less.

12.3 CREATION AND CONTROL OF THE $M1$ MONEY SUPPLY

The $M1$ money supply is the product of the monetary base B (also called high-powered money) and the $m1$ money multiplier, or $M1 = m1 \cdot B$. The monetary base consists of currency outside banks plus bank reserves (currency held by banks plus bank deposits at the Fed). The Federal Reserve exerts control over the $M1$ money supply by changing the reserve requirement and therefore altering the $m1$ money multiplier and/or by changing the monetary base through open market operations. The reserve requirement is rarely changed. When the Federal Reserve purchases Treasury securities, *ceteris paribus*, the monetary base increases; it decreases when Treasury securities are sold. When an addition to the monetary base increases bank reserves, there is a multiple increase in checking deposits and therefore the $M1$ money supply. The $M1$ money supply increases by the expansion of the monetary base when there is an increase in currency held by the private sector equal to the increase in the monetary base. Thus, the effect on $M1$ of an increase in the monetary base depends upon the $m1$ money multiplier. The $m1$ money multiplier equals $(1 + k)/(k + r_D + e)$; k is the currency ratio, the ratio of currency held by the private sector (C) to checking deposits (D); r_D is the reserve requirement for checking deposits, the ratio of reserves (R) that banks must hold relative to the amount of checking deposits issued; and e is the excess reserve ratio, the amount of excess reserves (E) that banks hold relative to the amount of checking deposits issued.

EXAMPLE 12.2 When Federal Reserve Banks purchase Treasury securities value at $100,000 from the banking system, the following changes occur on the balance sheets of these institutions:

Federal Reserve Bank

Δ Assets		Δ Liabilities	
Treasury securities	+$100,000	Deposits of depository institutions	+$100,000

Banking System

Δ Assets		Δ Liabilities
Treasury securities	−$100,000	
Deposits at Fed	+$100,000	

The banking system's reserves have increased $100,000 (it now holds excess reserves); deposit liabilities have not changed, but earning assets have decreased by an equal amount since the Fed pays no interest on deposits. The banking system can reduce excess reserves by lending and issuing checking deposits. (We shall assume a 10% reserve requirement on checking deposits.) If the banking system lends until excess reserves equal zero, checking deposits D will expand by an amount equal to the banking system's holding of excess reserves E divided by the reserve requirement on checking deposits r_D, i.e., $\Delta D = \Delta E/r_D$, assuming no change in the amount of currency held by the private sector. Loans and checking deposits thereby increase by $1 million: $\Delta D = \Delta E/r_D$; $1 million = $100,000/0.10. The Federal Reserve's purchase of $100,000 in Treasury securities from the banking system expands the $M1$ money supply $1 million.

EXAMPLE 12.3. Suppose Federal Reserve Banks purchase Treasury securities valued at $100,000 in the open market; at the same time, households decrease their holding of Treasury securities by $100,000 and increase their currency holdings by $100,000. These transactions have the following net effect upon the balance sheets of households and Federal Reserve Banks:

Federal Reserve Banks

Δ Assets		Δ Liabilities	
Treasury securities	+ $100,000	Federal Reserve notes	+ $100,000

Households

Δ Assets		Δ Liabilities
Treasury securities	− $100,000	
Currency (Federal Reserve notes)	+ $100,000	

Because the expanded monetary base is held by households rather than the banking system, there is no increase in checking deposits. The $M1$ money supply increases $100,000.

EXAMPLE 12.4. Suppose $r_D = 0.10$ and $B = \$200,000$. Bank reserves equal $100,000 when currency outside banks is $100,000. Checking deposits total (1) $750,000 when banks hold excess reserves of $25,000 or (2) $1,000,000 when banks hold no excess reserves. The $M1$ money supply, which is the sum of currency outside banks and checking deposits, is therefore (1) $850,000 when banks hold excess reserves of $25,000 or (2) $1,100,000 when banks hold no excess reserves.

EXAMPLE 12.5. The $m1$ money multiplier is 3 when $r_D = 0.10$, $k = 0.20$, and $e = 0.10$, since $m1 = (1 + k)/(k + r_D + e) = 1.20/(0.20 + 0.10 + 0.10) = 3$. The $M1$ money supply equals $600,000 when the monetary base is $200,000, since $M1 = m1 \cdot B$; $M1 = 3(\$200,000) = \$600,000$. An increase in k, r_D, or e reduces the value of $m1$. Thus, the $M1$ money supply depends not only on the quantity of B supplied by the Fed but the demand for B represented by the currency preferences of the private sector, the reserve requirement placed on checking deposits and the excess reserve preferences of the banks.

12.4 THE QUANTITY THEORY OF MONEY

Monetary theorists have used the equation of exchange $MV = py$ to theorize about the long-run determinants of the price level. In the pre-Keynesian (pre-1930s) period, y was assumed to be at its full-employment level. The velocity of money was believed to be influenced by factors such as population density, physical means of transporting money, spending habits, and the payment mechanism, which most agreed changed slowly over time. Velocity was therefore believed to be unchanged in the short run. An increase in the nominal money supply, under these circumstances, would result in a proportional increase in the price level. In the Cambridge k version of the equation of exchange, written as $M/p = (1/V)y$ or $M = kpy$, the Cambridge k focuses upon the demand for money rather than its velocity. As initially presented, the Cambridge k is a stable function of y; an increase in the nominal supply would thereby impact the price level and not output. Keynes related the demand for money not only to output but to the rate of interest. In doing so, the Cambridge k would now vary with the rate of interest, and a proportionality between the nominal money supply and the price level was less likely.

EXAMPLE 12.6. Suppose the demand for money is solely a function of real output, and the private sector wants to hold money balances equal to 10% of their real income. When the nominal money supply is $20 and real output is $100 (which is also the real income of the private sector), the price level must be 2.00 since $M/p = k(y)$; $\$20/p = 0.10(100)$. Now suppose the nominal money supply increases from $20 to $40, *ceteris paribus*. With no change in k or y, the price level must also double, increasing from 2.00 to 4.00 for there to be equilibrium in the supply and demand for real money balances.

12.5 THE TRANSACTION DEMAND FOR MONEY

Although money expenditures by households, businesses, and government are more or less continuous, money receipts tend to be periodic. Hence, idle money balances are held to meet a relatively continuous flow of expenditures. The size of these holdings is influenced by the frequency of money receipts, expenditure patterns and the rate of interest, *ceteris paribus*. The amount of transaction balances held is found from the formula $Mt = (1/2)(Y/365)\gamma$, where Mt is the average money balance held for transactions, Y is nominal disposable income, and γ is the number of days in a pay period. Example 12.7 shows that the average transaction ($M1$ money) balance held is positively related to the length of the pay period.

When there is an opportunity cost in holding transaction balances (liquid financial assets, such as money market deposit accounts, generally yield a higher net return than transaction balances), the formula for $M1$ demand is $Mt = (1/2n)(Y/365)\gamma$, where n is the number of transfers from a substitute liquid asset account to an $M1$ transaction balance. Mt varies inversely with the number of transfers. Example 12.8 shows that, for a \$14,600 annual income and a 7-day pay period, Mt is \$70 when there is one transfer per pay period (\$140 is withdrawn weekly) and \$10 when there are seven withdrawals during the 7-day pay period. The optimum number of transfers depends upon revenues and costs associated with transfers. In Fig. 12-1 we assume a fixed cost a per transfer; total transfer costs therefore equal an, depicted by curve C. Total revenue R in Fig. 12-1 is given by the formula $R = i[(n-1)/2n](Y/365)\gamma$, where i is the annualized return on substitute liquid assets. The optimum number of transfers is n_1 (see Fig. 12-1) where net revenue N is at its maximum. The optimum number of transfers increases when i, Y, and/or γ rises and/or a falls. The $M1$ balance held increases when a, Y, and/or γ increases and/or i decreases (see Example 12.9). γ and a are unlikely to change in the short run; hence, the average $M1$ balance held is a function of the rate of interest and nominal income. In Fig. 12-2, the transaction demand for money appears as a family of schedules where Mt, Mt', and Mt'' represent the transaction demand for $M1$ balances at higher income levels.

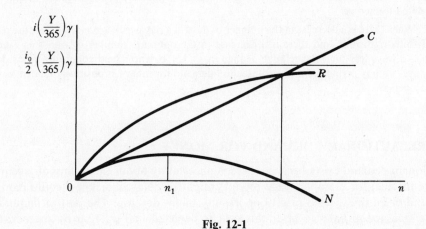

Fig. 12-1

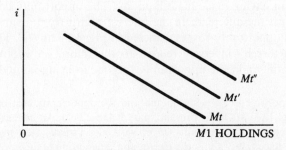

Fig. 12-2

EXAMPLE 12.7. Suppose a household's annual disposable income is \$14,600 and income is spent uniformly during the year. When the household is paid daily, the average $M1$ balance held is \$20 $[Mt = (1/2)(Y/365)\gamma;$ \$20 = (1/2)(\$14,600/365)1]. When paid weekly, the average $M1$ balance held is \$140; when paid biweekly, it is \$280.

EXAMPLE 12.8. Suppose a household's annual disposable income is \$14,600; income is spent uniformly during the year, and the \$280 weekly income is directly deposited to a savings account. When the household withdraws \$280 in cash weekly from its savings account (number of transfers n is 1), the average $M1$ balance held is \$140. $[Mt = (1/2n)(Y/365)\gamma;$ \$140 = (1/2)(\$14,600/365)7.] However, should the household make daily cash withdrawals ($n = 7$) of \$40, the average $M1$ balance held is \$20. $[Mt = (1/2n)(Y/365)\gamma;$ \$20 = (1/4)(\$14,600/365)7.]

EXAMPLE 12.9. The transaction demand for $M1$ balances is influenced by the fixed cost per transfer, the rate of interest, the level of income and the number of days in a pay period.

Situation I: When the fixed cost per transfer increases, *ceteris paribus*, the cost curve C in Fig. 12-1 pivots leftward, and there is a decrease in the optimum number of transfers. Since a decrease in the number of transfers results in a larger transaction balance held, the transaction demand for $M1$ balances is positively related to the fixed cost per transfer.

Situation II: When the rate of interest increases, *ceteris paribus*, the revenue curve R in Fig. 12-1 shifts leftward, and there is an increase in the optimum number of transfers. Since a higher rate of interest reduces the transaction balance held, the transaction demand for money is negatively related to the rate of interest.

Situation III: When annual income increases, *ceteris paribus*, the revenue curve in Fig. 12-1 shifts leftward, and there is an increase in the optimum number of transfers. The effect that this has on the money balance held depends on the relative change in n and Y. From the formula for the optimum number of transfers, $n = \sqrt{(i/2a)(Y/365)\gamma}$, we find that the relative increase in n cannot exceed one-half the relative increase in income. When the relative increase in the optimum number of transfers is less than the relative increase in income, there is an increase in $M1$ balances held as income expands. The transactions demand for money is positively related to income.

Situation IV: When there is a decrease in the number of days in a pay period, *ceteris paribus*, the revenue curve R in Fig. 12-1 shifts rightward, and there is a decrease in the optimum number of transfers. Since the relative change in n is always less than the relative change in γ, $M1$ balances held for transactions decrease as the number of days in a pay period falls. The transaction demand for money is positively related to the number of days in a pay period.

12.6 THE PRECAUTIONARY DEMAND FOR MONEY

A precautionary demand exists because there is uncertainty about the timing of receipt and expenditure of future income; for example, wage receipts might be delayed, sickness could require increased expenditures, and/or an unexpected profit opportunity might develop. The cost of illiquidity is greater the smaller the transaction balance held; this cost is depicted in Fig. 12-3 by the negatively sloped schedule EC. The expected cost of illiquidity is a function of the amount of the transaction balance held, the expected income level, the uncertainty about the receipt and expenditure of future income and the opportunity forgone in having inadequate liquidity. The opportunity cost of holding a transaction balance is $i(M1)$, where i is the difference in the interest return from a substitute store of value and a transaction balance. This opportunity cost is depicted in Fig. 12-3 as OC. The money balance held as a precautionary balance is thereby inversely related to the return on alternative assets and positively related to income, uncertainty and the opportunity forgone in being illiquid.

EXAMPLE 12.10. The expected cost of being illiquid and the opportunity cost of being liquid are depicted by schedules EC and OC in Fig. 12-3; M_0 is the precautionary balance held. An increase in the return from substitute assets (e.g., money market deposit accounts) shifts OC upward, and a smaller $M1$ precautionary balance is held. An increase in expected income, uncertainty about the receipt and expenditure of income, and the opportunity forgone in being illiquid shifts EC rightward, and there is an increase in the $M1$ precautionary balance held.

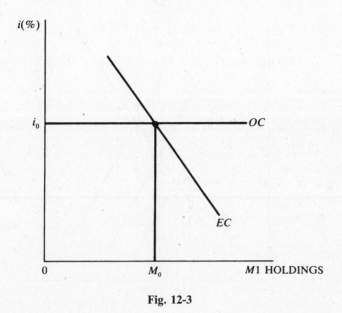

Fig. 12-3

12.7   THE PORTFOLIO DEMAND FOR MONEY

Keynes assumed that wealth holders have only two portfolio options: $M1$ balance and/or long-term bonds. Bonds are an imperfect store of value since a change in the market rate of interest affects the bond's price and its short-term return. Money is held in an investor's portfolio to the extent that the return on a long-term bond is uncertain and an investor is risk-averse. Portfolio alternatives are now categorized as real assets, equities, long-term bonds, and liquid financial assets; an $M1$ balance is a small subset of the liquid asset category. Investors' demand for liquid assets varies with the investors' aversion to risk and their perception of variability of return from nonliquid assets. However, the inclusion of an $M1$ balance in a portfolio as a store of value is less likely, since substitute financial assets, included in the $M2$ and $M3$ definitions of money, are equally safe stores of value and generally provide a higher return than an $M1$ balance. Hence, a portfolio demand for an $M1$ balance is unlikely, and economists generally associate a portfolio demand for money with the $M2$ and $M3$ definitions of money.

12.8   MONEY SUPPLY OR INTEREST RATE MONETARY POLICY

The Federal Reserve's choice of an interest rate or money supply monetary policy depends on the stability of the IS and LM schedules. Changes in autonomous consumption, investment, and net exports and a change in the interest sensitivity of private sector spending shift IS. LM shifts when there is an autonomous change in the demand for money and/or a change in the interest sensitivity of the demand for money. Example 12.11 demonstrates that a money supply monetary policy is called for when IS is more unstable than LM. An interest rate monetary policy is more effective in controlling the level of output when LM is less stable than IS.

EXAMPLE 12.11.   Equilibrium output is y_0 for schedules IS and LM in Fig. 12-4. When the LM schedule is stable, equilibrium output exists between y_2 and y_3 for shifts of IS between IS_1 and IS_2. Equilibrium output fluctuates between y_1 and y_4 when the Federal Reserve, in following an interest rate monetary policy, keeps the interest rate constant at i_0. In this static framework, then, a constant nominal money supply, with fluctuations in the rate of interest, has a greater stabilizing effect on output than does one where the rate of interest is held constant. Nominal money supply targeting is called for when the goods market schedule IS is more unstable than the money market schedule LM.

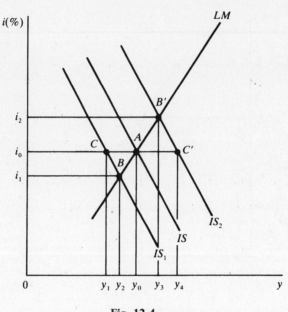

Fig. 12-4

Solved Problems

THE FUNCTIONS OF MONEY

12.1   Explain the following functions of money: (*a*) unit of account, (*b*) medium of exchange, (*c*) standard of deferred payment.

   (*a*)   Money is used to measure economic phenomena. In hiring resources and/or buying or selling goods and services, money facilitates economic decision-making by serving as a common expression of value.

   (*b*)   Labor is paid a money wage rather than goods for its services. Workers use this money income to obtain goods and services of their choosing. Money's medium of exchange function results in the efficient allocation of resources; and economic welfare is maximized by an efficient distribution of the resulting output.

   (*c*)   Money allows individuals to save and lend their saving to borrowers. For example, a dollar-denominated debt instrument (repayment is to be made in dollars) is created when a saver lends dollars to a borrower, and the borrower promises to repay the lender a fixed sum of dollars at a future date.

12.2   (*a*) What is meant by the term *liquidity*? (*b*) What are *near monies*?

   (*a*)   Liquidity is the ease with which an asset can be converted to a medium of exchange and there is minimal loss of nominal value. A savings account in a deposit institution is liquid since it is easily converted to an $M1$ balance without loss of nominal value. Although a long-term bond may be sold quickly, it is less liquid because the bond's market price (nominal value) depends on the market interest rate at time of sale.

   (*b*)   Near monies are financial assets which cannot be used as a medium of exchange but are close substitutes for a transaction balance. The following near monies are transferable into an $M1$ balance with no loss of nominal value and are therefore liquid stores of value: savings deposits, money market mutual funds balances, money market deposit accounts, time deposits and U.S. government savings bonds.

12.3   (*a*) Explain money's store-of-value function. (*b*) Are $M1$ money balances the only financial asset, which can serve as a store of value? (*c*) Are long-term bonds a store of value?

   (*a*)   Money allows the postponement of spending to a later period with no loss of nominal value, i.e., money can be held for extended periods with no change in the nominal value of the sum held.

   (*b*)   An $M1$ money balance is not a unique, liquid store of value. Various bank deposit accounts also retain their nominal value over extended periods, since the bank promises to repay the sum deposited.

   (*c*)   A long-term bond has a fixed nominal value as do all debt contracts. However, its market value varies inversely with the current long-term rate of interest. Thus, a long-term bond is not a good store of value when funds are needed prior to the bond's maturity and the current market rate is above the level which existed when the bond was purchased.

DEFINITIONS OF MONEY

12.4   Why is there more than one definition of money?

   Money is an asset which serves as a unit of account, standard of deferred payment, medium of exchange and store of value. Focusing on the medium-of-exchange function, money consists of financial assets which can be used as a medium of exchange; $M1$ is a transactions definition of money which includes currency outside banks, checking accounts, and travelers' checks. Financial assets other than $M1$ balances are good stores of value. Thus, the existence of store-of-value substitutes for $M1$ balances has resulted in the Federal Reserve's publication of $M2$ and $M3$ measures of the money supply.

12.5   Federal Reserve definitions of the $M1$, $M2$, and $M3$ money supply are as follows: $M1$ is the sum of currency outside banks, checking deposits and traveler's checks. $M2$ is the sum of $M1$, savings deposits, money market deposit accounts, small-denomination time deposits, and noninstitution money market mutual funds. $M3$ is the sum of $M2$, large-denomination time deposits, overnight and term repurchase agreements and Eurodollars, and institution-only money market mutual funds. From the data in Table 12-2, find $M1$, $M2$, and $M3$.

Table 12-2

(1)	Currency outside banks	$ 30
(2)	Checking accounts	262
(3)	Travelers' checks	4
(4)	Savings and small-denomination time deposits	852
(5)	Noninstitution money market mutual funds	175
(6)	Large-denomination time deposits	340
(7)	Institution-only money market mutual funds	35
(8)	Overnight and term RPs and Eurodollars	42

$$M1 = (1) + (2) + (3)$$
$$= \$30 + \$262 + \$4 = \$396$$
$$M2 = M1 + (4) + (5)$$
$$= \$396 + \$852 + \$175 = \$1423$$
$$M3 = M2 + (6) + (7) + (8)$$
$$= M2 + \$340 + \$35 + 42 = \$1840$$

CREATION AND CONTROL OF THE M1 MONEY SUPPLY

12.6   Why are most payments made by check rather than with currency?

>   Currency is a bearer instrument which must be delivered to the payee. A check can be mailed or funds from a checking account can be wire transferred to a payee. Payment from a checking account is therefore safer, more convenient, and more efficient.

12.7   (*a*) What is a reserve requirement? (*b*) Which bank deposits are subject to a reserve requirement?

>   (*a*)   A reserve requirement mandates the holding of reserve assets. For example, a 10% reserve requirement on checking deposits mandates that a bank must hold reserve assets of $10 when its checking deposit liabilities are $100.

>   (*b*)   Currently, the Federal Reserve imposes a 10% reserve requirement on only check-writing deposits. Other bank liabilities are not subject to a reserve requirement.

12.8   Why does the banking system increase checking account liabilities when it has excess reserves?

>   Excess reserves exist when banks hold more reserves than are required. Since reserves are a nonearning asset and banks seek to maximize profits, banks attempt to keep reserve assets at their required level. For the banking system, this is achieved by increasing checking deposit liabilities whenever there are excess reserves. Thus, banks make loans and/or purchase securities, and thereby increase checking deposits, until the amount of reserves held equals the amount that is required.

12.9   (*a*) What are the components of the monetary base? (*b*) What happens to the monetary base when the Federal Reserve purchases Treasury securities in the open market, *ceteris paribus*? (*c*) Find the change in the *M*1 money supply when the Federal Reserve purchases $1000 in Treasury securities in the open market and the reserve requirement on checking deposits is 0.10. (*d*) Find the change in the *M*1 money supply when the Federal Reserve purchases Treasury securities valued at $1000 and households increase currency holdings $1000?

>   (*a*)   The monetary base consists of currency outside banks plus reserves held by the banking system (currency held by banks plus bank deposits at the Fed). An alternative definition is currency in circulation plus deposits of the banking system at the Fed.

>   (*b*)   The monetary base increases. The Fed purchases Treasury securities and pays for them by issuing currency and/or crediting the deposit account of banks at the Fed. Thus, the expanded monetary base is held as currency outside banks or as reserves by the banking system.

>   (*c*)   As the T-account below shows, the banking system's reserves (deposits at the Fed) increase $1000. Since it now has $1000 in excess reserves, checking deposit liabilities and loans can increase $10,000. (Recall $\Delta D = \Delta E / r_D$.) The *M*1 money supply increases $10,000.

Banking System

Δ Assets		Δ Liabilities
Treasury securities	—$1000	
Deposits at the Fed	+ $1000	
Loans	+ $10,000	Checking deposits + $10,000

Federal Reserve Banks

Δ Assets		Δ Liabilities
Treasury securities	+ $1000	Deposit of banks + $1,000

(*d*)   Currency outside banks has increased $1000; there is no check deposit expansion, since additions to the monetary base are held as currency outside the banking system. The $M1$ money supply increases $1000.

12.10   (*a*) What happens to the monetary base when the Federal Reserve acquires assets other than Treasury securities, *ceteris paribus*? (*b*) What happens to the monetary base when the Federal Reserve purchases gold, sells foreign exchange, lends (discounts) to banks?

(*a*)   The Federal Reserve's purchase of any asset expands the monetary base, *ceteris paribus*. In the T-account below we see that purchases of Treasury securities, gold, foreign exchange, and/or other financial or real assets increase Federal Reserve note (currency) liabilities and/or deposits of banks, both components of the monetary base.

Federal Reserve Banks

Δ Assets			
Treasury securities	+		Δ Liabilities
OR		Federal Reserve notes	+
Gold	+	OR	
OR		Deposits of Banks	+
Foreign exchange	+		
OR			
Other financial and real assets	+		

(*b*)   The monetary base increases when the Federal Reserve purchases gold, decreases when it sells foreign exchange, and increases when it lends to banks.

12.11   The competing uses of the monetary base (the demand for the base) include currency held outside banks, excess reserves held by banks, and reserves held by banks to meet the reserve requirement on checking deposits. Derive a formula for the $M1$ money supply and the $m1$ money multiplier, given the following behavior for the demand for the monetary base:

(*a*)   The private sector's desire to hold currency C is a fraction k of checking deposits D, or $C = kD$.

(*b*)   Banks' willingness to hold excess reserves E is a fraction e of checking deposits, or $E = eD$.

(*c*)   There is an r_D reserve requirement on checking deposits or $R_D = r_D D$.

The supply of the monetary base is B; from the behavior specified in items (*a*) through (*c*), the demand for the monetary base includes currency held outside banks C, the banks' desire to hold excess reserves E, and reserves required for checking deposits R_D. Thus,

$$B = C + E + R_D$$

Since $C = kD$, $E = eD$, and $R_D = r_D D$, the equation above can be presented as

$$B = kD + eD + r_D D$$

Solving for D, we have

$$D = B\left(\frac{1}{r_D + k + e}\right)$$

which is a formula for the volume of checking deposits. By definition, $M1$ equals $C + D$. Substituting kD for C since $C = kD$, we have

$$M1 = kD + D$$
$$= D(1 + k)$$
$$= B\left(\frac{1 + k}{r_D + k + e}\right)$$

Letting the sum in parentheses ( ) be the $m1$ money multiplier, $m1 = (1 + k)/(r_D + k + e)$. The $M1$ money supply is an $m1$ multiple of the monetary base. $M1 = m1B$.

12.12 (a) Find the $m1$ money multiplier and the $M1$ money supply when $B = \$200$, $r_D = 0.10$, $e = 0.10$ and $k = 0.20$. (b) Find the $m1$ money multiplier and the $M1$ money supply when $e = 0$ and $k = 0.20$.

(a)
$$m1 = \frac{1 + k}{r_D + k + e}$$
$$= \frac{1 + 0.20}{0.10 + 0.20 + 0.10}$$
$$= 3$$

The $M1$ money supply is \$600. [$M1 = m1B$; $\$600 = \$200(3)$]

(b) The $m1$ money multiplier increases to 4.00 when e declines to 0 and k is 0.20. The $M1$ money supply is then \$800.

THE QUANTITY THEORY OF MONEY

12.13 (a) Explain the following variables used in the equation of exchange $MV = py$: nominal money supply M, velocity V, general price level p, and real output y. (b) Why is the equation of exchange a tautology?

(a) The nominal money supply ($M1$ definition) consists of all financial assets used as media of exchange, specifically currency outside banks, checking deposits and travelers' checks. Velocity is the average rate of turnover of the nominal money supply in effecting transactions. The general price level p measures the price level for final output. Real output is the final market value of all goods and services measured in constant dollars.

(b) The equation of exchange is true by definition. MV represents the amount spent on final goods and services, and py is the nominal amount received from the sale of final output. Since, *ex post facto*, the amount spent equals the amount received, MV must always equal py.

12.14 Compare the equation of exchange with the Cambridge equation.

The Cambridge equation is $M = kpy$, where k is the proportion of nominal income held as a cash balance. The equation of exchange and the Cambridge equation are alternative ways of expressing the relationship between the money supply and the nominal value of aggregate output. By rewriting the equation of exchange as $M = (1/V)py$, we derive the Cambridge equation with $1/V = k$. These equations differ in their focus on the use of money: "at what rate V does the private sector spend money balances?" in contrast to "what is the private sector's demand k for money balances?"

12.15 Suppose the nominal money supply is \$400, the general price level is 1.00, real output is at its \$2000 full employment level and k is 0.20. Why does the general price level increase to 2.00 when the nominal money supply increases to \$800?

The \$400 nominal money supply is willingly held (the demand for money equals the supply of money) when the nominal money supply is \$400, k equals 0.20, the general price level is 1.00 and real output is \$2,000. When the nominal money supply doubles to \$800 and there is no change in either the price level or real output, households hold larger (\$800 rather than \$400) nominal balances, and k is increased to 0.40. Holding excess money balances, households increase spending. Because output is at full employment, prices rise in response to the increased demand. Prices rise until the general price level is 2.00 and nominal output is \$4000. When nominal output is \$4000, k is returned to the desired 0.20 level, and the supply of money equals the demand for money.

THE TRANSACTION DEMAND FOR MONEY

12.16 (*a*) Why is there a transaction demand for money? (*b*) From Table 12-3, find the average money balance held for situations (1), (2), and (3) when weekly income is $140.

  (*a*)   Money balances are held to budget expenditures over a pay period. The average money balance held depends on the timing of expenditures, the level of income and the length of the pay period γ.

  (*b*)   The average money balance held over a pay period is the sum of the average daily money balance held divided by the number of days in the pay period. Expenditures are uniform in (1), concentrated in the latter part of the week in (2) and concentrated in the earlier part of the week in (3). The average money balance held for the one-week period for situation (1) is $70, $80 for (2), and $40 for (3).

Table 12-3

Average Daily Money Balances Held			
	(1)	(2)	(3)
Monday	$130	$140	$100
Tuesday	110	130	80
Wednesday	90	120	60
Thursday	70	110	30
Friday	50	40	10
Saturday	30	20	0
Sunday	10	0	0
Sum	$490	$560	$280

12.17 When spending is uniform over a pay period, the equation for the average $M1$ balance held during a pay period is $Mt = (1/2)(Y/365)\gamma$. (*a*) For the five situations in Table 12-4, find the average money balance held during each pay period. (*b*) What is the relationship of Mt to Y and γ?

  (*a*)   The average money balance held for a pay period equals $(Y/365)\gamma$. The average money balance held per pay period is as follows: *A* $210; *B* $420; *C* $840; *D* $315; and *E* $420.

Table 12-4

Situation	Y ($)	γ (days)
A	10,950	7
B	10,950	14
C	10,950	28
D	16,425	7
E	21,900	7

(b) Mt is positively related to Y and γ; an increase in Y, *ceteris paribus*, raises the average money balance held during a pay period, as does a lengthening of the pay period (an increase in γ).

12.18 Suppose a household is paid $140 weekly and spends this income uniformly over the pay period. Find the average $M1$ balance held during the pay period (a) when income is held as an $M1$ balance prior to expenditure or (b) one-half of the period's income is deposited in a money market deposit account at the beginning of the period, with the balance transferred during mid-period to an $M1$ account. (c) When expenditures are continuous, show in Fig. 12-5 for the situations described in part (a) and (b) the $M1$ balance held at any time during the pay period.

(a)   Table 12-5 presents the daily average money balance held when spendable income is held as an $M1$ balance. The average $M1$ balance held during the seven-day period is $70. [$490/(7 days) = $70]

(b)   Table 12-6 presents an alternative scenario where one-half of the income is placed in a money market deposit account for one-half the period and then transferred to a transactions balance. The average $M1$ balance held during the pay period is now $35.

(c)   When only transaction balances are held, a $140 $M1$ balance is held at the beginning of the pay period and 0 at the end; line AEB in Fig. 12-5 measures the quantity of $M1$ held at any time during the pay period. When money market deposit balances are held for one-half of the period, line $CDEB$ measures the $M1$ balance held at any time during the pay period.

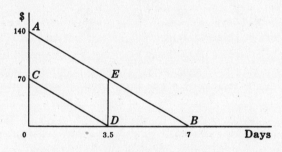

Fig. 12-5

Table 12-5

	M1 Balance Held ($)		
	Start of Day	End of Day	Average
Monday	140	120	130
Tuesday	120	100	110
Wednesday	100	80	90
Thursday	80	60	70
Friday	60	40	50
Saturday	40	20	30
Sunday	20	0	10
Sum			490

Table 12-6

	M1 Balance Held (\$)		
	Start of Day	End of Day	Average
Monday	70	50	60
Tuesday	50	30	40
Wednesday	30	10	20
Thursday	10	60	35
Friday	60	40	50
Saturday	40	20	30
Sunday	20	0	10
Sum			245

12.19 The average transaction balance held in an $M1$ substitute (Msub) and in $M1$ is found by the formulas

$$M\text{sub} = \frac{n-1}{2n}\left(\frac{Y}{365}\right)\gamma \qquad \text{and} \qquad M1 = \frac{1}{2n}\left(\frac{Y}{365}\right)\gamma$$

where n is the number of transfers from an $M1$ substitute to an $M1$ account. (a) Find the average balance held in an $M1$ and an $M1$ substitute account when a household is paid weekly, receives \$14,600 annually and (1) one-half of the weekly income is invested in an $M1$ substitute for one-half of the period, (2) two-thirds of the weekly income is invested in an $M1$ substitute and one-half is transferred to an $M1$ balance after one-third of the period and the other one-half is transferred after two-thirds of the period, or (3) three-quarters of the weekly income is invested in an $M1$ substitute and one-third is transferred after one-quarter of the period, one-third after one-half of the period and the last one-third is transferred after three-quarters of the period. (b) What happens to the average $M1$ balance held when a household makes an increasing number of transfers between its $M1$ substitute and $M1$ account?

(a) The average balances in an $M1$ substitute and an $M1$ account are calculated below.

(1)
$$M\text{sub} = \frac{n-1}{2n}\left(\frac{Y}{365}\right)\gamma = \frac{1}{4}\left(\frac{\$14,600}{365}\right)7 = \$70$$

$$M1 = \frac{1}{2n}\left(\frac{Y}{365}\right)\gamma = \frac{1}{4}\left(\frac{\$14,600}{365}\right)7 = \$70$$

(2)
$$M\text{sub} = \frac{n-1}{2n}\left(\frac{Y}{365}\right)\gamma = \frac{2}{6}\left(\frac{\$14,600}{365}\right)7 = \$93.33$$

$$M1 = \frac{1}{2n}\left(\frac{Y}{365}\right)\gamma = \frac{1}{6}\left(\frac{\$14,600}{365}\right)7 = \$46.67$$

(3)
$$M\text{sub} = \frac{n-1}{2n}\left(\frac{Y}{365}\right)\gamma = \frac{3}{8}\left(\frac{\$14,600}{365}\right)7 = \$105$$

$$M1 = \frac{1}{2n}\left(\frac{Y}{365}\right)\gamma = \frac{1}{8}\left(\frac{\$14,600}{365}\right)7 = \$35$$

(b) The average $M1$ balance held over a pay period declines as a household makes a larger number of transfers from an $M1$ substitute account to an $M1$ account. Thus, holding Y and γ constant, the average $M1$ balance held is negatively related to the number of transfers made from an $M1$ substitute account.

12.20 (*a*) What determines the optimum number of transfers between $M1$ substitutes and $M1$ balances when there are costs associated with acquiring $M1$ substitutes and then transferring them to $M1$ balances? (*b*) What happens to the optimum number of transfers when there is (1) a decrease in the rate of interest, (2) an increase in annual income, or (3) an increase in the fixed cost per transfer?

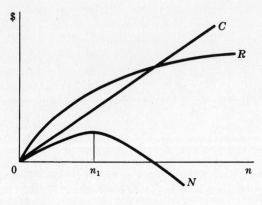

Fig. 12-6

(*a*)   For ease of analysis, we shall assume that $M1$ balances generate no revenue and incur no costs, whereas there are costs and revenues associated with $M1$ substitutes. Suppose there is a fixed cost per transfer between $M1$ and $M1$ substitute assets; cost schedule C in Fig. 12-6 represents the total costs associated with n transfers. Schedule R is the revenue associated with holding $M1$ substitutes, given a rate of interest, an income level, and a fixed pay period. The optimum number of transfers occurs when the net revenue ($N = R - C$) from $M1$ substitutes is maximized; this occurs in Fig. 12-6 when there are n_1 transfers.

(*b*)   (1) Revenue curve R shifts rightward, which causes the net revenue curve N to shift downward. There is a reduction in the optimum number of transfers. (2) Revenue curve R shifts leftward, causing an upward movement of the net revenue curve. There is an increase in the optimum number of transfers. (3) Cost curve C pivots leftward, shifting the net revenue curve downward. There is a decrease in the optimum number of transfers.

12.21 Suppose the total cost of transfers is $C = an$, and the revenue from holding $M1$ substitutes is $R = i[(n-1)/2n](Y/365)\gamma$. (*a*) Derive a formula for the optimum number of transfers. (*b*) What happens to the optimum number of transfers and the average $M1$ balance held when there is an increase in income?

(*a*)   The optimum numbers of transfers occurs where $R - C = N$ is maximized:

$$N = i\left(\frac{n-1}{2n}\right)\left(\frac{Y}{365}\right)\gamma - an$$

Differentiating with respect to n,

$$\frac{dN}{dn} = \frac{i}{2n^2}\left(\frac{Y}{365}\right)\gamma - a$$

The maximum condition exists where dN/dn equals 0. Thus,

$$0 = \frac{i}{2n^2}\left(\frac{Y}{365}\right)\gamma - a$$

and solving for n,

$$n = \sqrt{\frac{i}{2a}\left(\frac{Y}{365}\right)\gamma}$$ Formula for the optimum number of bond transactions

(b) From the formula $n = \sqrt{(i/2a)(Y/365)\gamma}$ we see that $\Delta n = \sqrt{\Delta Y}$. Thus, if Y doubles, the increase in n equals $1.414n$. Since the relative change in n is less than the relative change in income, the quantity of money held for transactions is positively related to the level of income.

THE PRECAUTIONARY DEMAND FOR MONEY

12.22 (a) Why is there a precautionary demand for money? (b) What is the cost of being illiquid? (c) What is the cost of being liquid?

(a) Precautionary money balances are needed when income receipts and expenditures are uncertain. "Extra" money balances are needed should income not be received on time or unplanned spending develops.

(b) The cost of being illiquid is the cost associated with not having an adequate $M1$ balance to acquire goods and services. The cost of being illiquid is related to one's income (and therefore the level of expenditures) and the uncertainty associated with $M1$ receipts and disbursements. Obviously, increased uncertainty about the timing of income receipts and expenditures raises the cost of not holding $M1$ balances.

(c) The cost of being liquid is the interest forgone in holding money rather than a substitute interest-bearing asset.

12.23 Suppose schedule EC in Fig. 12-7 represents the expected cost of being illiquid; OC represents the cost of being liquid. What happens to the precautionary demand for $M1$ balances when (a) there is a decrease in the return from $M1$ substitute assets, *ceteris paribus*; (b) the household sector is pessimistic that the business expansion will continue, *ceteris paribus*; (c) there is an increase in expected income, *ceteris paribus*.

(a) A decrease in the return from $M1$ substitutes causes the OC curve to shift downward; larger $M1$ balances are held.

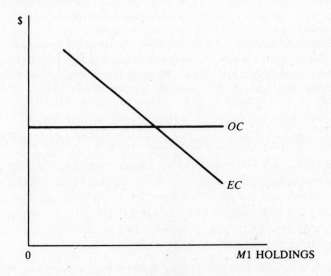

Fig. 12-7

(*b*)   Less certainty about the future shifts *EC* rightward; larger *M*1 balances are held.

(*c*)   An increase in expected income shifts *EC* rightward; larger *M*1 balances are held.

THE PORTFOLIO DEMAND FOR MONEY

12.24   Relate the transaction and the portfolio demand for *M*1 balances to the medium of exchange and store of value functions of money.

The *M*1 money supply consists of transaction balances, which are the medium of exchange. *M*1 balances can also serve as a liquid store of value in that they retain their nominal value.

12.25   Explain Keynes' original presentation of the portfolio demand for money.

Keynes assumed that investors had only two store-of-value alternatives: money and/or long-term bonds. Given these portfolio alternatives, a portfolio demand for money exists because money serves as a better store of value than long-term bonds. When a bondholder sells a bond prior to maturity and the market rate of interest is higher than when the bond was purchased, the bond is sold at a price below its purchase price and there is a capital loss. Investors hold money rather than bonds when they expect the capital loss to exceed the interest return. Thus, the portfolio demand for money increases during a period of rising interest rates, when money is expected to be a better store of value than long-term bonds.

12.26   Is an investor more likely to have a portfolio demand for an *M*1, *M*2, or *M*3 money balance?

The *M*2 and *M*3 definitions of money include financial assets that yield a higher return than those in *M*1 and have no real discernible difference from *M*1 with respect to loss of nominal value. *M*2 and *M*3 balances therefore are nearly perfect store-of-value substitutes for *M*1 balances. Hence, the portfolio demand for money is more likely a demand for *M*2 and *M*3 balances than a reason for holding *M*1 money balances.

MONEY SUPPLY OR INTEREST RATE MONETARY POLICY

12.27   What might cause *IS* or *LM* to shift?

In the absence of economic policy, *IS* or *LM* shift when there is a change in investment, consumption or the demand for money. Increases in autonomous investment or consumption shift *IS* rightward, whereas decreases in the demand for money shift *LM* rightward. Investment schedule I_1 in Fig. 12-8(*a*) is associated with IS_1 in Fig. 12-8(*b*). An increase in autonomous investment shifts investment schedule I_1 to I_2 and *IS* rightward from IS_1 to IS_2. A decrease in the demand for money in Fig. 12-8(*c*) from L_1 to L_2 causes *LM* to shift rightward from LM_1 to LM_2 in Fig. 12-8(*d*). When the investment, consumption, or demand for money schedules are unstable, there is uncertainty about the location of *IS* or *LM* in space.

12.28   Suppose goods equilibrium schedule *IS* in Fig. 12-9 is stable; *LM* is located between LM_1 and LM_2 because of an unstable demand for money. (*a*) Suppose the Federal Reserve follows an interest rate monetary policy and maintains the interest rate at i_0. Find the possible output levels for this i_0 interest rate monetary policy. (*b*) Suppose the Federal Reserve keeps the nominal money supply constant; find the possible output levels when equilibrium in the money markets exists between LM_1 and LM_2 because of an unstable demand for money. (*c*) Is an interest rate or a money supply monetary policy more desirable when equilibrium in the goods market is stable and monetary equilibrium is unstable?

(*a*)   To maintain an i_0 interest rate, the Federal Reserve must expand or contract the money supply whenever the interest rate rises or falls below this level. Thus, the actual *LM* schedule is the horizontal

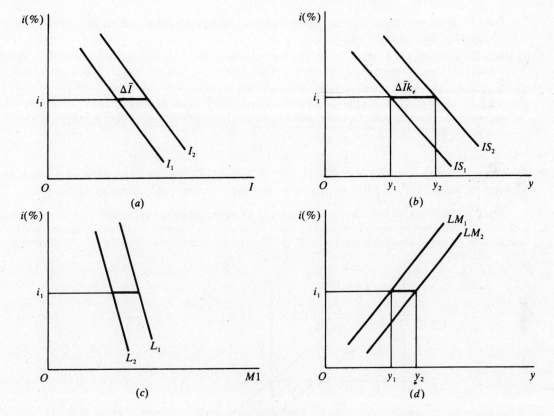

Fig. 12-8

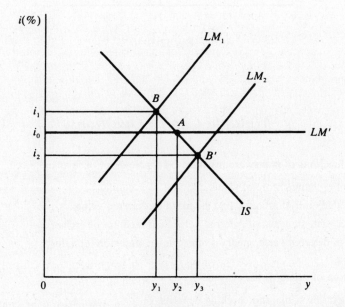

Fig. 12-9

line LM' at interest rate i_0. With the goods market schedule stable at IS, y_2 is the only output level for an i_0 interest rate monetary policy.

(b)   Equilibrium output is y_1 when the money market schedule is LM_1 and y_3 when the money market schedule is LM_2. A money supply monetary policy produces a range of equilibria between y_1 and y_3.

(c)   In parts (a) and (b), an i_0 interest rate monetary policy produces only one output level, whereas output exists between y_1 and y_3 for a money supply monetary policy. When IS is stable and LM is unstable, an interest rate monetary policy is more desirable because it generates a more certain output level.

12.29   The money market schedule is stable at LM in Fig. 12-10; the goods market schedule exists between IS_1 and IS_2. Is an interest rate or money supply monetary policy more desirable?

A policy of keeping the interest rate at i_0 results in an output level between y_1 and y_2, whereas holding the nominal money supply constant results in output y_1. A money supply monetary policy is more desirable because of its greater control of output.

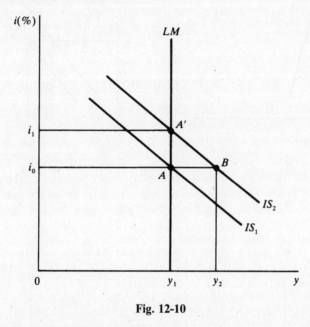

Fig. 12-10

Multiple Choice Questions

1.   The following functions of money are provided by a unique set of financial assets:

(a)   Medium of exchange, store of value, and unit of account.

(b)   Store of value, unit of account, and standard of deferred value.

(c)   Unit of account, standard of deferred value, and medium of exchange.

(d)   Standard of deferred value, medium of exchange, and store of value.

2.   The $M1$ definition of money is the sum of

(a)   Currency outside banks and checking deposits.

(b)   Currency outside banks, checking deposits, and travelers' checks.

    (*c*) Currency outstanding and checking deposits.

    (*d*) Currency outstanding, checking deposits, and money market deposit accounts.

3.   The Federal Reserve controls

    (*a*) The monetary base through open market operations.

    (*b*) The monetary base through reserve requirements on deposit accounts.

    (*c*) The money multiplier through open market operations.

    (*d*) The money multiplier through reserve requirements on deposit accounts.

4.   When the reserve requirement on checking deposits is 0.10 and the Federal Reserve purchases government securities valued at \$100,000, the $M1$ money supply

    (*a*) Is unchanged.

    (*b*) Increases by \$100,000.

    (*c*) Increases by \$1,000,000.

    (*d*) Increases by an amount determined by the money multiplier.

5.   According to the quantity theory of money,

    (*a*) An increase in the nominal money supply causes a proportional increase in the price level, *ceteris paribus*.

    (*b*) An increase in the nominal money supply causes a proportional increase in real GNP, *ceteris paribus*.

    (*c*) An increase in the real money supply causes a proportional increase in the price level, *ceteris paribus*.

    (*d*) An increase in the real money supply causes a proportional increase in real GNP, *ceteris paribus*.

6.   The average $M1$ balance held for transactions is

    (*a*) Negatively related to the length of the pay period and positively related to the income level.

    (*b*) Positively related to both the length of the pay period and the income level.

    (*c*) Negatively related to both the length of the pay period and the income level.

    (*d*) Positively related to the length of the pay period and negatively related to the income level.

7.   When holding $M1$ balances involves an opportunity cost, the average $M1$ balance held is negatively related to the return on

    (*a*) Currency, *ceteris paribus*.

    (*b*) Travelers' checks, *ceteris paribus*.

    (*c*) Money market deposit accounts, *ceteris paribus*.

    (*d*) Demand deposits, *ceteris paribus*.

8.   Which of the following statements is incorrect?

    (*a*) The precautionary demand for money is unrelated to income.

    (*b*) There is a precautionary demand for money because of uncertainty about the receipt of future income.

    (*c*) The precautionary demand for money is affected by the opportunity cost of holding $M1$ balances.

    (*d*) There is a precautionary demand for money because of unexpected expenditures.

9.   According to Keynes, there is a speculative demand for money because

    (*a*) People like to speculate in the stock market.

(b)   There is considerable risk in holding $M1$ balances.

(c)   Money, at times, may be a better store of value than long-term bonds.

(d)   Money always provides a certain, higher return than long-term bonds.

10.   The Federal Reserve should follow a money supply monetary policy when

(a)   The IS schedule is negatively sloped.

(b)   The LM schedule is largely insensitive to the rate of interest.

(c)   The location of IS in space is more certain than that of LM.

(d)   The location of LM in space is more certain than that of IS.

True or False Questions

11.   _____ The financial assets included in the $M2$ definition of money serve as a medium of exchange.

12.   _____ $M1$ is the sum of currency in circulation, travelers' checks, and check-writing deposits.

13.   _____ An increase in the reserve requirement lowers the value of the $m1$ multiplier.

14.   _____ The Federal Reserve increases the monetary base when it purchases Treasury securities.

15.   _____ The value of the Cambridge k is 0.25 when the velocity of money is 4.

16.   _____ The transaction demand for $M1$ balances is positively related to the number of days in a pay period.

17.   _____ Precautionary balances are held when there is concern about a decline in the stock market.

18.   _____ Larger money balances are held when there is increased uncertainty about the future.

19.   _____ There is a portfolio demand for money because money is a better store of value than interest and dividend-yielding financial instruments.

20.   _____ An interest rate monetary policy stabilizes output when the location of IS is uncertain.

Answers to Multiple Choice and True or False Questions

1. (c); **2.** (b); **3.** (a); **4.** (d); **5.** (a); **6.** (b); **7.** (c); **8.** (a); **9.** (c); **10.** (d); **11.** F; **12.** T; **13.** T; **14.** T; **15.** T; **16.** T; **17.** F; **18.** T; **19.** T; **20.** F.

Chapter 13

Consumption

Chapter Summary

1. Keynes' introduction of the consumption function in *The General Theory* resulted in considerable empirical research of household consumption. Cross-section studies of consumer spending showed that many lower-income households dissaved while most higher-income households saved. Time series data, however, showed that the U.S. economy's average propensity to consume is constant over time. A number of theories were advanced to explain the constancy of the aggregate APC and the differences of the APC among households.

2. According to the permanent income hypothesis, consumption is a function of both current and expected income, i.e., consumption is a function of permanent income. At any point in time, current income includes a permanent and a transitory component. When consumption is related to permanent income, consumption is a fixed percentage of income, and the APC does not change over time. When consumption is related to current income, the APC may be above or below 1.0. It may be greater than 1.0 when current income has a negative transitory component; it is below 1.0 when current income has a positive transitory component.

3. The life-cycle hypothesis relates consumption to lifetime income. Since income is normally low during one's initial working years and high during the later ones, lower-income individuals tend to dissave while higher-income individuals save. Thus, the APC is frequently above 1.0 for lower-income individuals and below 1.0 for higher-income individuals.

Chapter Outline

13.1 THE KEYNESIAN CONSUMPTION FUNCTION

Keynes postulated that consumption was subject to a "fundamental psychological law" whereby a change in consumption is less than a change in disposable income, i.e., the marginal propensity to consume is less than 1. In linear form, consumption is presented as $C = \bar{C} + cYd$, where c is the marginal propensity to consume and $\bar{C}$ is the influence of nonincome determinants on consumption. Keynes categorized consumption's nonincome determinants into subjective (psychological) and objective (wealth, installment credit, and income distribution) factors, but he speculated that these nonincome determinants were of minimal significance in explaining short-run consumption. (See Problem 13.4.) Cross-section studies of household spending have supported Keynes' hypothesized behavior: (1) household saving is largely explained by income; (2) high-income households tend to save, and low-income households tend to dissave. The nonproportional relationship of consumption and disposable income suggest that rising aggregate income levels should be associated with a higher national saving rate, i.e., the average propensity to consume (APC) would decline as income rose (Example 13.1). Time-series data show, however, that over long periods the U.S. economy's APC is constant (the relationship of consumption and disposable income is proportional). Milton Friedman's permanent income hypothesis and Franco Modigliani's life-cycle hypothesis are post–World War II consumption theories which reconcile the cross-section evidence of individual saving rates with time-series evidence of a constant APC. Both theories explain consumption by relating consumption to expected rather than current income.

EXAMPLE 13.1. Suppose the consumption equation is $C = \$40 + 0.80\,Yd$. The APC and MPC for a range of disposable incomes are given in Table 13-1. The relationship of consumption and disposable income is non-proportional, since the APC declines as income increases.

Table 13-1

Yd (\$)	C (\$)	APC	MPC
200	200	1.00	...
400	360	0.90	0.80
600	520	0.87	0.80
800	680	0.85	0.80
1000	840	0.84	0.80

13.2 THE PERMANENT INCOME HYPOTHESIS

Households are likely to smooth consumption over a business cycle in the same way that they smooth expenditures over a pay period. Hence, consumption is a function of both current and expected income. According to the permanent income hypothesis, current income Y consists of permanent Y^p and transitory Y^t components, i.e., $Y = Y^p + Y^t$. Permanent income is that which households expect to receive over an extended period, whereas transitory income consists of any unexpected addition to or subtraction from permanent income. The permanent income hypothesis is consistent with cross-section and time-series data. Higher-income households are savers because their current income includes positive transitory components, whereas transitory income is negative for dissaving, lower-income households. When we relate consumption to permanent income, a fixed, proportional relationship exists regardless of the distribution of permanent income. However, when we erroneously relate consumption to current income, we obtain a nonproportional relationship, since current income may include a positive or negative transitory component. Friedman used adaptive expectations to arrive at estimates of permanent income, with Y^p a weighted average of current and previous period permanent income. For example, applying a weight of j to current income and $(1 - j)$ to previous permanent income, we have $Y^p = j(Y) + (1 - j)Y^p_{-1}$. The theory also maintained that, regardless of the permanent income level, each household consumes approximately the same proportion of its permanent income. Hence, regardless of the distribution of income, aggregate consumption can be presented as $C = c(Y^p)$, with c the aggregate marginal propensity to consume.

EXAMPLE 13.2. Table 13-2 presents the fluctuation of a household's current income over a business cycle; years 1 and 5 are periods of recession, and years 2 through 4 and 6 through 8 are periods of economic expansion. Suppose this pattern is repetitive; the household's income averages \$12,000 over the business cycle, designated permanent income in the third column. Transitory income, presented in the fourth column, is the difference between the second and third columns. If the household's marginal propensity to consume permanent income is 0.90, \$10,800 (the fifth column) is consumed each year. $[C = c(Y^p); \$10,800 = 0.90(\$12,000).]$ The household's APC is constant at 0.90 in the sixth column when we relate current consumption to permanent income; however, it fluctuates over the business cycle in the last column when we relate consumption to current income.

Table 13-2

Period	$Y(\$)$	$Y^p(\$)$	$Y^t(\$)$	$C(\$)$	C/Y^p	C/Y
1	10,000	12,000	−2,000	10,800	0.90	1.08
2	11,000	12,000	−1,000	10,800	0.90	0.98
3	12,500	12,000	500	10,800	0.90	0.86
4	14,500	12,000	2,500	10,800	0.90	0.74
5	10,000	12,000	−2,000	10,000	0.90	1.08
6	11,000	12,000	−1,000	10,800	0.90	0.98
7	12,500	12,000	500	10,800	0.90	0.86
8	14,500	12,000	2,500	10,800	0.90	0.74

13.3 THE LIFE-CYCLE HYPOTHESIS

Modigliani's theory of consumption maintains that households stabilize consumption over time as they relate consumption to expected lifetime income. A household thereby saves while employed to accumulate wealth which will allow for consumption during retirement. When consumption and annual earnings are constant during employment years, a fixed percentage of annual income is saved for retirement, and an individual's *APC* is constant while employed (Example 13.3). However, when a household's annual income increases each year and plateaus prior to retirement, less is saved during the initial working years and more in later years. A new entrant into the workforce, whose income is expected to increase over time, is likely to have an *APC* greater than 1, whereas the *APC* for an individual near retirement is less than 1. This behavior is consistent with cross-section studies where many lower-income households dissave and many higher-income households save. The aggregate *APC* would be constant over time when the labor force consists of equal proportions of young, middle-aged, and older workers, which is also consistent with time-series data. The following factors could change consumption behavior: the interest return on financial assets, inherited asset endowments, age at retirement and expected number of years in retirement.

EXAMPLE 13.3. Suppose an individual enters the labor force at age 25; annual disposable income until retirement at age 65 is $30,000; and life expectancy is 75 years. If this person has no initial asset endowment, there is no interest return on financial assets, there is no private or public pension benefit program, and the individual plans to spend income uniformly during his or her lifetime, $6000 is saved annually during the years employed and $24,000 is consumed annually. [Lifetime earnings of $1.2 million (40 years times $30,000 a year) spent uniformly over 50 years equals annual consumption of $24,000.] The individual's *APC* is 0.80 while employed ($24,000/$30,000 = 0.80). At retirement, savings equal $240,000, and annual consumption is $24,000 during the 10 years of retirement. (When interest is earned on the amount saved, individuals save less while employed, and their *APC* is higher.) Fig. 13-1(a) presents an individual's consumption of $24,000 throughout her or his lifetime and annual saving of $6000 while employed. Fig. 13-1(b) shows the accumulation of financial wealth during years of employment, which peaks at $240,000 on retirement; financial wealth is consumed during retirement.

13.4 OTHER FACTORS AFFECTING CONSUMPTION

Recent writings on consumption consider the effect that bequests, liquidity constraints, interest rates, and the formation of expectations have on consumption. A large proportion of the wealth accumulated by individuals is not consumed during retirement but bequested to heirs. Research suggests that many of these bequests are involuntary because of longer but uncertain life expectancies and uncertain expenditures (especially those for medical care) during retirement. Imperfect credit markets have been a

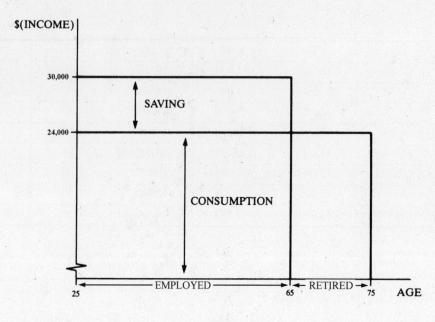

(a)

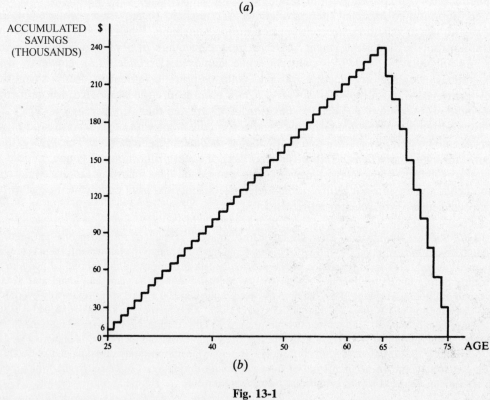

(b)

Fig. 13-1

financial constraint to individuals who, in the early years of employment, wish to borrow against future income to smooth consumption over their lifetime. Although little association has been found between the rate of interest and the saving rate, it appears that the rate of saving is positively related to the rate of inflation. The forward-looking permanent income hypothesis has been reformulated; it uses a rational expectations approach where plans are adjusted as new information about the economy becomes available.

Solved Problems

THE KEYNESIAN CONSUMPTION FUNCTION

13.1   (*a*) Explain Keynes' subjective factors which affect consumption. (*b*) What effect will the following events have on the consumption schedule? (1) An impending war is expected to result in a shortage of goods and adoption of a rationing system. (2) A substantial increase in the price of oil is expected to push up the consumer price index. (3) There is a consensus that the recession is over.

   (*a*)   Subjective factors are psychological factors which affect the willingness to buy goods. Buying attitudes are influenced by factors such as advertising, attractiveness of products, expectations about the price level, availability of goods, and income.

   (*b*)   (1) Households are likely to "hoard" goods before an actual shortage develops; increased demand shifts the consumption function leftward. (2) Households are likely to increase purchases prior to an expected increase in the price level; the consumption function shifts leftward. (3) When consumers believe that economic recovery is near, they are more willing to spend; the consumption function shifts leftward.

13.2   Explain the following objective factors identified by Keynes: (*a*) wealth, (*b*) consumer installment credit, and (*c*) income distribution.

   (*a*)   A household's ability to consume is directly related to its possession of wealth. Households add to their wealth (stock of financial and real assets) by saving. By saving annually, *ceteris paribus*, household wealth increases consumption, and the consumption function shifts leftward. Rightward shifts of the consumption function are likely to occur when wealth is destroyed by a stock market "crash."

   (*b*)   The cost and availability of consumer installment credit affects the buying capacity of individuals. When credit is more readily available and/or costs less, individuals are more likely to borrow and, in the aggregate, save less. Increased consumer borrowing, *ceteris paribus*, shifts the consumption function leftward.

   (*c*)   A change in income distribution affects aggregate consumption when all income recipients do not have the same marginal propensity to consume. An income redistribution from wealthy to lower-income households, effected through increased taxes taken from higher-income households and returned to lower-income households through welfare payments, shifts aggregate consumption leftward.

13.3   (*a*) From Fig. 13-2, prove that consumption function C' is proportional and C'' is nonproportional. (*b*) What happens to the national saving rate when income increases and the consumption function is proportional or nonproportional?

   (*a*)   A consumption function is proportional when the *APC* is constant and nonproportional when it changes with the level of income. The *MPC* is constant along a straight-line consumption function; the *APC* does not change when the *APC* equals the *MPC* at more than one point along the consumption schedule. Schedule C' intersects the vertical axis at the origin. Consumption function C' is proportional because the *APC* always equals the *MPC*. (Note that the *APC* and *MPC* are equal when the change in income is $0Yd_1$ or $0Yd_3$ along schedule C'.) Schedule C'' intersects the consumption axis at consumption level C_2; the *APC* exceeds the *MPC* at income level $0Yd_1$, whereas the *APC* equals the *MPC* at income level $0Yd_4$. Consumption function C'' is therefore nonproportional.

   (*b*)   The *APC* is constant at each level of income when the consumption function is proportional; thus, the national saving rate (average propensity to save) is also constant for all income levels. The *APC* declines as income increases when the consumption function is nonproportional; the saving rate is larger for higher income levels.

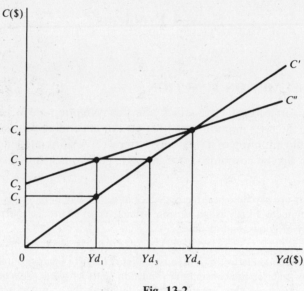

Fig. 13-2

13.4 Why was Keynes' consumption theory considered unsatisfactory?

Keynes presented consumption as principally a function of current disposable income. Subjective and objective factors which might affect consumption over time were not incorporated into the theory in a systematic manner and were considered unimportant even in the long run. This theory proved unsatisfactory because it could not explain, other than by chance, the statistical long-run proportionality of consumption and disposable income.

THE PERMANENT INCOME HYPOTHESIS

13.5 Do the data in Table 13-3 support the permanent income hypothesis?

Table 13-3

Consumption ($)	360	390	420	450	480
Current income ($)	400	440	480	520	560

There is no basis for support or contradiction. The permanent income theory maintains that consumption is related to permanent rather than current disposable income. The data are for current disposable income, which may or may not equal permanent disposable income.

13.6 Suppose the long-run APC is 0.90 but one obtains the following APCs by relating consumption to current disposable income: 0.91, 0.89, 0.88, and 0.92. Use the permanent income hypothesis to establish whether current disposable income has a positive or negative transitory component.

The permanent income theory contends that current income consists of permanent and transitory components, i.e., $Y = Y^p + Y^t$. When the long run APC is 0.90, $C = 0.90(Y^p)$. Thus, Y^t is 0 when $C/Y = 0.90$. $C/(Y^p + Y^t) > 0.90$ occurs when Y^t is negative, and $C/(Y^p + Y^t) < 0.90$ when Y^t is positive.

Current income includes a negative transitory component when C/Y is 0.91 or 0.92 and a positive transitory component when C/Y is 0.89 or 0.88.

13.7   Table 13-4 presents current disposable income for Household A. (*a*) Present in the third column of Table 13-4 permanent income for years 4 through 10 when Y^p is an unweighted average of income for the current and past three years. (*b*) Present in the fourth column consumption for years 4 through 10 when $C = 0.90 Y^p$. (*c*) Present transitory income for years 4 through 10 in the last column of Table 13-4.

Table 13-4

Year	$Y(\$)$	$Y^p(\$)$	$C(\$)$	$Y^t(\$)$
1	10,000			
2	11,000			
3	12,000			
4	10,000	10,750	9,675	−750
5	13,000	11,500	10,350	+1150
6	14,000	12,250	11,025	+1750
7	15,000	13,000	11,700	+2000
8	11,000	13,250	11,925	−2250
9	16,000	14,000	12,600	+2000
10	17,000	14,750	13,275	+2250

13.8   Plot the following data from Table 13-4: consumption and current income; consumption and permanent income. Comment on the data plotted.

The plotting of consumption and permanent income is noted by *xs* in Fig. 13-3, and consumption and current income are noted by dots. Consumption and permanent income have a linear, proportional relationship. The relationship of consumption and current income is nonproportional and gives the appearance of actual points on a leftward-shifting consumption function.

13.9   (*a*) According to the permanent income hypothesis, what is the likely behavior of transitory income and the rate of saving over the business cycle? (*b*) In the permanent income and life-cycle hypotheses, consumption consists of nondurable goods and services. Purchases of durable goods, which have a life greater than three years, are included in the definition of saving. What would you expect to happen to the rate of saving when durable good purchases are included in the definition of consumption, and households use transitory income to purchase durable goods?

(*a*)   Transitory income should be positive during an economic expansion and negative during an economic contraction. When the saving rate is calculated by comparing saving to permanent income, the rate of saving (*APS*) should be constant over the business cycle. However, when saving is related to current income, the rate of saving should increase during an expansion and decrease during a contraction.

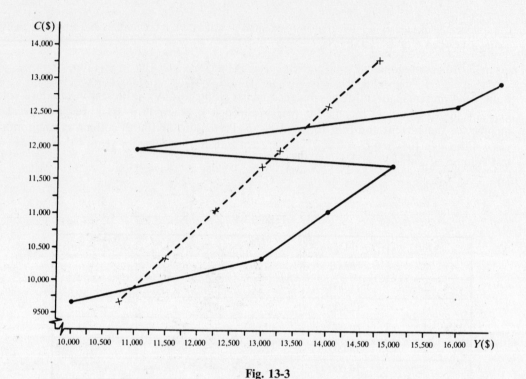

Fig. 13-3

(b) The saving rate should decrease during an expansion and increase during a contraction when durable good purchases are included in the definition of consumption and saving is compared to permanent and/or current income.

THE LIFE-CYCLE HYPOTHESIS

13.10 Suppose assets provide no interest return and that no public or private pension system exists. Suppose an individual enters the labor force at age 20, has a $20,000 annual income until retirement at age 65, has a life expectancy of 75 years, and has no initial endowment of assets at age 20. (*a*) Find annual consumption when this person spends income uniformly over his or her lifetime. (*b*) Find the *APC* during the individual's working years and the endowment at retirement. (*c*) What happens to the *APC* during the person's employment years when the retirement age is raised to 70, *ceteris paribus*? (*d*) Find the *APC* when the retirement age is 65 and life expectancy is 80.

(*a*) Lifetime earnings equal $900,000 [$20,000 (45 working years)]. Annual consumption is $16,363.64 when lifetime earnings of $900,000 are spent uniformly over the expected lifetime of 55 years.

(*b*) The average propensity to consume is 0.818, or $16,363.64/$20,000 during the employment years. The endowment at retirement is $163,636.20 (annual saving of $3636.36 times 45 working years).

(*c*) By raising the retirement age to 70, the person can work 50 rather than 45 years. Lifetime earnings now equal $1 million. When consumed over 55 years, annual consumption is $18,181.82. The average propensity to consume is 0.909 during the employment years.

(*d*) When the retirement age is 65 but life expectancy increases to 80, lifetime earnings of $900,000 are spent uniformly over 60 rather than 55 years. Annual consumption is then $15,000, and the *APC* during the employment years is 0.75.

13.11 Suppose assets provide no interest return, and no public or private pension system exists. Suppose an individual has an inherited endowment of $200,000 when entering the labor force at age 20, has a $20,000 annual income until retirement at age 65, and has a life expectancy of 75 years. (*a*) Find this person's annual consumption when lifetime earnings plus inherited endowment is spent during his or her lifetime. (*b*) Find the *APC* during the employment years. (*c*) Compare the consumption and saving rates in part (*a*) and (*b*) of Problems 13.10 and 13.11. Why do they differ?

   (*a*)   Lifetime earnings equal $900,000. When lifetime earnings are added to the inherited endowment, the individual has $1,100,000 to spend over a lifetime. Annual consumption is $20,000, or $1.1 million lifetime earnings/55 years.

   (*b*)   The *APC* during his or her working years is 1.0.

   (*c*)   The individual in Problem 13.10 part (*b*) has no initial endowment and therefore must save for the 10 years of retirement; $3,636.36 must be saved annually to provide for the planned level of consumption during retirement. The individual in Problem 13.11(*a*) and (*b*) has a $200,000 inherited endowment which is sufficient for the retirement years; the individual therefore can consume his or her entire income each year during the employment years. Without an inherited endowment, the individual in Problem 13.10 has a higher saving rate throughout the employment years than does the person in Problem 13.11.

13.12 Suppose assets provide no interest return, there is no interest cost in borrowing, and no public or private pension system exists. Suppose an individual enters the labor force at age 25, has a life expectancy of 75 years, spends income evenly over his lifetime and has no initial endowment of assets. (*a*) Find this individual's yearly consumption when $25,000 is earned each year during the first 10 years of employment, $35,000 is earned annually during the second 10 years, $45,000 during the third 10 years and $50,000 during the last 10 years. (*b*) Find this person's *APC* during the employment years and the endowment at retirement.

   (*a*)   Lifetime income is $1,550,000. Consumption is $31,000 a year when this individual spends his entire income uniformly over his lifetime.

   (*b*)   During the first 10 years of work, the individual's *APC* is 1.24 ($60,000 is owed by the end of the tenth year of employment). The *APC* during the second 10 years of employment is 0.886 ($20,000 is owed after 20 years of employment). For the third 10 years, the *APC* is 0.689 (accumulated savings is now $120,000). The *APC* for the last 10 years of work is 0.62; the endowment at retirement is $310,000.

13.13 Suppose an individual enters the labor force at age 25, has a $25,000 annual income until retirement at age 65, has a life expectancy of 75 years and has no initial endowment of assets at age 25; no public or private pension system exists. (*a*) Find this person's annual consumption when earnings are spent uniformly during a lifetime and there is no interest return on assets. Also find the *APC* during the employment years and the endowment at retirement. (*b*) The sum of $1 paid annually into an annuity for n years is $[(1 + r)^n - 1]/r$, where r is the annual rate of interest. What is this person's endowment at retirement when $5000 is saved annually and the rate of interest is 2% or 5%? What most likely happens to the *APC* and therefore the amount saved annually when there is an interest return on savings?

   (*a*)   Lifetime income is $1 million, or $25,000 times 40 working years. Annual consumption is $20,000, and annual saving is $5000 when this income is spent uniformly over this person's life. During the employment years, the *APC* is 0.80; the endowment at retirement is $200,000.

   (*b*)   When the rate of interest is 2%, the sum of $1 paid annually into an annuity for 40 years is $60.402; thus, the sum of $5000 paid annually into an annuity is $302,010.00. When the rate of interest is 5%, the sum of $1 paid annually into an annuity for 40 years is $120.79; the sum of $5000 paid annually into an annuity is then $603,950. The *APC* during the employment years is likely to be higher when interest is earned on savings. The *APC* is also likely to increase with the interest return on assets.

13.14 Holding other factors constant, explain the effect that the following variables might have on saving during the employment years: retirement age, life expectancy, age at entry into labor force, inherited asset endowment, and interest earned on financial assets. Assume that consumption is based on lifetime income and is uniform throughout one's lifetime.

An individual's saving rate increases during employment years the earlier the age of planned retirement, the longer the person's life expectancy and/or the later the person's entry into the labor force, *ceteris paribus*. When consumption is uniform over one's lifetime, there are fewer working years during which one can accumulate an endowment for retirement when one retires early and/or is a late entrant into the labor force. A person's saving rate during the employment years must also be greater when there is a longer life expectancy because of the need to accumulate a larger endowment during the employment years to support the individual during retirement. Inheriting an endowment reduces an individual's need to accumulate a personal endowment; hence, the larger the endowment inherited, the lower the saving rate during the employed years. The saving rate during the employment years is negatively related to the rate of interest, since wealth accumulation for retirement is greater the higher the interest earned on savings.

OTHER FACTORS AFFECTING CONSUMPTION

13.15 Why might an individual bequest accumulated wealth to heirs and not consume it in its entirety during retirement?

Bequests may be voluntary and/or involuntary. A voluntary bequest occurs when it is planned, whereas a bequest is involuntary when the individual dies before spending the endowment allocated to the retirement years. Parental concern for the economic welfare of children and/or grandchildren may induce parents to set aside a portion of their endowment for heirs upon death. In doing so, heirs can have a higher standard of living during their lifetime, since consumption over their lifetime is not solely dependent on income from their own employment. Consumption during retirement and age at death are uncertain. Spending during retirement depends upon an individual's need for health care. Because these needs and costs are unknown, individuals must set aside a portion of their retirement endowment for this purpose. Obviously, if the retiree has continuous good health, the allocated sum is not spent and is therefore left to heirs. Similarly, age at death is unknown. Hence, the endowment must be adequate to support an unexpected long life; bequests occur when life is equal to or shorter than one's expectancy.

13.16 How can liquidity constraints restrict consumption?

Individuals who expect income to increase throughout their working years borrow during the initial working years to smooth out consumption over their lifetime. The ability to borrow, however, depends not on the individual's but on the bank's perception of future earnings. When the bank's expectation is below that of the individual, consumption during early employment years is constrained, and consumption is at a lower level than what the individual has planned. When this occurs, consumption is more closely tied to current disposable income than expected income over.

Multiple Choice Questions

1. There is a proportional relationship between consumption and disposable income
   (a) When the *APC* is the same for all levels of disposable income.
   (b) When the consumption function is a straight line through the origin.
   (c) When the *MPC* equals the *APC* for all levels of disposable income.
   (d) All the above.

2.   Changes in subjective or objective factors

    (*a*)   Never affect the consumption function.

    (*b*)   Always cause downward shifts of the consumption function.

    (*c*)   Always cause upward shifts of the consumption function.

    (*d*)   May cause upward or downward shifts of the consumption function.

3.   Keynes considered subjective and objective factors

    (*a*)   Important determinants of consumption.

    (*b*)   Unimportant determinants of consumption.

    (*c*)   Determinants of investment.

    (*d*)   Determinants of business' willingness to supply.

4.   According to the permanent income hypothesis, all increases in

    (*a*)   Permanent income are saved.

    (*b*)   Permanent income are consumed.

    (*c*)   Transitory income are saved.

    (*d*)   Transitory income are consumed.

5.   When current income includes a negative transitory component, relating consumption with current income will produce

    (*a*)   An average propensity to consume that is lower than the long-run average propensity to consume.

    (*b*)   An average propensity to consume that is higher than the long-run average propensity to consume.

    (*c*)   An average propensity to consume that equals the long-run average propensity to consume.

    (*d*)   None of the above.

6.   The permanent income hypothesis is consistent with cross-section and time-series data because

    (*a*)   Higher-income households are savers, since their current income includes positive transitory components.

    (*b*)   Higher-income households are savers, since their current income includes negative transitory components.

    (*c*)   Lower-income households are savers, since their current income includes negative transitory components.

    (*d*)   Lower-income households are dissavers, since their current income includes positive transitory components.

7.   According to the life-cycle hypothesis, consumption is related to

    (*a*)   Current income.

    (*b*)   Past peak income.

    (*c*)   Expected lifetime income.

    (*d*)   Price expectations over one's lifetime.

8.   Suppose a 25-year-old individual expects to earn $25,000 annually until retirement at age 70. When income is spent uniformly during the individual's lifetime and life expectancy is 80, the

    (*a*)   Individual consumes $22,000 a year during the employment years.

    (*b*)   Individual's endowment at retirement is $204,545.

    (*c*)   Individual saves $4000 a year during the employment years.

    (*d*)   Individual's lifetime income is $1.3 million.

9.   Suppose an individual intends to spend income uniformly during her or his lifetime. During the employment years, the *APC*

(*a*)   Is constant when annual income is unchanged.

(*b*)   Decreases with age when annual income increases during the individual's employment years.

(*c*)   Increases with age when annual income decreases during the individual's employment years.

(*d*)   All the above.

10   Which of the following best describes the reasons for involuntary bequests?

(*a*)   Interest rates had increased in recent years.

(*b*)   There was considerable uncertainty associated with expenditures during retirement.

(*c*)   There were substantial gains in the stock market.

(*d*)   Individuals wanted to leave an inheritance to their children.

True or False Questions

11.   _____ Keynes identified psychological factors which influence consumer willingness to buy goods and services as subjective factors.

12.   _____ According to Keynes, a sudden drop in consumer confidence shifts the consumption function rightward.

13.   _____ There is a nonproportional relationship between consumption and income when the consumption function intersects the vertical axis above the origin.

14.   _____ According to the permanent income hypothesis, consumption is a fixed percentage of current income.

15.   _____ According to the permanent income hypothesis, transitory income is saved.

16.   _____ Mandatory retirement laws lower a household's *APC* during the years that the household is employed according to the life-cycle hypothesis.

17.   _____ The life-cycle hypothesis suggests that high-income households have a high *APC*.

18.   _____ According to the life-cycle hypothesis, a desire to bequest wealth to heirs lowers a household's *APC* during the years the household is employed.

19.   _____ According to the life-cycle hypothesis, a household's *APC* during its working years is inversely related to the real rate of interest, that is, the higher the real rate of interest the lower the household's *APC*.

20.   _____ Involuntary bequests are the result of uncertainty.

Answers to Multiple Choice and True or False Questions

1. (*d*); **2.** (*d*); **3.** (*b*); **4.** (*c*); **5.** (*b*); **6.** (*a*); **7.** (*c*); **8.** (*b*); **9.** (*d*); **10.** (*b*); **11.** T; **12.** T; **13.** T; **14.** F; **15.** T; **16.** T; **17.** F; **18.** T; **19.** F; **20.** T.

Chapter 14

Theories of Investment

Chapter Summary

1. In the rigid version of the accelerator theory of investment, capital is a fixed multiple of output. An economy adds to its capital stock, and there is net investment, when output increases. Because the capital–output ratio is greater than one, net investment is subject to greater fluctuation than output.

2. The economy's desired stock of capital depends upon expected output, the user cost of capital and labor's real wage. When output and the real wage are unchanged, the desired stock of capital is inversely related to the user cost of capital.

3. In the flexible accelerator theory of investment, the capital–output ratio increases when the user cost of capital decreases and decreases when the user cost of capital increases. The effect upon net investment of an increase in expected output is thereby magnified when the user cost of capital decreases and is reduced when the user cost of capital increases. Net investment due to an increase in the economy's stock of capital is also influenced by the production capability of the capital producing industry, uncertainty of projections, and the availability of financial capital.

4. Tobin's q-theory of investment explains net investment by the ratio of the market value of corporate financial assets to the replacement cost of corporate real assets, i.e., by the q-ratio. Firms increase their capital stock, and there is net investment, when the q-ratio is greater than one.

5. The amount of inventory held by a firm is related to its level of sales. A rigid inventory-sales ratio theory of inventory investment is incomplete in that it does not include the influence of uncertainty, the rate of interest and the availability of materials.

Chapter Outline

14.1 THE ACCELERATOR THEORY OF INVESTMENT

The accelerator theory of investment explains net investment in terms of increases in expected output. In the *rigid version* of the accelerator theory, firms maintain a stable relationship between the stock of capital and output. This relationship is presented as $K = vY^e$, where K is the stock of capital, v is the capital–output ratio (the ratio of the desired stock of capital to expected output), and Y^e is expected output. Additions to the economy's capital stock, i.e. net investment In, take place when output is expected to increase. Hence, $In = v\Delta Y$. Because v is greater than one, net investment fluctuates when growth of expected output is uneven over time (Example 14.1). Firms must also replace worn-out equipment, since a portion of an economy's capital stock depreciates in the course of producing current output. Thus, gross investment may change because of the need to replace some of the existing capital stock and/or the need to add to the economy's stock of capital (Example 14.2).

EXAMPLE 14.1. When $v = 2$, net investment is twice the change in expected output $(In = 2\Delta Y)$. Suppose the capital stock and actual output are $1200 and $600 in period 0 and expected output in successive periods is $610, $625, $635, $640, and $640. Table 14-1 presents the net investment (capital additions) which is necessary in successive periods to keep the capital output ratio at 2. Net investment is $20 during period 1 because output is expected to increase $10 during that period; net investment is $30 during period 2 when output is expected to increase $15; net investment is $20, $10, and 0 in periods 3, 4, and 5.

Table 14-1

Period	Expected Output	Net Investment
0	$600	$0
1	610	20
2	625	30
3	635	20
4	640	10
5	640	0

EXAMPLE 14.2. Suppose the capital–output ratio is 2. The $2000 capital stock, accumulated uniformly over 10 periods, has a uniform, useful life of 10 periods. Beginning in period 11, firms must replace worn-out capital; thus, replacement investment is $200 per period for periods 11 to 20 (Table 14-2). Gross investment consists of net investment and replacement investment. Gross investment increases from $200 during period 11 to a peak of $400 during period 14 due to uneven increases in expected output between period 11 and 16. The variability of gross investment is greater when the initial capital stock does not wear out evenly during the ten periods.

Table 14-2

Period	Expected Output	ΔY	Net Investment	Replacement Investment	Gross Investment
11	$1000	$0	$0	$200	$200
12	1050	50	100	200	300
13	1125	75	150	200	350
14	1215	100	200	200	400
15	1300	85	170	200	370
16	1325	25	50	200	250
17	1325	0	0	200	200

14.2 THE DESIRED STOCK OF CAPITAL

The business sector's desired stock of capital K^* depends on expected output Y^e, the user cost of capital u, and the real wage paid labor w, i.e., $K^* = f(Y^e, u, w)$. In determining the business sector's desired stock of capital, it is customary to keep labor compensation constant. When real output changes, the desired stock of capital is a function of the user cost of capital and the marginal productivity of capital. (See Problem 14.10.) When output is unchanged, the desired stock of capital depends on the user cost of capital and the cost saving associated with employing fewer workers and more capital to produce a specific level of output. Thus, the demand for capital can be presented as a schedule of the marginal productivity of capital or as a schedule of the marginal cost benefit from capital. The marginal cost benefit schedule is used in this section. (See Problems 14.9 and 14.10 for marginal productivity of capital analysis.)

The user cost of capital (stated as a percentage) is the real cost of using capital for a specified period of time. The user cost of capital consists of the real rate of interest (the real financial cost associated with acquiring real capital) and the rate of depreciation (real capital used in producing output). User cost can be specified as $u = r + d$ or as $u = i - \pi^e + d$, where r is the real rate of interest, d is the rate of depreciation of the capital stock, i is the nominal rate of interest and π^e is the expected rate of inflation. The user cost of capital is lowered by increasing the real money supply and/or by a fiscal action such as an investment tax credit or an acceleration of the rate at which a machine is depreciated for tax purposes. (See Problem 14.7.)

EXAMPLE 14.3. Suppose a machine's purchase price is $100,000, the firm's cost of securing funds to purchase the machine is 8% or $800 a year, and the machine depreciates (wears out evenly) over 10 years at an annual rate of 10%. The machine's user cost per annum (cost of using the machine for one year) is thereby 18%, or $u = r + d$ and $18\% = 8\% + 10\%$. The user cost of capital is below 18% when the monetary authority lowers the real rate of interest by increasing the nominal money supply. Fiscal actions also affect the user cost of capital. Because depreciation is a precorporate income tax expense, depreciation of a machine at an accelerated rate for tax purposes reduces the cost of using the machine over its lifetime. An investment tax credit, which reduces the net purchase price of a machine, also lowers user cost.

An increase in the capital stock, *ceteris paribus*, decreases the need for labor. For example, an increase in the capital stock from K_0 to K_1 in Fig. 14-1 decreases the need for labor from L_0 to L_1 when output is $500. A reduction in workers employed results in a cost saving, which is measured as a dollar cost benefit or as a

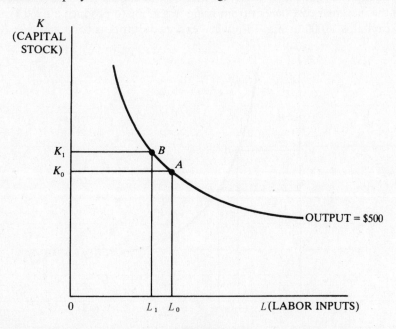

Fig. 14-1

marginal cost benefit when the dollar cost saving is related to the dollar cost of the capital addition (Example 14.4). A marginal cost benefit schedule is presented and labeled *MBK* in Fig. 14-2. Because capital and labor are imperfect substitutes, capital additions result in declining cost benefits. Hence, in Fig. 14-2, the marginal cost benefit schedule *MBK* is downward sloping. The marginal cost benefit schedule in Fig. 14-2 shifts rightward from *MBK* to *MBK′* when there is a higher level of output.

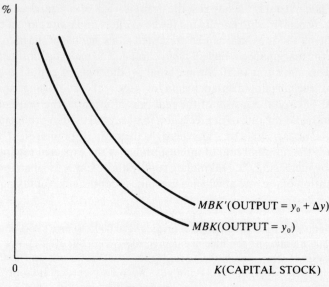

Fig. 14-2

EXAMPLE 14.4. Suppose a decrease in the employment of labor and an expansion of the capital stock from $500,000 to $600,000 reduces the annual cost of labor from $750,000 to $730,000. There is a 20% marginal cost benefit in expanding capital from $500,000 to $600,000 when the capital addition has a 10-year useful life ($20,000 labor saving/$100,000 capital expansion = 20%).

The desired stock of capital exists where the user cost of capital (the cost associated with a capital addition) equals the marginal cost benefit from using less labor to produce a fixed level of output. The desired stock of capital is $1000 in Fig. 14-3 when expected output is $500 and user cost is u_0. At user

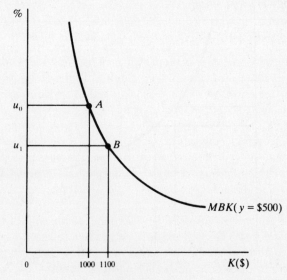

Fig. 14-3

cost u_1, *ceteris paribus*, the desired stock of capital is \$1100. The decrease in the user cost of capital from u_0 to u_1, *ceteris paribus*, makes the production process more capital-intensive and increases v, the capital–output ratio.

EXAMPLE 14.5. The desired stock of capital is \$2000 in Fig. 14-4(*a*) when user cost is u_0 and expected output is \$2000. When user cost is lowered to u_1, *ceteris paribus*, the desired stock of capital increases to \$2100. The u_0 to u_1 decrease in user cost increases the capital–output ratio from 2.0 to 2.1. In Fig. 14-4(*b*), the desired stock of capital is initially \$2000 for schedule MBK when user cost is u_0 and expected output is \$1000. A \$50 increase in expected output shifts the marginal cost benefit schedule from MBK to MBK'. When user cost is constant at u_0, the desired stock of capital increases to \$2100; the capital–output ratio remains at 2.0.

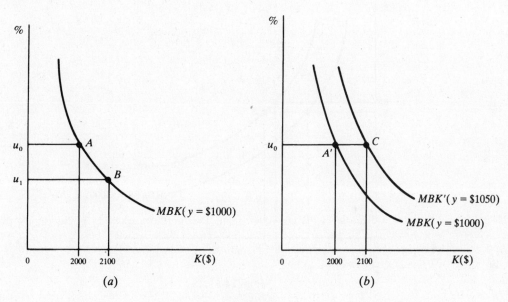

Fig. 14-4

14.3 THE FLEXIBLE ACCELERATOR

The flexible accelerator theory of investment amends the rigid accelerator model: the desired stock of capital is affected by the user cost of capital; and additions to the desired stock of capital may occur over time. First, we consider the effect of a change in expected output and user cost on the desired stock of capital. An increase in expected output increases net investment by $In = v\Delta Y$ when there is no change in the user cost of capital. The production process becomes less capital-intensive, however, when an increase in expected output is accompanied by a higher user cost and there is no change in the cost of labor. The lower capital–output ratio reduces the effect that an expected increase in output has on the desired stock of capital (Example 14.6). Production constraints and/or firms' willingness and ability to add to their stock of capital may be distributed over a number of periods. Thus, net investment in any period may be only a fraction of the change in the desired capital stock. A distributed lag for net investment is presented by the equation $In = \lambda(K^* - K_{-1})$, where λ is the fraction of the change in the desired stock of capital which takes place each period (see Example 14.7). The value of λ depends on factors such as the production capability of the capital goods industries, confidence in the projection of higher output and ability to obtain the financial resources necessary for acquiring capital. (See Problem 14.13.)

EXAMPLE 14.6. Suppose the marginal cost benefit schedule MBK in Fig. 14-5 is associated with a $1000 level of real output; user cost is initially u_0 and the desired stock of capital is $2000. A $100 increase in expected output shifts the marginal cost benefit schedule rightward to MBK'. When user cost remains at u_0, the desired stock of capital increases from $2000 to $2200. [Note that v, the capital–output ratio, remains constant, and net investment is explained by the rigid accelerator model: $In = v\Delta Y : \$200 = 2(\$100)$.] However, when the user cost of capital increases, as output expands from $1000 to $1100, *ceteris paribus*, the desired stock of capital increases from $2000 to $2150. Net investment is $150 instead of $200; there is a decline in the capital–output ratio from 2.00 to 1.95, and the production process becomes less capital-intensive. [Note that this analysis assumes no change in the real wage. The production process would be more capital-intensive (v would increase) if an increase in the real wage is greater than the relative increase in user cost.]

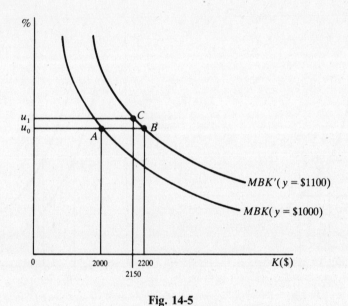

Fig. 14-5

EXAMPLE 14.7. The desired capital stock expands in Example 14.6 from $2000 to $2150 when expected output increases $100 and user cost rises to u_1. Suppose net investment in any period is 50% ($\lambda = 0.50$) of the difference between the actual and desired capital stock, i.e., $In = \lambda(K^* - K_{-1})$. Net investment in the initial period is $75, or $0.50(\$2150 - \$2000)$. When λ is unchanged at 0.50, net investment is $75, $37.50, $18.75, and $9.375 in successive periods, and the desired stock of capital is reached over time. Net investment during successive periods is presented in Fig. 14-6(a); the eventual $150 expansion of the stock of capital is presented in Fig. 14-6(b).

14.4 TOBIN'S q-THEORY

James Tobin advanced a dynamic theory of business investment by relating net investment to a q ratio—the ratio of the market value of corporate financial assets to the replacement cost of corporate real assets. He reasoned that firms add to their capital stock when $q > 1$, since firms enhance profits when the acquisition cost of real assets is less than the financial cost of acquiring them, i.e., the user cost of capital is less than the cost benefit from capital additions (see Example 14.8).

EXAMPLE 14.8. Suppose a firm finances all assets by the issuance of common stock. Currently there are 1000 shares of common stock outstanding, and the market value is $40.00 per share. The firm's market value is therefore $40,000. If the replacement cost of the firm's real assets is $40,000, the q ratio is 1.00, and there is no benefit in adding to the firm's stock of capital. However, suppose a decrease in the real rate of interest causes the market value

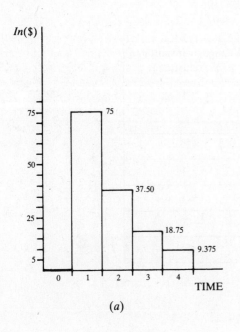

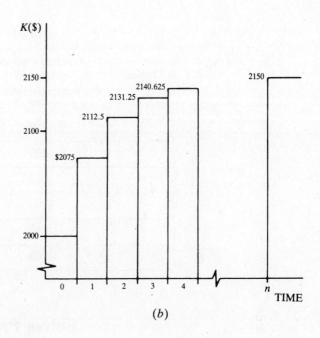

Fig. 14-6

per share to increase to $50, *ceteris paribus*. The q ratio is now 1.25, since the user cost of capital is below the cost benefit from capital additions. The firm could purchase additional capital at a price of $10,000, financing the acquisition by issuing 200 additional shares of stock at $50 a share. This is beneficial to current stock holders since a 25% (that is, $40,000 to $50,000) increase in real assets is financed by only a 20% increase ($50,000 to $60,000) in equity.

14.5 INVENTORY INVESTMENT

The practicalities of production and distribution require that firms carry an inventory of raw materials, goods in the process of production, and finished goods. Variables that affect inventory levels include expected sales, the cost of holding inventory, possible delivery delays of raw materials, and uncertainty about the economy. Inventory investment can be presented as a stable function of expected sales when variables other than expected sales are unchanged. In doing so, the rigid accelerator theory is used to model the change in inventory investment over time, e.g., $\Delta Inv = n\Delta R$, where ΔInv is the change in inventory investment, n is the inventory–sales ratio, and ΔR is the change in expected sales (Example 14.9). The model has limitations, as does the rigid accelerator theory, because variables are assumed constant which could change n, the inventory–sales ratio. For example, n would most likely decrease when there is increased uncertainty about future sales, there are increased costs in holding inventory, and/or there is greater availability and therefore more rapid delivery of raw materials. (See Problem 14.19.)

EXAMPLE 14.9. Suppose the desired inventory–sales ratio is 0.25, and the expected change in sales in successive periods is presented in the second column of Table 14-3. The change in inventory investment is presented in the right column. The change in inventory investment is larger or smaller to the extent that the inventory–sales ratio of 0.25 changes over time.

Table 14-3

Period	Expected Change in Sales ($)	Change in Inventory Investment ($)
1	+200	+50
2	+300	+75
3	+100	+25
4	0	0
5	−100	−25
6	−200	−50
7	+300	+75

Solved Problems

THE ACCELERATOR THEORY OF INVESTMENT

14.1 (*a*) What is a capital–output ratio? (*b*) Is the capital–output ratio constant over time?

(*a*) A capital–output ratio is the amount of capital resources needed to produce output; it is found by dividing the economy's stock of capital by its level of output.

(*b*) The economy's capital–output ratio may change over time for any of the following reasons: a change in the cost of producing real capital, a change in the cost of financial capital, a change in the cost of human and natural resources, a change in the taxation of financial and real capital and a change in technology.

14.2 (*a*) Find net investment for periods 1 through 5 when the capital–output ratio is 3; output is initially $100, and increases in successive periods are as follows: period 1, $120; period 2, $140; period 3, $155; period 4, $165; and period 5, $170. (*b*) What happens to net investment when incremental output is smaller each period?

(*a*) $In = v\Delta Y$; thus, net investment is $60 in period 1 $[In = 3(\$20)]$. Net investment in successive periods is presented in the right column of Table 14-4.

(*b*) Net investment decreases when incremental output is smaller in successive periods.

Table 14-4

Period	Change in Output ($)	Net Investment ($)
1	+20	+60
2	+20	+60
3	+15	+45
4	+10	+30
5	+ 5	+15

14.3   What objections are there to the rigid version of the accelerator theory of investment?

A number of objections may be made with respect to the rigid version of the accelerator theory of investment: (1) The capital stock is unlikely to respond immediately to a change in expected output. Willingness to add capital depends on the confidence business has that output will increase. Firms are unlikely to add plant capacity when there is a high probability that increased output will be temporary and/or not materialize. In addition, there may be lags in capital additions because capital takes time to build and/or order backlogs exist in capital-producing industries. (2) Technology may alter the amount of capital needed and therefore the capital–output ratio. Technological change, which makes capital more productive, results in the substitution of capital for labor and increases the capital–output ratio. (3) The cost of capital and/or other economic resources may change. For example, an investment tax credit lowers the cost of capital, whereas an increase in the cost of labor encourages the substitution of capital for labor. Either of these events makes the production process more capital-intensive and increases the capital–output ratio.

THE DESIRED STOCK OF CAPITAL

14.4   (*a*) What is meant by the desired stock of capital? (*b*) How is the desired stock of capital influenced by expected output, the user cost of capital and labor compensation?

(*a*)   The desired stock of capital is the optimum quantity of capital demanded by businesses to produce a specific level of output.

(*b*)   Holding user cost of capital and labor's real compensation constant, the desired stock of capital is positively related to expected output. Recall that the desired stock of capital is a fixed multiple of expected output, *ceteris paribus*, in the rigid version of the accelerator theory of investment. Holding real output and labor's compensation constant, the desired stock of capital is inversely related to the user cost of capital. Profit-maximizing firms substitute capital for labor when the user cost of capital decreases, *ceteris paribus*, i.e., firms substitute less costly capital for labor whose cost has not changed. The desired stock of capital is positively related to labor's real compensation. With no change in user cost and output, an increase in the real wage raises the relative cost of labor. Hence, capital is substituted for labor, and the business sector's desired stock of capital increases.

14.5   (*a*) What is meant by the term user cost of capital? (*b*) Can capital maintenance affect the user cost of capital? (*c*) How does monetary policy affect the user cost of capital?

(*a*)   The user cost of capital is the cost of using (renting) real capital over time. It consists of the depreciation cost of real capital plus the financial cost of raising the necessary financial capital (debt plus equity funds) to purchase real capital.

(*b*)   Properly maintained capital has a longer, more productive life than capital with no preventive maintenance. Depreciation cost is lower when capital is maintained; poor capital maintenance raises the user cost of capital.

(*c*)   When inflationary expectations are unrelated to a change in the nominal money supply, an increase in the nominal money supply reduces the real rate of interest, the firm's cost of financial capital and its user cost of capital.

14.6   Suppose a machine's rate of depreciation is 10% and the cost of financial capital is 13%. (*a*) Find the user cost of capital. (*b*) Is the user cost of capital the same for each firm?

(*a*)   The user cost of capital is the sum of depreciation and the cost of financial capital; the user cost of capital is 23%.

(*b*)   The user cost of capital may differ because real assets do not depreciate at the same rate, and perceived riskiness of the firm's operations affects its cost of financial capital. For example, suppose a longer-lived machine has a depreciation rate of 8% rather than 10%, and the cost of issuing financial capital is 10% rather than 13%. The user cost of capital is then 18% rather than 23%.

14.7   Explain how a fiscal stimulus, such as an investment tax credit or acceleration of the rate of depreciation for tax purposes, affects the user cost of capital.

An investment tax credit or an accelerated rate of depreciation for tax purposes lowers the user cost of capital. An investment tax credit permits business to reduce its tax liability by $X\%$ of the purchase price of new equipment in the year purchased. For example, a 5% investment tax credit allows a firm to reduce its tax liability $5000 when it purchases new equipment that costs $100,000. Through an investment tax credit, the government subsidizes (reduces the price of) new equipment, which lowers the user cost of the machine over its lifetime. Allowing business to accelerate the rate at which it can depreciate equipment also reduces the firm's tax liability and subsidizes newly purchased equipment. Although equipment may have an annual 10% rate of depreciation over a 10-year period, government might allow business to depreciate newly purchased equipment in 5 years. In doing so, the firm's taxable income is reduced during the first 5 years, and the firm has larger cash flows from the investment during earlier years.

14.8   Production functions Y_1, Y_2, and Y_3 in Fig. 14-7 present the combinations of capital and labor used to produce three levels of output. Output Y_3 is greater than Y_2, which is greater than Y_1. For user cost u_1 and real wage w_1, L_1 labor and K_1 capital are employed to produce output Y_1. (a) Holding real wage w_1 and real output Y_1 constant, what happens to the employment of labor and capital when the user cost of capital falls from u_1 to u_2, *ceteris paribus*? (b) Holding real wage w_1 and labor L_1 constant, what happens to capital and output when the user cost of capital falls from u_1 to u_2, *ceteris paribus*?

(a)   The u_1 to u_2 decrease in the user cost of capital alters the least-cost combination of labor and capital for producing output Y_1. Capital is substituted for labor, with output Y_1 now produced by employing L_2 labor and K_2 capital in Fig. 14-7. The production process becomes more capital-intensive.

(b)   When the employment of labor is unchanged and the user cost of capital decreases, output increases to Y_2 in Fig. 14-7, and K_3 capital is employed.

14.9   (a) What is a marginal productivity of capital schedule? (b) What is a marginal cost benefit from capital schedule? (c) Explain the difference between a marginal productivity of capital schedule and a marginal cost benefit from capital schedule.

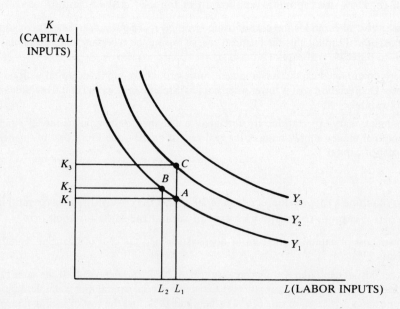

Fig. 14-7

(a) The marginal productivity of capital is the incremental output associated with an additional unit of capital, holding constant the amount of other factors. Due to the law of diminishing returns, each additional capital input is associated with decreased incremental output. Thus, the marginal productivity of capital declines as capital is increased. The marginal productivity of capital is measured as a rate of return by relating the dollar value of incremental output to the cost of a capital addition. A marginal productivity of capital schedule (MPK) is presented in Fig. 14-8.

(b) The marginal cost benefit from capital is the cost saving associated with using less labor, holding output constant. Because capital and labor are imperfect substitutes, capital additions result in declining cost benefits. The marginal cost benefit from capital is measured as a relative cost benefit by relating the cost saving from hiring less labor to the cost of the capital addition. A marginal cost benefit from capital schedule (MBK) is presented in Fig. 14-9.

(c) The MPK and MBK schedules in Figs. 14-8 and 14-9 represent demand for capital schedules. The MBK schedule holds real output constant, and allows the employment of labor to change; the MPK schedule holds labor employment constant, and allows real output to change.

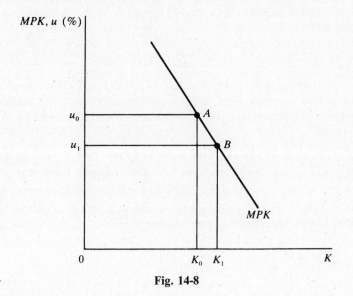

Fig. 14-8

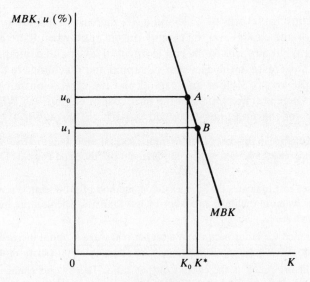

Fig. 14-9

14.10 The desired stock of capital is K_0 along schedule MPK in Fig. 14-8 when the user cost of capital is u_0. (*a*) Suppose the nominal money supply increases, there is no change in inflationary expectations and the user cost of capital decreases to u_1. Explain what happens to the desired stock of capital. (*b*) What is net investment as a result of the decrease in the user cost of capital? (*c*) What fiscal measures would also lower user cost? (*d*) What has happened to the capital–output ratio?

(*a*)   At user cost u_0, the desired stock of capital is K_0 where the marginal productivity of capital equals the user cost of capital. When user cost falls to u_1 in Fig. 14-8, the marginal productivity of capital is greater than user cost u_1 for capital stock K_0. Capital is added until the return from capital equals its cost, i.e., until the desired stock of capital increases from K_0 to K_1.

(*b*)   Net investment equals the change in the desired stock of capital; thus, net investment is the difference between K_1 and K_0.

(*c*)   The user cost of capital could be lowered by fiscal measures such as an investment tax credit, an acceleration of depreciation rates and/or a reduction in the corporate income tax rate.

(*d*)   The capital–output ratio has increased. In moving down a marginal productivity of capital schedule, the percentage change in capital exceeds that of output. Hence, the capital–output ratio rises as the user cost of capital falls.

14.11 The desired stock of capital is K_0 along schedule MBK in Fig. 14-9 for user cost u_0. (*a*) Suppose economic policy lowers user cost from u_0 to u_1. What happens to the desired stock of capital? Why? (*b*) What is net investment as a result of this decrease in user cost? (*c*) What happens to the capital–output ratio?

(*a*)   The desired stock of capital increases from K_0 to K^* in Fig. 14-9 as user cost declines from u_0 to u_1. Because the cost of capital relative to that of labor has decreased, firms substitute capital for labor.

(*b*)   Net investment is K^* less K_0, the difference between the desired stock of capital at user cost u_1 and u_0.

(*c*)   The production process becomes more capital-intensive as capital is substituted for labor in producing a fixed level of output. The capital–output ratio increases.

THE FLEXIBLE ACCELERATOR

14.12 Suppose there are constant returns to scale and a 5% increase in output. (*a*) What happens to the employment of labor and capital and the capital–output ratio when there is no change in the cost of factor inputs? (*b*) What happens to the employment of labor and capital and the capital–output ratio when there is a decrease in the user cost of capital and no change in the real wage? (*c*) What happens to the employment of labor and capital and the capital–output ratio when there is an increase in the real wage and no change in the user cost of capital? (*d*) What happens to v in the equation $In = v\Delta Y$ for the situations described in parts (*a*) through (*c*).

(*a*)   Since there is no change in the cost of factor inputs, there is no change in the least-cost mix of labor and capital. Output increases 5% as does the employment of labor and capital. The capital–output ratio is unchanged.

(*b*)   A decrease in user cost indicates that the least-cost method of producing is now more capital-intensive. Capital increases by more than 5% and labor by less than 5% when output increases 5%. The capital–output ratio increases.

(*c*)   Capital is substituted for labor because of a higher real wage. Capital increases by more than 5% and labor by less than 5% when output increases 5%. The capital–output ratio increases.

(*d*) v in the equation $In = v\Delta Y$ is the capital–output ratio. There is no change in v in part (*a*) and an increase in its value in parts (*b*) and (*c*).

14.13 What is the flexible accelerator theory of investment?

> The flexible accelerator theory of investment retains the dependency of net investment upon expected output but qualifies the relationship by also linking the desired stock of capital to the user cost of capital and by introducing a lag structure for capital additions. A decrease in the user cost of capital increases the capital intensiveness of production; hence, a higher capital–output ratio increases the desired stock of capital. The change in the desired stock of capital is probably distributed over time because of limited capacity in the capital producing industries.

14.14 (a) Suppose the user cost of capital and the real wage is constant. An increase in expected output raises the desired stock of capital from K_{-1} to K^*. Why might capital additions of $(K^* - K_{-1})$ occur over time? (b) The lagged effect of capital additions can be presented by $In = \lambda(K^* - K_{-1})$. What determines the value of λ?

(a)   Capital additions may be distributed over time because of capacity constraints in the capital-goods industries, business uncertainty about increased output, financial constraints to expansion, and expectations about monetary and fiscal policy. Capital additions are not instantaneous. Capital expansions must be planned. Orders must be placed. Backlog orders may exist in the capital goods industries. And in some industries, it may take a year or longer for capital to be built. Capital expansions may be deferred because of uncertainty about expected sales. No firm wants to overexpand; therefore, a firm may not immediately expand productive capacity unless it is relatively certain that a higher output level will be sustained. Financial constraints may also limit the rate at which capital is added. Firms do not have unlimited financial resources; hence, the availability of funds acts as a constraint to capital expansion. And firms may accelerate or slow capital additions depending on expectations about monetary policy (current and expected cost of funds) and fiscal policy (availability of investment tax credits and accelerated depreciation).

(b) λ is the fraction of the change in the desired stock of capital which occurs each period. Its value depends on the variables discussed in part (a). The faster the delivery of new capital, the larger the value of λ. Similarly, λ is larger when the firm has adequate cash flows available to undertake capital additions and is certain about continuance of a higher output level, and monetary and fiscal policy are supportive of capital additions.

14.15 Suppose the capital stock is initially \$1000, output is \$500, and the capital–output ratio v is 2. (a) Find the desired stock of capital when there is no change in expected output but v increases to 2.1 due to a decrease in the user cost of capital. (b) Find the desired stock of capital when there is no change in the user cost of capital (v remains at 2) and expected output increases 10%. (c) Find net investment for four successive periods for parts (a) and (b) when $In = \lambda(K^* - K_{-1})$ and $\lambda = 0.50$. (d) Recalculate net investment for part (c) when $\lambda = 0.60$.

(a)   The desired stock of capital is a multiple of expected output, i.e., $K = vY$. With output remaining at \$500 and v increasing to 2.1, the desired stock of capital increases from \$1000 to \$1050.

(b)   A 10% increase in expected output raises Y from \$500 to \$550. With no change in v, the desired stock of capital increases from \$1000 to \$1100.

(c)   When the desired stock of capital increases \$50 in part (a) and $\lambda = 0.5$, net investment during four successive periods is \$25—$In = \lambda(K^* - K_{-1})$, $In = 0.5(\$50)$, $In = \$25$—\$12.50, \$6.25, and \$3.125. When $\lambda = 0.5$, a \$100 increase in the desired stock of capital from part (b) results in net investment during four successive periods of \$50, \$25, \$12.50, and \$6.25.

(d)   When the desired stock of capital increases \$50 [part (a)], net investment during four successive periods is \$30, \$12, \$4.80, and \$1.92 when $\lambda = 0.60$. Net investment during four successive periods is \$60, \$24, \$9.60, and \$3.84 when the desired capital stock increases \$100 [part (b)] and λ is 0.60.

TOBIN'S q-THEORY

14.16 (*a*) What is Tobin's q-theory? (*b*) Relate Tobin's q-theory to changes in the user cost of capital.

  (*a*) Tobin's q-theory explains net investment by relating the market value of financial assets (the market value of the firm's equity and debt) to the replacement cost of the firm's real assets. The firm adds to its capital stock when the market value of its financial assets exceeds the replacement cost of its real assets ($q > 1$) because the incremental return from a capital addition exceeds its cost.

  (*b*) The market value of a firm's securities is directly linked to the real rate of interest. The market value of the firm's equity is the capitalized value of the earnings generated by real assets, i.e., $MV = E/k_r$ where MV is the equity's market value, E the earnings generated by real assets and k_r the market-determined rate of return for earnings of a given level of risk. Holding E constant, MV varies inversely with k_r. Hence, a decrease in the real rate of interest reduces user cost and increases the market value of the firm's financial assets because of a lower value for k_r. If $q > 1$ after the decrease in the real rate of interest, the reduction in user cost is associated with capital additions, since the market value of the firm's financial assets exceeds the replacement cost of its current capital stock.

14.17 Suppose a firm is totally financed by equity; it is earning $2.50 per share; its capitalization rate k_r is 20%; there are 10,000 shares outstanding, and the replacement cost of the firm's real assets is $125,000. (*a*) Find the firm's market value and q ratio. (*b*) Find the firm's market value and q ratio when the capitalization rate falls to 18% due to a decline in the real rate of interest. (*c*) What has happened to the relationship of the user cost of capital to the marginal cost benefit from capital? (*d*) Why does a decline in the real rate of interest increase the firm's desired stock of capital?

  (*a*) The market value of the firm is equal to the earnings per share divided by the capitalization rate, with the sum multiplied by the number of shares outstanding. The market value MV is $(E/k_r)10,000$ or ($2.50/0.20)10,000 = $125,000. The q ratio is 1, the ratio of the market value of the firm's financial assets to the replacement cost of its real assets.

  (*b*) The market value increases to $138,888.89 or ($2.50/0.18)10,000. The q ratio increases from 1 to 1.11.

  (*c*) The user cost of capital is below the marginal cost benefit from capital assuming that the user cost of capital initially was equal to the marginal cost benefit from capital.

  (*d*) The firm's cost of funding real asset acquisitions exceeds the return from real assets; there is an increase in the firm's desired stock of capital.

INVENTORY INVESTMENT

14.18 Suppose the desired inventory-sales ratio is 0.20; the change in inventory investment is presented as $\Delta Inv = 0.20(\Delta R)$, where ΔR is the change in sales. Find the change in inventory investment when sales are currently $1900 and are expected to reach the following levels in successive quarters: Q1.1, $2000; Q1.2, $2100; Q1.3, $2100; Q1.4, $2400; Q2.1, $2200; Q2.2, $2350.

  The change in inventory investment is $20 during Q1.1: $\Delta Inv = 0.20(\Delta R)$; $\Delta Inv = 0.20($100)$. The change in inventory investment for successive quarters is presented in the right column of Table 14-5.

14.19 (*a*) A firm holds inventories (materials, semifinished goods, and finished goods) to ensure that there is no disruption to the production and sale of output. Explain how the following variables might affect a firm's inventory–sales ratio: cost (interest and storage) of holding inventory, uncertainty about projected sales and availability of material supplies. (*b*) Suppose a firm's inventory–sales ratio is 0.20 and current sales are $2000. Find the change in inventory investment when there is no change in expected sales but the firm increases the inventory–sales ratio to 0.25 because of possible delays in receiving materials from suppliers.

Table 14-5

Quarter	Change in Sales ($)	Change in Inventory Investment ($)
Q1.1	+100	+20
Q1.2	+100	+20
Q1.3	0	0
Q1.4	+300	+60
Q2.1	−200	−40
Q2.2	+150	+30

(a) An increase in the cost of holding inventory should decrease the inventory–sales ratio; higher financing and/or storage costs, *ceteris paribus*, have a negative effect on profits. Firms therefore attempt to produce and sell output with lower inventories. Uncertainty about sales, *ceteris paribus*, should lower the inventory–sales ratio. Firms will keep inventory levels as small as possible when there is a high likelihood that sales will not occur. Scarcity of materials, *ceteris paribus*, encourages firms to keep larger inventories to maintain production and sales levels; the inventory–sales ratio would increase.

(b) Concern about delays in receiving materials will increase inventory holdings. The increase in the inventory–sales ratio from 0.20 to 0.25, with no change in expected sales, raises a firm's inventory investment $100. [Inventory investment is increased to 0.25($2000) from 0.20($2000).]

Multiple Choice Questions

1. In the rigid version of the accelerator theory of investment, net investment in successive periods is as follows when the capital–output ratio is 2 and the expected increase in output is $15, $20, $20 and $15.

   (a) $30 each period.
   (b) $15, $20, $20, and $15 in successive periods.
   (c) $30, $40, $40, and $30 in successive periods.
   (d) $7.50, $10, $10, and $7.50 in successive periods.

2. Which of the following statements is true?

   (a) Gross investment is more stable than net investment when replacement investment is constant over time.
   (b) Net investment is more stable than gross investment when replacement is constant over time.
   (c) Replacement investment equals $v\Delta Y$.
   (d) Net investment is greater than $v\Delta Y$ when the capital–output ratio decreases.

3. The user cost of capital is

   (a) The real rate of interest.
   (b) The nominal rate of interest.

(c)   The real rate of interest plus the rate of depreciation.

(d)   The nominal rate of interest plus the rate of depreciation.

4.   Which of the following economic policies will *not* lower the user cost of capital?

(a)   A 5% increase in the nominal money supply, which causes a 5% increase in the expected rate of inflation.

(b)   The introduction of an investment tax credit.

(c)   An increase in the rate at which firms are allowed to depreciate machinery for tax purposes.

(d)   A reduction in the corporate income tax rate.

5.   The marginal cost benefit from capital is the

(a)   Incremental output associated with an addition to the stock of capital.

(b)   Cost saving associated with employing less labor inputs and additional capital inputs to produce a fixed level of output.

(c)   Incremental cost of capital associated with the addition of a unit of capital.

(d)   Incremental profit associated with the addition of a unit of capital.

6.   A decrease in the user cost of capital will result in the production process becoming

(a)   More capital-intensive and the capital–output ratio decreasing.

(b)   More capital-intensive and the capital–output ratio increasing.

(c)   Less capital-intensive and the capital–output ratio decreasing.

(d)   Less capital-intensive and the capital–output ratio increasing.

7.   A distributed lag for net investment may be due to

(a)   A decrease in the capital–output ratio.

(b)   An increase in the capital–output ratio.

(c)   Limited, short-run production capabilities in the capital goods industry.

(d)   A decrease in the expected level of output.

8.   Tobin's *q*-theory of investment indicates that firms add to their stock of capital when

(a)   The replacement value of their real assets exceeds the market value of their financial assets.

(b)   The market value of their financial assets exceeds the replacement value of their real assets.

(c)   The market value of their real assets exceeds the book value of their financial assets.

(d)   The market value of their financial assets exceeds the book value of their real assets.

9.   When the inventory–sales ratio is 0.25, a

(a)   25% increase in expected sales results in a 100% increase in inventory.

(b) $25 increase in expected sales results in a $100 increase in inventory.

(c)   100% increase in expected sales results in a 25% increase in inventory.

(d) $100 increase in expected sales results in a $25 increase in inventory.

10.   Which of the following results in an increase in the inventory–sales ratio?

(a)   A decrease in the cost of holding inventory, *ceteris paribus*.

(b)   An increase in the probability of delivery delays for materials, *ceteris paribus*.

(c) An increase in expected sales, *ceteris paribus*.

(d) An increase in the uncertainty of expected sales, *ceteris paribus*.

True or False Questions

11. _____ The rigid version of the accelerator theory of investment relates net investment to the level of output.

12. _____ When the capital–output ratio is 2, a $20 increase in output results in a $10 increase in capital.

13. _____ The desired stock of capital is the amount of capital firms wish to hold to produce a specific level of output.

14. _____ The user cost of capital is the cost of using financial capital.

15. _____ An increase in the rate at which capital depreciates lowers the user cost of capital.

16. _____ A decrease in the real rate of interest decreases the user cost of capital and increases the desired stock of capital.

17. _____ In the flexible accelerator theory, an increase in the user cost of capital lowers the capital–output ratio.

18. _____ In the flexible accelerator theory, an increase in the real wage increases the capital–output ratio.

19. _____ Firms do not add to their stock of capital when the q ratio is 0.9.

20. _____ An increase in the rate of interest should increase the inventory–sales ratio.

Answers to Multiple Choice and True or False Questions

1. (*c*); **2.** (*a*); **3.** (*c*); **4.** (*a*); **5.** (*b*); **6.** (*b*); **7.** (*c*); **8.** (*b*); **9.** (*d*); **10.** (*b*); **11.** F; **12.** F; **13.** T; **14.** F; **15.** F; **16.** T; **17.** T; **18.** T; **19.** T; **20.** F.

Index

The letter p following a page number refers to a solved problem.